WHITHER FANON?

Cultural Memory

in

the

Present

Hent de Vries, Editor

WHITHER FANON?

Studies in the Blackness of Being

David Marriott

STANFORD UNIVERSITY PRESS

STANFORD, CALIFORNIA

Stanford University Press
Stanford, California

Library of Congress Cataloging-in-Publication Data

Names: Marriott, D. S., author.
Title: Whither Fanon? : studies in the blackness of being / David Marriott.
Description: Stanford, California : Stanford University Press, 2018. | Series: Cultural memory in the present | Includes bibliographical references and index.
Identifiers: LCCN 2017042249 (print) | LCCN 2018012527 (ebook) | ISBN 9780804798709 (cloth :alk. paper) | ISBN 9781503605725 (pbk. :alk. paper) | ISBN 9781503605732 (ebook)
Subjects: LCSH: Fanon, Frantz, 1925-1961. | Black race—Philosophy. | Imperialism—Philosophy. | Philosophy, West Indian. | Philosophy, Black.
Classification: LCC B1029.F354 (ebook) | LCC B1029.F354 M37 2018 (print) | DDC 199/.729—dc23
LC record available at https://lccn.loc.gov/2017042249

Cover design: Rob Ehle
Cover illustration: Wikimedia Commons
Typeset by Bruce Lundquist in 11/13.5 Adobe Garamond

Contents

Foreword

> However painful it may be for me to accept this conclusion, I am obliged to state it: For the black man there is only one destiny. And it is white.
>
> FANON, *Black Skin, White Masks*, trans. Markmann, 10

I resolved to write this book so as to provide a fresh examination of what this destiny might be, but not to affirm it, nor to refuse any of the suffering that comes in its wake, nor to pass off as disavowed an acceptance that Frantz Fanon clearly found so hard to acknowledge. If I were to be asked what this destiny signifies for me here now, writing this sentence, I would have to say at the outset that I do not know; and to that extent it could be said that this destiny is not really readable at all, insofar as the event of its meaning has yet to occur. My aim in this book, far from offering yet another interpretation of what this destiny might be, is to subvert both the ease with which this destiny could be dismissed or affirmed, and the imposition of a prescient point of view from which this destiny could be read or known. By presenting the concepts through which Fanon remains faithful to the difficulty of thinking blackness as a future tense, I have become more and more convinced that to have no certainty of judgment is the only certitude that Fanon's conclusion demands.

On the other hand, to see whiteness as the destiny of blackness is to question everything. To see the future of blackness in its absolute disappearance is also to imagine it as a thing obliterated. But what happens to this future whiteness when, blackened, it too learns of its origin? Indeed, for my purposes, Fanon's sentence communicates an extreme irony: if the only appearance of whiteness in the world comes from blackness, that raises the question of what it means to desire to see oneself as white or black and to recognize race as a destiny that allows one to grasp one's essence and existence. However painful the discovery, to receive race as a destiny is to forget that race confers no certitude in this world and that the only proof of its meaning is illusion and suffering; to affirm race as a destiny is to deny that it reveals a void and that it is nothing but an ellipsis, or caesura, through which being defends itself against the anguish and ecstasy through which its existence takes shape. The conclusion that race has no immediate knowledge, and can only be approached as the experience of its infinite deferment, is the object of this book. In what follows I am concerned not with a history of that deferment but with the relation between reading Fanon and what I take to be the pessimistic revelation of his thought.

This is not to say simply that race has no significance, but that what it accomplishes as a revelation at each and every moment is repeatable only as its difference from itself. In the same way, if blackness has a destiny, that destiny depends on the discomfort of knowing that its appearance always coincides with self-oblivion, and to that extent its existence is conditional on what remains heterogeneous to it. The plea for race to be a destiny (whether in the idiom of assent or that of obligation) intrinsically has to do with the wretchedness in which blackness came into being in the world and that continues to define the anti-blackness of the world. In saying this, I am not judging the world, nor the dogma by which the world worlds itself as world. I am not questioning the validity of anti-blackness as the content of the world, as if the world could be judged solely according to its hatred of black people. Nor am I asking that blacks be taken as the exception that proves the rule of what it means to be in the world.

But what I am saying is that anti-blackness is the discourse through which a singular experience of the world is constituted. Such experience is not ineffable: anti-blackness is the thing against which the universal, the human, the ideal, etc., is enunciated and created; it is the means through which the racial discourse of being is articulated as spirit. I say being because the essence of anti-blackness is not representation, but the structure by which racial ontology is literally inscribed on each act of enslaved, non-sovereign being. Anti-blackness is thus not the image of that which is excluded from being—even if that exclusion is always experienced as anguish—it is the body, the corpus, the mortis, that has to be cast off for the racial truth of spirit to reveal itself. In this sense, anti-blackness is the bearer of an immanent fault, defect, *lapsus* at the level of its very being, as Fanon teaches us. This defect is real; it is not imagined, projected, fantasized, etc. What characterizes this flaw, which does not proceed from any actual racist encounter, is that there is no resistance to this outcome by which blackness is suddenly relegated to a debased, decreated form. Why do I say this? For Fanon, blackness can only find its ontological fulfillment by no longer being black—or by entering its own abyssal significance. Now that this book is finished, I see signs of this everywhere, including in myself, and I detest its effects at the same time as I am fascinated by this desire not to be black. But what does it mean for me to say that I am compelled by a desire that forces me to choose between adherence and rejection but that leaves me unable to positively do so, a desire that forces me to suspend decision, without for all that abolishing it?

This book is the narrative of that fascination, the danger it signifies, and its contradictory inner meaning, which I have yet to overcome and whose parody and hypocrisy I continue to perform as if they were a destiny. This is, in a sense, why I believe that Fanon's conclusion above is still to be read. This is the *whither* on which this book is based. In the current discourses of fear and terror, in which the slightest suspicion of a black presence can be steered into mass hysteria and hatred, and all the more readily when the object of distrust hovers uncertainly between the known and the unknown (though we pretend to know who the real enemy is), paranoia and destruction soon teach us that the future will always return in the form of negrophobic malice, in whose aggression black identity is attacked and scorned.

I think that everyone is aware of this, even though I also believe that most people are anti-black not because they are avowedly racist but because such is the insecure being of their world. For no one can have lived long among whites without noticing that when things are not going well, most white people, however liberal they may be, are full of wisdom concerning "the minority problem" and do not hesitate to offer advice. No suggestion they hear is too extreme, ridiculous, or absurd to follow. For when they see a black person they are afraid, and anything they see that reminds them of a black presence seems to provoke or remind them of an unhappy outcome, thus they call blackness a bad omen, even though they have been disappointed a thousand times in their non-black lives. The moral contagion associated with blackness exists in a kind of cultural hysteria and was studied by Fanon with reference to stereotypical codes and signs and the obsessional hatreds of power. Negrophobia occurs when the cultural signs (of blackness) and phobic beliefs are no longer simply juxtaposed but aligned, when the rational and affective borders of the subject are no longer segregated from other stereotypical signs but are concentrated in a regressive insecurity: "methods of thinking and feeling that go back to the age at which he [the negrophobe] experienced the event that impaired his security."[1] Fanon's analysis of negrophobia under the rubric of a "regression" (in relation to an imaginary encounter or crisis) explores the ways in which fantasy exposes the fragility of racial identity independently of any actual act or behavior. In the same way, one can say that every racist encounter is dependent on phobia, the set of responses according to which the subject is overwhelmed by its own projections and fears. Again, if the negrophobe sees blackness present in their ordinary intimacies, it causes great consternation or astonishment; they believe it to augur a potential invasion that a UPS driver or mailman is black, and they think it not untoward to report this fact on their neighborhood watch bulletins, advising their neighbors to be attentive and mind their property. It is as if they were addicted to the idea that all that blacks want to do is invade them and all the spaces they occupy, repeatedly. They develop an infinite number of stratagems to make this superstition true, inventing extraordinary interpretations of black behavior as the keenest, most blatant example of an anti-white obsession.

This being the case, we see at once that it is especially those who see blackness in the world as an unsolvable enigma who are most prone to this anti-black superstition, especially when they find themselves exposed to a black person, are strangely disordered by that, cannot emotionally resolve the experience, and so trot out the most implausible excuses that they were only acting in self-defense when they reviled, attacked, or killed the young, the unarmed, and the innocent. They swear that their violence is justified, while any black response to their violence is not, and that their fear is racially blind because anyone in danger of their lives would have acted the same way to save themselves from a being that appears to them inhuman. Entering into these unexpected regions, it is not clear to me whether these delirious beliefs are merely the phantoms of a diseased imagination, or white pleas of self-defense are merely the childish projections of an insecurity in which wishful thoughts rediscover themselves as murderous acts, or anti-blackness is the expression of a psychic prematurity that is allowed to achieve its task at the expense of others. Or are these just several means of expressing the same symptom? There is nothing here that I did not already recognize as the consequence of an anti-black hysteria: when all is said and done, anti-blackness not only subjects the whole world, it also gives itself over to a murderous ravishment, one that discerns good government in the refusal of the racially undeserving; this is the oldest law of white superiority, and that one can find this law to be the essence of the West, its history, and its traditions, and only a fool, madman, or rebel would seek to go against the laws of nature (which always support the avarice of the racially strong and their merciless treatment of the racially weak). Like a destiny, in other words, anti-blackness opens a coincidence between black social death and the play and performance of whiteness as spiritual power—the surcease of the one becomes natural when its expenditure organizes the ontology of the other: it is sufficient merely for the idea of blackness to be obliterated for whiteness to establish itself as Being, at the point where its essence can be defined by a feeling of triumph. It is blackness that makes men irrational, and whiteness that preserves the good that enhances the polity.

Hence, fear is the root from which anti-blackness is born, maintained, and nourished. This fear appears to be a point of defense but the nature of the phobia—that blackness is contaminating—is precisely to include the threat of eradication within the language of contagion. If anyone wants to go further into the matter and consider particular examples, let them contemplate the disparity by which the countless deaths of nonwhite peoples are collectively commemorated and reported. Although perhaps anti-black by cultural upbringing, such a reader need not confront the facts of each of these cases to learn that the vast majority of black deaths are deemed to be natural facts, or part of the nature of things, whereas the death of whites connotes a tragic loss of being. Fanon himself says: "seven Frenchman killed or wounded at the Col de Sakamody" solicits so much more "indignation of the civilized conscience" than "the sacking of the Guergour duoars, the dechra Djerah [or] the massacre of the populations who had truly provoked the ambush."[2] Many similar examples could be given to show with complete clarity that white people regard blackness as *in essence* an unsolvable, barely nameable, enigma, to which they assign malicious desires of which they are afraid (since blackness is understood to be a disorder within natural life); that all the things that they have ever worshiped under the influence of anti-black superstition are nothing but the fantasies of despondent and fearful minds; and that blacks have the most to fear from these hateful, murderous delusions, which would rather see them repeatedly sacrificed than to suffer the deaths of a few white subjects. But I think that is well enough known to everyone, and I will not go further into it here.

Since negrophobia (a word I borrow from Fanon) is the cause of anti-black fear and distrust, it follows that not everyone is prone to these feelings of insecurity (despite the widespread theory that everyone is frightened of difference). It also follows that negrophobia must be just as variable or invariable as the affective pre-logic that reproduces it, and that it can only be sustained by fear and hatred, anger and deception. This is because such affect springs not from reason but from passion alone, in fact from the most powerful of the passions. Having reflected on all these things—that any racial certitude is not only misrecognized but held onto by many as a form of defense against insecurity, and that interracial enmity is often seen as a struggle for self-preservation, the murderous destruction of black presences is deemed to be self-protection, and anti-blackness is fought out in the streets and workplaces with intense passion, generating the bitterest antipathies and struggles, which leave no one safe—I have to say that all these incidents prove to me that Fanon's diagnosis of blackness *as an experience without a destiny* has yet to be grasped.

I do not claim to offer an exhaustive treatment of all the arguments Fanon uses to explain negrophobia nor give a full account of the clinical system that he devised in order to try to intervene against it. Instead, I began by inquiring: What is Fanon's *socialthérapie*? In what manner does the clinic reveal to Fanon his politics and vice versa? What did he make of the cure, how did the crisis of colonial war affect his practice, and did he remain bound to this clinical method in the wake of this crisis? Having asked these questions, I was able to conclude that the political carries weight because it also appears as a clinical symptom with regard to questions of freedom, servitude, and transfiguration, and that within the Fanonian clinic the political itself comes to be seen as both the failure and possibility of black revolutionary thought that I present here. Fanon became aware that he was creating a revolution in the field of clinical thought towards which the entire tradition of sociotherapy was leading, particularly that of Fanon's teacher Tosquelles, but the tradition had to be entirely rethought in terms of what I call "the vertiginous blackness of being," which defined the extreme violence and perversity of colonialism. Fanon recapitulated all the clinical teachings of colonial psychiatry that had preceded him, as well as the radical experiments of the Tosquelles school, by synthesizing their schemes with the revolutionary concept of racial subjugation and resistance, which he was the first to clinically work out.

Once I had understood this, I sought to know why it was that Fanon's clinical work was often excluded from a consideration of his politics. Was it because that clinical work entailed conceptions of revolution as itself a kind of hysteria? I realized that Fanon's psychopolitics revealed nothing but the failures and limits of either the clinical or the political to grasp the phenomenon of colonial war. Accordingly I needed to keep in mind how the two were bound together to understand Fanon. Next, I decided to reread Fanon's theory of violence to ask whether we should conclude from it that Fanon was, as some have claimed, a naïve apologist for terror. To that end, I began to consider whether the response to colonial violence or the violence of the colonial state was simply part of a means-ends thinking that defined the political tradition, or whether it was indeed something different. Thirdly, I also inquired into whether Fanon's descriptions of the minds of those affected by violence and the widespread use of torture and detention were understood by critics of his theory of violence. I found nothing in Fanon's writings that explicitly converges with, say, a Sorelian understanding of violence, nor anything that is reductively Sartrean. I also found that Fanon teaches a very simple thing, which is understood by the dispossessed everywhere (and is therefore decidedly the most difficult lesson), and that he had explained it in a style that they could recognize and supported it with the sort of reasons that might most effectively sway people's minds towards resisting the forces that oppressed them: namely, *that to exist as black is to experience the extremity of a dereliction in which the future and the past converge in an interminable war of guilt and condemnation,* in which one's part is the constant corpsing of one's social role. In this way, I became completely convinced that Fanon wishes the colonized to be absolutely free, but that this is a freedom that has nothing to do with political sovereignty; instead, for Fanon, each citizen should stand on their own feet and be able to look the enemy in the eye without trembling. I wrote this book in order to demonstrate, conclusively, how Fanon's clinical work should be interpreted, proving that we must derive all our knowledge of it and of its politics from what I see as Fanon's unprecedented interpretation of desire and politics in terms of their mutual imbrication, and not from anything we might discover about them separately.

Accordingly, I begin with Fanon's meditations on sociotherapy. After this, I go on to show the forms of negrophobia that have arisen out of anti-blackness and how Fanon conceives them. I discuss the fact that he considered racism not as an existential concept but from a structural reading of how language, being, economy, sexuality, and image all come together in an anti-black thematics. The first argument concerns the corporeal: that is to say, the fanatical, phantasmatic, and thereby somewhat fetishistic discourse about the black body. Roughly speaking, this corporeality has three major phases. First, there is epidermalization, the literal blackening of the skin. Then, in response to this blackening, comes the morbid rigidity that Fanon describes as petrification, as part of a more general description of how motor capacity is literally inhibited in the colony. Finally, there is the sociogenic, where the intent is no longer to know the body as affect but rather to show how culture responds to the *nègre* in its foreignness, or even the fundamental hostility of culture to the nonwhite subject. This concern is no longer for the body as sensorium, or imaginary prosthesis, but for the sociopolitical difference that comes to be lived as such.

This perspective, which pursues the meaning of blackness through cultural narratives and signs, is the symptomatic reading of the political emergence of negritude in Fanon's clinical practice. The first phase is associated with Sartre, Merleau-Ponty, and Tosquelles; the second with Hegel, Lacan, Freud and Guex. The third phase, Fanon's own, is seen as the innovation of his work in sociogeny. These phases are then taken up in terms of their consequences for discussions of war, trauma, desire, and guilt. In Algeria, and more broadly the African world, subjects of colonial war presented symptoms that forced Fanon to reflect on the cultural language of revolution both antecedent and contemporary. The madness in which each subject was held, itself being the sign of a delirious insecurity, is not to be confused with Fanon's early work on the psychoneuroses. The symptoms that went to make up these psychoses were distinct, traceable, and yet somehow profoundly unreadable: they were codes without a grammar or index. It suffices to recall the example of the white torturer who visits Fanon not because he is tormented by remorse or suffers from moral disquiet, but because he knows himself to be a torturer and does not fear the consequences of torturing. On the contrary, he considers torture to be not an affliction but his duty; his only complaint is that he cannot seem to stop doing it even at home! Torturing men and women whose cause he believes is unjust, whose race he detests, and of whom he understands nothing is not what moves him. It is the sheer *jouissance* that comes from separating the other from the unendurable limit of its being that drives him on.

It was not these men whom Fanon sought to cure but rather those whose loyalty to the anti-colonial cause, which they valued more than mere life, caused them to progressively lose their authority over themselves. Their freedom of judgment disappeared into an antithetical form of thinking, whilst their speech held a delusory paranoia, as if they were the enemy they sought—to the point where they could not judge or think where fantasy began and where reality ended. That they did so in a psychotic delirium informs some of Fanon's major clinical insights which I attempt to study here. Against the dissociation of such desire, which brought fundamental changes to his *socialthérapie*, and precisely in those areas where desire punishes worse than law, Fanon also came across opposing examples, of men and women who could not entirely offer themselves to the revolutionary demands of the war and whose delirium was consequently made worse by therapy. The resistance and indifference of such patients to the usual methods of social therapy caused Fanon to revise his practices for these patients. Just as these patients could not freely enter into the war of liberation, so their therapy stopped before the liberation of their symptom—these boundaries could not shift, causing them to turn away from the codes and protocols of the clinic (in relation to performing different roles) to ways of acting and talking that were so tormented by their deliria that the usual methods of therapeutic intervention had to be revised to include the avowal of what was utterly essential to the symptoms by which these subjects articulated themselves. It was not a case of providing more specific signs of cultural integration—be they secular or religious—for these people, but of understanding what kept their dependencies intact, the fantasies that preserved their servitude, and why engaging in therapy meant risking the unbinding of the very codes that preserved their equilibrium. It was precisely to intervene against these codes and fantasies of continued subservience that Fanon sought more poetic modes of therapeutic intervention (as outlined in several clinical essays), where the rules by which these subjects could receive meaning from the world and make sense of it were rearticulated at a different level. Here the clinic becomes a kind of disarticulating space that offers, at the same time, an unprecedented rearticulation of negative hallucination and the forms of distortion issuing from it, forms that are contiguous to the symptom (and sometimes even holding it in place), which provide for and maintain those symptoms at various levels of utterance. It was to undo such impasses that Fanon sought to revise his sociotherapy.

I also explore how Fanon turned to poetics to interpret what he calls invention and which alone is given a political authority to decide who is free and who is imprisoned, who is abject and who is sovereign. I conclude that invention is how we are entitled to think both what Fanon wished to be his future and the psychopolitical form through which the future must be thought, and then to take up this task as one of the more urgent questions we face today, given the present disenchantments of blackness.

After establishing these points, I move on to the more obvious political writings, describing them at some length to show by what means and by whose decision whiteness assumed the force of law in the colony and how blackness came to be known as a valueless, indebted form of being. The major thinkers and themes studied in Part Two have little concern for the clinical questions above, since they are persuaded, in their reading, that the existence of the wretched is self-evident, inscribed in the nature of things by cultural politics and the history of Western modernity. But I do believe that something goes missing here, something in the way Fanon's work is being used, in itself, to keep the disquieting complexity of the psychical from the consideration of the sociopolitical. My mission here is not to interrogate this absence but to understand it, somewhat in the sense in which Fanon considered his work to be promiscuous regarding all methods.

I bring this study to a close, therefore, by returning to one of my opening terms: the fall, the catastrophe, through which blackness has unfolded from its origin in the Middle Passage until its awaited arrival in the New World, an arrival for which we are still waiting, because such a possibility has to be invented if it is not to be missed.

Having thus demonstrated the two main foci of the book (the Fanonian clinical object and its political being), I conclude, finally, that the Fanonian object of knowledge is simply what it means to be black. It is therefore entirely distinct from an historical claim, both in its object and in its principles and methods, and has nothing whatsoever in common with identity. Each of these foci (the reinvention of which we cannot yet speak and its political expression) has its own province; they do not conflict with each other; and neither should be subordinate to the other. Fanon often says of himself that he is the one who waits, the one who does not inaugurate but the one who anticipates catastrophe. This claim, uncommon amongst black philosophers, rings true for Fanon in a way that will be of much concern for us. But this awaiting also seems to me to be a suspense and an anticipation of waiting itself. Of course, during Fanon's lifetime and after him, there were many thinkers who did not think as he did and who developed the concept of race as an end and a last redemptive word. We might think of W. E. B. Du Bois, for example, or the group of writers belonging to what has come to be known as negritude. But it is Fanon who for me completes what constitutes the ontological fulfillment of blackness; it is he who thinks it in its endangered impurity, its lack of right, and in a way that continues to determine the problems and refutations that will regularly punctuate the critical era of black political thought.

This awaiting has not yet been completed, and to say that it is over, or that Fanonism is no less a moment of conclusion, is as absurd a claim as saying that anti-blackness is no longer valid as a practice in the West. Does not the completion of the post-racial vision, for those who announce it, in fact signify racism's full retrieval and repetition in the daily roll call of those shot, maimed, and tortured for the most trifling of reasons? The metaphysical end of race points to the task of its permanent return in the form of the real; what still needs to be thought is the blackness of the body that consumes itself as it burns, a body that is permanently set on fire. Therefore, I do not claim that Fanon forbids a new humanistic vision of the world— but this is a vision that is expressly and necessarily not a plea for a white world, nor is it a plea for a black philosophy of identity. The abyss that conceives itself as nothing, as a void, does not await the white light of reason, for it is already penetrated by dark potentialities. It is this darkness to come, what I call the Fanonian moment, a moment that is always awaited, always to come: the abyssal.

WHITHER FANON?

Introduction

Whither Fanon?[1]

It is true that we could equally well stress the rise of a new nation, the setting up of a new state, its diplomatic relations, and its economic and political trends. But we have precisely chosen to speak of that kind of tabula rasa which characterizes at the outset all decolonization.

FRANTZ FANON, *The Wretched of the Earth*, trans. Farrington, 27

By "whither," my basic question is not what is to be done (with Fanonism), a question that fails to question the distinction between means and ends. I am thinking less of a telos or destination to which one has to hold or train oneself than of a question of incomprehension, deferral, and perpetual challenge. This is why I think that Fanon is still to be read. The attempt to subject or limit Fanonism to the horizon of a judgment, to make it make sense, to lead us to a thought, a destiny, to where we want leading, is for me a decision that is always in question. And I say at once that this is not where I would like to begin, for the experience of what it means to read Fanon, or to reduce his rigor to a question of method rather than an experience of contestation and challenge, reveals certain presuppositions that must be opposed, linked as they are to a certain evocation of Fanonism as a kind of knowledge that must be in some way already familiar, already experienced without difficulty. Opposition to this idea of reading—which takes up an essential part of this book—is necessary for me to understand what is most important about this "whither," as an evocation whose spirit of decision comes without guarantees or ends.

I – Fanon's messianic decolonial revolution

The time has come, it seems, to talk of Fanonism as a thought whose time has come and gone, a thought whose significance must accordingly be grasped and seized if the opportunity offered by this thought is not to be missed. And the proof of that is given among many other signs (including a flurry of recent pronouncements on the demise of the nationalist-humanist project) by the fact of Fanon's humanism, his messianic belief in revolution as a redemptive moment, which could not but invite the reflection that decolonization never was, nor could ever be, simply redemptive, that this is indeed to confuse *the* moment of revolution with a telos or eschatology.[2] And it seems that any attempt to think about the postcolonial moment as messianic or redemptive has to accept this critical melancholia from the start. Whatever Fanon thought about it, it is suggested that he implicitly claimed that decolonization is invariably a thought of national liberation—*any* decolonial struggle, however resentfully or apologetically, lays claim, usually explicitly, to *freedom-as-national-sovereignty*—and that anti-colonialism can only affirm itself as this opening towards the new nation whose time is always liberatory and whose arrival in general leads to a paradoxical suspension of time or tabula rasa that is also a radically new beginning. Independence is, accordingly, the time for a new humanity, the colonized whose time has come—and explicit claims to redemption or recovery are, one might suspect, no more than a further twist to this "narrative of liberation."[3] For there is nothing for which Fanonism has come to be so well known as the demand for a new sovereignty, nothing could be more Fanonian than the affirmation of the coming revolution whose proud claim is to redeem colonized humanity. The proud or messianic claim to nationhood is just the claim that the colonized will be gathered up into a greater identity, and, as is clear from Fanon's remarks on the Algerian War, anti-colonial resistance is always a demand for an end to the alienation to which colonialism gives rise. Alienation, which will return as a question in a moment, becomes the most appropriate way of thinking this link of recognition and liberation in Fanon: for on the one hand, recognition in revolution is all about reclaiming repressed humanity; and on the other, the decision to go against the colonial regime, and to stake one's life on the struggle, is crucial to discovering the meaning of freedom in the eminently Hegelian sense of *The Wretched of the Earth*, and especially via the chapter on violence, where freedom as a concept seems to be bound up with the teleological movement of force. And the suspicion would be that if this is the case then it would have a radical impact on our continued understanding of Fanonism itself: *The Wretched of the Earth* seems to propose concepts of freedom and sovereignty within a national-humanist schema that can only be fulfilled by a teleological movement of violence and force.[4]

It may, then, seem curious, in the context of this reservation about Fanonism (which is something that could be traced in several recent works, where Fanonism is called into question precisely because of its national-humanist affirmations)—it may seem curious in this context that Fanon should himself remain so resolutely anti-foundationalist in his characterization of anti-colonialism, and especially in his affirmation of decolonization as the tabula rasa that reverses appearances and renders the first last and his disconcerting insistence on the "wretched," whose meaning is at the furthest remove from national-humanist sovereignty. If the most apparently revolutionary subject *always might* be the least sovereign, then the passage from revolution to sovereignty is no longer so secure. The wretched can become recognized only to the extent that there is at least the suspicion of a non-coincidence between national-humanism and those who fall short of it, between the nation as telos and the *post*colonial nation as the necessary self-interruption of teleology. If Fanon needed to say or to announce that the time has come for a complete and utter tabula rasa, then he implies that in some way that necessity, the having-come of the time that has come, is not so redemptive, not so predictable. If he needed to tell us that the revolutionary moment is a tabula rasa, then this implies that decolonization itself is a time when things are decomposing or dissolving, or when the inherited metaphysical distinctions between ethics and politics, say, or sovereignty and subjectivity, are being erased. And on the other hand, more straightforwardly, this motif of erasure describes a situation in which the new humanism has not yet been determined, something that is, then, radically *unwritten*, and whose structure is enigmatic, and outside of teleology or eschatology. The arrival of the wretched is in this sense always at least potentially not synchronized with the time in which new sovereignty arrives: it is time for the wretched *only when* in some sense they are untimely. Fanon's *The Wretched of the Earth* of course presents itself as arriving at just the wrong—and therefore right—time, and the same can be said for the wretched—just because their arrival suggests a challenge to the political, then maybe the concept of liberation is also dislocated? The revolutionary moment in its arrival arrives as a force or representation; but the chance of erasing what is being produced suggests that force and meaning are not pure idioms of affirmation but revelations whose traces can always be *unscribed*, so that anti-colonialism can, by extension according to the dictionary, signify also a blank slate. But the possibility of the revolution's being the right moment depends on at least the possible (and in fact necessary) dissonance between the moment as event and the moment as the arrival of a new inscription (roughly: what makes it possible for an event to arrive necessarily includes the possibility that it can be erased; this necessary possibility means that it is never completely inscribed; or, what makes it possible for an event to appear in representation necessarily includes the possibility of its disappearance; this necessary possibility means that it never completely appears): and this dissonance then opens the possibility that *any* moment could be written and simultaneously erased, that the question of sovereignty is always the experience of the more or less muted expectation that it too can be suspended, and that the various fantasies we may have of revolution as the unerasable are secondary to this fundamental structure of the relation between time and tabula rasa. If I am right that this is just an analytical consequence of the concept of tabula rasa, then we could link it rapidly to the famous Benjaminian notion of *die rechtsetzende Gewalt*, the moment, itself as timely as it is untimely, at which, according to Benjamin, revolution erupts into a lawmaking violence that fundamentally alters both law and time.[5] The chance of revolutionary violence being lawmaking, given that it interrupts and suspends state law, generates in Benjamin the thought of a messianic time whereby, in the Jewish-Marxist tradition on which Benjamin is drawing, the very foundation of law is suspended over an abyss, suspended before a law that is not yet determined.[6]

II

I want to suggest that it is time today, the right moment, to think about two broad ways of dealing with this situation in Fanonism. The first, which is massively dominant in the Marxist-phenomenological tradition (and especially perhaps the Sartrean tradition), attempts to map the *philosophical* importance of Fanonism in terms of a phenomenology of *experience*, giving rise (or birth) to a drama of freedom and alterity, recognition and authenticity.[7] The second, traces of which can be found no doubt throughout that same tradition but which might be seen more obviously in, say, David Scott, or Achille Mbembe, accentuates the political or ethico-theoretical limits of that dramatization for thinking the postcolonial moment today. I want to suggest that the function of the first type of view is, to state it bluntly, to apprehend blackness as an existential concept: decolonization and humanism, for example, each has its telos or ideal outcome, and this end is the overall prospect of a free community of human beings in the wake of history: "For Europe, for ourselves and for humanity, comrades, we must turn over a new leaf, we must work out new concepts, and try to set afoot a new man."[8] The problem of this "new humanism" inevitably opens the question of a non-humanistic opening to humanism, where, almost by definition, the real interest lies: Fanon's persistent location of blackness as a necessary contamination of traditional political thinking and ontology is proof enough of that. If we are right to suggest that racism interrupts the movement toward the human, and paradoxically makes ontology irrelevant for understanding black existence, then clearly ethics and politics (insofar as they are grounded on this humanism) cannot simply be invoked, even negatively, as a model for thinking black existence. But this puzzle is not insurmountable if philosophical thought can come up with an anthropological description of black experience that is both idiomatic and singular, even if the radical singularity of that description remains bound to colonialism as context. It is this task that, up till now, has oriented phenomenological readings of Fanon; Lewis R. Gordon (focusing explicitly on black lived experience as a series of embodied meanings) discusses Fanon in the context of a dialectics of recognition, referring to freedom, obviously enough, as an existential analytic. Of course not all of Fanon's texts encourage the kind of existential analytic that this attention to experience might seem to promote: Fanon, who famously links the violence of colonialism to language, visuality, and sexuality, thinks of *black* life as a moment of suspension or lived impossibility in which the subject is made excessively, and therefore insufficiently, aware of *being-as-lack* or *defect*: this is the point of many of Fanon's reflections on the unconscious, of course. But the experience of this lack or defect (which can also provoke despair, anguish, disillusion) remains somewhat of a mystery precisely to experience because it cannot be embodied. Such a stress on lack, deferral, and the question of psychic morbidity that cannot be separated from them is of course strictly Fanonian, as many readers know: yet

I have wondered why this question of defect (first explicitly thematized in *Black Skin, White Masks*) has been insistently read as loss, or as something that can be existentially grasped and so restored in some significant sense (I have also wondered here about why Fanonism is seen too immediately, and comfortably, as a discourse of restitution). And this structure brings out another feature of the thought of Fanonism as a thought whose time has passed—Fanonism is, in this second tendency, typically referred to as a phenomenological discourse whose urgent questioning (the moment of separation of authenticity from bad faith, the past from the present, the moment at which all becomes clear, at which the temporal and the contingent resolves into the universal and the absolute) is no longer "ours." On this view, the truth of Fanonism no longer awaits the messianic moment, which will resolve difference into a definitive moment of identity and resolution: Fanonism is judged instead to be a romance of emancipation, whose thought is no longer able to think the postcolonial as such and whose anticolonialism remains tied to the thought of the nation as telos.[9] My unresolved question in this book will be that of whether it is possible to think Fanonism without being committed to this narrative of liberation, or the thought of a deferred universal-humanism, of time having an end in dialectical resolution; and, relatedly, whether it is possible to think of a Fanonism that is not surreptitiously mortgaged to a thought of racism in its understanding of the politics of life.

III

In order to keep things relatively simple, I shall concentrate for this first type of thinking about Fanonism on Ato Sekyi-Otu and Gordon and for the second on Scott and Mbembe. It will rapidly become clear that I do not think that the relationship between these two types of thought is simply oppositional or contradictory, nor indeed that there is, in Fanon's body of work, a time for one and a time for the other. With luck, we may hope to understand a little more clearly how and why Fanonism, as a thinking of emancipation, is also and thereby affirmative of a narrative that liberates.

Let me begin by recalling some crucial features of Sekyi-Otu's "African-situationist" reading of Fanon in *Fanon's Dialectic of Experience*.[10] The main gesture of the book is one of reclaiming Fanonism from the illicit "Fanon of the postmodernist imagination," or of rescuing Fanonism from being misused or even abused outside the home of post-independence Africa.[11] Any temptation we, or some of us, may have had to read Fanon as a non-dialectical, anti-foundational, psychoanalytic thinker is sternly put in its place as an irresponsible, because politically ill-formed, nihilism, and this judgment, handed down to us by a vigilant *"postindependence reader,"* seems to stretch to all diasporic metropolitan readers who have, presumably, not "witnessed the desolation of the world after independence."[12] Not only does Sekyi-Otu maintain that Fanon's entire output is formalizable as a set of dramatic narratives (ignoring any explicit attempts that have been made to show that Fanonism is, both conceptually and textually, neither a philosophy nor an hermeneutics), but he tells us repeatedly that Fanonism is essentially, and unashamedly, a *dialectical* humanism whose true philosophical import is the universal. Accordingly, Sekyi-Otu has no qualms whatsoever in determining Fanon's entire output as a dramatic narrative that is dialectical in form:

What, then, does it mean to read Fanon's texts as if they constituted a dialectical dramatic narrative? Briefly and provisionally put: It means, first, that the relationships between utterance and proposition, representation and truth, enacted practice and authorial advocacy, are rendered quite problematic. It means, furthermore, that an utterance or a representation or a practice we encounter in a text is to be considered not as a discrete and conclusive event, but rather as a strategic and self-revising act set in motion by changing circumstances and perspectives, increasingly intricate configurations of experience. . . . We shall encounter instances in which seemingly privileged pictures and rhetorics are reviewed, renounced, and replaced in the course of a movement of experience and language of which Fanon is the dramatist, albeit in the role of a passionate participant and interlocutor. The result is a critical and visionary narrative that provides a vantage point from which we may measure the promise and performance of postcolonial life.

And it is the language of *political* experience that I propose to feature as a principal subject of Fanon's dramatic narrative.[13]

This insistence on a "dialectic of experience" is a leitmotif of Sekyi-Otu's book, and is essentially argued against the rival postmodern Fanon, although Sekyi-Otu does also make his reading rely on a series of hermeneutic gestures, separating the "increasingly intricate configurations of experience" from any misguided attempt to "bestow upon utterances in his [Fanon's] texts the coercive finality of irrevocable propositions and doctrinal statements," or dialectics from axiomatics.[14] Fanonism, Sekyi-

Otu seems to imply, is only apparently systematic, and attempts to secure its systematicity have tended to violate its dialectical performativity:
that is, Fanonism is endlessly self-revising, but *not strategic enough* to traverse dialectics in the hermeneutic ways that Sekyi-Otu, paradoxically
enough, claims are *more* properly Fanonian. This problematic of performance, and all that it implies, also has institutional and professional implications for the "ownership" of Fanonism by Fanonians: Fanon's work
may annoy political theorists by being so disciplinarily promiscuous, so
open, despite its very real difficulty, to readers of all sorts, including post-
modernists and post-independence readers, but dealing with that annoy-
ance by a making a claim for proper ownership—*"our* Fanon,"[15] or "I
claim an authentic Fanon"[16]—is always likely to confuse reading with a
phantasmatic appropriation or criticism of Fanon. As an example: Sekyi-
Otu spends several pages in his prologue and introduction refuting Homi
Bhabha's view of Fanon's early work as giving up on the political and the
social in favor of the private and the psychic, and does indeed refute the
view that the latter has any priority for understanding the lived experience of the black, but Bhabha makes an easy target in this respect (if only
because he has, along with many other psychoanalytic readers of Fanon,
opposed "a dialectic of deliverance" to the languages of "demand and desire"), and there are much more complicated ways of trying to talk about
the relationship of Fanon and psychoanalysis than Bhabha's.[17] It is easy
to argue that "Fanon ultimately gives psychoanalytic language no more
and no less than an analogical or metaphoric function, as distinct from
a foundational or etiological one" if the only other possibility is "the primacy of the psychic and the psychological," or some other kind of psychological essentialism.[18] But the point here is to claim that the language
of neurosis (and this is just what Fanon's dialectic of experience helps us
to understand) is, in its analogical or metaphoric dependence, never simply secondary to "the language of political experience" whose priority is
(in the sense both of revolutionary possibility and of state retribution)
never simply decipherable, or *readable*, without the detour of (racial) figure or the figurability of psychoanalysis, and in fact this is a key insight
of Fanon's work. The problem with Sekyi-Otu's approach is, paradoxically enough, its prescriptive performance of Fanon's dialectical narrative as politics: Sekyi-Otu's commitment to performance, dialectics, and
post-independence African politics leads him to provide an anything-but-

dialectical account of Fanonism and appears to break the rules of reading he has set himself (which should prevent the privileging of certain pictures or rhetorics). Sekyi-Otu wants to argue that whereas in "*the* psychologizing reading of Fanon" what was at stake was a univocal concern with the psychic and the psychological, in his dialectical concern with narration and performance he moves beyond the "analogical and metaphoric" function of psychoanalytical language, to the more originary example of the political.[19] Sekyi-Otu's understanding is that Fanon takes colonialism as having to do with a "perversion" of the politics of life (he uses the term within scare quotes at first, but soon stops that and never thinks through the difficult implications there may be in relying on a psychoanalytically determined concept to describe the political: the non-metaphorical use of perversion is presumably what makes the priority of the political's relationship to psychoanalytic metaphoricity possible), and that Fanon seeks to overcome that "perversity" (of state, time, space, class, race, and gender) by formulating what Sekyi-Otu repeatedly calls, in a strong singularizing gesture, "an incipient dialectical critique of truth."[20] It seems to follow that if we are to read this reading, we should ask the question, why should *politics* (as a dialectical-hermeneutic performance) suggest an originality of prescription whose claim to epistemological rightness, as Sekyi-Otu asserts, subsumes both analogy and metaphor? When he writes that "it is the language of *political* experience that I propose to feature as the principal subject of Fanon's dramatic narrative," he seems to be unaware that he is performing prescription in precisely this privilege given to the "political" (in italics); and in so far as this referential dimension of the political is taken to be definitive of the Fanonian text, and thereby any possible reading of those texts, then it seems important to resist this "presumption" that the meaning of the political could ever be so simple or secure. Simply assenting to this reading is thus, in view of the passage read, which opposes the performative dimension of the Fanonian text to the "coercive finality of irrevocable propositions and doctrinal statements," a failure to read dialectically.[21]

This is not all. A necessary corollary of this particular reductive form of politics is that when we do finally arrive at Fanon's "narrative," Sekyi-Otu has largely to shift abruptly from anti-dialectics to dialectics, and *de*-psychoanalyze Fanon's thought. In this complex setup, colonialism is deemed to be an anti-dialectical *space*, that is, a zone of "reciprocal exclusivity," in Fanon's phrase, that resists Marxian notions of time as labor, and anti-colonialism is judged to produce a new dialectical *structure* of class and national emergency that is the starting point for a new universalism—it is a bold presentation, but the psychic costs of colonial war are never discussed as such, and the opposition between space and time simplifies what Fanon himself says about the experience of space and time in the colony (as a kind of dead, petrified spacing of time), and in the postcolony (as the moment of tabula rasa where thinking is recalled to time and the becoming time of the nation transforms the space of ethical and political life). The point is that not only in his explicit reflection on violence, perversion, politics, and race, but also in his own clinical study of the psychoses that closes *The Wretched of the Earth*, Fanon necessarily escapes the type of simple opposition and naming that Sekyi-Otu presupposes in his account. To the extent (and Sekyi-Otu does have some fine passages on this) that Fanon refuses metalanguage in the name of "truths that are only partial, limited, and unstable," to the extent that this refusal is of a piece with his reinvention of political concepts in the colony so as to measure up to the racialization and globalization of capital (i.e. the colonial bourgeoisie and proletariat cannot be contextualized according to traditional Marxist thought), then it is entirely misleading to suggest that Fanonism or Fanon's text "proposes a classical dialectical resolution of these aporias" that Sekyi-Otu has to assume.[22] This resolution situates Fanonism in terms of (a particular dramatization of) "immediacy as a 'territory of mediation,'" and specifically in terms of the lived immediacy of racism (the "perverse genealogy" of which is then reflected by dialectical cognition), that is then made to enter into an "authentic project of particularity" as Fanon plots the emergence of a national consciousness beyond both nationalism and race.[23] The curious effect of this, which means that the reader of Sekyi-Otu's book is called upon to view Fanonism as a series of contingent positional statements, is that a compelling and at times brilliant account of Fanon's anti-dialectics is presented in tandem with a set of claims about a dialectics of *experience* as though the "perversity" grounding the whole analysis were, from the start, separable from Fanonism's "*aborted dialectic*" which, because of the Hegelian metanarrative itself, can only appear as finite, transient, aporetic.[24] There is really no way that Sekyi-Otu can understand in this perspective the fact that Fanon's descriptions of pathological racism should be worked out in and through a psychoanalysis of perversion, a reading that shows that *no* concept can attain to the value of (non-perverse) mastery, and that this situation is originary to the history of colonialism itself.

Whence the necessity for a "universalizable truth": Sekyi-Otu is committed to a vision of Fanonism as a *"political pragmatics of the sign,"* whose first move is to critique colonialism's language of exclusion, in so far as that language is founded on "separation and subjugation," and subsequently to reveal the conditions of possibility for a national consciousness whose universal structure might then be built.[25] Language emerges as an issue in these analyses, let us remember, because of the reciprocally exclusive structure of colonial domination: the anti-dialectic or drama that is necessarily violent and that, to the extent that it brings into being the "inaugural figuration" of colonizer and colonized, relies on a figural mode (of separation and subjugation) that has, in the words of Fanon, "ontological implications" for life in the colony.[26] Sekyi-Otu sees these implications as fourfold: (1) identifying why things "are never perceived in themselves" but are devoured, haunted by race (the words are Fanon's); (2) describing how native speech never participates in this world of signs and is transformed into a pre-ontological language without articulation, a language of shrieks and sighs, clicks and mimicry; (3) assuming that these "highly alienated meanings" must signal the hypertrophy of subjugated life as body, voice, word, and gesture are each absorbed into forms of domination; and (4) being surprised to find how modern technology (i.e. the radio) allows the transformation of native speech into a new way of making itself audible that simultaneously absorbs and expels the colonizer's language and represents a new somatic-semantic event.[27] These factors had purchase at a time of colonial war, writes Fanon, because they "unified experience and gave it a universal dimension"; and so, by virtue of this disjunction, the world of false appearances and the chaos of simulacra were negated by the "message of truth" that the nation awaited.[28] And here we find an interesting twist: the "new language of the nation" is to be neither French nor Arabic, neither native nor foreign, tribal nor modern, but the space for their multiple *mediation* as signs of a new meaning-bearing event that is radically indeterminate (as Ronald Judy points out, this new expression transcends both the *arabisant* and the *francisant*[29]). To that extent, however unifying the discourse of the emerging nation may be to the colonized, and however pressing the transformation of signs may be to native signification, it can never in principle enter directly into this "dialectical transcendence" of word by nation, as Fanon paradoxically attempts to make it so enter through his claims that it was "created out of nothing" (*créé de rien*).[30] Sekyi-Otu ascribes this *ex nihilo* to "poetic excess," but the possibility of the nation appearing as such out of nothing, and quite independently of any dialectics of emergence, raises again the founding power of the tabula rasa as something inexpressible, and not inscribable into political structure but defining it; this creating out of a void, or hiatus, goes far beyond the forms of reciprocal exclusivity and their determination by dialectics.[31] The curious effect of this, which means that the revolution is always separated from its various materializations in presence, means that the dialectic is presented as always *haunted* by a void or lack that it cannot absorb nor exorcise. The upshot is that, in contrast to Sekyi-Otu, who writes a phenomenological anthropology of Fanonism as the "gathering of the universal," Fanon writes of the ontological implications of a revolutionary hiatus that is groundless, whose untimeliness is irreducible to dialectical forms of antagonism, and whose creativity can only be evoked in the absence of institutions or rules, ideologies or statements.[32]

IV

The ontological implications of Fanonism are also the dominant concern of Lewis R. Gordon's brief, yet incisive account in *Fanon and the Crisis of European Man*. For it is indeed the question of existence, rather than, say, the complexity of being and truth, that gives the book its main theme and is the focus of an explicit concern with "humanity and reason" and their respective crises in the texts of European philosophy: "By Europe, we mean Edmund Husserl's description of a place" (in the *Crisis of European Sciences*); and by crisis, Gordon means *krinein*, the crisis of European Man's decision not to decide (a crisis that Fanon "embodies").[33] It is tempting to speculate that if the man of color symbolizes the "sickness" of "European Man" then this sickness is of a piece with what is arguably Gordon's most powerfully reductive gesture in his reading of Fanon, which consists in presenting Fanonism as essentially a philosophical anthropology of bad faith that is also philosophy's diagnosis and cure.[34] Gordon knows and understands French existential phenomenology and its influence on many aspects of Fanon's thought (such as the idea of a "sociogenesis" of black affective life, or the relation between ontology and existence) that many commentators have failed to explicate accurately.[35] As I shall suggest, though, these insights are bought at the price of a number of powerful but reductive decisions Gordon has taken about Fanonism as a philosophy: in fact, in so far as Fanon's "questioning of the question of man" is, following Husserl, "a philosophy critical of the West within the West," that questioning seems to become, despite Gordon's claims to the contrary, solely an interpretation of European philosophy's interpretation of humanistic crisis, a reflection that allows philosophy to see its own racial thought or structure at long last— the same goes for the famous interpretation of Sartre's "*Orphée Noir*" in *Black Skin, White Masks*—but then Gordon seems to know this in so far as he explicitly presents Fanon as a black existentialist who allows philosophy to see, as if for the first time, the "existential reality" of race.[36]

For it is indeed philosophical anthropology, rather than any ontological concern with Being, that gives the book its particular thematics (historical, existentialist, humanist, etc.), and via an explicitly Husserlian-Sartrean inflection:

Bad faith becomes a feature of all dimensions of crisis. . . . Every black person *faces* history—*his* or *her* story—every day as a situation, as a choice, of how to stand in relation to oppression, of whether to live as a being subsumed by oppression or to live as active resistance towards liberation, or to live as mere indifference. This conception of history is rooted in daily life. . . . There is no question of elevating one's value beyond oneself into a spirit of seriousness. There is, instead, the recognition of how one's *actions* unfold into one's identity in relation to the socio-temporal location of one's experience.[37]

Such a stress on duplicity, resistance, and indifference and the question of decision that cannot be separated from them is especially Fanonian, as Gordon knows: Fanon's "liberating praxis" is thus taken to be a *philosophical* response to *forms of bad faith*, indeed Gordon explicitly thematizes Fanon's life as an existential struggle against nihilism and Fanon's political thought as an attempt to restore black life to an experience of radical immanence (via praxis, revolution, restitution, therapy, etc.), so as to free human being from the crisis of "racist reason."[38] The argument here, rather as in Sekyi-Otu, starts from the view that blackness is the anthropological response to racist ontology and that Fanon's importance lies in the way he draws attention to this visible-invisible characterization of blackness as non-being, as a way of rejecting racial ontology whenever it appears: the point being that Fanon does not simply respect the question of existence as secured by philosophy's signature, but is happy to find philosophical moments in, say, the

everyday. Now it takes only a moment's reflection on Fanon's most sche-
matic presentations of black experience to realize that this must be, from
the start, a partial and inaccurate presentation, insofar as the rejection of
ontology is very precisely and explicitly to do with *failed reciprocity*, not just
in the Hegelian-Kojevean schema of freedom through mediation but in the
sense of a "lack" or "defect" at the common root of being and thought, and
whose "morbid universe" is fundamentally foreign to a phenomenology
of embodiment, as *Fanon and the Crisis of European Man* has it.[39] However important Fanon's meditations on bad faith may be, it is a bold reader
(but Gordon is nothing if not bold) who takes as his central concept for
the explication of Fanonism a phenomenological notion of *krinein* or *kri-
sis* despite what Fanon himself says is his irreducibly "psychological" approach (in the first pages of *Black Skin, White Masks*, the sociogenic, far
from being opposed to psychoanalysis, is in fact revealed as its very essence:
that is, Fanon's "clinical study" explores the interdependence of the two as
the twin poles of a reversible message as he moves from a "lytic" reading of
symptoms to a genetic reading of how egos are traversed by socio-symbolic
structure). If, as "The Lived Experience of the Black" famously claims, but
as Gordon does not see fit to pursue, there can be no ontological resistance to the white world because the black is an "overdetermined" subject,
a subject who is essentially derealized (by imago, culture, unconscious, and
world), then making existence the center of one's account is quite a statement, but also a sign that something is being simplified. Given the philosophical complexity of much of Gordon's argumentation, this may seem a
churlish complaint, so I shall try and justify it in what follows.

Gordon's third chapter opens with the need to contextualize racism in
the sense of a *perverse* anonymity:

Racism renders the individual anonymous even to himself. The very standpoint
of consciousness, embodiment itself, is saturated with a strangeness that either
locks the individual into the mechanism of things or sends him away and transforms him into an observer hovering over that very thing. Thus, to be seen in a
racist way is an ironic way of *not being seen* through *being seen*. It is to be seen
with overdetermined anonymity, which amounts, in effect, to invisibility. For to
be seen in a typically human way is to be seen as a point of epistemological limitation; one's subjectivity is called upon as a point of meaning. . . . The perversion of anonymity—overdetermination—seals off such affirmations [of reciprocal
recognitions].[40]

A necessary corollary of this perverse anonymity (which determines Gordon's project as a whole, of which he tries to situate Fanonism as a particular reading) is "alienated embodiment": "like his identifiers, the Negro finds himself facing the objective alienation of his embodiment *out there*" (that is, in the racist world).[41] I cannot here unpack all the implications of this deceptively simple picture. One, on which Gordon is insistent, is that this strangeness comes more or less violently—but always violently—from the outside which, just because the black is overdetermined from without, remains more or less a situation of objectification and denudation. But there are a number of reasons for resisting this way of looking at it. For a start, the way overdetermination is described in *Black Skin, White Masks*, it is clear that this "strangeness" is no longer describable as a question of encounter at all. As Fanon shows repeatedly in "The Negro and Psychopathology," the feeling of estrangement is not simply a result of contact: "Frequently the negro who becomes abnormal [*s'anormalise*] has never had any relations with the White man. . . . Has there been a real traumatism [*traumatisme effectif*]? To all of this we have to answer: *no*."[42] Elsewhere Fanon refers to the singular experience of the self or ego being invaded and breached by the "unidentifiable and unassimilable."[43] Fanon goes on to suggest that this manifestation *within* of something that cannot, so to speak, be owned or possessed, seen or intuited, is of the order of a radical de-situating of the ego, that necessarily interrupts—evacuates, empties—the very possibility of transcendental reflection on the seer and the seen. Anonymity is essentially *pervertible*, then, not because one is enslaved to a black appearance, but because one is—wishfully, unconsciously—already a slave to the *imago* of whiteness and that this pervertibility is the condition (to be violently affirmed) of what it means to be a black subject. "In the Antilles," Fanon suggests, "perception always occurs on the level of the imaginary. It is in white terms that one perceives one's fellows."[44] To be black, then, is to be originally violated by a whiteness that comes from the inside out, and this anteriority necessarily follows from an intimacy that is already perverse. I think it would not be hard on the basis of these observations to show that the way overdetermination is determined here can already be read, with the help of Fanon's work on the psychoneuroses, as marked by a kind of intimacy that remains radically alien to the subject, a sort of self-interrupting *that within* in which the subject cannot reflect itself as a subject, a *décalage* that can never appear as such, never give itself to a phenomenology of *seeing*, but that nonetheless haunts both seer and the seen, an intimacy that also marks a crucial shift in Fanon's relation to phenomenology.[45]

Gordon especially struggles with this shift and, casting in his lot with the phenomenological tradition (which he clearly thinks according to Husserlian "reduction"), appeals to a notion of perversion (a point he shares with Sekyi-Otu) that is marked in advance by its opposition to psychoanalysis. Perverse anonymity is, then, the concept that Gordon goes on to suggest defines the black existential attitude and, in the context of a later essay, the reason why Fanon turns away from psychoanalysis: although this schema has been quite common in reading Fanon, and consists in saying that "politics" is Fanonism's true *telos*, Gordon's argument is curious because, in opposing existentialism to psychoanalysis, and despite Fanon's refusal to separate them, he has to remove what he calls psychoanalysis from what Fanon calls his psychopathology of race.[46] Thus, psychoanalysis is reproached for its inability to think blacks as "perverse anonymous objects," a failure that gets further reduced to saying that "Only the white, whether female or male, can be historically situated on the symbolic level," partly no doubt because black existence is, from the start, understood to be never neurotically alienated, but alienated in so far as it is black.[47] What is properly black is thus what is properly, perversely alienated and somehow beyond a psychoanalytical reading of language and culture. For Gordon, Fanon gives us the insight that blackness always means what it is—*the black*, and this singularizing typicality, operating what Gordon calls "below the symbolic," dictates a number of consequences for Gordon's understanding of the relations between psychoanalysis and phenomenology in Fanon's works.[48]

Let us be clear. Fanon's first explicit engagements with the notion of a black divided subject come not in relation to Freud, but via the motif of *déréalisation* in Sartre, and he always associates this motif with problems of the *pour soi* as Sartre wields that concept (as a self-presence that is always separated from itself: "The *pour-soi* has no being because its being is always at a distance";[49] and whose *soi* is only *soi* insofar as it is necessarily "an elsewhere in relation to itself,"[50] that is "*diasporique*" or dispersed; and which can only be truly *for* itself, as a synthetic construct of consciousness, insofar as it is object-less, a nothing or nihilation [*néantisation*], and this is its very possibility as a subject). But it is Sartre's description of the *pour soi* as a being "always in abeyance, because its being is a perpetual deferring" that Fanon analyzes most fully in his reworking of this motif.[51] Fanon identifies in the colonial subject a voidlike nothingness-of-being that is also linked to the problem of self-deception [*mauvaise foi*] in Sartre (a link that will allow him to develop thoughts on how the black subject is always belated and dispersed, is *irrealized* and yet forever haunted by its non-appearance, and can only acquire a certain density of being by taking on the tragic neurotic role [of an imaginary whiteness]—which is also why phenomenology can never be grounded in the experience of this subject for its truth is literally void). Whence the notion, in the pages of *Black Skin, White Masks* on psychopathology, of a subject who is "possessed" by culture—by its racist "impersonation" (*impersonation*; the word is from Sartre's *L'Imaginaire*)[52]—who is no longer the subject of its experiences, and whose narcissism, or style of being, can only move from abjection to abandonment: this is a subject whose situation is one of mimicry or personation, and who "fucks [whiteness] to render himself imaginary" (*baise pour s'irréaliser*; the words are again from Sartre).[53]

Fanon draws a number of consequences from Sartre's "eidetic analysis of self-deception."[54] First of all, he says that this "zone of nonbeing" refers to an unconscious schism or *décalage*, and later, in a reading of René Maran, claims that this dereliction or lack is simultaneously the work of racist culture. Later he will say that the colonial subject is an alienating synthesis of *ressentiment* and *agressivité*, and whose *vécu* nonetheless reveals, as it were, how an impersonated whiteness is the necessary consequence of a personated blackness: "For the Black [*le Noir*] no longer has to be black [*noir*], but must be it in the face of the White [*en face du Blanc*]."[55] And: "It's no good: I am a White Man. For unconsciously, I guard against what is black in me, that is, the totality of my being."[56] In this familiarly disconcerting analysis of identity, Fanon describes a self that is white and yet totally black, a self embattled by an unconscious distrust (white *and* on guard) of its black identity (the "I" *and* its totality); and to the extent that this is a self traversed by an uncanny doubling (white *and* black), then it is clear that black cannot simply be made white because to be black is to be already, unconsciously white. We're back with the notion of an irreducible perversity here, with an ego whose mask hides nothing, for nothing (absence, simulation, impersonation, irrealization) is its imaginary synthesis—and the very thing that makes it identifiable as an image of being is what fissures it and deforms it as a ghostly double of being.

It would appear, then, that the self-deceived black is caught up in a tragic interplay: like the actor he is, he can only reveal himself as a (black) subject via the oblique confirmation of an imaginary whiteness whose power and culture he wants to acquire; just as the blackness that he constitutively hides from, and whose dense opacity haunts him as a dereliction, can only be borne in so far as it is determined as a persona or mask that hides the whiteness within, and first of all because the ego is spectator here to an unconscious that degrades and despises the *nègre*. This opposition between blackness and whiteness is not between bad faith and sincerity but between two indeterminate positions: thus it is, for example, impossible to say whether unconscious distrust is more sincere than egoic self-deception (at least in Gordon's sense of being able to decide what is decidable), or whether the white, which the imago pares away to reveal, is not more feigned than the black that it masks. The play between persona and mask, desire and distrust, mimicry and personation, has become impossible to unravel into an unequivocal meaning (of crisis or decision).

We have thus come back to the question of whether decision, even in its most duplicitous or indifferent forms, is too simple a reading of demand *and* desire (the demand for recognition, the unconscious desire that interrupts it), for if they are no more separable from each other than from the distrust that signifies the problematic join between them and whose intimacy bequeaths the advent of doubling and division, then does it even make sense to argue for a decision that isn't already implicated in perversity? Alienation emerges as an issue in *Fanon and the Crisis of European Man*, let us remember, because of anti-black racism: whence the stress on decisionism. The problem with this approach is its pursuit of an equally singular notion of redeemed life: Gordon's reading of black liberation as the authentic choice of a mundane life (if only we [blacks] could simply *be*) is anything but a Fanonian reading of how illusions sustain desire, or how desire sustains the illusion of immediacy. Whence the title of Fanon's first book. We protect ourselves from the real (of racism) behind suitably contrived illusions or masks. (And the existentialist pursuit of authenticity is just one more example of self-deception, a pursuit that ends up with the ego taking itself to be the ground of Being, and ipseity the experience itself of unconditioned liberty. Even Sartre, in his early work, considered sincerity to be a version of bad faith.) To the extent (and Bhabha has some brilliant passages on this) that Fanonism is a concern with the duplicitous languages of demand and desire, to the extent that racism is not simply a refuge from desire but also somewhat its provocation, then it is entirely misleading to suggest that because one is typically negro or white so, by the same token, are one's fantasies, hatreds, intuitions, and beliefs. This severely normative presentation itself relies on a version of black psychic life as perversely anonymous, which is quite as debilitating as the projections of anti-black racism that Gordon chides with such authority. Further still, if it is true that Sartrean notions of absolute freedom and universal responsibility remained crucial for Fanon, then we must assume that the *pour-soi*, like the tabula rasa, evokes a process that eludes all identity and all description and can only be *for* itself in so far as it is nothing, that is without object and a void-based invention. This does seem, in the context of some of the political writings, to be justified. But I would suggest that if Fanon does have a tragic conception of existence (both Sekyi-Otu and Gordon think this), it is because he breaks decisively with Sartre's early conception of absolute freedom (as a thinking that preserves the illusions of the ego), but equally with Sartre's later, more dialectical conception of emancipation (which also retains the thinking of the subject as a sovereign act or decision). Despite the influence of Sartre, Fanon's notion of liberation is much more aporetic—and that is because the black subject is the thought of difference suspended between immanence and transcendence. One consequence of this is that Gordon's own placing of Fanon in a tradition of phenomenological thought remains too historicist and yet not sufficiently historical.

V

History, aporia, narrative: so far we have seen how the Marxist-phenomenological tradition of reading Fanon, in its reliance on an hermeneutic narrative of experience, has tended to exclude the psychopolitical from the problem of the political in Fanon's work. This reading tends to purge Fanonism as a complex thinking of violence, power, and sexuality, but in so doing it fails to comprehend the violent affects of its own interpretation, and one plausible way of reading Fanon's work as a whole is that it shows up an irreducible phantasmatic racialism even in the most theoretical or speculative domains of psychoanalysis and philosophy. In a way that is not at all a "reduction" in the sense of phenomenology mentioned earlier,

Fanon on this account would reveal a *fantasy* or *fetish* in the philosophical concept of race itself, so that *all the philosophical readings of Fanonism* could be taken to be examples of an unavoidable *ressentiment*: namely the very thing that allows philosophy to think the concept of race is precisely what forbids it from understanding those dimensions of race that refuse to be contained in the historico-hermeneutic narratives with which philosophy has traditionally distinguished race as a "philosophical" concept.[57] This tension, according to which the philosophical concept of race is itself constituted by a form of racist disavowal, could be followed throughout Fanon's work in various forms: the relation between fantasy and experience, time and labor, knowledge and desire, violence and freedom, dialectic and tabula rasa, and so on, the point being that no term should be reduced to or separated from its opposite if we are to understand Fanon's rigorous thinking on the temporalization and affective dimensions of race. This aporetic thinking has consequences for the analysis of Fanonism as a *narrative* or eschatology. The category of narrative has been crucial to recent readings of Fanon (its reference seems to be shorthand for a kind of dialectical-hermeneutic faith), but as a category it cannot do justice to Fanon's interest in the contingent, the singular, or the violent impropriety of his own thinking on revolution or race. Fanon's thinking of tabula rasa disallows this teleological narrative, or at least complicates it to the extent that what decolonial violence amounts to is an affirmation of the endless interruption of the political as such. Perhaps it is not yet time for this suggestion. Maybe we can take another step, accepting the priority of narrative, but questioning its claims as an understanding of the Fanonism at stake today.

We can sharpen up all these points by turning to those readings that insist on analyzing Fanonism as a political story of liberation whose time has passed or is no longer in question.[58] In *Refashioning Futures*, David Scott presents a generalized critique of Fanon's narrative of liberation, casting doubt on what he insists is a key figure of Fanonian discourse: *alienation*. Scott does not justify his privileging of the term with any references from Fanon himself, which is not surprising, because it is hardly a common word in Fanon's writing. Yet Scott is prepared to claim that the very concept of alienation, as the key term of Fanon's counter-positioning of power and freedom, is an intrinsic part of the latter's "metaphysics of self and power."[59] This alienation is a discursive and not materialist reality in that it gives rise to a concept of a repressing power that is absolute and to-talizing, as is the case with colonialism. *All* acts of anti-colonial liberation are therefore attempts at overcoming alienation:

A narrative of liberation, on this view, works through the construction of a certain economy of discourse, the central elements of which are not hard to identify: it operates by constructing, for instance, a teleological rhythm in which the various moments and maneuvers that constitute the struggle are identified in their succession; by constructing a repressive power that denies the subjugated their essential humanity, and whose absolute overcoming constitutes the singular objective and destiny of the struggle; by constructing a subject who moves from alienated de-humanization to self-realization; and by constructing a "beyond" in which there emerges a new and unencumbered humanity.[60]

This narrative of liberation is, Scott argues, the most familiar, if problem-atic, idiom of Fanonism. It is a story in which collisions between power (the repressive nation-state) and subjects (the anti-colonial revolutionary) appear as mutually antagonistic terms in a narrative of heroic romance, revolutionary struggle, and self-realization. Only romance (most typically in the form of a utopian imagining of the future) adequately captures this story of "a triumph of good over evil, virtue over vice, light over darkness, and of the ultimate transcendence of man over the world in which he was imprisoned by the fall" (and simultaneously the collapse of history into al-legory), and the revolutionary subject remains the privileged agent of this narrative.[61] Romance denotes an historical faith in progress that is, accord-ing to Scott's argument, to be grasped as an inadequate way of thinking about the relationship between past and future. For Scott this narrative is no longer of discursive use, and we therefore need to move on from its "emplotment," for only tragedy (and not anti-colonial nationalist ro-mance) provides an adequate perspective on those moments of historical crisis and transformation defining *our* postcolonial sovereignty today (it is worth noting how often Scott uses the collective pronoun to contextual-ize his history of the present, having deemed colonialism's future a future past). The problem with this approach is its negative determination of te-leology as history: Scott's commitment to an anti-teleological reading of history leads him to provide, in his critique of Fanon, a teleological history of postcolonial tragedy (first was anti-colonial romance, then came post-colonial tragedy, then came the conceptual contextualization of this shift as elegiac history, so instead of optimism and faith we now have instability and crisis: the question then becomes whether this melancholia is not itself a specifically romantic narrative of historical crisis, which also means that if there is a question here of a choice to be made, Scott's reading of Fanonism as part of a romantic tradition already falls foul of his tragic determination of it). What is going on here? Here again, as with alienation, it would appear that Fanon gets revolution slightly wrong, which would on this account be because he has an uncritical faith in history, produced as a liberatory narrative that Scott is generous enough to outline for him and us. It is a crucial feature of Scott's account that anti-colonial nationalists (Fanon being his prime example) are not *conscious* of conflicting, often irreconcilable demands between resistance and liberation other than via an essentially negative, totalizing view of power—Fanonism represents a vision of power that turns it into a question of negation or acquiescence, but that vision also fails to appreciate, according to Scott, how power often shapes resistance in ambiguous ways:

At the same time that I want to appreciate the problem-space in relation to which the Fanonian narrative is articulated, I also want to resist some of its normative implications, in particular those that bear on how we seek to derive affirmative claims about the preferred forms of political community in *post*colonial society. In the Fanonian story the idea is that the colonized are alienated from a harmonious identity; that this alienation is fostered by colonial institutions that repress the colonized self and prevent the colonized people from achieving a higher and unifying consensus. The redemptive project of overcoming colonialism is to return the natives to themselves. But who exactly are these "natives"? What is their gender? What is their ethnicity? What is their class? What is their sexual orientation? What are their modes of self-fashioning? My worry is that the Fanonian story underwrites too much—or gives too much space to—the normalized centrality of a specific identity, even though an identity argued to have suffered particular injuries under colonial domination. . . . I am arguing, in short, that the Fanonian story licenses too unreflective an idea of an essential native subject.[62]

Scott's stress in this passage on the "normative implications" of Fanon's narrative is no doubt necessary: there's an obviousness about the link of liberation to realized identity (one is alienated because one's humanity has been denied by a repressing power) that would tend to equate the experience of post-independence with a new sovereign identity. But the argument that the essential humanity of the colonized has been concealed or repressed seems to encourage the idea that this is Fanon's only view of the subject, while discouraging at least one pivotal aspect of the Fanonian story: and that is quite simply the concern with the unconscious, which precisely involves positing a subject that is irreducibly alienated from itself. Or perhaps, paradoxically, a subject whose future liberation exceeds the political concept of liberation, which is also to do with a resistance whose paradoxical structure cannot be measured by the normative terms of resistance whatever they may be. So perhaps, for Scott, the "Fanonian problematic of liberation . . . is, of course, simultaneously a liberation of colonial desire," but what if that desire precisely involves something altogether more agonistic and intractable?[63] Although I shall not here attempt to follow Scott's discussion of a subject "in the grip of a repressed truth buried under the ponderous weight of a repressing colonial power," it is clear to me that this is not Fanon's last word on the subject: from the stress on psychoses as one of the necessary symptoms of colonial war in the concluding chapter of *The Wretched of the Earth*, through the rereading of the concepts of dreamwork and fantasy in Fanon's disagreement with Mannoni, via analysis of *Prospero and Caliban*, to the therapeutic discussions of *"dépersonnalisation"* in relation to the clinical sessions at Blida-Joinville and Charles-Nicolle, Fanon has in fact constantly been writing about unconscious desire, *without making any teleological predications*.[64] What I shall be attempting to do here is no more than an elaboration of that structure. In the final chapter of *The Wretched of the Earth*, on "Colonial War and Mental Disorders," for example, Fanon's concern is with how anti-colonial revolution, far from producing emancipated subjects, can also produce subjects who are radically dispossessed (from which it seems to follow that the word "disorder" now replaces alienation, a word that occurs much less than Scott assumes).[65] The understanding that colonial war "is singular even in the pathology that it gives rise to" leads Fanon to recognize the power of psychoses in producing a kind of egological "vertigo," and therefore a "haunted" subject that forces him, in spite of himself, to rethink the distinctions between ethics and politics, or, in his own words, "the question of responsibility within the revolutionary framework."[66] Alienation presumes an existential crisis that can be repaired, an identity or coherence that can be restored (which is why, in his late work, Fanon will say that colonial war gives rise to a pathology whose singularity cannot be mapped in this way, and why it is possible for him to now talk of a kind of *vertiginous* subject, a subject destroyed and hypnotized by the extreme literal violence of the war that he or she nonetheless embodies—this is what justifies Fanon in his objections to the whole discourse of responsibility in the revolutionary context, especially in his psychiatric work with patients, and gives some substance to the sense that their disorders are absolute, and represent "cases where the whole of the personality is disrupted definitely"—disorders that no amount of emancipation can ever make up for).[67]

Scott's narrative of liberation, however, appears to overlook these aspects of Fanonism, and is concerned only with the relation of alienation to emancipation in general (which is why Fanonism is reduced to a thought of the normative implications of difference rather than, say, a thinking on the perversity of *difference* within colonialism per se), and why, as Scott himself says, liberation is considered to be solely a matter of self-realization. This is all rather strange: even on Scott's own account, desire is never simply liberated. The subject subsumed under this concept is called unrepressed and free: these are not words that Fanon uses to describe the colonial subject: the names he gives (and here we return to the questions about the unconscious) do not name anything like an essence, but draw on terms borrowed from Freud, Lacan, and Ferenczi (terms that invoke a negrophobogenesis at the level of personhood and culture; see Alice Cherki's helpfully clear expositions of these borrowings in her *Frantz Fanon: A Portrait*).[68] To clarify: Fanon's political writings are all written in tension with a certain psychoanalytic thinking: his anti-colonialism is explicated on the basis of the clinic and vice versa; they are thought simultaneously. By far the most useful discussion of Fanonism and psychoanalysis is provided by Vicky Lebeau's analysis of Fanon's *psychopolitics*, weaving together questions of the real and fantasy on the basis of a non-oppositional difference between dreamwork and culture.[69] We take it that this relation to psychoanalysis is familiar to all readers of Fanon, and that there is no need to explain again why it is simply a mistake to assume that this signals some unfortunate collusion with a naïve and voluntarist idea of the subject (an error that recurs whenever Fanon's work as a psychiatrist is in question, and in fact this particular type of contextualization tries to situate Fanon in terms of a particular reading of the psychoanalytic tradition, and specifically in terms of a psychological inflection of that tradition by biographical history).[70] This is too simple an account of what Fanon means by subject, and scarcely justifies the larger claims that Scott and others read into it. In principle at least the difference between Fanonism and psychoanalysis cannot be simply formulated in terms of a resistance to the unconscious or Oedipus (criticisms of Fanon's thinking on the grounds that it is non-psychoanalytical, as if that automatically disqualified it, have, in my view, simply failed to appreciate the political stake of Fanon's reworking of terms such as "narcissism," "phobia," "affect," and "resistance" in his structural account of racial subjects). For Scott, Fanon gives us a vision of freedom as negation in a straightforwardly Hegelian manner, and this oppositional political narrative, operating on what Fanon will *always* clinically reinscribe, dictates a certain number of consequences for Scott's thought.

Historicism emerges as an issue in these analyses, let us remember, because of the structure of liberation itself: the teleology or decisionism that necessarily supervenes in the situating of revolution as an *end* is, to the extent that it is not programmed by a "history of the present," an irruptive cutting of temporal continuity which, as we are here talking about liberation, it seems natural to refer to as a new beginning. But this beginning has two aspects: (1) the future is the future (and not just a future past) to the extent that it is radically unwriteable (erasable or even heterogeneous to the teleological work of time itself) and is therefore what appears (though never as such) in the arriving of any event whatsoever. (2) But in that arriving from the future (the structure of which implies that history is not just a weave of traces and memories outside of time, but moments that materialize from out of their irremediable disappearance), the tabula rasa also opens in return a movement of temporalization that is never simply present, or timely. The revolution, insofar as it is always timely in its untimeliness and not just the teleological outcome of what went before, brings neither redemption, nor erasure, but the messianic promise of a new *écriture*. The question of historicism arises not when I have historical faith, but when I pretend to know the end: and the knowledge thus essayed or risked—and in these circumstances claiming to know the beyond of colonialism is always a risk—promises a story of liberation that will certainly never be liberated from narrative, but will remain illusory (the illusion of having been liberated from history, of which illusion Scott's notion of romantic allegory would be a particularly refined example, moves from an insistence on the future to come—which, as Scott rightly says, is both revolution's promise and its fate—to a sense, paradoxically enough, that there is nothing more teleological than the presumption that emancipation could ever account for its end non-teleologically).

It is easy to see that this notion of the *post*colonial is not straightfor-wardly historical at all: Scott's idea, that we no longer confidently inhabit the present, relies on the centering of romance as an always already in-habited present and the determinations of past and future as mere mod-ifications of it. If, as Fanon claims, the only concept of anti-colonial emancipation is that of a tabula rasa—and so an inscription that escapes the entire thematics of responsibility, genealogy, or history—and if there-fore Scott himself does not escape teleology in his periodizing of history as romance or tragedy, then it looks as though the type of radical question of a "future present" implied here bears a relation to anti-colonialism that is at best strategic. One indication of this is the ease with which this thought of a postcolonial present converts into a thought of historic crisis, as Scott tries to reimagine the problem-spaces of colonialism. But what this implies is that crisis only has an historical privilege in the tragic situation ("tragedy sets before us the image of a man or woman obliged to act in a world in which values are unstable and ambiguous. And consequently, for tragedy the relation between past, present, and future is never a romantic one in which history writes a triumphant and seamlessly progressive rhythm, but a broken series of paradoxes and reversals in which human action is ever open to unaccountable contingencies—and luck"), and cannot communi-cate historical change as Scott needs it to with what he portentously calls the unstable paradoxes of postcolonial modernity.[71] The "tangible ruins of our present" are always in some sense an allegorical image, but one that cannot be thought beyond allegory: the very melancholia of these reflec-tions means that deciding what is absolutely past is already to enter the game of an allegorical present that the analysis was designed to reshape, and that is itself essentially part of the historical *ressentiment* of the postco-lonial intellectual.[72] Scott is unable to resign himself to any narrative of the past based on allegory, and unable to renounce any narrative of the present that would do away with allegory—his writing thus ends up allegorizing this torment as tragedy. This in no sense implies that melancholia rather than resistance is the appropriate pathos for writing about postcoloniali-ty, but that the urging of a crisis in the traditional narratives of liberation maintains a relation with liberation that is not here thought through, and just because of the disenchantment with Fanonism as allegory.

This refined blind spot has at least two consequences for Scott's presen-tation of Fanon. One is that it is still, and in spite of itself, unduly historicist (in terms of Fanon's alienated modernity, at least), and runs the risk of implying in pedagogical fashion that it is impossible to understand Fanonism without first understanding anti-colonial romance and nationalism, whereas a necessary and paradoxical consequence of Fanon's analyses of colonial culture and its traditionalism is that this is simply not the case—as I have argued elsewhere, Fanon, just because of his readings of education and family life, also presents a reading of power as the always interruptive moment of agency, which is not to be confused with coercion or seduction (a point Scott admirably explicates in a later essay on the work of Talad Asad).[73] Another, more important consequence is that Scott, like Sekyi-Otu before him, is pushed by this singularizing narrative of liberation into the desire to articulate the thought of Fanonism as an allegorically understood notion of redemption, for one of Scott's most insistent claims is that it is just this that is increasingly determining, and will increasingly determine, our experience of the tragic present. (The irony is, never is Scott as close to Fanon as in his refusal of historical allegory, and never is Fanon as tied to his future critic as when he pretends to have nothing more to do with history as eschatology, as in the concluding pages of *Black Skin, White Masks*.) This is why, entirely consistently with his analysis, Scott arrives at a number of reservations or hesitations about Fanonism, the matrix of which is stated as the suspicion of Fanon's "metaphysics of self and power."[74] And this is what is developed via a reading of Foucault, where Scott convincingly shows how the latter provides a way of thinking "politics as ethics" and, in the context of general claims about the *productive* impact of power on the colonized, goes on to suggest that Fanon is nevertheless limited to the view that "lifting the lid of repressive power [is what is needed so] that the self can be set free," a view, so he claims, that means that Fanon is thus unable to see how "every political order produces an exclusion" (the originary articulation of a difference on which political identity depends), and so remains deluded in his metaphysics of liberated identity.[75]

The fundamental doubt Scott is voicing here is that Fanon is still too tied to the metaphysics of authenticity he is deconstructing, or at least that is the way it looks: the Fanonian problematic of liberation is thus seen to be undermined by an inability to escape this narrative thematization of its particular predicament. Given everything that Fanon says about fantasy, phobia, and violence, it simply cannot be true that he fails to understand the politics of exclusion, and nor can it be true, as Scott claims, that there is a lingering metaphysics of authenticity in Fanonism (an argument that seems to forget Fanon's characterization of identity as a mask which only serves to hide further illusion). On the other hand, Scott's intrinsic interpretation claims to be a new theory of politics, but often presupposes a politics of theory of which he is not himself aware. Of course, within the polemical circumstances in which it was written, *Refashioning Futures* has to overstate the opposition between narrative and history. From the start, the fascination with present crises is counterbalanced by a deep pessimism that remains rooted in a generational sense of historical discontinuity, although it reverses the movement of history from one of romance to one of tragedy. Narratives of liberation, we are told near the beginning of the book, are no longer able to capture the destructions and contradictions of the present. This description of present crises can only be metaphorical, and is therefore necessarily inadequate. Scott's reservation really says no more than that he is more interested in postcolonial tragedy than in anti-colonial romance, and tries dogmatically to justify that interest, and its concomitant prescriptions, by claiming with Foucault that "the general theme of liberation" is not sufficient anymore to "our" experience of historical crisis.[76] And one perverse side effect of this is that Scott returns to something like a humanism about "us" (the elegiac postcolonial intellectual that he assumes all of us to be) that he could not possibly want to support.

One answer to this confusion is to argue that, even in their most historical forms, tragedy and romance are both operative in Fanon's texts, but as metaphors for *ressentiment*, defined here as an inauthentic attitude toward time: "I am not a prisoner of History. I should not seek there for the meaning of my destiny. . . . The tragedy [*malheur*] of man is that he was once a child."[77] If, as seems to follow from these thoughts, romance is just as generative and imprisoning as tragedy, and tragedy is just as foundational a telos of the subject as romance, then the apparent duality Scott ends up with evaporates into a narrative that is not too romantic or too tragic just because it is still politically married to a generational notion of melancholia or despair (I note, in passing, that whereas for Scott, it is romantic to consider the future in terms of redemption, for Fanon the decolonial moment can only be understood as the collapse and abandonment of all given meanings, all compensatory forms of commitment, including that of tragedy itself). These genealogical metaphors have nothing to do with Fanon's desire to wipe out colonialism, in the hope of reaching at last a point that could be called a new present, a new inscription that marks a new departure (the tabula rasa). It is this historical awareness of the present as necessarily self-interrupting, as irrevocably ruptured and discontinuous, that leads Fanon inexorably to a concern with a temporality diametrically opposed to that of narrative (whether dramatic, dialectical, or existential). This does not of course mean that the tabula rasa can not still be thought in narrative terms, on the contrary, but as the figure for a teleology without telos, as the figure for the necessary interruption of all thought of purpose or final ends, the tabula rasa does resist any narrative or archaeoteleological schema that would reduce it to a final meaning, and this is both its strength and weakness.

VI

But perhaps more important for thinking about the question of the political, as his late works establish, is Fanon's account of violence and sovereignty: it is an account that seems to upset all traditional political philosophies and, no doubt for the same reason, has tended to produce extremely violent readings.[78] One of the most powerful, and least violent, responses has been that of the Cameroonian scholar Achille Mbembe. In what has become a seminal reading, Mbembe's *On The Postcolony*, published two years after Scott's *Fashioning Futures*, discusses African postcolonial sovereignty as a convivial and yet extravagantly violent politics of *commandement*, in which both the rulers and the ruled derive intense sensual pleasure of one sort or another.[79] Mbembe links this violence to Fanon's thinking on time, simulacra, and superstition, only to argue that "we are witnessing an epochal change, a surreptitious passage to another temporality[,] and this entry into another temporality requires, evidently, new postulates of understanding" (other than Fanon's?).[80] And yet, in his introduction, in the context of questions of time and temporality, Mbembe says, in a way that complicates any linear narrative: "In the case of the postcolony, to postulate the existence of a 'before' and an 'after' of colonization could not exhaust the problem of the relationship between temporality and subjectivity"; and, "As an age, the postcolony encloses multiple *durées* made up of discontinuities, reversals, inertias, and swings that overlay one another, interpenetrate one another, and envelope one another."[81] Or again, analyzing "De la scène coloniale chez Frantz Fanon," in 2007, Mbembe says, again referring to the postcolony as an epochal moment, that Fanon was unable to "anticipate the postcolony," an inability linked, wrongly I think, to Fanon's reading of how the colonial subject becomes *"subjugated"* (*l'assujettisement*) by his desire, a subjugation that places him outside of himself (*"hors de soi"*), and this assertion is restated at the very end of the paper: in so far as he failed to pay enough attention to this "little secret," Fanon, says Mbembe, was unable to think, despite all appearance of attentiveness to image, affect, fantasy, and so on, precisely what made power in the postcolony the producer of so much death, desire, and hilarity.[82] Are we dealing with two different notions of *durée* here? But why doesn't Mbembe (or at least his insistence that, in Africa today, "the postcolony is first and foremost a temporality which can be narrated"[83]), make that clear? As the understanding not only of Mbembe's book but also of one of the most enigmatic statements in the whole of Fanon ("For the black man there is only one destiny. And it is white,"[84]) would seem to depend on some clarification of this question, we had better take our time. This is still all about narrative and history, and suggests a problem in how Mbembe *writes* these multiple *durées* as narratives that will not fit easily into any historical scheme.

Mbembe knows all this too. Arguing that he is in some sense continuing (as much as criticizing) Fanon's quarrel with historicism, Mbembe also thematizes black lived experience as a problem of time rather than identity. One consequence of this is that just as Fanon determines black lived experience very broadly as a *not-yet* (a *defect* that renders the language of ontology extremely problematical), in *On the Postcolony*, Mbembe aims to outline a preontological language of black *Dasein* as a life that is not, as such, living (a necessary corollary of this is the form of politics Mbembe will later call "necropolitics"). Lived temporality is, then, the theme that will on Mbembe's account be central to any account of Fanonism. Mbembe's reading of what is at stake here will clarify the issue. Discussing the links between psychic life and racist culture, most clearly laid out by Fanon in *Black Skin, White Masks* (1952) and *The Wretched of the Earth* (1961), Mbembe writes, quite correctly, that the African becomes the bearer, in spite of himself, of "hidden meanings" (*significations secrètes*) circulating in a general economy of signs and images.[85] Mbembe defines the colonial situation as one in which power becomes a kind of enigmatic mirror to instinctual and emotional life, in which the colonized see reflected the promise of unlimited wealth and sensual pleasure: "it is this idea of an *imaginary without symbolic* [the fascination and lure of the fetishized image behind the mirror] that is the 'little secret' of the colony, which explains the power of the colonial potentate."[86] The colonial potentate, in Mbembe's rereading of Fanon, introduces a new libidinal economy of desire and a new order of truth. The flow of desire must be regulated, but also created. But if the potentate offers wealth and abundance, it would seem that this investment in ceremonies and largesse also falls within a relationship of debt (*une relation de dette*): as sovereign the potentate is himself indebted to the mirages, coercions, and vanities he feeds on, just as the indigene is placed in a position of complete servitude with respect to the potentate: colonial sovereignty therefore cannot *strictu sensu* be abstracted from the various stages of indebtedness and expenditure through which it circulates and manifests itself.[87] Mbembe names this (with a nod to Bataille) the "accursed share" (*part maudite*) of the colony.[88] This accursed share is instituted in violence, out of *sacrifice*, and this violence brings together "logic (*reason*), fantasy (*arbitrary*), and cruelty" in the instinctual form of the *commandement*.[89] In a brilliant article called "Provisional Notes on the Postcolony," Mbembe, wondering what happens when conviviality and punishment, obscenity and excess essentially replace law and civil society, suggests that the indigene bear witness to the potentate's fantasy in the indebted servitude and venality in which their instinctual life situates them as subjects to be either fucked or killed. The relation between the *commandement* and its subjects is then, says Mbembe, neither one of coercion nor of resistance, but that of an "illicit cohabitation" and/or mutual connivance.[90]

In Mbembe's reading, the oddness of the *commandement* is that it brings together orgiastic excess and obscene enjoyment into some sort of hallucinatory interplay (in this form of power the opposition between the real and the imaginary cannot be sustained, indeed they are *one and the same* as the imaginary is realized and the real made imaginary: Mbembe is attacking what he sees as the opposition between fiction and truth in the political discourse of modernism, with its emphasis on the oneness of truth, and stressing that the decision to erase the real [*de rayer du réel*] and to de-realize [*de dé-réaliser*] reality is precisely what defines colonial sovereignty).[91] But the matter is more complicated than this opposition would suggest: Mbembe is arguing that verisimilitude is not simply opposed to falsehood in the colony, for the point is that what is true and what is masked cannot be recognized as such even when it is *literally* the case that the fictions that "claim to be true" represent or signify what is also known to "produce the false," and that *everyone knows this to be the case.*[92] The whole classical opposition between being and appearance is thus rendered oblique in the colony and reveals, more or less violently, how the potentate is both double and doubly heterogeneous to truth. Fanon himself first discusses racist culture as giving rise to an affective prelogic in which blacks appear as monstrous and terrifying, and intraracial dreams and desire reveal or manifest a sociogeny of lies and fabulation: in the colony, where the real is the imaginary (arbitrary and cruel) and the imaginary is real (bewitching and terrifying), what appears is neither simply random or irrational, nor necessarily *conscious* or perceived—for the fetish or phantasm of power depends, at least in part, on a truth that is neither oppositional nor contradictory but (simultaneously) always both empty and full. And, more crucially, at some point this voracious plenitude-emptiness must attempt to take itself as real and fictionalize its own institution or origin, stating its appearance as the empty real (of appearance) whose power might also be said to *enforce* this situation wherein the true and the false have no interiority or depth at all. On the other hand, in so far as there is *commandement*, then it is necessarily the potentate who decides what is the essence of the lifeworld. Whether this be figured in terms of nightmarish punishment or not, it is clearly a situation of violence, if only in that the potentate is he who decides what is the state of exception (this collusion of complicity and truth defining the *commandement* as the place of truth, and vice versa).[93] Paradoxes proliferate in this situation: Mbembe shows how duplicity and indebtedness structure everyday life to the exclusion of anything else: if the colonist is the enemy, then it is not entirely clear who in this perspective is the neighbor or friend.

How does all this relate to Fanonism? The question of the *commandement* returns a little later in the context of an argument that moves from recognition of the role played by fantasy and force in Fanon's analysis of colonial necropolitics, to the sense that in the postcolonial epoch it is the brother and not the colonist who is now the enemy, and that the sovereign right to kill is being exercised in a fratricidal manner against one's own people first (which, as Mbembe implies, is perhaps why Fanon couldn't anticipate the postcolony). One consequence of this is that Mbembe's own placing of Fanon as the thinker of necropolitics implies that in some way Fanon was wrong about the post-independent nation-state: or, more mysteriously, that Fanon somehow underestimated how colonialism interacted with the perverse *jouissance* of the colonized. On this view, the postcolony would indeed require new postulates for understanding other than Fanon's. The ease with which such a characterization can be constructed suggests that something is being simplified. Fanon himself was one of the first to determine an oedipal crisis in the colony in which very broadly the (white) father is also master and the (black) brother is also both enemy and friend. Fanon does indeed use Oedipus, in his early work, to suggest the perverse experience of all genealogical filiations in the colony, which are, above all, based on relations of force, rape, and unconscious self-hatred. (If there is a crisis in the whole classical notion of Oedipus, in which the father is never simply a father, but always both brother and rival, then this crisis also blurs the difference between sovereign and enemy, between a rule founded in legitimacy and a rule founded in illegitimacy and force.) The point is that not only in his explicit reflections on inheritance, narcissism, and hatred, but also in his own psychoanalyses of aberration in *Black Skin, White Masks*, Fanon necessarily complicates this kind of assignation. The issue thereby becomes: is Fanonism simply a narrative (of destitution and reconstitution), or is it a question; namely, what does it mean to be an ex-slave? Mbembe clearly struggles with this either-or and—casting Fanonism as a thinking on the margins of the postcolonial archive, library, episteme, but also presenting Fanonism as a thinking absolutely crucial to the "post" that comes after, and which is inclusive of a new *durée*—ends up with a certain indecisiveness as to the proximity and distance of Fanon himself: is he our contemporary, enemy, or friend? Here again, as with Scott, it would appear that the wish to assign Fanonism a certain historicity is more or less secretly ruled by the radical untimeliness of Fanon himself, in the sense that all of these disagreements are to do with the problem of *inheritance* he theorized explicitly as a problem of suffering and time.

Now in fact Mbembe also uses the term *durée* to address this particular question of temporality or historicity, and more specifically to locate a configuration of multiplicities that breaks simple linear temporality by opening each moment to a multiple inscription. Mbembe, unlike Scott, does not locate the *durée* in opposition to some teleologically periodizing history, but neither does he comprehend the temporal complexity of the tabula rasa Fanon is attempting to address: it may well be that the very term *"durée"* is so strongly identified with a certain Bergsonianism that it cannot fail to be another periodizing term, but it seems clear that the tabula rasa Fanon is attempting to "write" is prior to the temporal organization of history as narrative that Scott (and to a lesser extent Mbembe) has to presuppose. Just as the philosophical urge of Mbembe's book leads him to write the African *durée* as a series of entanglements and displacements, so here he is led to use a vulgar notion of time to describe a world in which time appears as essentially unreal, as a *not-yet* in which everything remains to be invented, a monstrous appearance that Fanon diagnosed as lived *through* teleological illusion. This is why Fanon saw his project in terms of a generalized unmasking or dis-illusionment (and why he clears the way, in turn, for an unconditional affirmation of the real behind the mask). Contrary to Mbembe's assumption that fiction is what gives us access to the real, the Fanonian real has no "double" or mirror-reflection, and authorizes nothing other than what it is: the absence at the center of each representation or image. The real, in brief, cannot be presented nor written—and thus made recognizable—for, lacking any double, it remains resistant to any identification (including that of the *commandement*). And, as is quite often the case with Fanon, such non-coincidence is explicitly linked to the untimeliness of the revolutionary moment.

Some care must be taken here to avoid hasty misunderstanding: at first sight, Fanon is suggesting that colonization rests on a simultaneous grasping of the imaginary in the symbolic and vice versa, and on the presupposition that the image of the Other, more or less obliquely, reveals or manifests the hidden or concealed disorders and conflicts of the colonial subject. As Mbembe shows, an underlying assumption here is that the opaque, the hidden, exists prior to and independently of the image: the image is the accidental ("arbitrary") means of access to the hidden (its "little secret"), and ideally should be read psychoanalytically. Mbembe, on the other hand, is saying that the life world of the colony, in its irreducible opacity, can only aggravate or confirm the inaccessibility of the truth of the image. And this presupposition that the more familiar the idiom in its more or less brutal or obscene guise, the more starkly it shows up the arbitrariness of the potentate's image, just because the idiom used makes all *commandements* in the colony look either blind or perverse—this presupposition presents very little to be read here beyond the fact that this perversity is everywhere and every aspect of life in the postcolony is included in it, and remains curiously complicit in preserving the enormous swath of its delusion. The arbitrariness that the image of the potentate reveals involves, then, a certain affirmation of force against any content or specificity whatsoever, an arbitrariness that the colonized nonetheless affirms. We might in any case wonder if it is by chance that Mbembe uses allegory to reflect on the timeliness or untimeliness of his reading of Fanon in the final chapter of his book.[94] (And indeed this chapter—"God's Phallus"—is essentially an extended meditation on how divine sovereignty appears in time as a moment in whose interruptive force there is either *parousia* or epiphany, telos or *eskhaton*).

In this chapter, Mbembe links the historical violence of the colony to the foundational violence of divine sovereignty. The messianic moment is revealed in the guise of arbitrariness and absolute power, but this is a moment also marked by torture (crucifixion) and death. We are back with Walter Benjamin"s notion of messianic or sovereign violence—on the other hand, in so far as the "the *imaginaire* of state sovereignty in the colony" is a form of law-preserving violence, the founding violence that legitimates the right to conquest, then it necessarily converts itself into an "authorizing authority" by emptying the precolonial past of "any substance" and by abrogating the future to itself, a construal that it repeats ad infinitum: colonial sovereignty, acting as both authority and morality, thus reconstitutes its denial of right into the assertion of right (this combination of violence and regulation defining the notion of race war [*une guerre des races*] and the conversion of sovereignty into necropolitical force).[95] It is this right to dispose that connects colonial sovereignty with sacrificial reason and divine will, and provides an understanding of why "those who command and those who are assumed to obey" come together in an "anti-community" defined by "mutual brutalization."[96] (And indeed Mbembe here refers to Fanon's reflections on the effects of torture on both perpetuators and victims during the Algerian War to illustrate this point.)

If one pursues the analogy a little further, then colonial sovereignty requires this "phantasmatic device" (*dispositif fantasmatique*) to present itself as a miraculous foundation—the truth is not what is at stake here, but (Mbembe's analysis of) the founding gesture of colonialism.[97] Colonization, in its guise of arbitrariness, is a phenomenological miracle of power and mystery: in Mbembe's analogy, in the limitless and violent representations of itself, in its interweaving of enjoyment with voracious appetite and phallic desire, and in its overflowing narcissistic fantasy of the indivisible (sovereign) subject, the colonial potentate authorizes himself as absolute ruler.

Mbembe's suggestion is that if the violence and masquerade of colonial sovereignty is a fantasy that has become real, this real fantasy was also contingent on the animalization and/or thingification of the native, the power to summon and cancel or annul life, and the desire to sever being from its existence and so render it into nothing but flesh. We can complicate this picture (and note that to do so we must jettison any simple notion of phenomenology), so far as Mbembe is concerned, by noting that his reading of will and decisionism in the colony does not allow for the affirmation of the messianic as a radical cut in history. Fanon's attempt to affirm a messianic moment as one that remains (like the real) radically indeterminable, and so prior to any notion of the messiah, the tabula rasa, for example, that cannot be mapped on any teleological schema, is the first casualty of this construal of the postcolony as the place where the real and the imagined are assumed to be one and the same, which is why the analogy between the potentate and messiah leaves Mbembe looking as if he is too wedded to the analysis of their complicity rather than the political question of how to prise them apart.[98] It seems more plausible to suggest that Mbembe remains ambivalent about what he calls "the Fanonian cul-de-sac," which he describes as somewhat of the order of an (Hegelian) logic of freedom through death and sacrifice, or more generally "the dead-end of the generalized circulation and exchange of death as the condition of being human."[99] In his *On the Postcolony*, this anti-Hegelianism is more or less marked by mimicry of Bataille's notion of expenditure in whose "disposing-of-death-itself" Mbembe finds a poetics, as against a dialectics, that exceeds the whole notion of sacrifice but only in so far as it "cannot be read literally."[100] This does not of course mean that Mbembe is somehow doing no more than evoking Bataille against, say, Hegel. But it follows from everything we have seen that, while being concerned to stress the exemplary discontinuity of the revolutionary moment, it strikes me as odd that Fanon should be consistently read as committed to a teleological "narrative of freedom" rather than to maintaining freedom as a difficult question that cannot be resolved.[101] Finally, I would like to say that it is precisely this question that will always *come after* the question of how we ought to read Fanon, a reading that cannot be entirely predicted or known in advance, and in whose future inheritance we necessarily remain bewildered and perplexed.

If Fanonism is a poetics, it cannot be underwritten by dialectics, or by the current state of things as understood or known. The tabula rasa as we know cannot be totally laid bare nor can it stop the movement that brings into being the most obscure notions and apprehensions: what never disappears entirely, either during the rebellion or after, are the traces that link what is known to its perpetual dissolution; accordingly, the tabula rasa signifies both experience and its dissolution. Moreover, I maintain that it is in the context of his clinic that Fanon first apprehends this poetics of dissolution—its grammar, tenses, and modes, which I outline in Part One.

PART ONE

PSYCHOPOLITICS

Prologue

According to the etymology, the word *disavowal* should be linked to the root of *disclaimer*, meaning to deny a claim (undoubtedly there exist ways of denying a claim that maintain what is denied without confronting it).[1] Thus we find ourselves immediately at the heart of the most important problem of Fanon's political and clinical writing: why do people disavow what could truly liberate them? Is it possible to conceive of another "reality" (as opposed to its disavowal) that goes beyond this fixed and determined belief? We know that Fanon sought, in accordance with his work as a revolutionary clinician, to bring human decision to the status of the real, from the perversions of fantasy to the responsibility of praxis—the moment of such encounter is doubly articulated in his work, as a *socialthérapie* founded on that of the group where the patient-actor is compelled to give up their defenses and commit themselves to a new articulation of self, subject, and world. So too he believed that in this encounter with the group the one thing we should be suspicious of is the language of catharsis; Fanon immediately suggests that a cure does not necessarily follow from a change in reality—indeed, his conception of praxis is resistant to the languages of therapeutics and hermeneutics and, as we know, he presents truly revolutionary activity as antipathetic to lived experience, in that it necessarily forces us to exist and act in ways that induce a moral and existential "vertigo," and this for two reasons.

Firstly, in so far as colonial racism is part of a defensive view of the world, it also disavows certain attributes of the racial other. Hence whatever follows from the encounter with that other (that is, from otherness itself in so far as we understand it to be expressly the seat of anxiety) results also from a vertiginous capacity for racist disavowal. Hence the decreeing of these others as other may quite correctly be said to follow from an inverse reflection: because this image depends especially on the power of projection, it can be very clearly conceived as a projection outwards of a kind of primal splitting of the subject in its encounter with difference. The existence here of a kind of racial fetishism, in so far as the subject perceives something to be missing from the other, is key to this encounter with the other as we have just defined it. Secondly, I have said that the structural motif of disavowal informs Fanon's telescoping of hysteric anxiety in colonial racism because he defines and explains it as a proximate defense; indeed, a general consideration of racial anxiety and its connectedness with a disavowal of reality is crucial to Fanon's formation as both a clinician and political thinker.

Thus from both sides the disavowed is felt to be a defense with respect to reality: *it is a judgment that fluctuates wretchedly between anxiety and fear.* By definition, this scene, its reality, gives a special status to that of psychoanalysis: "Indeed, I believe that only a psychoanalytical interpretation of the black problem can lay bare the anomalies of affect that are responsible for the structure of the complex."[2] And yet there are those who think that Fanon's clinical thought is extremely rudimentary in comparison with psychoanalysis and those who think that psychoanalysis cannot explain the ineffable necessity of political acts or decisions. Now even—and above all if—the clinic is in a certain manner the *limit* of Fanon's politics, it permits the consideration of what this "psychopolitics" might represent. How does politics inform Fanon's therapeutics? And what of psychoanalysis in the colony? How does Fanon's reading of Freud, Mannoni, or Lacan, say, inform his politics?

Such are the questions that I wish to raise by submitting disavowal to an analysis of the messages it may contain. We will start with this word *vertigo.* Why? Because even though it seems to be only a metaphor for certain psychoses, it signifies something veritable in the life of the colony; namely, the ways in which the subject feels itself to be commanded as if by a law, which constrains it, which it fears and yet must follow in order to avoid something worse. Vertigo therefore seems to be an index of what madness and revolution have in common during a time of total war, and refers to a rupture at the level of the subject's awareness of itself as a subject. Vertigo is a response—implicit—to the ontological void opened up by the ruptures of decolonization as episode, event, or catastrophe. This is why it threatens to violate the workings of disavowal. If vertigo is the sign of crisis, we can be sure that its essence is that of a command prescribed to the subject from the other and is consequently the affect of an abeyance that makes life as such impossible for certain subjects, or at least aporetic. A distinction can be made, however, between a symptom awaiting form—referring to the ways in which fantasies fill in a void experienced as constant and perpetual, and those moments when a subject is called to fill in the void that is its own being residing in the world (for example the hatreds, paranoias, and suspicions due to fears of the other)—and the way in which total war makes the psyche into its informant (willing or no) via these feelings of acting at the behest of a law and under the threat of boundless fears and desires (the vertigo of acting steadfastly on one's own and yet at the same time under another's command, and therefore under a judgment whose authority comes both from within and without).

To say that vertigo is a kind of index of the real,[3] or evidence of a law that the subject is more or less incapable of grasping, is evidence of one of Fanon's enduring concerns with how negrophobia—and later psychosis—forms an index of affect, or semblance, that brings with it an anguish-laden atmosphere under which the subject lives as if subjected. To say that the unconscious is, accordingly, put in the role of an informant, however, does not mean, at least on the level of desire, that its activity is purely one of complicity, or betrayal, but that it serves to authenticate the reality of colonial war as referent, or event, and so embeds a phantasm of the real as its rationale and meaning.

1

Psychodramas

"The atmosphere of permanent insecurity in which the refugees exist . . ."

FANON, *The Wretched of the Earth*, trans. Farrington, 224

I think that every reader of Fanon is aware of this "atmosphere," even though I also believe that people do not often agree on what constitutes it. How does one read Fanon's psychopolitics with respect to this atmosphere? Since Fanon's relationship to psychoanalysis remains strangely disconcerting to critics, let us begin by considering it. Although this relationship is far from straightforward, I would not presume, as David Macey does, to say that Fanon simply reduces fantasy to trauma and mental illness to social alienation.[1] Although this is not the worst example of what might be called a "skeptical" reading of Fanon's relationship to psychoanalysis, it might be regarded as typical. In what follows, I will attempt to show why this point of view is tendentious and misguided in its choice of oppositions. Since Fanon's relationship to psychoanalysis cannot be usefully understood outside of the institutional contexts in which he wrote, studied, and practiced, let us begin, accordingly, with those contexts.

Since the best part of Fanon's work as a clinician was done during a period of war, it is certain that, if we truly want to understand his work in *socialthérapie*, we should try to imagine as much as possible the effects of war on Fanon's clinical work. Furthermore, since all our historical knowledge of this work depends on a limited series of clinical writings, some of which were co-authored, and since we are in doubt as to whether Fanon's clinical ideas received a clear and distinct final version, all of what follows is necessarily circumspect. Again, since Fanon's clinical work was on the psychic effects of colonial war, it is certain that this work involves and expresses a conception of a psyche at war, or as a warring self-relation, and that consists in war altogether. This also follows from the fact that, just as the early work was taken up with the aftermath of the war against fascism, the later work is necessarily taken up with how colonial culture continues that war by other means. Let us try and sum up the different clinical messages these wars contain.

The first forays in *socialthérapie* were under the tutelage of François Tosquelles's experiments in *thérapeutiques institutionnelles* and immediately focused on the means by which the clinic could question the prescribed rules, as it were, of group psychology; the main innovation was to transform the clinic from a carceral, or juridical, disciplining of the subject, into a space of free, albeit limited, therapeutic intervention, where the foundations of mental health could be reconnected to rules for living.[2] At Blida-Joinville in Algeria, for example, and, later, the Charles-Nicolle hospital in Tunis, where Fanon served as *chef de service*, or director, the transformation of the clinic was undertaken not just at the level of instituting day wards or occupational therapies or allowing patient-led workshops, courses, or discussion groups. These innovations, although wholly essential to maintaining the link between life inside the hospital and life outside it, were no guarantee of any significant intervention in the scene of the symptom, but all belonged to the effort of getting both patients and doctors to reflect on their existence as a group, in both its veridical and cultural dimensions. Françoise Vergès is thus right to address these innovations as Fanon's attempt to overcome the opposition of the hospital as carceral and the hospital as therapeutic institution, innovations that represented a revolution in the medical history of the colony.[3] She is also right that Fanon proposed a new methodology in 1952 to counter the theses of the School of Algiers regarding the weak affective and moral life of Algerians.[4] But the idea that a "successful" therapy could only take place in a "common culture" shared by patient and therapist is decidedly more complex than she suggests.[5]

Taken in its entirety, what accounts for the specific character of Fanon's *socialthérapie*, and what was truly unprecedented about it in Algerian medical history, was the constant interrogation of the group as a veridical dimension of the real, since it sought to make being-there part of a group process wherein an awareness of the patient's "phantasms" "force[d] him to confront reality on a new register."[6] What we have here is a situation organized so as to force the group to become aware of the difficulties of its existence as a group, and then to render it more transparent to itself, to the point where each member is provoked into an awareness of the relation (albeit previously disavowed) between phantasm and the real. It is then at the level of the phantasm that the *real unreality* of life in the colony could be fully understood: its reality is that of a group phantasm, even though that reality is never experienced as illusion; its reality is that of a kind of imaginary evasion, from which the reality of each member is sheltered. Finally, this is also why Fanon's *socialthérapie* is a development of Tosquelles's *thérapeutiques institutionnelles*. Whereas the latter wanted the psychiatrist to be an actor among actors, and in this scenography of exchange "the persistent and irreducible *sociality* of the patient" became the founding principle of the practice, in Fanon's colonial clinic the psychodrama was substantially different; the necessity was not just to set up an analogy between the clinic and society, but to deduce the phantasms defining both.[7] As can be seen in books such as *Studies in a Dying Colonialism* and *Toward the African Revolution*, Fanon's major concerns are: first, to trace that sociality, through a genealogy of the group, to racial phantasms and divisions; then, to show that out of this group psychology could emerge the terms of a "transvaluation" of the colony and its modern exclusions; and finally, to show that these terms simultaneously reconfigure and transvaluate the violent history of the colony and its reactive affects.

My concern here lies not with this representation but with how it conceives of another, equally vital point: what was different about Fanon's use of these methods in Algeria, a "difference with many consequences," Vergès avers, is that in the colony corporeality and affect were necessarily shaped by racist discourses of heredity and fate.[8] She notes the "difficulties" that Fanon's *socialthérapie* came up against in Algeria. Referring to these difficulties in an article jointly authored with Jacques Azoulay, Fanon writes: "A leap had to be made, a transformation of values had to be carried out. Let us admit it; it was necessary to go from the biological to the institutional, from natural existence to *cultural existence*."[9] In light of this, several critics have argued that institutions of Arabic and Islamic culture—their symbolic authority and meaning—forced upon Fanon a need to revise his methods, as did the question of language, etc. "The solution was to train the psychiatrist in local culture, language, and customs. But, more important, the psychiatrist could not, in a colonial situation, *exercise his technique*."[10] What does this mean if not that the talking cure relies on a common lexicon of cultural signs and symbols in order for the recipient to hear the message, to be the subject of a reading, to be articulable as such, within a hermeneutic system of determination? What seems to go missing here is the insistence on the group itself as symptom, and the dialectical determination of the symptom in its differentiations, thus preventing a deeper symbolization of the group as a precursor to the philosophical-political project of its transvaluation. I propose to call this insistence a transvaluation and this is exactly how Fanon also comes to grasp it, and what he seeks solutions for.

Now if, for Fanon, "madness was one of the means man has of losing his freedom," and since colonialism was a systemic deprivation of freedom, liberation from the latter should not be confused with freedom from madness, far from it.[11] The moment of liberation, of decolonialism, without which, in fact, freedom is not possible, is always a complex network of displacements and valorizations, and to suggest otherwise is to forget the psychotherapeutic terms in which colonialism is to be transvaluated. I would also add that the question of freedom was never just a question of analytic technique, but was always supplemented, for Fanon, by persistent and urgent questions concerning the cultural meanings of his role as both a therapist *and* a black man. Such questions, politically and analytically necessary, were not to disappear during the struggle, but persisted in ever more malignant and desperate forms.

This is why freedom is not the aim and goal of Fanon's *socialthérapie* and, hence, why, in his account of liberation, the image is that of a group absolutely compelled by its transvaluation as it expiates its own subjection. However insistent the idea of freedom is, it does not allow relief for the modern subject in its desires and exclusions. Are not the affective anomalies that Fanon indicated are at the base of racism (the vertigo, the lysis, the morbidity, etc.) not blunted in their memory if freedom is the only arbiter of their relevance? Does not the belief that alienation is "entirely the result of social, cultural, and political conditions" make readily apprehensible what remains profoundly resistant at the level of the group?[12] Indeed, if Fanon's role as a revolutionary was in tension with his work as a clinician (the politics of the one being in tension with the resistance of the other), such a view fails to see the obtuse angle between them, which Fanon believed opened the field of the signifier totally, that is infinitely, in both domains.

Here the notion of limit situation, which I will come back to, is of relevance. Even if one accepted this tension, what I think gets overlooked here is Fanon's insistence that a leap had to be made, both analytically and politically, in order for a new society to emerge. This is not so much a politicization of psychiatry, but an acknowledgment that the practice of psychiatry in the colony was already political in its diremptions, not so much in the way passion and suffering were endured, but in the ways in which they were institutionally construed and understood. It follows from this, first, that power does not supersede resistance, or at least that decolonial politics arises from but can never overcome the subject's *unknown* relation to itself in the histories and mediations of its desires and resistances. Secondly, the experience of revolutionary responsibility, as we learn from *The Wretched of the Earth*, is always full of anxiety, or feelings of uneasiness dominated less by fear than by anxiety-ridden persecutions and ravishments that find their movement and impulse in a *demand* that the subject very much desires; for in this way doing one's duty willingly becomes the experience of incalculable feelings of calamity and revenge. The concept from which this message was taken is none other than that of moral "alienation": the only knowledge required to decipher the symptom is the knowledge of how it derives from guilt (here an economy of blood-debt, duties, and punishments). In fact, this alienation can itself be further broken down, for the alienated life is not simply the form of the symptom but also, by its performance, an additional signified, that of a cortico-visceral "mortification."[13] The clinic's role is thus twofold (at least in this particular context): rehabilitational and disalienating. Since, however, we have here a more complex set of factors, namely, that of the clinic itself as a symptom, we shall see:

1. That the patient is understood not just as a patient but also as a social actor undergoing processes common to all.

2. That putting aside the carceral nature of the clinic, we are left with the idea (even if the activities are experienced as falsely artificial) of the clinic as a kind of psychodrama. This image straightaway provides a series of discontinuous messages. How, according to what "theater," are the different spheres of therapy and society strung together along the same therapeutics? What are the rules by which madness is to be inferred, treated, and judged? First (the order is important as these steps are not linear), the idea that madness should be taken as evidence of a sick society is only part of the story. Since the colonizer is an occupying force, it is certain that Fanon conceived of the clinic as

a kind of refuge, as much as the psyche of the colonized feels itself to be under siege (like a garrison keeping watch over a conquered city—a phrase that Fanon uses in *Black Skin, White Masks*)—since we know that for Fanon colonial war and terror can freely combine together: as for example in the many examples he gives that readily juxtapose psyches under siege from a combinatory of actual civil war and certain traits of character. Belief in the besieged itself implies two consequences: that the symptom has a social nucleus and that colonialism is the catalyzer for mental illness. Catalyzer and nucleus are here linked by a simple relation of implication, they are bound together like actors to their roles. The function of psychodrama is thus to show how the two come together reciprocally. It is this last relation that needs to be considered further—first because it defines the very framework of Fanon's use of therapy (its dramaturgy, or performance); second, because it is the main conduit through which he works toward a restructuring of the unconscious and of psychoanalytic categories.

3. We shall also see that Fanon institutes "sociogeny" as a combinatory of cultural life and therapy. This combination forms the central problem of his *socialthérapie*. Is there a cultural logic lying behind the temporality of the symptom? Readers of Fanon have been divided on this point. Jacques André, whose analytic study of Fanon is still ahead of most of the work done today, is totally committed to the idea of the irreducibility of the real: he sees Fanon refusing the phantasm in the name of reality and for this reason is convinced of the necessity of rooting Fanon's clinical work in anti-illusion.[14] Yet Fanon himself, in his contrast between dreamwork (defined by translation and transposition) and historical narratives of trauma (defined by actual death and slaughter), was reluctant to give primacy to reality over phantasm, as we have already shown. All contemporary readers of Fanon's clinical work (André, Bhabha, Bulhan, Lane, Macey, Vergès)[15] could subscribe (while differing on other points) to André's proposition that Fanon's phrase "real fantasies" is somewhat of an oxymoron, and one without very much useful purpose for our understanding of unconscious ambivalence and resistance. These readings tend to dechronologize the narrative continuum from symptom to culture and to relogicize it, to make it dependent on certain formal categories; or, rather, more exactly, and to be clear, the task of therapy,

as Fanon saw it, was to succeed in giving a structural-genetic description of such real illusions—it is the reality of the phantasm, or the way reality is maintained as phantasm, that needs to be accounted for. The more we observe such real fantasy, the better we shall be able to understand how its symbolic representations come to be implanted as part of the habits of a culture where racial paranoia and psychosis come to be counted as common sense.

To put it another way, one could say that Fanon's various clinics were precisely this attempt (as practice and discourse), just as his clinical writings insist that the racist phantasm only exists functionally, as a remnant of the real. Reality belongs not to the unconscious strictly speaking but to the signifiers that reach the mind as a given; both psyche and symptom are *occupied* by the time of the real, "real" time being an irreal, phantasmatic time disavowed as such, as Fanon's clinical writings show. It is as such that readers of Fanon's *socialthérapie* must deal with it.

4. Finally, we see that the reward of such sociogeny is to know colonial social law itself, that is, to know its true working in damaged minds; the penalty of not knowing these things means continued enslavement to various commandments, or an inconstant and mortified mind.

If we now summarize the main points above, as I have just explained them, we shall see that:

1. Fanon's clinical writings do not regard "psychic conflicts as politically determined," but these conflicts do reflect a crisis in the real that is inseparable from Fanon's notion of otherness, a crisis whose impact also comes from a certain convergence of fantasy and the real (with or without a reference to trauma).[16] It is also the aftermath of a world war that saw the European account of white supremacy as the justification for a virulent pro-colonialism. Change in the life of the colony, thanks to the emergence of new movements of resistance, begins to put into question this ethnic model of democracy and its racist account of the human. Such movements motivated the thought of many anti-colonial thinkers in the Caribbean, such as Aimé Césaire, to name only him. And so Fanon's response to these changes is at once radical (in questioning the founding concepts of psychoanalysis) and hypercritical in so far as Fanon is keen to put colonial psychic reality back in its "time . . . and in its place."[17] As for this place

and its timeliness, they are impossible to tie down to a naïve ontologism or historicism. It is therefore all the more surprising to hear Fanon's efforts at restoration criticized for being non-psychoanalytic, or merely sociological, lacking psychoanalytic nuance, and for ontologizing otherness (whatever that means).

2. Keeping in mind that the more nuanced insight seems to be one's ability to tell fantasy and reality apart, these critics seem troubled by what is for me one of Fanon's more important insights, and that lends itself to a deconstructive reading of this very distinction (and its nuance): the real *is* fantasy, for Fanon, and vice versa, as we shall see.

3. But this deconstruction is in some way part of the opposition to what Fanon believes to be the leading fantasy of neocolonial psychoanalytic psychiatry: that drives, cultural traits, etc., are *not* political, and that it is the strength of psychoanalysis—but whose psychoanalysis?—to precisely oppose the fallacious legitimacy of such thinking. But what is the politics of this refusal, and what precisely is being disavowed in Fanon's allusion to it, or wish to go beyond it? This is one of my questions. It is a question about the possibility of psychoanalysis in the colony (and postcolony). And I would say that Fanon studies loses nothing from admitting that psychoanalysis is, in some sense, impossible in the colony; and also that those who would rush to condemn that admission perhaps have not really grasped the originality of this question. For Fanon the possibility of psychoanalysis is always a question of *praxis* (and not just one of legitimacy, authority, or hermeneutics), and praxis is never simply a question of procedure, or method, or technique, but one of force, advent, desire, and ideology.

Fanon's clinical writings concern the question of guilt, responsibility, right, and justice. It even means to inaugurate, and we shall be able to describe this more rigorously in a moment, a psychopolitics of transformation (and one that should never be confused with the ego-juridical fantasy of reparation). And this praxis seems to be organized around a series of distinctions that all seem interesting, provocative, necessary up to a certain point but that all, it seems, remain radically open, incomplete.

First, there is the distinction between two kinds of psychic violence: the violence that brings fantasy, or dreaming, to a halt, the one that institutes and positions the psyche as a "depository" of cultural hatred and the violence that allows fantasy to get going, or be discharged, via the vengeful sadistic fantasy that maintains, confirms, insures the permanence of the racist status quo of the colony. For the sake of convenience, let us call the first that of the *colonisé*, and the second that of the *colon*.

Next there is the distinction between the violence that is disavowed (implicit meaning: white anti-blackness) and the violence that annihilates disavowal, which is termed anti-phobic (implicit meaning: black, it seems to me).

Finally, there is the distinction between guilt as the principle of "historicity" (a word that we shall come back to), or how one becomes who one is, and justice as a principle of a more ethical positioning. A last point: Fanon's primary critique of psychoanalytic psychiatry is in terms of ethics.

Having made these points, we must now ask: what then is the logic that makes fantasy real? It is this that this current book on Fanon is actually trying to work out and that has so far been a relatively marginal focus of debate. Three main directions of research can be seen. The first (Macey et al.) is more properly psychoanalytically orthodox in approach: it aims to reconstitute psychoanalysis as instituted by Freud, to retrace the choice of the oedipal neuroses that inevitably face the individual at every point in his or her psychosexual development and so to bring out what could be called the genetic logic of race, since it grasps the symptom as the expression of oedipal dramas. The second (Bulhan et al.) is ethnopsychiatric: its essential concern is to demonstrate paradigmatic oppositions between therapeutics and politics which, in accordance with Bulhan's definition of the clinic, are extended along the line of a new revolutionary development in the treatment of the post-colony. The third (Tosquelles, Cherki, et al.) is somewhat different in that it sets the analysis at the level of power and authority (that is to say, at institutional, cultural life), attempting to determine the rules by which therapy respects, varies, and transforms the basic predicaments of the sociopolitical.

There is no question of choosing among these approaches; they are not competitive but concurrent, and at present are in the throes of historic elaboration. The only compliment we will attempt to give them here concerns the psychical dimensions of Fanon's analysis. Even leaving aside the actual use of psychodrama, the nucleus of symptoms and catalyzers, there still remains the notion of a violent occupation of the psyche (which also manifests a telling evacuation) and this violence cannot be mastered by the orthodox analyses just mentioned, which until now have worked on the major articulations of illusion or fantasy as displacements or repressions. Provision needs to be made, moreover, for a description sufficiently close as to account for all of Fanon's clinical thought on projection, for the use of therapy in all those psychodramas. We must remember that "psychodrama" cannot be determined by the use of actual theatrical production in the clinic, only by the (doubly implicative) nature of performance. A psychodrama, no matter how dramatically it is performed, on the one hand itself comprises some important functions (acting out, speaking, putting on a role, etc.), while on the other, taken as a whole, it must be linkable—at the very least as a performance—to the major signifiers of the symptom. The performance of the secret behind the part or persona is at war with the mask of the ego, hereafter referred to (following Fanon) as an occupied city.

What we should think about this is readily deduced from the essay on "Medicine and Colonialism" where Fanon considers the relation between Muslim patients and French doctors and psychiatrists.[18] For example, he says that the two are bound together by a relation of enmity; the sequence opens when one of the patient's symptoms is considered to have no antecedent and closes when the proposed "cure" is judged to have no consequence. Fanon's focus is on the point where the different understandings of illness between patient and doctor become diremptive, a difference whose essence is that of race and that obviously results in a closed circle of enmity and distrust. Indeed, it being impossible to separate psychical reality from colonial ideology without moving into unreality, resistance to the cure as prescribed is due not to the patient's acting out but to the affirmation or negation of the colonial world of medicine, and its necessary truth. The sequence indeed is one where ideology decides what is reality (of illness *and* cure). Determining the major factors of this enmity, Fanon and subsequently Tosquelles have been led to name both as masks; the masking operation is equally inevitable in the case of the clinic as in everyday life, those mini-dramas that often form the finest grain of resistances and collaborations. Are these masks solely the province of the therapist? In other words, are they purely therapeutic tools? No doubt they are, dealing as they do with the codes and trauma of transference. Yet at the same time they can be imagined as forming part of an inner metalanguage of resistance and rule in the patient or doctor who grasps every therapeutic intervention as a collaboration or a subjection: i.e., to cure is to subject; to be ill is not only to resist the language of authority, it is also to reconstruct it. The mask is therefore a subterfuge or a camouflaging word or counter-colonial scheme of redoubt that covers a wide variety of meanings and shades of meaning. The masking language of racism comprises from the start these essential headings: the law that structures desire is inextricably linked to its administrative authority; any therapeutic intervention that initiates a deduction prescribes from the moment it appears, in the information to which it gives rise, the entire process of seduction as we have learned it from Fanon as that fashioned by the language of colonial authority.

However minimal their importance, these dramas, since they are made up of real fantasies (that is to say, in fact, phobias and paranoia), can be said to always involve moments of camouflage, risk, and secrecy, and it is this that justifies analyzing them. It might seem futile to include in a radical program such thoughts of therapeutic acts that go to make up a new kind of institutional therapy, but precisely at every one of these crisis points a resistance—and a politics—is discernable. Tosquelles has some illuminating things to say on this aspect of Fanon's clinical work (as does Cherki), but the meaning of the bifurcation between persona and part is linked to a more general suspicion for Fanon, who instinctively fears that therapy (of whatever persuasion) can become a booby trap. The patient is thus, one can say, in danger of becoming a deployed unit on behalf of the colonial status quo, its justification contained in his illness as both its necessity and truth. It is also a question of not opening up the colonized to further surveillance: therapy is criticized in its collaborative function, when subsumed under hegemony, but so is the cure itself in so far as it constitutes a new front in the war against the colonized, when each new treatment, ready to function as a kind of advancing army, is deployed in a war of pacification against native populations. For example, here is a typical clinical sequence: symptom, distrust, prescription, further demoralization of the colonized. It could even be said of Fanon that he himself grasped the impossibility of therapy in the colony, how a whole network of subterfuges structure the cure in this way, from the smallest matrices to the largest functions of social life. What is in question here, of course, is a hierarchy that remains within the diagnostic level of mental health: it is only when it has been possible to have the symptom widen its resistance, step by step, to include familiar European signs and connotations, that the psychodrama of mistrust is over—the pyramid of functions by which the Arab, or African, is judged to be deficient, then touches on the next level (that of certain racist stereotypes that stand in a relation of redundancy to anything resistant, or singular). There is both a syntax within the sequences and a subrogating syntax between the sequences, at one and the same time. It is for the same reason too, namely the deficiency of a certain aetiology, that Fanon wants to restore the symptom (of difference) to its proper time and place, that is, not as a universal truth, and so a challenge to the decrees of psychoanalysis as ever adequately universal in their truth.

What needs to be noted here, however, is that the psychopolitical effects of these aetiologies can easily become imbricated in one another: a phantasm is not yet completed when already, cutting in, the first term of the real may appear. Symptom and cure move in counterpoint; functionally, the phantasmatic structure of the real is fugued: thus it is that fantasy at once performs and masks itself. Within the single ego, the imbrication of forces can indeed only be allowed to come to a halt with a radical break if the occupying forces which then compose it are in some way recuperated at the highest level of the superego (which is rarely the true form of the cure, given that cultural authority's representative is deposited there). One can recognize here the pattern (of a real made up of multiple fantasies): the phantasm is a narrative broken at the egoic level but is unitary at the level of unconscious performance (something that can be verified in the corporeal or in the body's motility or movement). The level of psychodrama (which provides a major part of Fanon's experimental therapeutics) must thus be capped by a higher level from which, step by step, resistances draw their meaning—the level of praxis and national-civic disobedience.

From the clinical perspective, *socialthérapie* is thus a question of ending the division between individual alienation and group paranoia, thereby restoring the symptom to its sociopolitical context. The question of remedy is thus not solely a hermeneutic problem, but a question of how the symptom is *lived* as collective experience. It goes without saying that the group is the point at which the symptom acquires authority, but also the place where the subject undergoes agitation and contestation, and in whose communication it returns to itself shattered, forced to renounce the previous forms of its racially diminished life, including the nativist forms of ecstasy and ravishment, whose dramatization up to this moment has been essential for maintaining colonial authority.

The Clinic as Praxis

I emphasize these things because one must see how Fanon's North African clinics were adapted to transforming the equally irrational beliefs of colonial psychiatry. For, as I mentioned above, the profession had at this time proved instrumental in the creation of a racist semiology of the *colonisé*. So it was no surprise that Fanon saw his role as contrary to these beliefs and doctrines, but also opposed to the politics by which the profession sought to preserve the psychical as a purely scientific area of study. Fanon did not believe that the mental breakdown of the colonized could be grasped by thinking of the mind alone without any reference to the social forces occupying it.

In his articles on neuropsychiatry, the notion of racial heredity is discredited and made entirely subsidiary to the notion of culture: there may be organic factors in an individual's history, writes Fanon, but there is no causal relation between biology and symptom, a view he expresses when first introducing the notion of "sociogeny" in *Black Skin, White Masks*. Later theorists have sought to flesh out this word, which until recently has not played a significant role in Fanon studies, but they fail to see sociogeny as linked to Fanon's interest in how a person acquires psychological consistency, or how they become a person who is white or black, in short a fully institutionalized racial being, even should they do nothing and of course even before being racially marked as a subject. (This question is also at the heart of Fanon's psychopolitical work on *socialthérapie*). How individuals stop being subordinate to their racial characters embodies immediately psychological affects, dramatizations, and aporias, whence these affects can be drawn up into aetiologies, as can be seen in the diagnostic lists of several articles. Since from the very outset, Fanon's sociotherapeutic analyses show the utmost reluctance to treat character as a simple essence, even merely for purposes of classification, it follows that he should also deny the theory of organism, then prevalent in psychiatry, any diagnostic importance, a point of view that he never veered from or modified. Without leaving the corporeal out of analysis altogether, Fanon considered the body to be a psychosomatic complex or typology based not on naturalism but on the history of collective complexes assigned to it by culture (in this he was clearly influenced by the early work of Lacan and Merleau-Ponty).[1]

Since madness is lived in the register of meaning, Fanon was therefore concerned with the specific intersubjective meanings of racial madness, that is, as we have already said, the ways in which racism makes people mad. On the one hand, he says that all delusional phenomena (whatever one calls them—hypnagogia, hallucination, salvinizations, heautoscopy, etc.) form a necessary plane of discourse, outside of which the slightest reported somatic disturbance ceases to be intelligible except in certain racial discourses, so that it can be said that there is not a single mental illness in the colony without a register of racial meaning, or at least without the discourse of race. Yet on the other hand, these extreme pathogens or biological agents can be neither described nor classified as purely symbolic—whether the illness be considered as a purely historical, or intersubjective, form, limited to certain complexes (those most familiar to us it is true), in which case it is necessary to include in the account the very large number of experiments Fanon did using lithium, comprising biological agents but not psychosexual complexes (experiments that were included in his medical thesis but excised from *Black Skin, White Masks*).[2]

Fanon's critiques of neuropsychiatry, much concerned with how it defined people in terms of biological essences, had striven, using various hypotheses, to define the human being not as an essence but as a social process. The mental positivist however cannot understand this; it seems misguided to him because mental disorders have their root in the organic. For Fanon, every organic or mental disorder (whether primary or secondary) can be related to history and alienation (understood in the psychiatric and not the Marxist sense); when a sequence involves racism (as is usual in the colony), it comprises multiple perspectives; in short, every disorder is the coalescence of both neurology and psychiatry. Fanon, analyzing a Muslim patient, starts not from the stereotypes of colonial psychiatry but from the three major relationships in which the patient can engage and that he calls the "cortico-visceral" (adaptation, situation, alienation). The treatment brings these relationships under two rules: rules of *reaction-derivation*, when it is a question of accounting for other relationships, and rules of *action*, when it is a case of describing the transformation of the genesis of the symptoms in the course of the treatment. There are many examples, in Fanon's clinical writings from 1951 to 1960, where it is the dissolution of the personality (its vertigo) that is classified and reconstituted.

Finally, Fanon proposed to describe and classify the processes of an illness not according to what their repressed source might be but according to their effects (whence the name *socialthérapie*), inasmuch as they participate in three somatic-mental axes (also to be found in his writings on neuroses), which are the socius, space (the body), and reconstruction. Since this reconstruction derived from the occasional use of shock therapy (as a preparation for psychotherapeutic work), it, too, is bound by a paradigmatic structure to the very notion of *socialthérapie* that Fanon practiced (with Tosquelles) at Saint-Alban and Blida-Joinville; and since this work defines the clinic as the socius, it can be asked to what extent shock therapy was mobilized or used as a substitution or replacement for therapy.[3]

The three articles Fanon co-wrote with Tosquelles have many points in common. The most important, it must be stressed again, is the use of shock therapy to counter participation in the psychotic dissolution of the personality according to a succession of dissolutions (the shock acting as a second dissolution), this succession being typically classified as part of the psychological reconstruction of the personality; which is why the second dissolution through electroconvulsive therapy, despite ethical concerns, has here been called reintroducing the patient to the shock of the real: the word *real* is not to be understood in the sense of the reality that forms the outside to the hospital but in the sense of the real in which the work and the organization of the clinic represents a major articulation of praxis (of meaning, communication, and struggle). In other words, it is not so much that the hospital stands in for the real but that, in so far as it reintroduces the sufferer to his or her own desire without fear of punishment or of penalty, it forces him or her to confront the real of institutional life (a point often forgotten).

We have now explained what institutional therapy in the colony chiefly consists in and what changes were made by Fanon; for Fanon, *socialthérapie* was based on the idea that it was necessary to treat the institution itself in order to cure the patients. For this to take place the clinic had to provide more than a mere facsimile of quotidian life (as we have shown above), but it first had to adapt the sufferer to the temperament and sanctions of institutional life before treatment could proceed to therapy. Fanon did not believe the former would ever be enough without therapy. Hence his abiding interest in psychoanalytic techniques and practices.

We conclude therefore that although the emphasis, in Fanon's clinical work, is heavily cultural, the knowledge on which this depends arises both from the place of racism in the mind and from the emphasis on the visceral nature of its affects (not to mention its corporeal "malediction"). This last point, however, is coextensive with a whole theory of the colonial body; it is a body in pieces, or it is a haunted semblance that eludes signification insofar as it is essentially irreal: even in its utterances it is not necessarily an *I* that is speaking, but a *colonial thing* under the command of some other. This corporeal image arises from several of Fanon's case histories. I propose to expand and explain its ramifications in what follows.

ADDENDUM: A CASE STUDY

According to Alice Cherki, in 1958 Fanon wrote "an extremely significant case study" which "is surprisingly reminiscent of Freud's famous 'Rat Man' and owes much to certain findings of Ferenczi."[4] With regard to Fanon's own reading of Freud or Ferenczi, Cherki has little or nothing further to say, nonetheless she writes: this "report reveals" that the *idea* of transference makes Fanon feel "extremely uncomfortable" because he finds "his centrality burdensome."[5] Aside from the fact that this entire passage is itself already transferential, given the ease with which Cherki claims to know the meaning of Fanon's unease, and by reference to a discomfort whose interpretation is at once transferential and all too predictably unaware of its *own* projection, why this insistence on the discomforting idea—rather than the intense emotional affect—of transference? What might we consider is being addressed here within this transferential reading of a discomfort that, we are told, "does not stop transference from occurring"?[6] (There is nothing to be done with such transference but to perform its discomfort it seems.) Two possible answers come to mind.

The first is historical and concerns Fanon's changing relationship to psychoanalysis from 1952 to 1958: for Cherki, that relationship became "much more nuanced."[7] Hence, she writes of Fanon's changing relationship to the Oedipus complex, homosexuality, and the unconscious, but also his acquisition of a specific kind of analytical knowledge, or technique, according to which he acquired an "extremely attuned ear": she refers to Fanon's concern with the "repetitive patterns of signifiers," "the denials and lapses" or parapraxes, and, finally, the question of transference, as if all of these things had not already been discussed, with considerable authority, in *Black Skin, White Masks*.[8] Where does this discomfort with transference come from? Cherki sees it as a sign of Fanon's reading in search of personal answers! Now in fact, Fanon's concern with transference, in its earliest occurrence, was essentially defined by a concern with how the black can only perform itself as a subject insofar as it is able to project and so reflect itself as a white persona or mask. If transference is, according to Freud, understood as "the most primordial form of emotional tie to an object," in Fanon's analyses of black psychoneuroses transference is reconceived in specular terms, as an imaginary relation to an image, or an imago in which the black is already masked, that is to say, made irreal or artificial. By the same token, what Freud defined as an affective and essentially blind emotional tie becomes in Fanon a concern with the unwitting repetition of an artificiality that also denotes an inner nothingness. Cherki's contribution to this narrative is unduly biographical, and nowhere more so than in her transferential relation to Fanon's discomfort. Here we find posited, apropos of a case history that has never been published, an analysis that recalls one of Freud's most difficult, enigmatic texts dealing with torture, anality, and homosexuality: that of the Rat Man. What we have here is a form of disavowal, and less a negation, present in Fanon's wish not to be seen as the patient's father but to be his doctor; or, as Cherki cites it: "In the fullness of time, he stops responding to the patient's wish—'I would have liked you to be my father,' by saying, 'I cannot be your father, I am your doctor.'"[9] She concludes (and with an ease that raises further questions about whose transference is being discussed here): "the young man in question made incredible progress. As did Fanon."[10] Let us call this wish not to be the father, Fanon's discomfort with the whole language of psychotherapy, its symbolic centrality and authority as both an organizing idea and institution; it is in this withdrawal that a new therapeutic is born as both an institutional project and a politics.

We know that 1958 was a period of exile and crisis for Fanon, in which there was, so to speak, maximum exposure to the political dimension of his therapy (and of his death—it was a year of assassinations and disappearances, including attempts to assassinate Fanon himself). It was during this year in Tunis that Fanon wrote *L'An V de la révolution algérienne* (translated as *A Dying Colonialism*), a book that includes the same therapeutic displacement of psychotherapy in the name of a new politics (of both the subject and the clinic); but it is certainly this same principle of (analytic) discomfort that comes to define Fanon's sensitivity to what he refers to repeatedly as hysterical suggestion, the use of hysteria as persecutory support in the colonized, with the ensuing misrecognition of their own reality. What we have here is a certain sequence—from Freud to Fanon, hysteric to revolutionary, psychotherapy to *socialthérapie*—that we can designate as the attempt to find the articulation of a certain authority and to analyze revolution itself as an hysterical event. The contraction of the colonized as a mortified body is central to this hysteria, which Fanon sees everywhere as the defining symptom of colonialism. Words are trapped in the corporeal imagos that captivate the subject, they become marked by a colonial ideology of the referent: the petrification of speech and language, dream and desire by which the *colonized* expresses the jouissance that discourse forms. At the same time the task is not simply to make the subject see what is hidden or repressed, but to make it recognize the imaginary dimensions of its history and language. The analyst's responsibility or ethics is to introduce the subject to that moment when it can confront the void of its own intoxication. On this point, Fanon offers a profound rethinking of the clinic as a collective therapeutic system adapted to the language and temporality of the colonized, whose petrified speech is the point of origin for the discourse of treatment and cure.

Nor is this all: catharsis of affects, body, petrification; in Fanon's case histories, torture has a force that the subject must carry as a *force de rupture* that is both an interrupted movement and an immobilization: this movement is thought differently from that of persona or mask and suggests a reconceptualizing of transference as an interrupted form of the *n'est pas* (by which is meant a rupture or void in the subject; I will come back to this).

This leads to a second major therapeutic development, as important to Fanon's political as to his clinical thought: that of the *mirror as mask*, which is not to be confused with his earliest insight into *the mask as mirror*. As we know, *Black Skin, White Masks* presents itself to the reader as a mirror of disalienation, in the sense of a corrective self-seeing. For the early Fanon, the progress of analysis is a progress in self-consciousness, and its dialectical mainspring is the analyst as a reflecting mirror of disalienation. It is the progression from blind (non-specular and thus hypnotic or, as Fanon notes, irreal) identification to true and authentic self-identification: the subject must free itself from the roles it plays and mimes through the alienation

imposed upon it by the racial imagos of culture, consequently the subject finally *recognizes itself* in its alienated delusory image and thus passes
from ignorance to knowledge. If in 1952 transference is the projection of
an intrusive, suggestive, petrifying image, it is the specular identification
through speech of the imprinted (and therefore invisible, unimaginable)
image hidden from its gaze that the subject is initially captured by: namely,
the alienated form of its (white-identified) ego. In his first book, Fanon
wants to hold a mirror up to that alienated subject, so that through the
reading of *Black Skin, White Masks*, it can be free from the constraints of
an imago of which it is unaware; until the moment when it can finally see
itself in the mirror and thus once again know itself in it, the subject will
remain the mime or suggestion of a racist self-reflection. Hence, the object of the cure is not to suppress the egoic image from which the patient
suffers but rather to authenticate it as the subject's own image, so that the
subject can recognize (rather than misrecognize) itself in it. In other words,
you *are* the *nègre* that you denounce; you are the sacrificial remnant of a
shame that preexists you and your being: the imposed "reality" of a white
object-relation. So in Fanon's earliest work, identification is conceived in
specular terms as a relation to an image, and analysis is conceived as the
simple dialectical dissolution of that specular image, and yet, in 1958, that
mirroring is seen as the manifestation of something rotten, or decayed, or
as something frozen, not quite living. Here reading is no longer a question
of recognizing oneself in the mask as mirror; on the contrary, the issue is
not to recognize oneself in the mirror, to shatter it and move on, but to see
beyond the void, or absence hidden by it, a deathliness, meaning by that
name a mirroring that, in relation to the object, has no reflection. What
difference is there between the de-alienating mirror of the analyst and the
captivating mirror of the specular image? On the one hand, the mirror
captures, freezes, and alienates the subject by expatriating it in an image
that dominates, subjugates and suggests it. On the other hand, and simultaneously, it permits the subject to see itself—that is, to separate itself
from its image by seeing itself in front of itself. Thus it should not surprise
us that disalienation has its own transferential politics like other organizations, and that disalienation in its petrified and petrifying form is incapable of knowing itself (dis-alienating itself) *except* in the mode of self-vision
(which is the mode of alienation, of being outside oneself).

This is what Fanon still seemed to believe in 1952, but by 1958 (if not
earlier), in his essays on *socialthérapie* and colonialism, he has completely

changed his tune: to return the image to the analysand is no longer to dis-
alienate him; rather, it is to risk trapping him in another objectification no
less imaginary than before, locking him into an endless aggressivity of depersonalization. It's an insight that comes to Fanon via his treatment of the
tortured and torturing subjects of the Algerian civil war. In 1958, the cure
becomes more aporetic. Here we come across Fanon's later presentation of
the object which, from 1952 to 1958, changes from an imaginary schema
to a schema of the real, from a specular disalienation to a more unnameable *n'est pas*. First of all, let us recall that the object in 1952 is conceived as
the expression of an imaginary dereliction, or as the focus of an interiority
constituted out of a wounded narcissism whose meaning represents a sign,
or rather the interlocution of a negrophobic disturbance. In the later case
histories, the basic dissymmetry between the *me* and *not-me*, explained by
disavowal, opens onto a more vertiginous absence between the *I* and the
it, and this absence cannot simply be represented by disalienation, nor is it
simply linked to colonial racism: consequently, the object here refers to a
deep, often circuitous fall or descent whose lapsus is received by the subject
as a mirroring without content, in which the subject is not reflected back
to itself as a diminished or distanced whiteness but as a no-thing, or non-
being, marked by the absence of what specifically constitutes *le vécu noir* as
the site of a specular reversal.

Lastly, this descent into the *n'est pas* that torture reveals leads Fanon to
an important shift in his notions of sovereignty and resistance. Hence, if
we return to the colony as a therapeutic project, we may better understand
Fanon's effort to try and distinguish a politics of the imaginary from that of
the real. The *n'est pas* is unthinkable in terms of presence, nor can it be represented or made present as a pathology. The corporeal schema is no longer
swathed in real fantasies or illusions that make the body into an allegory,
or fictive persona, but it takes on the form of a rigidification in which the
person is a dead object filled, so to speak, by its own vertiginous absence,
by its own force of disaggregation. These observations suggest that there is
something unfathomable in blackness that exactly coincides with what we
might call the unrepresentability of its *n'est pas*: just as there is a point at
which racial meaning can no longer signify, which has as its consequence
that no signifier escapes the abyss (of blackness), so Fanon is trying, by various ways, to figure this untranslatability as a new form of wretchedness.
It would be interesting to know at what moment wretchedness comes to
signify, for Fanon, an important change in his relation to psychoanalysis.

In *The Wretched of the Earth* the word no longer refers to a dialectical op-position between active and passive being, or *ressentiment* and resistance, but designates the way in which the subject is immiserated or affected by its own impossibility or nothingness. Contrary to the current trend to de-politicize Fanon's clinical thought, it is my argument that Fanon's clinical work on wretchedness, on those effected and affected by it, is an effort to describe an experience of non-sovereignty that is not conceived as a state of exception (or of escape) but as the (non)signifying place for *the one who is black*. With this proviso in mind, let us now turn to the sociodiagnostic categories that Fanon devised for interpreting blackness.

3

Negrophobogenesis

As will be seen more clearly in a moment, all negrophobogeneses are *reactions*; they imply, underlying their signifiers, a phobic chain of signifieds, with the negrophobe able to choose some and ignore others. Negrophobia poses a question of meaning and this question always comes through as a *décalage* in the subject, even if this rupture or gap is recuperated by society as an anxious (sadistic) response to blackness.

Fanon's work as a clinician was, from the first, bound up with the fact of his blackness. This is obvious perhaps, but something that is little spoken of. Why is that? Fanon repeatedly refers to his body as a transferential object to the extent to which a patient's questions and expectations, fears and interrogations, impose on him an immediate and obvious supplementary message, in addition to the symptomatic content itself, and that will impact the very possibility of treatment. Considered overall, this transference is formed through racist doctrine and belief and is the channel and point of transmission through which a racist notion of the therapist is communicated and reproduced. In such thought, whose source can be traced back to negative transference, the word "negrophobogenesis" refers to a resistance that is both unique and indelible but that manifests itself differently in Fanon's various case histories. In short, before a word is said or heard, racism already informs the work to be done in deriving the symptom, or, more exactly, its connotation, from the system and codes of culture. This is why the concept of negrophobogenesis necessarily immediately refers to a message supplementing clinical intervention, in the sense that what has racial *significance* is understood at a level that is unconsciously connected to ideology.

This being the case, we see at once that it is through the question of black corporeality that Fanon's engagement with psychoanalysis can be more justly appreciated. Fanon begins his first work by asking what it means to have "race" lodged in the body and what it might possibly mean to be free from such lodgment. Accordingly, he identifies several scales of racialization—epidermalization, petrification, sociogeny, and a post-humanistic account of the human. These different structures are co-implicated but, since they are structurally and politically heterogeneous, they necessarily have to be understood as separate from one another: here (in Fanon's various texts) the racialized body is made up of several racist fantasies or "myths"; each myth is contiguous to the others in so far as they fuse a Manichean logic —of self and other—with stereotypical languages and images of racial difference. Hence, in his study of racist texts—literary, philosophical, psychoanalytical, and political—Fanon shows how racism plays a key role in the dissemination of epidermal myths and how it has given the modern body a narrative and affective form that has been both systematic and singular.

Racism has been formative not only of the genre and form of lived experience but also, more fundamentally, of the very notion of embodied experience itself. In *Black Skin, White Masks*, Fanon writes: "wherever he goes, the Negro remains a Negro." The point being that the racialized body has often been the point of reception through which racism has become readable and natural but also, more tellingly, or more worryingly perhaps, the racialized body has also formed a complex limit to the experience of the body as first of all belonging to a self. What follows will be a brief survey of what Fanon initially clinically defines as racial misrecognition and his attempts to restore that racialized body to a less phobic re-presentation.

1. *Epidermalization* (*épidermisation*) refers to the imposition of a second historical-racial schema on the corporeal schema proper. In place of the corporeal ego, which no longer has any meaning, the body forms an imaginary surface veiled (or disfigured) by hostilities. "The White [*Le Blanc*]," writes Fanon, has woven the black body out of a "thousand details, anecdotes, stories"—stories, and anecdotes, endowed with certain meanings or signs (such as fetish, phobia, stereotype, scopophilia): these meanings are linked to certain gestures, attitudes, expressions that remain if not arbitrary, at least entirely historical.[1] Hence it behooves Fanon to say that racist society projects onto the black body feelings and values that are equivalent to "a racial epidermal schema," whose signification is one of disfiguration, in which the very surface of the body, its skin, becomes a metonym for a

certain *historicity of hatred*.[2] As the corporeal schema crumbles, by dint of this dislocation, the dialectical movement between body and world gives way to feelings of disintegration as the subject takes these signs, words, and images—invested in the body by racist historicity and culture—as the "natural" denotation of reality. Consequently, racialization here signifies a rupture between body and world, between sense and symbolization. Fanon speaks about his body being turned inside out, and of succumbing to an impurity or flaw. With this we see how the black body as sensed becomes bound to the trauma of how it is known, in whose awareness it finds itself "collapsed," "fragmented," and "assailed" from without and within as part of the racialization of experience.[3]

In the experience of dislocation, it seems, the subject comes to grasp itself as *nègre*, which cannot be distinguished from the hatred defining it. How does Fanon read this consciousness? In what order, according to what progression? If, as is suggested by Fanon's turn to Freud and Lacan, there is no racialization without fantasy or phobia, without a kind of re-corporealization of anxiety, then the body is epidermalized in the very moment in which it is unable to resist this incorporation, which leaves it bare, denuded; better, it is only after it receives this phobic revelation of itself (that is to say, its anguished, traumatizing dereliction) that the *colonisé* encounters the intolerable real of blackness: "But when we say that European culture possesses an *imago* of the Negro [*nègre*] responsible for all the conflicts that may arise, we do not go beyond the real."[4]

2. *Petrification (pétrification)*. Fanon uses the terms "petrified" and "petrification" in the two opening chapters of *The Wretched of the Earth* to refer to a kind of hardening, or of being turned into stone; since the whole effect of colonialism is to mortify the "culture" and "*Erlebnis*" of black embodied life, it is evident that the colonized are not at liberty to simply express themselves, and conversely, what freedom they do possess is heavily restricted and restrained. The truth of petrification thus refers to the work of imposition within us, the sense of wanting to flee or speak but remaining frozen, under the weight of a certain *style* of embodiment (petrified, rigidified, inanimate, ankylotic), by which the body mimes or acts out the signs of its own subjugation and its own petrified perversion as a subject.

3. *Sociogeny (sociogénie)*. In his first book, *Black Skin, White Masks*, Fanon writes: "Beside [Freudian notions of] phylogeny and ontogeny stands sociogeny. In one sense, conforming to the view of Leconte and Damey, let us say that this is a question of a sociodiagnostic."[5] What is the content of

this sociodiagnostic? What does the sociogenic signify? By definition, the term clearly indicates a response to Freudian psychoanalysis, and it forms the basis for Fanon's dual turn from phylogeny and ontogeny to that of racialization. In fact, in the early chapters of *Black Skin, White Masks*, Fanon presents black life as an effigy (but one dazed by its appearance), as a being dispossessed by the racist connotation of the body that it is unable to evade or escape. Living under the law of white supremacy, blacks necessarily experience themselves as continually hated and, caught up as they are in a morbid fixation on the dominant culture, they remain suspended in an imaginary white projection of themselves, the better to appear "in" culture through their disappearance as a black. In such a divided state, there is nothing more abhorrent to these white-identified subjects than to see themselves as *nègre* and no greater disgrace than to fall into the "pit of niggerhood," the very definition of what it means to be a subject bereft, impotent, and socially benighted. In a more obscure way, blackness becomes the symbol of a veil that forces the *colonisé* to invent, to love, to mourn the loss of a whiteness buried within, an inner purity that is faded, absorbed, *in travail*. This innermost loss, identified with the master's language and culture, makes the relation to blackness *irreal* by making the *nègre*, who is both model and rival, *servile* to the white being that surpasses it.

Fanon also recognizes this, explicitly in *Black Skin, White Masks*, as a problem of time: or rather, the discovery that black narcissism is perhaps nothing other than an originary banishment that is regarded as the self's most prized, because ceaselessly desired, inheritance. For the same reason, we must especially note here that psychoanalytic theory is essential to sociogeny—its reinvention and objects—and indeed it is Freud's reading of fate and accident (or, in Lacan's terms, *tuché* and *automaton*) that seems to be crucial here.[6] Again, Freud's notion of *Nachträglichkeit* allows Fanon to explore, politically and ethically, the psychic and corporeal affects of colonialism: it is as the incongruous affect of a certain cultural inheritance that the black chooses itself as the expression of a white inner presence.[7]

What would it mean for the colonial subject to affirm itself as black in such relations (relations that are the daily expression of reproaches, and that attest to how detestation is firmly entrenched in anti-blackness)? This is, I think, the sense of the "I should not seek the meaning of my destiny there [in History]" remark in *Black Skin, White Masks*, to the effect that the meaning of any self-presence, viewed as black, has to cope with a hatred whose persistence and intensity involves a more complex articulation of symptom and culture. Turning to Fanon's discussion, we will see how the theme of the psyche and culture come together in the form of a mutual abhorrence that is itself a sign of a traumatic inheritance (this replication is, in my view, key to the various arguments of *Black Skin, White Masks*).

Which is to say: Fanon constantly wants to discover a reading of culture that is psychopolitical, but a psychopolitics that, in its analysis of unconscious fantasy and colonial reality, revises Freud's late reflections on the social bond to show how racist fantasy can not only be fully integrated and institutionalized, but remains as a kind of traumatic—albeit disavowed—memory in the unconscious life of the colonized. It is a psychopolitics, in other words, of the ways in which the unconscious is constituted by the real, but also of the ways in which the authority of the real is secured by social beliefs that are necessarily phantasmatic, as well as indignant and envious: the imagos and stereotypes by means of which the colonial subject hates and enslaves itself as a subject, affirms its immorality or malfeasance, and fails to know itself as anything but a masked, white-alienated subject.

4. To these three main concepts should be added the Manichean categories that accompany racialization. Three remarks should be made in this context.

Firstly, "it is the colonist who *fabricated* and *continues to fabricate* the colonized subject," and out of these fantasies the racialized body emerges as an object of fantasy, violence, and delirium.[8] In other words, and this is an important psychopolitical insight, the racialized body is an unconscious, fetishized symbol; it is a body that, structurally, does not need to exist in order for this symbolism to develop. The black man *is* a genital, phobogenic object: in the traditional oedipal figures of the father or mother racialization was not the principal message since, precisely, oedipal desire needed no racial symbol to manifest itself; in the relationship that holds, however, between racism and the racialized body, the oversexualization of the black body that comes to dominate colonial discourse perverts or overwhelms the body politic. As however this perversion is carried out unconsciously, the expression of negrophobia is chiefly founded on the phantasmatic messages of the black body, which appears in the minds of whites as a symptom of sexualized anxiety, almost as a kind of hallucination. Metonymically, the black man *is* a penis; and, "Whoever says rape says Negro" (*Qui dit viol dit nègre*); or "A Negro is raping me" (*Un nègre me viole*).[9] Driven by the collision or collusion between libido and stereotype, these fantasies illustrate how sexually loaded this body is, burdened by a mix of desire and revulsion, morality and imagination, libido and culture. Driven by the desire to either *whiten* (in lactification) or *blacken* (in negrophobia), these fantasies illustrate how the racialized body amplifies the racist work of culture; here, the fundamental denotation constituted by the black body is that of a naturalized sexual aggression in which the body is either violating or violated.

Secondly, the effect of being a symbol for the white-other results in an incorporation that divides the imago from the veil that conceals or absorbs it. The black has no "ontological resistance" to the ways in which s/he is presented or connoted, for blackness arrives as a destiny or fate, and its obscurity is not due to an absence but due to its absorption of an inner whiteness. Fanon's clinical strategy is to return that body, from being a symbolically incorporated object, to a resistant symbol of culture. The more the body experiences itself as the *predestined depository* of cultural and unconscious aggression, the less it seems able to resist the burden of negrophobia; caught as it were in the dynamics of racist oedipal desire, this body must innocent itself of this cultural investiture in the sexual and symbolic life of racism. This liberation has a less obvious role perhaps than Fanon's famous call for revolutionary violence: the freedoms accompanying decolonial violence, however, are palpably linked to a new kind of libidinal expenditure and protest; in the revolutionary moment the racialized body will no longer be enslaved to its stereotypical connotation, will distance itself from its former white identifications and desires, and will also overcome its former reified investments in a black, mystical essence. The liberated body, on the contrary, by its very disposition, by its opposition to the erotic politics of racialization, will divest itself of its symbolic body, that is, sacrifice itself to the real of revolution. Against the omnipresence of the racialized symbolic body, according to which the Negro is "the biological," "the genital," the predestined depositary and the phobogenic object of culture, Fanon will stress certain acts of decision that will lead to a new subject of culture, to be included in what he will call a "new humanism."[10]

It is impossible however (and this will be the final remark concerning racist lived experience) for the revolution to simply redeem this body politics; in the movement from racial symbolics to a new humanism, Fanon's conception of the body inevitably changes from a phantasmatic conception to a conception of a *"corps à corps"* (one's body is always already a body for others). In *The Wretched of the Earth*, the thematics changes from petrification to a kind of tabula rasa or disinvestment of the colonial subject:

"the proof of success lies in a whole social structure being changed from the bottom up."[11] What is the relationship of depetrification to this image of the tabula rasa? To all appearances, it is one of making explicit the "absolute depersonalization" undergone by the colonized, which in turn calls for an "absolute violence" of the tabula rasa aimed at the social structure (with its petrification of cultural life).[12] Hence Fanon's view of the revolution as a moment of tumult and ecstasy, in which depetrification allows (invents) the discharge of an entirely new libidinal expenditure that also allows new relations of love and pleasure and new forms of aesthetic culture (music, poetry, and dance) to appear. From social death to tabula rasa, for Fanon, destructive violence is the process through which the socially dead acquire a new symbolic form.

An analysis of Fanon's writings on decolonial war reveals this violence to induce a kind of vertigo or anguish, and a form of radical expenditure that is not exchangeable, and does not enter into a sacrificial logic (of the gift); here the new form of the human no longer enters into the purview of tragic politics or revolutionary dialectics but has the appeal of an almost ecstatic transformation or annihilation, preserving the rupture and movement of the tabula rasa. In the decolonial struggle, violence has a regulatory function insofar as it is detoxifying and destructive, creative and reinventive.

A last point: whatever the source of this violence, or its derivation from the complexes discussed above, it is clear that it had a major political and personal impact on Fanon's *socialthérapie*, since it was primarily as a clinician that Fanon had direct experience of this violence and its psychopolitical affect (as we have said). In the remaining sections of Part One, I shall explain why this *socialthérapie* cannot be distinguished from these violent affects nor, hence, from the psychic costs of colonial war.

4

Historicity and Guilt

We showed in the previous chapters that the sociodiagnostic of cultural hatred in the colony, and the mode of unreality in which it was lived, also included that of the hospital or clinic. It was thus seen that the focus of Fanon's institutional therapy consequently became an interrogation of cultural life, and the imaginaries forming it, by means of group-governed rules of transformation whose *modus operandi* began with a redrawing of the division between resistance (to treatment) and the therapeutic community as a new group idea, to which the decision and responsibility to belong was seen as a primary condition of recovery. As for this new group idea, or at least those implemented at Blida-Joinville, not all instituted measures were successful, with certain subjects remaining closed to the positive therapeutic effects of the new discipline.[1] Not everyone, in other words, invested in the authority of the new group. It is certain, therefore, that the problems raised by the classification of the mental character of the *colonisé* were never quite satisfactorily resolved. But since these problems, however defined, were the subject of further reflection by Fanon, it serves to establish the principle of group treatment that was his radical objective, and the theory of group cooperation, both evictive and elective, that held it all together. I propose now to adduce that theory through what Fanon, following on from Lacan, mentioned as the problem of relating to one's counterpart (or *semblable*).[2] Then, for yet greater clarity, I will show why language serves to establish and preserve the problem of human misrecognition (or *méconnaissance*); along the way, I will touch on the feeling of guilt produced in those forced to play a part or role that (literally) *corpses* them.

I. METAPHYSICS OF GUILT

Fanon's clinical writings teach nothing more clearly than that resistance is not the same as the reactions it provokes. Certainly there is ready agreement on the innumerable obstacles presented by linguistic and cultural differences between Fanon and his Arab Muslim patients. It is also evident that Fanon spent most of his career as a psychiatrist resisting the scientific reductionism of colonial psychiatry that he considered ignorant and that, even within works supposedly sympathetic to the "Musulman," forensic principles were often derailed by mystical hypotheses of degeneration. Again, the somatic model popularized by Poirot (and widely adapted by psychiatrists practicing in French colonial outposts) seems to not stand the test of time. Like any scientific racism, its value lies less in its canonic truth than in its regulated form of authority as governmental policy, to which it lends itself, thus holding out the hope of a scientific proof to the natural hierarchy of the races. A difficulty for *socialthérapie*, however, is that when cultural specificity has a high classificatory power (as in the case of racial aetiologies), it fails adequately to account for the multiplicity of patients' symptoms that may not really be concerned with racial identity, especially when analyzed by the non-native observer, which Fanon decidedly was.

The analysis of Muslim criminality proposed by Fanon and Lacaton, for example, avoids saying that Europeans and North Africans are inherently different but fails really to explain why native criminals deny the facts of their crime, when faced with overwhelming evidence, without also trying to prove their innocence.[3] The real difficulty posed by this denial is not a culture of lying but the place (and hence the experience) of when a lie becomes known as such. This distinction, whatever its formulation, forces Fanon to say that indigenous crime has a development, frequency, brutality, and savagery that surprise at first but that are driven by a special "impulsiveness."[4] What is this special impulsiveness that compels patients to lie? *Who* is the liar in this narrative? There appears here to be an ability to lie that is unaware of itself, and at the moment when it can no longer imagine itself as innocent. Is this so because this is a lie that always speaks its truth, or a truth that is always impelled to lie, or a truth that can only disguise itself as falsehood and error? Is there—or not—a privilege given here to psychiatric speech as a truism that can only repeat as inscrutable the speech of the native confessor?

The idea of confession has accustomed us to emphasize in one way or another—sometimes in a legal or juridical way—the notion of a hidden

truth being revealed. In colonial psychiatry what is revealed is a truism: natives lie because they, like children, are incapable of telling the difference
between lies and truth. So what is most deceitful about the native mind is
that it assumes a truth that, without knowing it, persists in error. For Fanon
what matters here is that lying is a form of resistance; more than that, the
native refuses to be seduced by the idea that there is any kind of shared
meaning as to falsehood and truth in the colony. There are no such contractual agreements as to standards of behavior or the social performance of
truth. There is on the contrary an absence of any affinity, even if this truth
is only accessible via mutual suspicion. Many practices, for example, set
the *colon-colonisé* as two adversaries in conflict over the same stake; but it is
not the same, for both mean different things by truth and its denial: truth
then is truly double (Fanon will later say "antithetical"), it is not reducible
or classifiable by any one rule or criterion. By knowledge and truth what is
revealed is a desire to either resist or subvert what passes for truth in the colony, and that accordingly affirms a native truth contrary to clinical knowledge and its racist concepts of superiority and hierarchy. It is as if the act of
saying "I am ill" is not only a challenge to the universal values and claims of
French psychiatry, but also to the power and interests of the dominant class
of Europeans that dismisses native veracity. This difference is all the more
interesting in that it relates truth to the structures of cure in such a way as
to detach it from any therapeutic desire or object, a cure in which two very
unequal opponents try to gain possession over a denial that circulates as
law; as though the superego, after the fashion of certain magistrates, were
to proceed with conviction but was unable to decide between a just cure
and a cure that is pure force: a judgment that has no agreed-upon sentence
form (and thereby is impotent, rotten). If therefore a privileged class of colonial psychiatrists can define what a lie is (as the subject of native desire
and of action), they need at least to be aware that such definition is one of
the very categories defining the ongoing occupation (grammatical and psychological, moral and juridical) of those accused of not knowing right from
wrong. Once again, it is doubtful whether such classification has any forensic value, but what it does permit is a clinical perspective on how "lying" is
performed by native psychopolitical life (wherein the meaning of the symptom is already decided, and the ends of the cure already known as the truth
of native experience, as Fanon's reservations confirm).

It will—perhaps—be the aetiology of these denials (accessible as symptoms) that will provide the key to Fanon's *socialthérapie*: but since these

morbidities can only be defined in relation to a carceral or stigmatic discourse, not to their stereotypical reality, Fanon will find their meaning (for those who suffer them) only if his therapy departs from the canonical descriptions of madness in the Maghreb, here classified as the ethno-topoi of various malfeasances, and he is then able to decode a radically new series of lytic narrations (in the sense of cultural messages or signs). Equally, the institutional pressure of his role as a black *French* psychiatrist treating Arab Muslims will also cause him to revise some of the founding tenets of Tosquelles's institutional therapy. I propose now to adduce that questioning through what I have just mentioned as the problem of therapeutic language and why, for Fanon, language serves to establish and preserve the problem of guilt and transgression, as a question of falsehood and truth.

It is evident from Fanon's oeuvre that language is related to two foci, that of delusion and that of obligation: that language use implants in us habits of disavowal and suspicion, reducing people and things to abstractions, and that anti-colonial speech itself imposes on us certain obligations, in the sense of a new meaning and understanding. We might say that the former, in addition to identifying difference, is coextensive with a defensive-defended attitude or world view, whereas the latter arises from a world view that we might call more open or ethical. Additionally, those who use language to separate and accuse and to deny the liberty or uniqueness of their neighbor or *semblable* are just as intolerant as those who stipulate beforehand what they believe to be the only certain and indubitable truth, regardless of the authority and testimony of the speaker. If the one incites hatred due to what it imagines to be the literal truth, or, conversely, condemns to non-truth what it sees as meaningless, we must especially note here that nothing separates them as dogmatic attitudes, for both require *their* truth to be revered by the *semblable*. Now what if these positions were to manifest themselves as psychopolitical attitudes, not so much in terms of narrow-mindedness but in terms of imputing to the *semblable* a secondary, or derivative, status, and precisely as a way of confirming their "scientific" authority and truth? The stakes could not be higher, as they concern nothing less than the very possibility of effective therapy in the colony and the therapeutic foundations of the cure deduced from it. Further, what would it mean for colonial psychiatry to subvert or resist its *own* racist values—or to measure nativist evidence against its own diagnosis without rejecting, dismissing, or perverting it as contrary to science and reason? A key illustration of this difference can be found in Fanon's response to

Octave Mannoni, a response that also sends us back to his critical engagement with psychoanalysis:

> Monsieur Mannoni adds: "Colonial exploitation is not the same as other forms of exploitation, and colonial racism is different from other kinds of racialism." He speaks of phenomenology, of psychoanalysis, of human brotherhood, but we would like him to consider these aspects in more concrete terms. All forms of exploitation are alike. They all seek to justify their existence by citing some biblical decree. All forms of exploitation are identical, since they apply to the same "object": man. By considering the structure of such and such an exploitation from an abstract point of view we are closing our eyes to the fundamentally important problem of restoring man to his rightful place.
>   Colonial racism is no different from other racisms.[5]

When I said above that there are those who claim to have a hold on native truth, or its jurisdiction, whose authority depends on the purely linguistic separation between the *I* and its *semblable*, I had in mind not just a veridical but also a political dispute about meaning. For such truth must apply both to the dispute and its witnessing. Or, in Fanon's words, to confuse the concept of a thing for its lived condition is a kind of blindness. I want to put a particular emphasis on this point, concentrating on it in this chapter, because very many people vigorously deny what is unique, or a uniquely particular truth, which they suspect of being a false concretization, and one that they refuse to recognize as having grasped the truth of the matter. From this they arrogate to themselves the license to accuse and condemn the experience of others as a falsely idolatrous claim and even to chastise them for forgetting their rightful reality. We shall see below in this present chapter that what they are in fact doing is dividing what is idiomatically unique from its lived experience and attempting to devise another path from the particular to the universal. What has not been grasped in this authoritarian claim to truth are the inner movements and excitations by which the *colonisé* encounters itself in the repeated denials of its own claims to truth; it is an experience analogous to vertigo.

I intend first to show that Fanon's response to Mannoni is not as clearcut as the above implies and that his demand is that Mannoni pay closer attention to what is essentially unique as against what is only apparently so. I also want to demonstrate that what Mannoni sees as a unique cultural example of the disposition and existential desire of the *semblable* must be reinterpreted due to his own prejudices that seek to interrogate the native from the point of view of a psychoanalytic authority that is falsely attributive. I speak expressly to why colonial exploitation can only be concret-ized in its universal relation to capital and why difference or the means by which colonial racism manifests its truth occurs especially in relation to language. This is why any language that would include the *semblable* is the most fantasized and the most alienated of all.

Let's begin with the above citation, which occurs in Fanon's forceful response to Mannoni's *Psychologie de la colonisation*—a Freudian-inspired reading of the Malagasy civil war. Mannoni puts forward a dependency theory that absolves the French from any responsibility for their colonial exploitation of the Malagasy. Fanon's response to this text is both political and historical, but he is mostly concerned with Mannoni's hermeneutics. In *Psychologie de la colonisation*, the relation between *colon* and *colonisé* is discussed in terms of that between symbol and symbolized; even though that relation is displaced with regards to its political meaning, the relation is always retrievable in the meaning of its psychic interdependency. Even though the relation itself opens up an aporia of violence and freedom, Mannoni remains convinced that the idiomatic meaning of dependency is the underlying cultural truth to which both sides of the civil war re-main literally faithful. In his response, Fanon therefore asks: what could it mean for psychoanalysis to be a faithful work of cultural translation, when it can never be faithful to the literal meaning of culture? And what does it mean for psychoanalysis to be literally present to this work and in a way that reveals its political complicity solely through its denial, a presence in which native truth always attests to its own servility? This is why, in oppo-sition to Mannoni, Fanon is not solely concerned with method, but rather with how cultural idioms come to be recognized as part of a metaphori-cally totalizing pattern that is wholeheartedly seen to signify non-racial, human truths. For such universalism, cultural idioms are under everyone's jurisdiction (they are everyone's truth), and to that extent they cannot be reduced to a particular truth, with the only exception being known aber-rations (such as racism) whose deeper meaning itself reveals what makes these truths universal in the first place. The universal, on this account, be-longs to everyone because everyone receives it as a force of law, and this is why everyone, in consequence, feels guilty with respect to its authority, since they are obligated to receive its truth in their particularity, and what arises from it: the authority to feel guilty or angry on the universal's be-half. On the same grounds, universal guilt—which I will come back to in a moment—is exclusively tied to those who possess the right to exercise it precisely because they are willing to forfeit their particularity. It follows therefore that those who have no special choice of right over mankind cannot feel guilt except through removing what is uniquely singular to them. And for this they are not celebrated, but despised and condemned. Furthermore, what I mean by the dominant truth here is plain enough, I suppose, from previous chapters. We showed there that the black experiences himself as excluded from the universal and often at the behest of a humanistic command, from which it follows that a universal truth is universal because it takes on a form that is white. I cannot see that it makes any difference here whether the claim is psychoanalytic and the uniqueness being denied is the Malagasy struggle for independence, or the rightfulness of black anger. It makes no difference how such justification takes place, provided that it possesses the supreme authority of its truth and subjugates difference to the highest onto-political point of the universal, its mastery glimpsed at the summits of such struggle.

Why then does Fanon insist on the universal in his response to Mannoni? If all forms of colonial exploitation are identical I must therefore now show why the refusal of the specificities of colonial racism also takes place as the refusal of the authority of the universal, and then I will be able to conclude why this appeal to the universal never quite arrives at either an appeal or a refusal (in so far as the movement from the particular to the universal is never simply a question of departure or arrival), and this is why the *semblable* is the figure through which this displacement takes place. The question of the *semblable* (as we shall see in a moment) is tied to the rhetoric of the right place, which is as usual more difficult than it seems. Accordingly, the phrase "rightful place" should not be read as an appeal to a more faithful translation, rather it reveals a tension between the trope and meaning of what is truly singular and any attempt at its universal restoration. To understand racism from a more concrete view than, say, phenomenology or psychoanalysis, one must know that its foundation is already the derived form of some mystical authority or decree. In other words, the common measure of all racisms is how difference comes to be decreed as difference in the history of humanism. But this decree, common to all racist forms of exploitation, legislates difference differently according to what concept or idea of difference is at stake—in other words, the concept of racism implies boundaries to objects that must be enforced as if their difference were somehow analytically *a priori*. To illustrate what he means, Fanon gives the example of anti-Semitism and says: "I cannot dissociate myself from the fate reserved for my brother. Every one of my acts commits me as a man. Every instance of my reticence, every instance of my cowardice, manifests the man."[6] There are a number of valuable associations that are being alluded to here. Fanon cites two of them, two that he sees as interrelated with the question of language, guilt, and disavowal.

1. The first that is explicitly mentioned is Jaspers's notion of "metaphysical guilt," which occurs in a long footnote to the discussion of Mannoni noted above:

When we wrote this we had in mind Jaspers's metaphysical guilt: "There exists a solidarity among men as human beings that makes each co-responsible for every wrong and every injustice in the world, especially for crimes committed in his presence or with his knowledge. If I fail to do whatever I can to prevent them, I too am guilty. If I was present at the murder of others without risking my life to prevent it, I feel guilty in a way not adequately conceivable either legally, politically or morally. That I live after such a thing has happened weighs upon me as indelible guilt. That somewhere among men the unconditioned prevails—the capacity to live only together or not at all, if crimes are committed against the one or the other, or if physical living requirements have to be shared—therein consists the substance of their being."[7] Jaspers declares that jurisdiction rests with God alone. It is easy to see that God has nothing to do with the matter, unless one wants to clarify this obligation for mankind to feel co-responsible, "responsible" meaning that the least of my acts involves mankind. Every act is an answer or a question: both, perhaps. By expressing a certain way for my being to excel itself, I am stating the value of my act for others. Conversely, the passivity observed during some of history's troubled times can be read as default on this obligation.[8]

This footnote, with what continues and concludes it ("the guilt of those who remained 'neutral' during the Occupation. In a confused way they felt responsible for all those dead and all the Buchenwalds"), deserves a longer analysis than I can offer here.[9] If the Jew, without exception, is Fanon's *semblable* or neighbor here, it is because he is never quite universal, insofar as he too has had to transfer his right of idiomatic singularity to that of the universal, but, in another sense, since the Jew can never be rendered black he can never be this *semblable*, and precisely because he never quite arrives at the particular. Consequently, in so far as the Jewish relation to racism is a relation of translation, a translating that allows him to pass for the universal, he too can be a demonstration of this guilt felt on behalf of the (white) universal. For, by that very fact, the covenant with the universal which Fanon understands to be racially metaphysical, and which has been the foundation of humanistic responses to the Holocaust, thereby abolishes black death from the purview of universal suffering.

By rendering black life idiomatically singular, the politics of the universal thus obviates any need to feel responsible for it. It most evidently follows from all of this that Fanon's notion of universal guilt is very different from the metaphysical form that Jaspers gives it. The expression of co-responsibility is clearly in dialogue with Jaspers's later, ostensibly more political work on guilt. In *The Question of German Guilt* one can see how Jaspers distinguishes between those who feel a kind of guilt that, he says, is not juridical-political, or ethical, but ontological in its relation to others, and those who deny this "indelible" aspect of human being.

What difference is there between, on the one hand, a victim of anti-Semitism, or in any case one who is hated and insulted because he is a Jew, and on the other hand the singular violence meted out to black Africans under apartheid? How does one discriminate, as Mannoni does, between one form of racialism and another? To stay with the question of abstraction or obligation, let me turn here to Fanon's somewhat ironic response to Jaspers's reference to God: "Every act is an answer or a question: both, perhaps. By expressing a certain way for my being to excel itself, I am stating the value of my act for others. Conversely, the passivity observed during some of history's troubled times can be read as default on this obligation." For Fanon the act that arises out of any limit situation is no more passive, or neutral, than the act that disavows its obligation to others, or defaults on this ethico-ontological decree. Both constitute communicative acts and values. How are we to distinguish between those whose feelings of guilt forced them to act and those whose guilt supposedly rendered them neutral during the Occupation and exterminations, so that, in this destitution of decision, neither praxis nor obligation carried any force—or, others would quickly say, they were neither authentic nor inauthentic? Fanon's distinction here is a subtle one—even though the theme of guilt is closely connected here to a pathology of difference—and is one in which the power and authority of a certain kind of racial reasoning plays a decisive role, for the guilt over European Nazism isn't simply a guilt over what it means to be human, especially not in a context where Fanon will demonstrate the claim that originally blacks were not considered to be the same life species as "us" Europeans.

2. The principal point of Fanon's analysis seems to be that racism is always a humanism, and so it is necessary to see how, like all world views

that are defensive or suppressive (of difference), humanism also relies on subterfuge in trying to justify itself, and that this justification is based on false certainties and spurious objectivity, be they religious or biological. It is difficult to decide whether the above reference to Jaspers also contains an implicit allusion to Jaspers's early works, *Psychology of World Views* (1911) and *General Psychopathology* (1913), where world views are, notably, seen as cages (*Gehäuse*), in which existence hardens itself against contents or experiences that threaten to transcend or imbalance its defensive rationality. It is precisely the forcefulness of such *limits* or antinomies through which we essentially remain barricaded in from more authentic possibilities, of subjective and objective life. To overcome these limits, new cognitive acts and experiences are required, not only to exceed or contradict reason's antinomies (a word that Jaspers borrows from Kant) but also, perhaps, to maintain a more authentic relationship to the real. The phrase "limit situation" (*Grenzsituation*) refers to such moments where, accompanied by feelings of dread, guilt, and anxiety, the subject confronts the possibility of going beyond his limits; by knowing that each act he commits is either an answer or a question he begins to excel himself, and by seeking to transcend the limits of reason he confronts the antinomy that defines *him*. For Jaspers, in short, each limit situation can be formulated as a reproach or a declaration, a moment of indecision or bad faith, and an act of decision in which everything is at stake, but in relation to which the feeling of community— its fidelity—cannot be determined without anguish and torment.

There are, to be sure, familiar existential accents in all of this, but the key emphasis is on how reason can only enforce its jurisdiction through disavowal, or through the passivity of a certain feeling of guilt, an enforceability that relies on an inauthentic form of communication that is both abstract and coercive, antinomic and regulative, and one that is singularly incapable of grasping, without foreclosing, this singular experience of itself. In love only with freedom, the subject cannot properly speaking commit itself without being wracked with anxiety.

Here Fanon is clearly distinguishing racist humanism, that is to say, a world view that excludes, from a world view that restores mankind to its rightful place via a decision that precedes reason's jurisdiction or reason's authority as arbiter.

There are several other passages, equally decisive, where the limits discussed concern anti-Semitic guilt as a kind of reactionary psychosis. I will cite just two of these passages. The first is a passage from Sartre's *Anti-*

Semite and Jew that Fanon cites, extolling it as masterful: "'In this situation there is not one of us who is not totally guilty and even criminal; the Jewish blood that the Nazis shed falls on all our heads.'"[10] The second is a citation from the neuropsychiatrist Henri Baruk that describes a "fine reactional phenomenon": "'Making rounds in the ward of my colleague, Dr. Daday, I encountered a Jewish patient who had been the target of taunts and insults from her fellow-patients. A non-Jewish patient had gone to her defense. The Jewish patient thereupon turned on the woman who had defended the Jews, hurling every possible anti-Semitic calumny at her and demanding that the Jewess be got rid of'."[11]

While the Sartrean passage evokes the same kind of metaphysical guilt as does Jaspers, Fanon's use of it is to illustrate *a pathology of difference* (difference as the relation between hatred and psychosis, psychosis and projection that represents a perversion of thought, of thought and desire, but also and especially of all those situations in which the force of guilt is affirmed through the greatest paranoia). And that is not all. The word *reaction* appears frequently in Fanon's work and is always accompanied by a rhetorical sensitivity, both illocutionary and perlocutionary, to racist language, to its "fixed concept of the negro," which is why "the first action of the black man is a *reaction*."[12] There are no doubt many reasons why the majority of these instances identify racism—for example—as a relation of force that foregrounds neurotic and psychotic responses (I will only mention these) that determine the relations between the racist self and the *semblable* as a form of pathological guilt. It goes without saying that these various references to reaction, philosophical and psychoanalytical, denote the principal motif of *ressentiment*, but also, and less obliquely perhaps, the themes of power, politics, and disavowal.

My concern here lies not with guilt per se but with its ethico-politico-juridical significance. In "Colonial War and Mental Disorders," for example, Fanon refuses to dissociate the practice of torture from an intrinsic ideology of complicity. As long as the French do not face the psychical or moral consequences of torture and its effects on the person tortured, the usual condemnations of torture (in the name of liberalism, humanism, etc.) will remain naïve and ineffectual. Fanon does not hide his disdain for the declamations of pacifist activism and for the proclamations of human rights that would like to exempt the consciences of the French from the bio-political realities of torture in Algeria ("the human legacy of France in Algeria").[13] This reference to the moral climate of a generalized "apocalypse" (people feel themselves "being caught up in a veritable apocalypse"), however incontestable it may be, allows no critique of the generalized effects of torture on a subjugated population during a period of total war.[14]

Psychiatry in its very notion of reactive psychosis allows Fanon to go beyond a purely moral critique of violence (à la Jaspers or Arendt) as critically impotent. For the same reason, he does not provide a critique of violence in the name of liberty, of what Fanon calls the "human legacy" of France, that is, a purely formal or empty legalism. These attacks against torture lack permanence and effectiveness because they remain impervious to how colonial war "is singular even in the pathology it gives rise to."[15] So any effective critique of colonial war must be able to name this singularity, in both its particular untimeliness (as a semiological, gnoseological, or therapeutic event) and its *uniquely* generalizable state of dislocation. That is one of the key concepts of Fanon's texts, but also among the most obscure, whether it is a question of putting the symptom back in its proper time or place or being caught up in the apocalypse of colonial war. That which causes psychosis, which has psychotic affects, and that which at the same time threatens the entire personality belongs inviolably to the time and place of colonial war because it is singular. The notion of singularity is important here but also difficult, for the singularity is not a secondary affect. Colonial war involves "frequent malignancy of these pathological processes."[16] This malignancy is neither harmless nor secondary, as psychiatrists of reactive psychoses believe. The malignancy turns out to be a threat disrupting the whole of the personality, including a "mass attack against the ego" whose force always leaves "as their sequel a weakness which is always visible to the naked eye."[17] The future of such people is always *mortgaged* (i.e., a dead pledge against the future, or a life that lives its historicity as dead). To get at the deepest meaning of such pledges, it will be necessary to meditate upon the essence of timeliness at the base of this sequence, but also upon the ego and its complex relation with those mass attacks launched against it by a sadistic superego.

Besides, these feelings of guilt seem to be unforeseeable, untimely, disturbing, and such untimeliness seems to be the most proper place for them. This appears to be crucially so if one considers, for example, the many texts dedicated to racism and guilt—Jaspers's *The Question of German Guilt*, or Sartre's *Anti-Semite and Jew*—that Fanon uses to complicate the opposition between guilt and moral conscience, between being affected and being disaffected; that is to say, the opposition between historicity, experience, and auto-affection on the one hand, and the foreignness of an alterity that dislocates the self, on the other. The most iconic example in the whole of Fanon's texts is the opposition between the corporeal imago and the racial epidermal schema (the incongruity of being affected when one is not affected at all), a *hemorrhaging* of the cogito into object that starts, as this one did, by splitting the ego within itself, as all that is felt to be proper to the self, or the property of its being affected, disappears from all registers of the subject as a coherent structure, marked by self-pleasure, and all that follows from this, such as the excised ruination of the self in its ability to feel itself as a self. This dis-location is neither self nor other nor even a disincarnating form of thought (as in paranoia or delusion), but it puts into question the very history of the experience of what it means to be a person. At the same time, Fanon says that "I rejected all immunization of the emotions."[18] For what he wants to be is simply a subject—and so a pure autoaffection which is thus opposed to the affect of being a nonsubject, which has no self-relation other than that of racist historicity. For to say that racism immunizes the feeling of being affected—and so leads to the disappearance of affect in the form in which one normally experiences inner life and the body—is to suggest an overwhelming sense of there being something missing, evanescent, non-existent.

If, hypothetically, racism removes this sense of *being someone*, which is precisely the case here, it does so by making the phenomenological self opaque to itself, it literally *blackens* (if one wants to see it that way) any self-relation. That is why, without necessarily any appeal to the unconscious, or the physiological, Fanon uses words connoting an inalienable hard surface or kernel that now occupies psychic space and that, it seems to me, refers to how one has been ineradicably affected by the other, altered to the point that the subject feels itself to be *cut off* from its own affectivity, or enclosed in a morbid, sterile zone, without access to what Fanon calls self-certitude, recognition, and more generally the world.

Allow me to add here, briefly, the following three points:

1. This encounter with the *gaze* of the other is no doubt necessary and inevitable, but unlike in Lacan and Sartre (Fanon's primary reference points here), the feeling of being looked at, of being under the gaze (*"sous la fascination"*), has as much to do with the effect of being removed from any affectivity of reflection as it does with the aggressivity, the hatred, that always comes with the fascination and idealization of one's mirror image.[19] Indeed, if the eyes of an imaginary white Other in this scenario are seen

as the only "real eyes," as the only gaze that could render one transparent, what would it mean to see oneself from this position, as a pure eye whose vision is not limited but absolute? It can only lead to a negation of one's facticity as black.

2. It is certainly not by chance that this being gazed at opens onto a question of historicity; the question of time—which has very much to do with guilt and criminality, as already mentioned—is one of Fanon's most compelling concerns. There are no doubt many reasons for this. But what seems to be the main focus here is how hetero-affection correlates to how the psyche is composed, without necessarily knowing so, out of discourses, idioms, and contexts in which it is literally hated, not to mention the belated form of a cultural hatred, although that discovery is always *nachträglich* in its eventuality.

3. Above all, beyond the principle of belatedness, Fanon announces right away a concern with how the object of hatred is "situated" *de jure* by racism, a point that he takes from both Jaspers and Sartre. If historicity refers to how a subject situates and authorizes itself at any one moment, it is important to note that the expression of any historicity is always historically bound. According to Jaspers, the very emergence of the subject into its situation is always limited by the relation between openness and determination: the subject is not the docile instrument of its situation, but is in a complex relation between the limit (*Grenze*), which cannot *not* be followed, and its situation, which has a sense of open possibility. The relation between limit and situation is not so much one of borders that must be followed in terms of what they include or exclude—in the sense of existing outside or before them and requiring a defensive force, power, or violence—but of how we are situated by our experience of being limited, finite; even though those limits may not necessarily be thought, they *must* be followed. To be human is to exist in the finite limits of existence. In other words, the concept or idea of limit, in the sense of its implication, is not that of a border to be policed or enforced, for a bird's eye perspective on what lies beyond one's limit is strictly impossible. To think limit in this way as border is to confuse the sense of transcendence with that of its knowledge. It is just what makes the thing unreachable, which is why the limit is a thinking of openness rather than that of a border to be justified or enforced. To be open, the subject must be brought up against the limits of itself: in itself, in its performative power, the subject is genuinely open. It is only when it imagines itself to be limitless, or absolute, that it walls itself into a violence

that is exclusive and enclosed. A limit and situation are thus always double, which is why Jaspers coins the term "*Grenzsituationen*" (limit situations): to be situated, in other words, is to be on one side of the limit, and the limit thereby gives one a situation. Our situation arises from that of limit rather than from the limit of our situation. Here the discourse comes up against the problem of guilt: guilt, in itself, is a limit situation, in so far as one can take refuge in it or it can open up the self to feelings of dread and anxiety, as the antinomian structure of such guilt opens onto an abyss in which the finitude of self is understood.

For Jaspers, the inability to perform universal acts makes us feel guilty for being human, for a powerless sense of injustice cannot be enforced; guilt thus points back towards one's situatedness as a finite and singular human being. Accordingly any act is, in itself, a leap into the unknown, suspended over an abyss. It is in this sense that I would be tempted to interpret, beyond commentary, what Fanon calls the performativity of invention. That said, I would take the word "invention" in another direction. Fanon's analyses of guilt, implicitly including racism as a "*Grenzsituation*," are actively concerned with the inter-institutional or mono-institutional nature of a nation's racialized delimiting of itself. His language is, for reasons already explained, not so much ethico-ontological as therapeutic-political, which presupposes that the limits by which people live are not so much chosen but *imposed* (an important word of his) in the sense of a violent, exclusionary power whose pathological foundationalism always conceives of the limit as delimited, in an antinomian sense of hierarchical differences. But the paradox is this: it is precisely this racist structure of law and social being in the colony that also insures that the universal is always the particular point of this situation. The violent reinvention of colonial authority during decolonial war is always the new drawing of a limit (such as authority, legitimacy, justice, etc.), and it is the universal that arises from it, but not vice versa.

In the light of these general reflections, let us now reconsider the phrase "rightful place." For Jaspers the idea of limit cannot itself be suspended (nor can the boundary or border between the concepts of limit and situation), except in the experience by which it is traversed, a move that seems to presuppose the limit of what is being thought here. For as soon as one is on the border or limit, one is no longer under its jurisdiction, and thus one is potentially free to redraw the frontiers or borders or make new rules for that which delimits one's situation. Fanon's own analogy between being and the given determinations that limit it is less philosophical, and more concrete, in so far as the concept of black life already presupposes that it has been delimited *as* life. The political approach to the question of black life (its death) already suggests, obliquely, that the subject is compelled by a drive that can *either* mortify *or* break down or lessen the effects of this mortis by limiting it. This means that the black body must be thought as already and essentially in fact mortified, or as lytically detoxified right from the beginning. And if this is a lysis, it is already mortified in the very concept of its lived limitation. But because a state of petrification is already potentially lytic, it is therefore both what cures and corrupts. The limit is thus no more than a name for the suspended crossing of a limit always already crossed. Blackness is always haunted by the mortis that composes it, which can never be absolutely abolished nor entirely established (which would come to the same thing). This is why Fanon, with his insistence on man's rightful place, is saying nothing more than that there is no distinction between black life and the prescriptions that subsequently limit/exploit it in its extreme illegitimacy.

I said a moment ago that it is through delusion and obligation that racist language manifests itself. Having already discussed obligation, as Fanon conceives it, let us now turn to delusion to demonstrate how Fanon further thematizes the problem of how racism manifests itself as feelings of guilt.

II. LANGUAGE—A PARA-NEUROSIS?

How the colonized are deluded in their obligations is a key problem here. We already know that Fanon wrote several papers on how, in the colony, the cure itself produces an experience of aporia. Because the therapeutic relation comes down to the racism shown to the patient by his European psychiatrist, communication and signification are rendered aporetic at the level of the signifier. (I will come back to this in Chapter Six, "Desire and Law.") This confusion between therapy and imperial rule (in both the diagnosis and treatment of mental disorders) forces itself upon Fanon in terms of a double aporia: as a French-trained psychiatrist in the employ of the state, Fanon was expected to take his clinical bearings from a common, general lexicon of theories; but as a clandestine member of the National Liberation Front (*Front de libération nationale*, FLN), he sought out different meanings and therapies and refused to be a recipient of the colonial message of his profession. But those new meanings that he sought out were also somewhat closed to him because he did not speak Arabic. We know that Fanon,

on his clinical rounds or visits, often questioned patients using Arab inter-
locutors or translators (people such as Jacques Azoulay and Charles Geronimi). The nature of such strategic intervention is neither a simple testimony
to cultural difference nor a simple proof (other categories being required
here) that such a relation straightaway prevented him from being able to
hear the unconscious of his patients, as if the latter ever simply appeared
in language. Above all, critics who have paid attention to this point have
used this example to question Fanon's analytical accuracy. Albert Memmi,
in a 1971 review article, for example, writes: "like the other foreign doctors,
[Fanon] had to hold consultation with his patients through an interpreter.
He knew better than anyone what constituted a psychiatric scandal."[20]

This scandal—the simultaneously alien and intimate character of
illocution—is not directed towards the validity of translating unconscious
Arabic content into French words, nor does it even indicate that there is always an *elsewhere* to meaning when one is dealing with an unconscious put
into words; no, the scandal deduced here is due to the evidence of Fanon's
(implicitly black) foreignness, whose difference is understood and comprehended as a scandalous practice of listening. It is also evident that Memmi
appears to take as obvious the fact that the need for translation necessarily
means that the only signification to be recognized here is that of a non-arrival with no genuine exchange. If we now turn to Fanon's own remarks on
language we come across a wholly different set of premises and inferences,
where the desire for meaning is shown to be an impossible desire for com-
municability and the purpose of language is to thoroughly veil the lexia,
diction, and accent that is inevitably determined as other or black. Consequently, the question of speech or locution is understood to be always a
question of trying to convince those who hear it of a non-racial dissemination, or of dissipating one's own doubts as to the *blackness* of one's speech
in the appearing-disappearing of its stereotypical foreignness.

Let us explain this more clearly. It is evident from communication in
the colony that the relation between *langue* and *parole* is discontinuous.
Even when the message is purely denotative, it is nonetheless overloaded by
delusionary signs (cultural, symbolic) of separation: linguistic performance
thus carries an additional signified, in much the same way that the intona-
tion of a heavily accented French carries a literal meaning and the separate
signification of one's niggerness, or one's lowly place in public life. Even if
a totally pure French were to be achieved, it would immediately join the
sign of an impurity, completed as it is by the black body that enunciates it,

while always under the suspicion of a third—racial—pretense, of putting on airs, where the image of an improperly spoken French is immediately determined as *nègre*. In *Black Skin, White Masks*, Fanon provides multiple examples of what happens when the desire for signification is not only not correct but is unwittingly so, where the subject is contemptuously thrown back into the pit of a nigger emergence, a sort of pit where meaning empties itself. For to speak French "means above all to assume a culture, to support the weight of a civilization," or to risk being crushed under that weight.[21]

From this I think it is clear that we are dealing here with a cultural lexicon whose signs—and punishments—are drawn from a cultural code where every performative is impregnated with a whole plenitude of virtualities: absence, mimicry, impropriety, exclusion, and corpsing. In *Black Skin, White Masks*, Fanon shows that French carries a promise—of worldly well-being, of honor, wealth, dignity, and health—that remains virtual by reason of the very racism by which the *colonisé* invest in its image and vilify those who fall short of its enunciation.

Fanon does not say that this attitude to the imperial signifier is false, or misplaced, or that black speech could be cleared of its connotations; on the contrary, it is from these stories of penalty, pretense, and punishment meted out on behalf of an imperial French culture that he deduces the truth of a black imaginary, or, in the last analysis, its delusion. From what we have just shown it very plainly follows that Fanon radically recasts the status of alterity and its limits, in terms of the traces that difference communicates as the *other scene of the universal*. It also follows that anyone who rejects this cultural imperative because he or she believes in a creolized French is also deluded. Fanon makes it clear here that the wish to possess a black civilization of signifieds is still forced to locate these articulations in relation to the *signifiance* of French writing, language, and culture.

Equally, there is also the native commandment not to speak Creole that relates to the way in which black speech seems to constitute a message that threatens—analytically—the content of the mind itself, as if speaking in dialect were to open the mind to signs and rules whose code is not linguistic, even when denoted, but that signifies a *lapsus* without cultural reward. This is why Fanon suggests that the signifier in the colony is racially disruptive: it signifies within the psyche a spiritual, alienated loss, which reinforces the idea of the naturalness of French (as *white* language, power, authority). The scene here, as I said, is not just one of connotation, but plays out the various ways in which what can be communicated (in dreams, neuroses, poetry) effectively proclaims and performs an occultation drawn from history. Hence, we readily understand why Fanon begins his study of black neuroses with a study of language, since it is through the specific character of its *signifiance* that he weighs the psychic costs of assimilation. Fanon's overriding concern was to offer a mirror to this heterogeneity and to distinguish the speech act that establishes a consciousness of being *over-there* (in France, as French), from that which establishes an awareness of *never-having-been-there* (in the colony), and one modeled on feelings of anxiety, irreality, and secondariness.

We should add, though, that when we say that there is an awareness in the colony of dislocation and belatedness, we do not mean that this awareness is always articulated, but only that the situation is determined by a singular historicity in which the reality of language can be understood as a kind of whitening and the sign is experienced as an elective elocution, or is seen to evoke only a white pretense, as if in every sign there were a trace, a "morphology," that gives the *colonisé*, as if by a precious miracle, a white interlocution, and a white reality from which its blackness is excluded. For in speaking French, "the Negro of the Antilles will be proportionately whiter—that is, he will come closer to real human being—in direct ratio to his mastery of the French language [*la langue française*]."[22] Speech in the colony recalls the structure of hallucination as described by Merleau-Ponty in the *Phenomenology of Perception*: "Hallucinations are played out on any other stage other than the perceptible world; they exist as if in a double exposure. . . . Any hallucination is first and foremost a hallucination of one's own body. 'As if I were hearing my own mouth.'"[23] The mouth hallucinated as a white pseudo-presence is crucial to Fanon's analysis.

Thus we see how language gets caught up in a game of appearances, masks, and concealments, where the supposedly primary addressee of one's discourse is put in the position of a purely virtual auditor, but above all of someone who will not mistake this address and the reason why it is so singular: the magical white interlocutor on which the performance depends and who will not mistake the difference between inferiority and civilization that is the reward of a properly spoken French. The point being not to reconcile Creole and French in some kind of cultural equilibrium, but to distinguish them in a radical opposition, this being the imperative of every idiomatic expression in the colony and the rule for how one speaks in conformity with one's duty not to be *nègre*, a lesson underscored by black family life.

For Francis Affergan, writing in *Anthropologie à la Martinique* (1983), these obligations create a "visceral attachment" to appearances.[24] For it is certain that in the colony, to address oneself in the language of the *semblable* is, it seems, to make a choice, and this choice is not just an anthropological fact but an ontological decision, to speak, to the extent that one appropriates and assimilates *la langue française*, syntactically, lexically, phonologically, according to the law of whiteness, inasmuch as speaking Creole condemns one to an inferior tone or idiom that is definitive and absolutely unsurpassable and that signifies a poverty of style, intellect, and culture.

On the other hand, for fundamental reasons, it is clear that to the extent to which the *colonisé* who goes to France is always aware he is speaking in a language in which he is forced to be "suspicious of his own tongue," and generally anxious about his "*diction*," concerned as he is with his "native" competence, that is, his understanding and interpreting, Fanon refers to several examples in which the act of speaking French leads to a comedic comeuppance for the subject, whose lapses are witnessed and ruthlessly exposed and judged. And however slight or minimal the mistake, members of the colonial community will be quick to point it out: "Only one choice remains for him: throw off his 'Parisianism' or die of ridicule."[25] It is as if his words have not only "betrayed" him, they have mobilized an army of stereotypes, lexia, and chatter ["*palabres*"] to confirm only one thing: that the means of masking the black *parole* under a white meaning has been undone, found out, and the more rarified the articulation the further the descent into black abysses of being. The ego is penetrated through and through by this reversion to pidgin ["*petit-nègre*"]; indeed, by this cultural and symbolic deflation the whole totality of one's utterances is reduced to a black "jabber" of thought.[26]

At first sight this stereotypical speech may appear extremely empty (or formulaic); what defines it is not its lexicon but its syntactical or rhythmic peculiarity (this speech becomes meaningful through the unusualness of repetitions, ellipses, parataxes, etc.), but also, so to speak, through how things come to be ordered and connected, and therefore the ways in which a culture—of *denegation*—comes to punctuate these syntaxes. Between these nodal points, these dispatches, disavowal plays the role of a guarantee. These guarantees are not, however, useless: it must be stressed again that they allow negrophobia to be practiced but in a denied form. Were the denial to be renounced as denial, the phantasm could not participate in the economy of the message; in fact, an apparently explicit denial always has a recursive function (Fanon uses the word *contre-coup*): it accelerates, delays, gives fresh impetus to the discourse (of renunciation) while maintaining its complicity with denial. For example, "You are not black, you speak French as well as I"; or, "Those Africans are truly savage, unlike us." This is why the language of phobia is both a path and that which leads astray (as the etymology of the word *perverse* suggests). Since what is traumatic always appears as an absence (or excess), the phobic catalyzer ceaselessly revives the semantic association of blackness with that which makes it most notable: the almost obsessive focus on the *genital-sexual*. Thus, in the final analysis, negrophobia has a constant function, which is, to use Fanon's term, to be a process where meaning is "predestined": it maintains the work between culture and symptom. A symptom cannot be altered without altering the cultural narrative that informs it, but neither can a culture fix the meaning of a phobia without altering its discourse. So much of Fanon's semiology of culture is taken up with the signs and discourses of how communication humiliates and bewilders.

As for the playing out of these tensions in the clinic, Fanon himself admits: "I myself have been aware, in talking to certain patients, of the exact moment at which I began to slip [into pidgin]. . . ."[27] Once again, the image presented is that of a *lapsus* whose unconscious meaning surprises the enunciator, for it suggests a moment in which the mask slips, and the signifier relapses into stereotypes, a moment in which the *Noir*, or better (since it is a question of cultural life in the colony) the *colonisé* is *exposed* in his utterance. At such moments, what is being put into words is something that French cannot but render precisely because it is unlocatable in French, even though it was there waiting to be named as a slip that is only formulatable *in* French as mutilation. In fact, Fanon refers to such moments as a sudden "collapse."[28] In this articulation of a therapeutic slippage, therefore, we can already glimpse a concern with how the reversion to stereotype has consequences, analytically; namely, a certain signification of the other that reproduces the total framework of the socius, its ideology, its racist semiology, to which correspond signifiers whose connotations are specified according to how they express the thought "'You'd better keep your place.'"[29] The most important thing, however, at least in reference to place, is that it is very hard to say just where the slip is located, sliding as it does between, on the one hand, phantasm and interiorization, signification and social inferiority as expressed by *créolismes* and *petit-nègre* formulations, not to mention the policing of these borders, or limits by public censure and ridicule; and on the other, the passage between idiom and symbolism, propriety and power, competence and hyperbolic failure, the excess and inadequation of black speech in the cultural life of the colony. In other words (and this would be a valid proposition for colonialism in general), the relation between cultural code and dialectal idiom involves endless slippages between language, *langue*, and *parole* that produce a kind of *affective allergy* at the level of the signifier and its meaning as speech act. For we see here that language is no longer the place of recognition, but of its impossibility, as Fanon teaches us.

However, returning to the word "scandal," let us state the conclusion we set out to prove, namely that, whatever the form that racist language takes, Fanon himself compares its *signifiance* to that of a "foreign body" or pathogen, which in turn produces a *Spaltung* or "rupture" in the rhetorical and embodied life of the *colonisé*, whose speech is thereby split between its meaning and affectivity, where the act of speaking French comes now to figure a bewilderment, not just about racism, but about the whole opposition between assimilationism and nativism, propriety and incompetence.[30] Nor is it surprising that this position comes from Fanon's engagement with negritude (which we will discuss in more detail in Part Two). If language is the *key that opens the door* of culture, it matters whether it opens onto a prison or leads back into a situation that is self-imprisoning.

These openings, I think, support my position with regard to the importance of language to Fanon's *socialthérapie*. It remains now to show how and why Fanon's analysis serves to preserve and maintain the image of a *colonisé* possessed by a syntagm which is not theirs and which is that of a dereliction in culture. I shall do so as briefly as I can.

III. TRANSLATING THE NATION

Language in the colony immediately yields a racial problem whose substance is moral-political; Fanon's lack of Arabic has been called a "scandal." The code from which this charge has been taken is none other than that of the French language; the only place from which Fanon's foreignness is required to be authentic is his knowledge of speaking and writing in French! (So Memmi's critique reinforces the very ethnocentrism that is ostensibly his target.) In fact, as Brian T. Edwards makes clear, Fanon's use of French can itself be further broken down, for in texts such as *Studies in a Dying Colonialism*, the "movement between Arabic and French—his inhabiting of the space in-between a firm sense of where one language begins and the other ends—produces an Arabized French that effectively repositions" both languages—but also, by this movement, places French in an in-between role.[31] Fanon's French is thus twofold or doubled in its *signifiance* (at least in his texts on Algeria): "Fanon's literary style doubles linguistically a fragmented French voice that will be the clear signal for the revolution."[32] This is because the lexical instability of this style is sustained by the hope that the new language of the decolonial nation will spring neither from Arabic nor French alone, a situation allowing the same wretched or supremacist state to endure, but from a new form of Arabized French, a way of speaking that has not yet been lexically set down. Such instability of diction, albeit lost in the English translation of Fanon's texts, is, as Edwards rightly notes, an effort to transcend the oppositions between foreignness and monolingualism, translation and homeland, localism and cosmopolitanism, etc. I would also add that it is an effort to transcend the imaginary contexts by which the mind tries to ward off, disavow, or foreclose the distressing reality of conflict, captivated as it is by superstition or deception. Having already discussed the relation between obligation and disavowal, I will go no further into it here. Since, however, we have here a lexical sign or style that is both an act of *truchement* (interpreting, translating) and an act of *truchement* as *turgeman* (translation), namely, that of speaking from the in-between, and not *about* it, it is by no means clear whether the relay is under the guise of a fragmented French or the clear signal of some Arabic revolutionary signified. What defines this signal is precisely that the relation between (Arab) signifier and (French) signified is less of an equivalence or quasi-identity and more in the way of a *transformation without destination*. In other words, the sign of this message is not drawn from an institutional index or lexicon, is not coded (by a dictionary), but denotes a message without time or place and, as such, is genuinely open. This peculiarity can be seen again at the level of reading; in order to read Fanon, all that is needed is to remember that natural languages are not necessarily bound up with either time or place, but are only perceived as such. That perception is imaginary, for we need to know neither local nor global sign systems to speak the new language of the nation. This message corresponds, as it were, to the letter of the nation as its literal message, as opposed to the symbolic message of the colony.

Hence, a new kind of idiomatic expression is the root from which the decolonial nation is born, maintained, and nourished. It is a speech in which the frighteningly difficult language of revolt is taken up by the masses and the security and justification of the colonial nation-state is put into doubt. As Fanon himself says, it is an idiom in which anxiety and superstition mingle with credulous fear and vengeance, people are swayed by fantasies of sacrifice and murder, and language itself becomes anxiogenic, or accused, not at the level of denotated description (a description seen as more *real*) but at the level of a suspicion that each sign is a secret, and each official message the suppressed scene of delirious fantasies and impulses.

To illustrate these points by particular examples, let us consider those essays in which this scenario is presented. In his extraordinary essay on Algerian radio, for example, Fanon shows how colonialism is not only the imposition of a second meaning on indigenous culture proper but represents a coded message that is realized at different levels of production and articulation (differentiation, justification, and rightfulness). It is thus possible to separate out various connotation procedures, bearing in mind however that these units of signification are not only linguistic signs but, strictly speaking, structures of feeling that lead to a modification of reality itself, that is, of the way in which everyday life is denoted (albeit in a series of displaced, even hallucinatory messages), in which scenes of differentiation (of self from other, settler from native) are translated into values of justification (of settler safety and security and superiority) that consequently conceal how the exclusionary entitlements of the settler community have no certainty from the point of view of sovereign rightfulness (the right to govern, rule, and dispense existence), which is why imperial culture needs to be continuously expressed and represented as a force without origin or code, thus necessitating a veritable decipherment by the *colonisé* of how power and its prestige intervene on cultural form at the levels of both investment and resistance.

1. *Linguistic message.* In "This Is the Voice of Algeria," Fanon shows how radio, whose technology is part of a sign system, whose operational validity derives from frequencies, signals, bandwidths, etc., is endowed with certain meanings by virtue of the practice of colonial society: the link between signifier and signified remains, if not entirely historical, at least entirely amplified by feelings and values whose signification (or resonance) echoes a given historical conflict between *colon* and *colonisé*.[33]

Formerly, before the colonial civil war, Radio-Alger had been a symbol of "a material representation of the colonial configuration."[34] From the moment of its appearance, the linking of transmission to power was evident, which is why the native refusal to take up the radio was never simply down to a religious and moral concern over content (a point of view evident in certain sociological approaches). For Fanon, on the contrary, radio content has a less obvious effect of connotation than radio as "a bearer of language" which "must be apprehended in the colonial situation in a special way."[35] The link between transmission and power is only possible to the extent to which each radio broadcast (from Radio-Alger) comes to be invested in as a sign or attitude for a certain society and for certain given values.

Here radio speaks with an old lost familiarity, as if one were hearing one's own voice—its timbre, its authority—coming back to one from mainland France, the homeland. Such presences require no translation, even though they mark a dislocation between the origin of those sounds and their manifestation in the colony. Since the French language is never simply a language but the ineradicable foundation or ground of settler society, it is important that these auditory manifestations, these loci of loss and authority, remain familiar and not foreign, that they not be penetrated by the uncouth and barbaric sounds of Arabic. French forms the limit of national identity by making audible these sounds by which the *colon* is constituted as a community speaking with one voice and tongue. The purity of this devotion has its roots, however, in dread and paranoia, the fear that the French of this community has already been transformed into its alien Other. For the settler, of course, Arabic has no rules or conventions to speak of, it is the sound of deformation, the sound of someone eating their own tongue which is by definition disarticulate. Hence the suspicion that the colony is a simulacrum of nationality, that it is *denatured* to the point of transforming civility into falsity, a dread that is brutally and dogmatically foreclosed.

Beyond the broadcasts themselves, it was already noted that the French spoken on Radio-Alger is the sign of a comprehensible familiarity, which is to say that the imperialist attitude that allows the distinction to be made between European and Arab, the civilized and barbarous, is the true historical message of Radio-Alger, while on the other hand this code refers to how the mere aural presence of the French language and culture is enough to ward off the "corrosive influence" of Arabization.[36] This is why Fanon says that Algerian society "never participates in this world of signs," but also why Arabic practices of listening appear to duplicate the phantasmatic fear that to listen to the voice of the other is to literally incorporate or digest it, to be sullied by its denotation.[37] In colonial Algeria, in short, the history of radio post-1945 and 1956 shows a dialectical movement between practices of listening and broadcasting through which the intelligibility of the Algerian civil war becomes audible, even when it is the *unheard* outcome of that war that is retroactively projected into the broadcast, so much so as to appear denoted there *as the sign of a new compensatory connotation*, or as the inaudible trace of a new projection-identification that is nonetheless heard as "a piercing, excruciating din."[38]

Here the radiophonic constitutes a code that has two resonances: one that is heard, that refers to clear, familiar signifieds; and one that is necessarily unheard, a kind of static or jammed signal that produces (invents) an entirely new signified whose noise amplifies a set of connotations that overloads the frequency typifying the "objectivity" and "naturalization" of colonial cultural life, burdening it with a cultural or moral message whose amplification calls for a new experience of listening. So if, before the onset of colonial civil war, Radio-Alger denotes for the European bourgeoisie the "feeling that colonial society is a living and palpitating reality," and, for the indigenous Arabic population, the alienating message of the occupier's presence, after the outbreak of civil war and the founding, in 1956, of *The Voice of Fighting Algeria* by the FLN, each radio transmission comes to illustrate the conflict over how the "first words of the nation" can record over or reincorporate the alienating presence in which that reality was heavily connoted "while at the same time renewing it."[39] Each radio broadcast is now experienced as the amplification of a multiply accentuated interruption that is palpably separate from the sound-image, in which the listener is confronted with a "produced static" that is less the ability to hear the new speech of the nation, or the "reality of colonial power." than the desire to hear the effect of its "rightfulness."[40]

Secondly, the effect of transmission differs according to the way in which it distances, or jams, the (de)colonial content of the sound-image. Fanon's point is very subtle here. If Radio-Alger brings the European settler community closer to France by becoming "one of the means of escaping the inert, passive, and sterilizing pressure of the 'native' environment," the closer *The Voice of Fighting Algeria* brings the reality of civil war to the ears of the Arab population, the less it seems to matter whether it actually connotes it, caught as it were in the hysterical demand for a new kind of listening in relation to which the clarity of transmission is only of a kind of secondary importance, almost without consequence.[41]

In the jammed signal of each broadcast Fanon sees the affect of an obligation to listen that is felt to be irreducible and spectral: "Every Algerian felt himself to be called upon and wanted to become a reverberating element of the vast network of meanings born of the liberating combat."[42] In the "phantom-like and quickly inaudible" voice of the *djebels* what matters is not what is denoted, but the desire to hear the "*felt reality* [of resistance] *and its power*" which accompanies the image of a liberated, sovereign nationhood.[43] In this new desire to listen to the radio, Fanon sees ample confirmation of a "presence felt, whose reality was sensed" in direct proportion to its jammed sabotage by the colonial authorities.[44] It is precisely because this jammed text can only be imperfectly heard that it becomes important for setting out the "reality and intensity of the national expression," messages and meanings that cannot be found in the actual broadcast, only in its "phantom-like character."[45]

Once again, we see how the denotative or referential functions of the linguistic sign here coexist with that which is absent, inaudible, but is felt to be the consequence of a materialization that obliges a certain listening (and certain disavowals): "Every Algerian, for his part, broadcast and transmitted this new language [of the nation]."[46] Radio thus has a substantive value, it is the means through which absence acquires an informational charge and, being primarily affective, is "the guarantee of a true lie," whose meaning lies hidden behind every modulation, every broadcast or static; but here the hallucinated message is no longer alienating but protective and friendly.[47] It is impossible, however (and this is a crucial point concerning the conflict), to separate obligation from resistance: in the movement from colony to national movement in the Arab world after 1952, the meaning of events is now experienced differently by *colon* and *colonisé*.

What is the relationship of these reverberating networks to the new language of nationhood? To all appearances, it is one of amplification, of providing a new relay or channel for a new group idea; the interrupted broadcast of *The Voice of Fighting Algeria* is thus transformed into a multiple set of revoicings by which the *colonisé* hear, as if for the first time, how their "spoken *words*" literally bring a new world into being.[48] In this "real task" of reconstruction, words and projection are as one, are fragments of a more general syntagm (of nationhood).[49] And yet at no point does Fanon say that these listenings are not hallucinatory, that is to say, what changes are the projections produced by these phantom-like communications. Just as the radio can lose its "anxiogenic and accursed character" for the *colonisé*, so can the French language lose its familiar character for the settler community.[50] In brief, it is not radio as mechanism that liberates but rather its revolutionary clarification, constituting a new kind of group listening that hears the connoted meanings differently (as struggle, say, or freedom).

This is why the founding, by the FLN, of *The Voice of Fighting Algeria* "at once acquired an essential [cultural-political] value."[51] This being the case, we see at once that the mass acquisition of radio sets by Algerians is a "sign of a radical mutation," in which a boundless desire for news of what "was going on" changes the meaning and nature of listening itself as an event or resistance to the "occupier's lie" and one that "participate[s] in a world of truth."[52] What is now performed is listening as the technique of a new group awareness in which the words, reports, messages of settler society lose their assurance and their certainty. On the other hand, what is also heard is a new language of the imagination combatting the "antique social arrangements" of Algerian Muslim society; in so far as *The Voice of Fighting Algeria* becomes part of the "new signaling 'systems' " of the Revolution, its political and ideological function lies in its affective mobilization, through which it directs the listener beyond local and religious differences, through the signifieds of colonial war, to the "consolidating and unifying" idea of an Algerian nation.[53] From which follows this paradox: the Arabized French of Fanon's own writing is an attempt to make audible the sound of what is yet to come, that has no denotation, but whose very blurred, distorted signal can be received as the auditory annihilation of the occupier's French, and one that moves the bodies of the *colonisés* to amplify it among the rocks and the *djebels*, the *souks*, and the *douars* (the hills, bazaars, and villages). In all these cases of consolidation, language clearly has a function of collective transformation and translation, but this transformation-translation is also a sublation, a dialectical transcendence, as the national-political group idea imposes unity on Arabic, Kabyle, and French signifiers, converting them into a veritable lexicon by which signs of the revolution are constituted. The nation is to be read as the creation *ex nihilo* of a new right to representation over sovereignty—in the face of French military and police power— in which the medium is indeed the message, incorporating this right into the "nation's new life."[54] With respect to this new life, radio has a de-repressive function in which, above all, the aural warfare of the airwaves is waged. Thus Fanon returns to the theme, already remarked upon, of how, through an essential distortion, events open onto a political future. Indeed, these eclipsing resonances, by invalidating what is assumed to be secure and permanent, are the conceptual equivalent of a stutter in the new speech of the nation, a jabbering that is now validated as the working through of a new historical eloquence. The stuttering suggests a new articulation of the future, of futural blackness, a revelation that cannot be embodied by him who utters it, for it is literally the working through of a new group idea, and one that preserves the difference between voice and body so as to penetrate otherwise unimaginable political scenes.

2. *Veiled/Unveiled Message.* We have seen that the radiophonic code reflects a new kind of message; it follows that not everyone heard this message in the same way. It also follows that this new kind of listening required leaps of imagination that can only be sustained by passionate deception. This is because the new language of nationhood was neither historical nor cultural but a projective distortion, and could only be heard through its hallucinatory repetition. Therefore it is easy to see why Fanon insists that both *colon* and *colonisé* remain captivated by aural hallucinations, by fears of the other's presence to which they remain loyal. And why language—Arabic or French—is called on to fill these tears and hiatuses in the whole auditory fabric of the real. In fact, because the colonized live in a wretched condition, they could never adhere to the French world of signs for long. It is only the new form of listening that comes with *The Voice of Fighting Algeria* that causes them to tune in, to go from credulity to engagement, to treat the radio as a weapon in the combat over meaning. Which is why, to a certain extent and paradoxically, radio noise or static is grasped as a meaning that is undivided, impenetrable, and henceforth liberated, a radiophonic non-meaning that produces a new voice or sign to which is attributed a new truth. Such projection is the cause of many ferocious tales and heroic exploits presented as if they were news. For, as is clear from Fanon's semiology of culture, the multitude is governed less effectively by reality than by fantasy. Hence they hear what they want to hear, under the pretense of listening, sometimes to affirm what they adore and at other times to deny what they fear and detest as the accursed scourge of the occupier's presence.

In his famous essay "Algeria Unveiled," Fanon turns his attention to how the wearing of the veil in colonial Algeria became the site of a similar "grandiose battle."[55] The veil plays out this tragedy, this "epic of colonial society," with its specific ways of existing and of adorning the true and the false, the real and the imaginary, enmity and disgust.[56] Fanon sees the veil as a sign of a reality that he, the French occupier, simplifies by attributing to it "religious, magical, fanatical behavior," not realizing that he too zealously shows the highest degree of fidelity to a reified image of the veil as a secret to be possessed and penetrated.[57] In his essay, Fanon downplays the religious significance of the veil, preferring to see it as a sign of national cultural resistance, or as the doubly displaced sign of a wish to conquer and possess that is itself the hallucinated perception of an unveiled Algerian woman, an erotics whose sadism leaves no room for reason.

Orientalist fantasy may indeed be the secret of this patriarchal vision of a veiled woman, who is so utterly essential to the desire to keep hidden and so to disguise the fear that the veil, paradoxically, keeps nothing hidden by virtue of its own doubly impenetrable character, a symbol that seems to call forth the fetishistic glorification of the wearer in Orientalist culture. Here, however, analysis must differentiate, for the fetishistic attitude toward the veil as hiding or "disguising a secret," or of "creating a world of mystery, of the hidden," is itself an attempt to disguise the sadistic pleasure that wants to rend and expose the colonial body to ritual humiliation by the French republican gaze.[58] For it is completely contrary to assert, on the one hand, that the veil is a secret without a code that must be forcibly exposed and, on the other, that it is a shackle or restraint from which the Algerian woman must be freed, and so exposed to a showing where, in her erotic mystique, she is publicly condemned to Western freedom. This demand to see can be read on three levels. Firstly, it is because the woman ostensibly "sees without being seen" that she must be seen, made to give and offer herself to the common gaze; there is nothing more necessary than to expose this desire to see without being seen, and the code forcibly needed to disclose it: "The European faced with the Algerian woman wants to see. He reacts in an aggressive way before this limitation of his perception."[59] In this image of the veiled woman that seems to necessitate a certain sadistic fantasy of pillage and rape, the veil-as-signifier does not so much reproduce these fantasies as "create faults, fertile gaps" through which such fantasy can emerge, without its ceasing, however, to disturb the link between the rending of the veil and the raping of its wearer: from this point of view, to penetrate the secret of the veil-as-signifier cannot be undertaken without raping the object that it covers up.[60] "The act assumes a para-neurotic brutality and sadism, even in a normal European."[61]

In other words, the erotic significance of the veil itself uncovers a para-neurotic desire to possess, to possess and brutally disclose. Finally, like all reaction formations, the occupier's desire to disclose produces in the native a principled resistance "with respect to a formerly inert element of the native cultural configuration."[62] However, if the word "inert" suggests that the veil does not become a contested sign or semiological fact until colonialism, the way in which it signifies either repression or fidelity, secrecy or piety has always been part of its history. Does the coding of the veil-as-colonial-signifier have consequences for our understanding of its history? It is certain that the "colonialist's frenzy to unveil the Algerian woman" is a struggle over sovereignty, since it at once establishes a new form of resistance with respect to the wearing of the *haïk*, and one that gives "new life to this dead element of the Algerian cultural stock"; consequently, the desire of the colonized to veil the Algerian woman constitutes a desire not so much to cover up but to hide by "weaving a whole universe of resistances around this particular element of culture."[63]But at the same time, in so far as the veil displays nothing but its own enigma, the relationship of the Algerian woman to her own mystery is profoundly modified: it is no longer the relationship between an inert passivity and a paternal mobilization projection (whether by the *colon* or by the *colonisé*) but one that is between two imperatives to action; to unveil, or sacrifice herself to the revolution, is not the same as unveiling herself to the gaze of the colonizer. If the former was a "wholly revolutionary step," the latter remains a "work of cultural destruction."[64] This is the core thesis that Fanon sets out to demonstrate in his essay.

In order to do so, it is chiefly necessary for him to say that the revolutionary Algerian woman necessarily unveils herself, and, by doing so, removes the vestiges of servitude to those who would confine her (be they men *or* women). In the actions she will go on to perform, her liberty is no longer in thrall to the oppositions between activity and passivity, secrecy and disclosure, for these relations are now *transformed* by the message that her unveiled body now gives: as she steps out into the street, with weapons concealed about her person, she "does not have the sensation of playing a role," the fetishistic role of masculine culture, for she assumes the authority of an "authentic birth in a pure state without preliminary instruction"; it is as though unveiling is the new (even utopian) beginning of a new kind of fidelity, a new sign freed from any cultural servitude; in short, she acquires the disturbing authority of a tabula rasa.[65] Only the paternalistic opposition of the FLN leadership to this new beginning can, it seems, allow this birthing, this radical mutation of piety and gendered servitude, bringing out what can now be seen for the first time, and so allow this sociological revolution in how the Algerian woman sees/represents herself. The type of consciousness that unveiling involves is indeed truly unprecedented, since it establishes not a consciousness of *passing* (from a native body to a European body, or from feminine to masculine), but an awareness of *passage* (to a new kind of experience of both self and body, an enigmatic feminine gaze impelled across the checkpoints of culture and tradition).

What we have is a new corporeal-political category: a new dimension of the body is invented and a new corporeal pattern assumed; "she has to create for herself an attitude of unveiled-woman-outside"; a self-creation that itself arises out of "a new dialectic of the body and of the world."[66] Moreover, what is understood by this expression, "unveiled-woman-outside," implies what we might call a distressing, but also potentially euphoric, modification in the manner of her being. It is true that Fanon also says that the unveiled body must be interpreted as a body-in-pieces, by which he means that whereas before "the veil covers the body and disciplines it, tempers it," and so reassures and protects it, without the veil the Algerian woman "has the impression of her body being cut up into bits, put adrift"; without being anchored by the veil, in short, "the unveiled body seems to escape, to dissolve."[67] Why does the body seem to escape? What does it mean for it to flow outside of itself? These are the questions that await us. Nevertheless, in both cases the situation is the same: to have the veil taken away is to undergo a separation of self and body, that is, the unveiled body is no longer my body and its gestures are no longer my gestures; this is a body that has been rendered invisible, hidden, by being disclosed, and its corporeality is now a message without articulation. Thus the body's illusoriness ceases to belong to the body and is dissolved by it. In the unveiled body outside of itself we thus have a complex situation.[68] The unveiled soma never quite coincides with the body; it is either too long or too elusive, and creates a hiatus in the body *qua* body. By virtue of this hiatus, the body is exposed to the world, completely naked to the meanings that enter it, penetrate it, and at the same time isolate it from the security of the home, the cloistered life that allowed it to be closed in on itself, inconceivable and impermeable. This is precisely an example of the phantasmal-spectral status earlier invoked. The unveiled body tries to look at itself from a point that is outside of itself, for it tacitly or expressly has become an "unfinished," "disintegrating" space, a space that has escaped the forms of piety that used to enclose it, and where the senses subordinate to theology can no longer be felt.[69] The role of the revolution is thus to rebind self and body, to give its muscular movements and expression a new method of articulation, a new depth and meaning, one that is directed to ethico-political life, but a life, a meaning, that can only conserve itself by becoming the opposite of the gesture (veil-unveil) that the Algerian woman sees herself performing.[70]

It is thus at the level of the unveiled body—this body that is outside it-self—that a real revolution in fidelity takes place and can be fully under-stood: its reality is that of a woman who has overcome all anxiety and hesitation, in whose splendor all rivalry and resentment is transformed, and in whose movement there is neither that of a sacrificial fetish nor imi-tative role, nor inert presence whose magical character lies always hidden. In describing the Algerian woman's new state, Fanon refers to a new code of *linkage*, for in her movement a new link is forged between armed and cultural resistance that is now essential, committed as it is to disclosing the political reality of the new Algeria.[71] As soon as this linkage is manifest (be-tween passing and passage), it raises profound questions about the power of image (to seduce, confuse, stupefy) and the purely spectatorial politics by which the veil becomes the sign of a fetishistic, magical misrecognition and/or the igniting spark on which all revolutionary discourse depends. This is perhaps why Fanon inadvertently says that it is only by showing herself to be an empty sign that the Algerian woman can defuse or disarm this warring distinction between a secret that is veiled and a mystery that is persecuted for its lack of openness. This would lend authority to the view that the distinction between modern Algerian femininity and its repressed traditional other is not a simple difference in ideology but two sides of a symptom. But of course this is the very thing that emerges from Fanon's critical examination of the veil-as-signifier: the desire to expose her in her essence and resistance, in her essence *as* resistance, gives way before a de-sire to unveil her as a "means," an "instrument" of cultural interpretation, which would explain how there can be in some sense a history of the veil that excludes her, without in any way providing any real break from the fetishistic logic that represents her, in which she is at once absolutely liber-ated and definitively suppressed, a politics of liberation that defines her as a message that has no other meaning than that of her emptiness.

At all events, to the extent to which "every contact between the occu-pied and the occupier is a falsehood," the Algerian woman plays a special role in the general structure by which all "pseudo truths" are transformed by the experience of revolution: she is the "fertile kernel" through which the occupied materializes its symbolic message and transforms the inert sclerosis of its own localism, which relies on her veiling, especially in the home.[72] It is she therefore who has kept alive the revolutionary spirit, not as piety or faith but as "humor" and fidelity. In accordance with this humor, Fanon himself says that "revolutionary war is not a war of men."[73]

Although he earlier states that her insurrectionism seems to spontaneously produce an iconic authenticity, there nonetheless remains a certain irony or humor in her attitude, an attitude suggesting a certain remove or distance from the "old mystifications" of Algerian and French patriarchy, one allowing her to distinguish truth from falsehood; this rigorous insurrectional humor is not the sign of an absence, but that which preserves the revolutionary spirit during a period of total war.[74] This is without doubt an important semiological paradox (and one that has something in common with the radio essay): the more she appears (as sign or image), the more her humor provides the means of masking her constructed meaning under the appearance of a meaning unveiled for all to see.

If our reading is satisfactory, the new language of the nation offers three messages: a linguistic message, a coded (veiled) message, and a non-coded, unveiled message. These messages represent more than an ability to speak the language of revolution, but they do manifest the desire, by the *colonisé*, to speak and be heard differently, at least to the extent that decolonialism authorizes and justifies this right to speak in a way that is foreign to both native and settler society, whose foreignness is constrained neither by Arabic or French but represents a new idiom for understanding the social contract and the conditions of law, and all that follows from these foundations. The linguistic message, like the cultural message of the veil-as-signifier, shares the same (national) substance as the other two and cannot be separated from them. It is certain that the distinction between nation and colony is not spontaneously a sign of revolution: the hearer of the new sign receives *at one and the same time* the prophetic message and psychical message, and it will be seen later that this corresponds to translation (our concern here). The distinction, however, has a therapeutic validity, analogous to that which allows the distinction between signifier and signified an antithetical meaning. If the distinction permits us to describe the structure of the nation in a clear fashion, and if this description paves the way for an explanation of the role of language in Fanon's clinics, we will take it to be justified. The task now is thus to reconsider Fanon's writing so as to explore it in its generality, without losing sight of our aim of understanding the overall clinical question of language. Given that what is in question is not a national language but a new situation for the nation, the order of messages will be modified a little by the inversion of the clinical and the political. Successively, then, we shall look at the clinical message, the political message, and the psychopolitical message.

IV. THAT WITHIN

"Truly such a bestowing love must become a thief of all values"

NIETZSCHE, *Thus Spoke Zarathustra*, 101

We showed in the previous chapter that what conjoins the temporality of politics and the time of the nation is a *new kind of speaking* that erases, annuls, what Fanon variously calls the inert, petrified subject whose mortification is neither *in* language nor *outside* it, but is comparable to a fractured, orthopedic suspension. This annulment-by-depetrification works in two ways: it is because language is a sign of failure in the colony, meaning by this a *misfiring*, that it has to be reinvented; and it is because language is a sign of a misrecognized *loss of black speech*, which appears here as a kind of childish jabbering, that it must be reconstituted, or added to. We will discuss the cultural implications of this loss in Part Two; here we will discuss Fanon's psychoanalysis of what he calls jabbering.

There is a failure to be cognizant of or, more important, to recognize the negrophobia of one's own words being presented here. Fanon very much insists on this; the negrophobe performs his anti-blackness before thinking about it, without thinking about it. But consider the reason for this: these *palabres* need not be marked with an intention, even a solicitation, to utter what the *colonisé* knows and understands to be a desire to speak in a way that assures him of white self-recognition. That is why he is in a situation of untruth, and an inessential relationship to himself: he tries to do everything he can to secure a recognition that can only misrecognize black existence as a state of non-being and non-truth. The black is "the eternal victim of an essence, of an *appearance* for which he is not responsible," Fanon writes, a conflict given symptomatic expression through language.[75] From the definition of racial misrecognition previously given, it follows that jabbering amounts to a kind of non-speech, that is, a failure to communicate, a failure to pronounce or make audible black identity as anything more than a distressing separation of the *colonisé* from his or her own body, creating a void, a *lapsus*, around which the unconscious is formed. Fanon refers to this void as *that within*, which denotes something "indefinable, irreversible."[76]

Here Fanon's discourse comes up against its limit: *that within* refers to something elusive and indefinable, its meaning reveals a failure of meaning or non-meaning that forms a void or gap that is henceforth irreversible. It is no accident that Fanon writes about this figure as a kind of vanishing point or ghost within the black corporeal imago (it is also sig-nificant that this reading grants an extreme importance to *Hamlet*: that is, that drama in which an unavowed lie reveals an unenacted truth and the actor, through the interrogation of meaning, discovers the violent found-ing act that enacts new speech and desire). The reference to the word "re-sponsibility" above also gives the game away, politically speaking, for it touches on what, in Fanon's Algerian writings, the appeal of a truly revo-lutionary event is when it cuts through the forms of representation. Ex-istentially, the former allows the *colonisé* to distinguish the true from the false, to tell apart the act that would liberate the nation's new speech from the act that aspires to resemble or shape it. The violence of insurrection thus discloses a conspicuous imperfection in the image of the *colon* that the *colonisés* reproduce as their reflected image. For this reason, revolu-tionary praxis does not reveal what is concealed or hidden, but shows how each glimpse of the other is distorted by what may indeed be called a cul-tural imaginary grounded in racial honor and worship. It is as if Fanon were saying that, since the black has lost the ability to experience a "world in which things happened, in which events existed, in which forces were active," he is akin to an actor who can only perform a role that doesn't belong to him, who can only speak through a voice that is not his own, a voice that is alien, phantasmal, delusional, a voice that exempts him from any obligation to speak in his own person or to act ethically.[77] We may even see, in this opposition between the *colonisé* and the unacted being, Fanon's most considered response to psychoanalysis, of which we shall speak at greater length below. In other words, my principal purpose here is to discuss the *failure* of black desire through Fanon's concern with *that within* and its psychophilosophical implications. I will discuss these im-plications at some length.

One must thus take this *that within* as inspiriting and haunting, and the first way to hear, read, interpret it, is to try and understand where it comes from, what it wants of us, knowing that it does so through several idioms (literary, psychoanalytic, philosophical, idioms in which it is neces-sary to delimit our relation to others [*autres*)], be they white or black, male or female: we shall come back to this later), and also knowing that this *that within* always addresses itself to the singular idiom of interracial sex and desire, to the singularity of the other as an implicated self-relation, despite or even because in recognizing the other the black can only misrecognize its own difference, or can only annihilate itself *as* black.

Consequently, consider these sentences from "The Man of Color and the White Woman," from *Black Skin, White Masks*: "Jean Veneuse [the main protagonist of René Maran's 1947 novel, *Un Homme pareil aux autres*] is not a Negro and does not wish to be a Negro. And yet, without his knowledge, a gulf has been created. There is something indefinable, irreversible, there is indeed *that within* of Harold Rosenberg."[78] This wish *not* to be black, the indefinable and irreversible nature of its affect, in short its affectivity, opens up a gulf in self-relation, or auto-affection, that reminds Fanon of *Hamlet* as read by Harold Rosenberg in a 1948 essay, "Du Jeu au je: Esquisse d'une géographie de l'action," in *Les Temps Modernes,* a journal edited by Sartre.[79]

The phrase "that within" thus condenses three incipient processes of reading—it occurs in a study of Maran's autobiographical novel, alongside a reading of Germaine Guex's psychoanalysis of abandonment, and in a dazzling reflection on the difference between "is" (*la réalité*) and "seems" (*l'apparence*). It now occurs to me that Fanon's attention to *that within* is part of a wider concern throughout his work with the black failure to act, or to close the gap between (black) appearance and (white) reality that Fanon compels us to notice. In any case, his rhetoric is not designed to overcome the gap that the actor-neurotic cannot but present in its impossibility. For this reason I do not doubt that Fanon's decision to present Jean Veneuse as if he were not a character, but the mouthpiece for Maran, is primarily rhetorical. If Maran will not speak in his own voice, Fanon will make him, if only to make his words sound different and convey what is distorted by his narrative. This is not so much an attempt to put *Un Homme pareil aux autres* back in its proper time and place as it is a desire to make the text speak as if Veneuse were Maran, in a kind of impossible identification that cannot be captured or rejoined. When Fanon turns to *Un Homme pareil aux autres,* he too is engaged not only in a reading of literature as symptom but also with the consequences of a black demand for vengeance that disguises itself as love and fidelity, loss and misrecognition. All this is buried in a highly condensed and opaque reference to Rosenberg's "Du Jeu au je" (and its remarkable reading of *Hamlet*).

It is easy to imagine why "Du Jeu au je" appealed to Fanon. Rosenberg's study of Hamlet's famous hesitancy or failure to act proposes that we think of the hero as one for whom "an empty space appears, a void of non-being," which is why he suffers an "ontological anxiety to get into the act" and to "decide whether the part assigned is really one's part."[80]

Only through action, it seems, can Hamlet separate being from its representation. But having offered this rather conventional reading of the play, Rosenberg proceeds to complicate it. For one thing, the distinction he draws between "is" (*la réalité*) and "seems" (*l'apparence*) is meaningless in the theater, for there what seems *is*; in life, unlike in the theater, it is real men, not actors, who die, and "each man's death is singular to him."[81] And for another, the imperfect doubling of being by appearance has two profound consequences; for the actor who only wants to play a part, performance is all, but for the man who desires to act, "there is that within which cannot be played by an actor," and which is radically particular to him.[82] It appears, Rosenberg continues, that *that within* is never itself present but testifies to the spectral effect whereby the dead (phantom) compels Hamlet to distinguish mere acting from the event that is "hiddenly particular" to him.[83] If, for Rosenberg, the philosophy of man as actor fails to separate being from event, in the sense that playing one's part is all, then *that within* is the means through which this falsity is vitiated and put into crisis. Hamlet's ghost thus manifests, historically, the difference between "what cannot be enacted at all and what cannot be enacted yet but will be enacted"; *that within* is thus a diremption *and* rupture, and one that reveals a double contradiction between Hamlet's nonperformed act and the act that reveals the necessity of an obligation that cannot be enacted yet.

Despite the difference of approach between Rosenberg's quasi-existentialism and Fanon's psychopolitical semiotics, both are likewise invested in the question of the event as uniquely defining, even revolutionary, but whose meaning never appears as such even as a visibly masked rupture. I imagine that Rosenberg's reading of Hamlet, as someone caught in a gap between two identities (or two stages of commitment) neither of which he can assume, resonated deeply for Fanon, as did the implication that *that within* denotes something that is truly inexpressible, that cannot be enacted, or performed, and that is in a relation of what Sartre called "transcendentality" to what *I* feel, or what I attest to having felt but which is never recognizable or representable as such.[84] If committed art transforms speech into action, in "Du Jeu au je," the drama of art is that it never goes beyond the illusion of having done so. As Fanon's reference to Sartre's *What is Literature?* makes clear, if the "real task" of literature is to get society to reflect and act, the concern here is less with what it means to reflect or to act than with whether it is ever possible for the black to really express himself when what he feels is unreality, or when he tries to speak in his own person and is prevented from doing so by the parasitical white ventriloquist who speaks through his mouth and person.[85]

Here I must point out that Fanon's use of "Du Jeu au je" is *importantly* not about the sequence from language to action but all about the secret suspicion that recognition and its customary consequence can only make itself readily comprehensible to the black in so far as he empties himself of all pleasure and reality. What Fanon discovers in Rosenberg and Maran is what Sartre discovered in the *Transcendence of the Ego*; that there is a whole hidden level of transcendentality that is manifestly haunting every self-relation and that is invariably linked to a *failure of self-certainty* in the courts of recognition. Both Fanon and Rosenberg indicate that the encounter with the ghost—its social death—is the beginning of a resolution to act that will be uniquely defining; but the meaning of that act is vitiated by the same double bind: in harping on black Hamlet's terrible situation, they uphold the act as "a free act of human decision," but one in which the subject "cannot decide unless it is decided."[86] Paradoxically, it is because the decision to decide—to cut through the "counterfeit presentments" of words that serve the impostures of the actor—is undecidable that it "unveils" itself as a revolutionary truth-event, even if that event remains indefinable and irreversible.[87]

That within is not a flaw to be discovered at being's expense, behind the arras as it were. Nor, forming the manifest end of representation's "empty show," does it merely designate a "transcendence" overcoming the opposition between man and actor.[88] Rather, both Fanon and Rosenberg acknowledge that no transcendence can "cure" this gap between convention and event by which black Hamlet is torn.[89] In the triangle of man-actor-ghost, they acknowledge that Hamlet, the *colonisé*, maintains *that within* as a kind of rupture that is both primal and irreparable, and one that, in the absence of rules and knowledge, remains an essential dimension of his inner truth. In this sense we may also say that *that within*, that is, the experience of a secret imperfection that is necessarily unrepresentable, irreversible, resembles a shared concern between the two theorists that is instructively tied to literary—and undeniably theoretical—commitments to a voice that does not know whether it is real or not, and to speech acts about which it is impossible to know whether they are revolutionary-artistic events or signs of madness.

The basic question then would be: when does one know that one is in a real situation? And how do we match our emotions to new events given that "it is not we but the plot that determines our actions"?[90] The formal implications of Fanon's *clinical* reading of *Un Homme pareil aux autres* is at issue here—indeed, it is as the signifier of a lost trace or gap in the psychological plots of colonialism that Fanon begins his reading of Maran's text. As if to insist on the necessity of reading the text as no more than its distorted appearance, Fanon focuses on *that within* as the means by which that which is said to be lost suddenly reappears as a rupture at the core of Maran's art. It appears, first, as a complicated series of narrative denials; second, as the beautiful hiding of a rupture (formed by what the black feels himself, symbolically, to be deprived of); and third, as the elegiac acknowledgment of an impossible desire (produced the moment the subject enters into white discourse).

Having written on *Un Homme pareil aux autres* elsewhere, let me here briefly summarize the main points of Fanon's reading.

Firstly, for Fanon, *Un Homme pareil aux autres* makes explicit a contradiction between desire and identification, between a desire to be the same as that which is felt to be conserving, one that positions the self as loved, and a desire that is felt to be annihilating, rejecting or condemning the essential relation between other and self so that instead of a relation of love, or recognition it is one of resentment, distrust, and revenge. But if the contradiction simply consists of wanting to be loved, of enacting or exacting revenge for being abandoned, we might say that it arises out of the fear of not being loved, that it conforms to a narcissism, and perhaps, by way of metaphor, that of its *failure* (in the sense in which Fanon says *Black Skin, White Masks* is concerned with narcissistic failures), but we would be wrong to say that this failure is itself narcissistic. Fanon begins his chapter on *Un Homme pareil aux autres*, for example, with the following event: "Out of the blackest part of my soul, across the zebra striping of my mind, surges this desire to be suddenly *white*. I wish to be acknowledged not as *Black* but as *White*. Now—and this is a form of recognition that Hegel had not envisaged [*décrite*]—who but a white woman can do this for me?"[91] Here Fanon proposes a relation that we should linger over, particularly because it links interracial desire to the enigmatic concept of *that within*. What would happen if the *blackest part* of the soul was discovered to be a drive to be white, and in such a way as to open an unbridgeable gulf between this desire and the blackest part from which it surges? Neither desirably white nor undesirably black, undecidably, it would no longer even be a means to love (a white-identified object) but would enter into an entirely other relation to both identification and object. At least if the blackest part that guarantees in no uncertain terms this whiter love is unable to tell apart the black stripes that darken from the white stripes that lighten, that visibly confirm the whiteness of black love, it follows from this undecidable relation that we can say that there is no way of absolutely knowing, or of making present, whether this desire for recognition is a decision both to reveal "what is hiddenly particular" and/or to conceal that which "denote[s] oneself truly" (the words are Rosenberg's).[92]

In short, for the black to be acknowledged as such, it must, in its difference and in its desire, be both other to the (white) love object it solicits and in conformity to the (white) recognition that destroys or suspends it, or at least reinvents and conserves it the better to sublate and negate it. The blackest part of the drive would thus denote not an alienating representation but the affect of its (non)appearing; but why should the *colonisé* experience this as a passive desire to be white in the form of a *méconnaissance*? Where does this resistance to blackness come from? Here we come back to a certain rivalrous relation to the racial *semblable* that appears to be essential here, a cultural symptom that is so intimately present that it no longer signifies an egoic imago or imaginary image but a culturalization of the drive. In this sense, too, it denotes an affect that is not experienced by the subject even though s/he obsessively performs and enacts it as their designated role. Fundamentally, there is something like a diremption between desire and drive that creates a gulf, a *décalage*, and this gulf gives rise to feelings of *abandonment* that Fanon, closely following the work of the analyst Germaine Guex, says belongs to a pre-oedipal order of object relations and identification.[93] "Since I was abandoned, I shall make the other suffer, and abandoning the other will be the direct expression of my need for revenge."[94]

The critical question remains open of whether the need to abandon arises out of a desire to eschew (the pain and hurt of abandonment) or whether the recourse to revenge is from this point of view an attempt to conceal precisely this outcome (of being ruined, re-marked, by the other's abandoning). Whether abandonment is the result or cause (could it be both?), Fanon cites Guex to say that the abandonic is "out of place, affectively speaking," and because he is "the Other," he is always on *guard*; "unconsciously [he will] do everything that's needed to bring about the expected catastrophe."[95]

Secondly, the notion of *that within* (as a "secret zone" within the self's first object relations) permits Fanon to ask why, in the *colonisé*, "the first characteristic seems to be the fear of showing oneself as one actually is."[96] Yet again, *that within* exposes a gap or rupture between this "game of appearances" [*piège des apparences*] and the false-semblant [*faux-semblant*] of an ego torn between the "specter" [*le spectre*] of the loss of love—the fear of being abandoned—and its own regressive-aggressive rivalry, at the level of fantasy, with the object that it believes has abandoned it (the words are Guex's).[97] From this perspective, the *colonisé* can do no more than to act out a profound conflict of identification: to put on their white masks they have had to forego their black skins, but here it is not the *colonisé* or even the *colon*, but blackness itself that masks the concealment; as every instance of *méconnaissance* stands revealed as a masked imperfection, a kind of white striping that enhances the black features beneath it.[98] For Fanon, Veneuse's "constitutional morbidity" is thus an "imposture," both philosophically and psychoanalytically, but this does not mean that it is any less real.

Doubtless, to grasp what this imposture means, one must distinguish it from a delusion that arises simply from an ideology of anti-blackness and the internal identification with that ideology. The surging forth of a desire to be white, real or imaginary, or real *because* imaginary, is a desire that divides the desire to be (to be seen as masked) from the desire not to be (unveiled as black). For if whiteness is the fantasy of a lost self-relation that the subject must find again in his object (the white woman), the decision not to be of the order of the abandoned, not to be lost, must be seen as black, even if the oscillation between the two desires is undecidable and both desires are felt to be equally imperative. For Fanon, what must be acknowledged here is the unique singularity of blackness as the example of a *catastrophe that has already happened*, but one that the *colonisé* cannot possibly be aware of uttering, even though everything he says can hardly escape the need to allude to it. The undecidable is not merely the oscillation or the tension between two desires, it is the experience of that which, though heterogeneously foreign to the order of race and representation, still obliges the subject to give itself up to this impossible desire that *haunts* every object relation and social tie. A recognition that did not go through the ordeal of abandonment would not be enough for the black neurotic, it would only be that which conserved itself, ignoring the obligation to attend to what is always lost and so never possessed (the beloved specter) and, moreover, cannot be reduced to the calculation that some blacks call love and which is really interracial revenge. That is why Hamlet's ordeal is related to that of Veneuse: they give themselves over to a spectral law that is never passed nor past, that can never be surmounted nor sublated (*aufgehoben*), and in which they remain caught up, an undecidability that persists in every desire and decision. Accordingly, *that within* removes the *colonisés* from any assurance of love or presence and puts into doubt any certitude or supposed conviction that would assure them of the justness of their decisions. Who can ever assure Veneuse that he is loved, or that love as such has befallen him: that it has not, through such and such a detour, followed the usual course of fetishistic calculation, or sexualized revenge, that marks all black desire for whiteness at the moment that blackness is, or is not, dispensed with or eradicated?

We can already see from this second accent that *that within* refers to a gap that is irreducible, irreducible because owed to the other, owed to the other before any contract, or object relation, because it has come, in its surging singularity, out of the blackest (most ghostly) part that is always other. *That within* seems to me to be beyond mediation or recognition; it is a demand without symbolism or exchange, without representation or affirmation, without object and without genealogy. We can only recognize it as the *limit* that identifies a desire, and a desire that is so insistently a fantasy of loss that *any* chance of reparation appears to be only another beguiling, ultimately ruinous, continuously fissured, rejection. A desire *not to be* (what Fanon calls elsewhere a *n'est pas*) is the "plot that has won against the man" in *Un Homme pareil aux autres*.

The key point here is not to generalize Veneuse as racially typical, but to understand him in the singularity of his black (hidden, masked) desire. There is no connection between his neurosis and "the amount of melanin in his epidermis," Fanon avers, even though the very forcefulness of his reading presents the political and cultural history of blackness as a discourse of epidermalization that complicates all kinds of biologism in favor of psychoneuroses.[99] I would hesitate to assimilate too quickly this notion of *that within* to a notion of lack or to similar constructions. In all the figurative and literal detours between (black) desire and (white) object in the novel, the desire not to have is articulated, retrospectively, as a desire to have without having, which is also why Veneuse's fear is not that of separation, but that of not-having his loss, which the white woman is being asked to both confirm and give up, confirm by giving him up as a lovable object.

One could hardly ask for a better encapsulation of Guex's thesis than this view of an egotistical love marked as lost because never truly retrievable *as* a loving self-relation. Moreover, while Fanon agrees with Lacan's attacks on the notion of "constitution," his decision to replace it with that of "structure" invites us to see in his reading of Maran a reference not just to an individual neurosis but also to a collective pattern: a pattern that registers sometimes as a drive, sometimes as an affectivity, and sometimes in the discord between them.[100] By structure he also means the ways in which anti-blackness should not be reduced to other racialisms (be they Orientalist or anti-Semitic). His reading of Veneuse as a kind of neurotic black Hamlet allows us to perceive and conceive an irreducible oscillation in Fanon's own response to *that within*: another way of saying this is that he runs the risk of saying that *that within* does have a specific meaning, for example, that is only incidentally raced because it exhibits the by now familiar conflicts of disavowal and obligation. Inversely, it is true that what Fanon says later about racism being incidental is not always incompatible with the belief that Veneuse is a neurotic who happens to be black precisely because, in imperial France, he is made to see blackness as an (unplanned, unwanted) flaw in the human being. In any case, the Fanonian critique of *that within* claims to exceed the two traditions of misrecognition (Hegelian and Freudian) and no longer to arise simply from repression and the failed struggle for recognition in the civil sphere of social life. It belongs to what he calls, in a rather singular sense, an out-of-placeness that is expressly related to Rosenberg's interpretation of *Hamlet*, and what may be considered the specter condemning the black in his historicity.

We have now reached the point where this out-of-placeness can be considered more generally:

1. Veneuse delays his confessions of love not just because he is uncertain about the other's desire, but because he needs to compulsively avoid his own desire. This avoidance is closely joined to the love letters written for the purpose of delaying any consummation or covenant (and from this point of view, the long letters that Veneuse writes to his white lover are where his desire has indeed become an objectification of the other's desire through the act of writing). From this it emerges that *Un Homme pareil aux autres*, as a collection of letters, gives evidence of a long epistolary excuse that is also a *jouis-sense* of deferral and concealment.

2. The abandonic thus substitutes thought (writing) for action; incapable of engaging himself in an act that would transform his situation, the abandonic conceals himself behind the white mask of his desire which, in the colony, is linked to the paternalism by which he devotes himself to his black African charges. This paternalism, and the renunciation that is in-

separable from it, is the means by which he gives up his private life and the promise of interracial sexual intimacy (even though in the novel he is happy to discharge himself in native women) out of love for the French empire.

3. It is evident finally that there *is nothing behind the social mask of his desire*, nothing behind the veil covering his essence, nothing but the mythological phantom of his own singularity and uniqueness: *that within*. All these symptoms therefore collude towards one end: to love by not-loving, and desire nothing but the idea of being desired. Faced by this aphanisis, Veneuse submits himself to the racist colonial social codes in order to maintain the white woman as the inaccessible love object that sets his desire in motion; she is Eurydice to his Orpheus, more real to him because lost and all the more valuable because of this renunciation. But what, exactly, has been renounced? The abandonic cannot at the same time renounce this renunciation and conserve its mythical dimensions, i.e., both his sacrificial narcissism and his most anxious demand—that he be dissociated from the sensuality and vengeance that, in the novel, are figured as black.

4. We conclude that the abandonic is *strictu sensu* incapable of any historico-political solution to the loss or injury experienced by the *colonisé*; hence the need to make the other responsible for his desire or, in sum, the scrupulously observed decision to avoid any uncertainty or risk.

Thirdly, *that within* is a phrase that appears in English in the original 1952 French text of *Peau noire, masques blancs*, that imposes itself on the text as a sort of obligation or symbolic force that defies translation. To this extent, it already concerns the question of race and representation as a question of language: if, at least, I want to make this blackest part of myself understood, it is necessary that I speak it in the *colon*'s language, or that the blackest part of my language must be represented and understood as something that manifestly whitens the text. And even if it were expressible in French, even if *that within* represents what both performs and exceeds the ethico-therapeutic limits of colonial racism, it always remains the consequence or effect of a theoretical or historical knowledge in suspense, interrupted by that which precedes it, that must precede it. The instant of *that within* is an abyss, says Fanon. It is the moment in which a gulf opens onto a moment of decision or a fateful period of waiting; that moment, writes Rosenberg, when "the fatal rupture of being from action" transforms "the situation in which he [Hamlet, Veneuse] is acting."[101]

That within is an interesting expression, about which I have already had a lot to say. But let us recall how the black *colonisé* is obliged to speak in the sense of colonial culture, in the sense of speaking the language of power and force, especially when, through accentuation and norms of propriety, French grants the native the authority to speak and be understood as a subject whose speech is indisputably part of the *work* of subjugation. In his reading of *Un Homme pareil aux autres*, Fanon repeatedly has recourse to allusion, both literary and rhetorical, in order to insist that Maran-Veneuse's adoption, and subsequent appropriation, of French, in its classical decorum, is the point at which his blackness ceases, at least to the extent that the moment at which he responds to the invitation to manifest his desire as a Frenchman, something that apparently no one has constrained him to do, is also the moment at which he is no longer a foreigner speaking French but a Frenchman who merely happens to be black. At bottom, the performative structure of these speech acts is itself founded on conventions of race and propriety that already presuppose the essential foreignness of black *parole*, that is to say, the dissymmetry between the status of *la langue française* in the metropole and colonial idioms. This is not without consequence, needless to say, for the way in which French literature is used to rigorously distinguish Veneuse from those (African) blacks who, in the novel, can only speak *petit-nègre* to the black Frenchman whose political and juridical status, paradoxically, is all to do with his talking and usage of French colonial idioms of power, address, and superiority. But for Veneuse, in more or less the same way, this cultural translation of black desire into white text, into the idioms of classical French literature, necessarily remains a translation, that is to say an always possible but always imperfect compromise between two idioms, at the heart of which he remains a foreigner to himself whose expression in language— *that within*—has no strict equivalent in French imperial culture nor black Martinican culture.

This question of blackness and idiom is doubtless central to Fanon's reading of *Un Homme pareil aux autres*. There are a certain number of questions here which return us to the idiomatic expression of obligation and out-of-placeness that we have already touched on. The first is to make sense of *that within* in terms of the analytic structure of its concept, in its decentered relation to racial misrecognition. What is the objective of this analysis, asks Fanon? To *"face the world"* (in a Sartrean sense).[102] And yet, echoing Guex, he says that the notion of a black abandonment neurosis has resulted in Veneuse being "put back in his place, his proper place."[103] There is a crucial difference implied here between the feeling of being out of place, of being deemed alien or alter, and the analysis and even the re-alization of that affective disquiet at the level of therapy and literature. To stay with the question of idiom, if the English words "that within" can-not be translated into French precisely because they signify, in French, an originary disjunction, that is because the blackest part of the drive (to be white) could not represent itself conceptually without the white anteriority that it so anxiously signifies as reparative, so that, in this initial moment, the subject is neither legitimate nor excluded, or, put differently, is not al-together white nor black. How are we to distinguish between a desire that is abjected by its own desire for legitimacy and the supposedly originary whiteness that must have established this desire for abject legitimacy?

Fanon will attempt to demonstrate his claim that even though the words *that within* signify a gulf, a *décalage*, a regression, and so forth, at the level of both experience and theory, they also signify the necessary fail-ure of translation when it tries to grasp this *that within* in the universalist idioms of phenomenology, psychoanalysis, and canonic French literature. For as we have seen, *that within* can only be briefly glimpsed on the path to experience, for its singularity is always ghostly (and to that extent dis-tant from all idioms), albeit one that exposes the subject to the depths of its anguish. How, without knowing it, can one renounce this renuncia-tion? How does one grasp what is in fact ungraspable, or overcome that which indicates the limits of possibility? What provokes these questions also compels Fanon to reread Hegel.

Hegel (I)

Hitherto our concern has been to understand *that within* as a figure of separation. We began our enquiry by showing how, via a certain reading of *Hamlet*, it was understood and explained as the violent inexpressibility of a commandment that does not have an origin or outcome in the playing of a role, but calls for a revo-lutionary event in which "all the gaps are closed."[104] Likewise, the profound mel-ancholy of *Un Homme pareil aux autres* suggested the neurotic fears, resentments, and jealousies of the abandonic as discussed by Guex, a defense mechanism that shows how neuroses of abandonment arise in interracial desire. Further, these neu-roses create in the *colonisé*, no less miraculously, a devouring love (for whiteness) that easily turns into jealous rivalry, a precariousness that comes to designate the whole of his being. Now since neither reading is subordinate to the other, as both turn on a failure to grasp the moment of decision as such, in its urgency and vio-lence, why does Fanon invoke interracial passion as a melancholy failure to act? I am tempted to say that this is all signaled in the reference to Hegel's *Phenom-*

enology of Spirit that opens Fanon's chapter on "The Man of Color and the White Woman," in which it is claimed that the desire to be loved by a white woman is a recognition that Hegel had not envisaged.

Now the first thing to say is that *Un Homme pareil aux autres* could easily be read as a failure of mutual recognition on the part of the interracial couple who encounter each other and precisely fail to recognize the other as self-relation, and therefore fail to see that the other is never simply other, but always an implicated self-relation. Guex too asserts this explicitly in her analysis of the abandonic, who is unable to recognize how his self-relation is mediated by what he idealizes or condemns in the other's relation to him or herself, whose rage and anxiety can only confirm how he both abandons and is abandoned by his own egotistical relation to himself, and who is most vulnerable when seduced by the other's denials and solicitations. In response to his insecurity, the abandonic is both equally slavish and enraged, and his relation to domination and dependence both unstable and reversible, which is why he bids the other to believe in the sanctity of his deceptions so as to avoid being abandoned by real declarations of love. This is why Veneuse has to quieten and deny *that within*, on precisely the same grounds: in order to prolong the assuredness that arises out of the misrepresentation of the other's desire— and the novel simply excludes the white woman's desire—the abandonic must defer or exclude his obligations to the world of others and things. For Fanon, as we have said, emotional sensitivity is a structural condition of life in the colony.

Since these motifs could be considered straightforwardly Hegelian, and particularly in regard to the theme of misrecognition, why does Fanon insist that *that within* in a strategic and vitally important, even decisive, way, derives from a desire that Hegel had not envisaged? I won't cite here the Hegelian texts at issue (see Part Two, Chapter Ten, "The Abyssal"), but is the difference to do with the irrepresentable? In the sense that *that within* is unknown to the self, it signifies a force and affect that never coincides with self-presence, even though it exposes the black *colonisé* to its irreparable deposing. For me, it is always a question of the differential force of blackness, of the relation between blackness and work, blackness and signification, in whose movement the dialectically defined relations of trial and recognition are suspended or exposed in their limitations. Now all this requires detailed exposition, but Fanon's point (spelled out at various places) seems to be that the internalization of a struggle between abjection and obligation is one that *precedes* the social antagonisms of desire. Blacks, when defined abstractly as victims of racism, lose their relation to desire, work, and otherness, their own and that of others. But when the passage from imago to identification is understood, in whomever is revealed as such, what becomes evident is that the *colonisé* must first be taught to misrecognize blackness as abject: on this interpretation, the *colonisé* must, so to speak, learn to recognize himself by cultivating the passions of anti-blackness. And he does so in the same manner and under the same conditions as Veneuse—for whom the blackest part denotes the power or force of a disturbing, enigmatic image in which the black learns to see himself, without being able to recognize himself in it—has done. He is consequently a narcissus (to speak in specular-imaginary terms) who has no reflection. What the black specular imago does then is to ob-ject him (as Fanon argues throughout his early work), by preventing him from acceding to the revealed nothingness of the other's desire. For in this moment the *colonisé* finds himself caught up in the pathos of a contradiction, which, though unconscious, is that of a life in conflict with itself: after all, *that within* is motivated less by a struggle over recognition or of penetrating what otherness means than by the conflict in which the self alienates itself from its own individuation. Fanon gives several examples of why this is the case.

a) In the subject's encounter with the signs and symbols of colonial culture, which Fanon talks about in his clinical writings, these signs acquire a meaning before a sense of alienation is formed by racism; indeed, they will come to express *de jure* a mistrust, a suspicion, that the subject disposes of *de facto* in the phantasms of narcissism;

b) the ideological foundations of colonial culture under the French turn on the question of time, or historicity, and the racist disavowal that forms a radical mutation of the subject (Fanon himself describes this as a vertigo that is *nachträglich*);

c) the explanation of a certain sociogeny (and this will later be applied to the combatants during the Algerian war) will become pivotal to Fanon's relation to psychoanalysis and to the neuroses and psychoses that he attributes to life in the colony (see Chapter Six, "Desire and Law");

d) blackness, as against the being that is black, is essentially constituted as the no-thing that *is* not (or *n'est pas*, a term that I discuss more fully below). Nor is it coincidental that this *n'est pas* is the mark of a negativity that cannot be phenomenalized as the work of negation in the sense in which Hegel gives it, and by virtue of the fact that its very enunciation and inscription signify how the blackest part cannot in any sense either be meant or give way to a definable or reversible meaning. For as we showed above, what is profoundly unsettling about blackness is not that it can only affirm itself by sacrificing its own presence or by veiling itself under the appearance of unveiling, or that it can only speak itself as a demeaned or distorted representation; no, what is unsettling is that its mode of appearing has no phenomenological certitude, that it cannot be placed or be made actually present as such. And this is its mode of affect. For it is indeed not a case of experiencing a "night in which all the cows are black," a night confirmed as the limit of reason, but a night in which nothing is the purest illumination of that which *is* not, a night in which the cows are highly uncertain, not of their appearing, but of their being as such.[105]

Now in order to find out what this all means, it is doubtless necessary to go back to what Fanon refers to as a black obscurity inhabiting the colonial subject.

"Out of the blackest part of my soul, across the zebra striping of my mind," Fanon writes, "surges this desire to be suddenly *white*. I wish to be acknowledged not as *Black* but as *White*. Now—and this is a form of recognition that Hegel had not envisaged [*décrite*]—who but a white woman can do this for me?" Since what is at issue here is an affectivity that presents itself to the ego as not merely a result but also an event, not merely a manifestation but also the production of a desire for what exceeds it, the interpretation of this surging must represent more than the purely passive consequence or result of previous cultural impositions and their dialectical role and history in identification. Admittedly, this desire to be desired by the other could also mean a desire for the desire of the other as explained by Alexandre Kojève, in his famous *Introduction to the Reading of Hegel*, who reformulates the desire for recognition as a desire to be recognized in the other's desire—who but a white woman can do this for me?—wherein desire signifies nothing "but a revealed nothingness."[106] However the interpretation of *that within* (that refers it to a pre-oedipal configuration) seems to me more accurate. We know that Fanon distinguishes the eventness of *that within* from a dialectical process of recognition. He also specifies that the performative power of its affect cannot be separated from the history and passion of a certain interracial desire: black man, white woman. Moreover, Fanon constructs this notion of *that within* on the basis of two determinations: it is indefinable (because its opacity cannot be reduced to that of a phantasm) and irreversible (because after it happens, or occurs, it is singularly true to you; one cannot not know this affect, or its truth, even if one tries to dissimulate or perform it differently, or replace it with an imaginary narcissistic certitude). *That within* is unrepresentable because it exceeds all objectivity and transcendence, including that *surging* within that neither arrives nor commences in the ego nor the world. Thus, according to Fanon, to grasp the blackest part philosophically as already identical to the whiteness implied in it, and thereby implying that whiteness is the true labor of its concept, would be to sublate it, and would have to draw the same teleological conclusion: namely, that there is but one destiny for the black, and it is white.[107] Every further stage, from the colonial to the postcolonial, would belong to an already whitened narrative, and every additional step from which the black might relate to itself would be that of the always already abandoned object. As a self-presentation, such a dialectic collects all prior usages and practices that govern the relation between black desire and its objects, and must proceed as if that desire is already realized as given and yet, at the same time, nevertheless infinitely suspended in its surging: the ontic status of *that within* would thus understandably become the work of alienation and ideology rather than something that is always at the threshold of its abandoning, both abandoned and abandoner—of itself, and of any other in its insecure being. This is without doubt because *that within* marks the point at which the *I* no longer recognizes its image, behind whose opaque, petrified being there is nothing but the mask of its concealment. As a pre-oedipal difference, however, blackness is essentially constituted by an incomplete, regressive identification that is before any object choice and thereby prior, by right, to the processes of socialization. It is not, as we have already noted, but the meaning of this *n'est pas* at the heart of its rhetoric is still to be explored.

I will come back to this *n'est pas* in Chapter Seven, on "The Condemned," but for now let us say that the blackest part of blackness is never absolutely black but only includes elements that blacken it: those words, scenes, anecdotes, fables, by which the *colonisé* is incontestably subject to the most abject misrecognition apropos of whiteness, or its concept.

If the struggle for recognition, as Hegel's speculative idealism conceives it, is also simultaneously a struggle to expose, via negation, one's self-relation to the other, according to the work of dialectical mediation, then there is something about *that within* that cannot expose itself; resistance to exposure in fact constitutes its limit situation. Hegel might say that this then is its object-like character, but *that within* possesses one element that defines it specifically: its phenomenality that is said to be spectral, corpselike; Fanon uses the phrase "affective ankylosis" to describe it, which signifies a painful stiffening; and, to the extent that *that within* testifies to the affect of something petrified or dead, we know that its remains are preserved forever on a stage littered with corpses.[108]

5

Racial Fetishism

It follows from the previous chapter, as we have pointed out, that blackness reveals a desire not to be *nègre*, and that this refusal arises out of a devotion to the institutions of anti-blackness, as Maran's *Un Homme pareil aux autres* abundantly shows. By definition, interracial desire is the point at which anti-black delusion and paranoia appear to manifest themselves. From the moment of the appearance of interracial desire in *Black Skin, White Masks*, the linking of neuroses and anxiety is frequent, though it seems to have been little studied from a structural point of view. One of the key opening assumptions that Fanon makes in his chapter on "The Negro and Psychopathology" is that "the Negro is a phobogenic object, a stimulus to anxiety."[1] What is the meaning of this anxiety and why (consequently) does it lead to what Fanon describes as "genuine insanity"?[2] Does the idea of blackness cause anxiety because of the ways in which it has been read as *inherently* obscene, or because of its resistance to any concept of meaning or agency? The problem could be posed ideologically as regards the theme of "The Negro and Psychopathology"—with the black playing the role of a scapegoat—including the relations between figures of evil, sin, guilt, etc., and discourses of incivility. In these accounts, blackness also connotes an identity that is constantly shifting, discontinuous, ungrounded; and having no stable referent, it has at once no meaning and all too much. Blackness as excess and blackness as privation, however, are not identical. My aim in this chapter is to pursue Fanon's work on anxiety, in relation to fetishism. In many examples taken from a variety of texts and sources, Fanon shows that there is an *imago* of the black (attached to the *hallucinatory* idea of a sexual potency), which everyone *knows* not to be true but nevertheless acts as if it were.[3]

Fanon's political-ethical task is to show how blackness, as a stereotype—idea, affect, fantasy—functions as a source of traumatic energy in the ideological life of the colony. Negrophobia and its fantasies appear to have taken over people's minds. Indeed this is why fetishism, as a defense against an intolerable idea, is also viewed by Fanon as an important element of negrophobogenesis and the many associations of blackness with savagery and licentiousness, evident across a range of historical discourses and texts. The language of cultural stereotypes teaches this very clearly, I think. If we peruse this language, we shall see how blackness is coterminous with a predation whose exorbitance is conceived of as a sexual-libidinal force that has neither right nor power and that threatens to put the self at risk. If one were to phrase this in economic terms, blackness would then be defined as a kind of primitive drive or energy thoroughly stripped of morality and restraint; a force or power that appears to be in excess of nature and, in so far as it is thus conceived, contains within itself nothing but a drive that ceaselessly expends itself without any thought of limit or reserve.

Having written on this elsewhere, I will not expand on the point here.[4] However, I believe that this libidinal economy has many fetishistic aspects, which therefore depend on a racialized model of anxiety. It is precisely because blackness is imagined to be a drive that can never be appeased, and that is continually present, that it becomes at once an excess at which the subject is brought, as it were, to the dizzying threshold of expiration. Put slightly differently, the stereotype that is blackness can be traced back—against the ego—against its racialized *representation*—to the *affective force of the self's own sexual self-relation*; that is, the resistance to the idea of blackness-as-phobic is the *same* resistance as the resistance to certain sexual ideas, ideas that have as their foundation a phobia that subsists through renunciation. For this is how it has come about that negrophobia testifies to the experience of blackness as a phobic idea, independently from any actual encounter with black subjects.

I. MLLE B.

In order to demonstrate these things in due order, I commence with the following case history of Mlle B., where it appears that a negrophobia is indeed present in every image and affect: as figure, symbol, translation, and transposition. Aside from being the longest case history in *Black Skin, White Masks*, this story of a young white woman, haunted by circles and tics, raises the question of what arises when the paternal signifier is swathed in images of blackness:

[An excerpt from session notes] Deep and concentric, the circles expanded and contracted to the rhythm of a Negro tam-tam. This tam-tam made the patient think of the danger of losing her parents, especially her mother. . . .

I told her to go closer to the circles, she could no longer see them. I told her to think of them; they appeared, but they were broken. I told her to go through the opening. "I'm not completely surrounded any more," she said spontaneously, "I can get out again." The circle broke into two pieces and then into several. Soon there were only two pieces, and they then disappeared. There were frequent throat and eye tics while she was talking. . . .

I do not want to elaborate on the infrastructure of this psychoneurosis. The questions put by the chief psychiatrist had brought out a fear of imaginary Negroes—a fear first experienced at the age of twelve.

I had a great many talks with this patient. When she was ten or twelve years old, her father, "an old-timer in the Colonial Service," liked to listen to programs of Negro music. The tam-tam echoed through their house every evening, long after she had gone to bed. Besides, as we have pointed out, it is at this age that the savage-cannibal-Negro makes his appearance. The connection was easily discernable. . . .

Lying in her bed and hearing the tam-tams, she virtually *saw* Negroes. She fled under the covers, trembling. Then smaller and smaller circles appeared, that scotomized the Negroes. These circles can thus be seen as a defense mechanism against her hallucinosis. Later, the circles appeared without the Negroes—the defense mechanism asserts itself by ignoring its determinism.[5]

From this strange case history, it is evident that the sound of the tam-tam is at the core of these hallucinations. These circles come to signify, whether consciously or unconsciously, something that is both repeatable and irremediable, but also something lost or missing. Distressingly, they also make visible a certain feeling of incommensurability that is inseparable from a feeling of danger and dissolution, whose cause Mlle B. can barely indicate aside from going round in circles: from the real and imaginary sounds surrounding her to the tics and spasms they invariably abut upon and encircle, from the reassuring tones of analytical speech to the loud cries of gendered inarticulacy, what emerges from these clinical notes is nothing less than an intrusion that is felt to be inescapable, but that nevertheless sees Mlle B. dissolve into further tics and anxieties. Consequently, these circles are an enigma, like blackness itself, whose pulsating rhythm, by Mlle B.'s own admission, makes her think of sex, loss, death, and sacrifice: as if behind the music there could be heard something else, namely, the inner echo of a childhood wound or trauma, that comes back to Mlle B., that resonates or seems familiar through the radio owned by her father, whose nightly penchant for black music is at the origin of these memories teeming with imaginary sounds and signifiers, so much so that, in a real and hallucinatory sense, Mlle B. "virtually *saw* Negroes" as she lay in bed.[6]

According to her session notes, Mlle B. was nineteen years old when she entered the psychiatric hospital at Saint-Ylie. On her admission sheet, we are told that her nervous disease consists of "periods of agitation, motor instability, tics, and spasms which are conscious but which she cannot control."[7] We also learn that her hospitalization is voluntary, although the chief physician, following Mlle B's. examination, will go on to say that she "should remain institutionalized."[8] Returning to the notes, we see that her treatment proceeds in accordance with this diagnosis of a nervous illness, for which Mlle B. receives waking dream therapy, but also in accordance with the knowledge that the tics "depend on what she is doing" and become ever more persistent when she is alone, even though they stopped "as soon as she was spoken to."[9] Throughout these sessions it is made clear that the circles seem to reveal something that is most anxiously *there*, where what is broken or opened up admits ever more perplexing topoi that frame or surround Mlle B., and from which there is no respite other than the analyst's speech. As Fanon's sentences suggest, it is precisely because the anxiety-affects of the circles can appear without the Negroes that he is put on the track of their unconscious, repressed meaning *as a defense*. How do the circles relate to negrophobic ideas? And why, precisely, does Mlle B. desire to enter them prompted by the concern that "something was missing"?[10] Not only is blackness unavoidable in describing this absence: what it means to *obsessively want to enter into the circle of negrophobia*, to be enclosed by it, to traverse it, is also what is at stake.

But we must take care here not to reduce everything to repression, as if nothing here was clearly stated. And here at the outset we must note that the tam-tam, whose rhythm refers Mlle B. back to a childhood memory, also produces feelings of intoxication in which she imagines herself *surrounded*, even without precisely knowing why, as she is led toward the point where the blackest rhythms exceed her capacity to bear them. In this (erotic) encountering, there is thus both literal fear and the wish not to be possessed by that fear, which only later fuses with anxiety as the self goes towards its wild transformation.

For it emerges, first, that this memory, even if subsequently clarified as the onset of anxiety, does not become traumatic until later. It is not until Mlle B. enters the world of work and adulthood, in brief, that this adolescent memory produces affects that stir something deep down in her, something that only then, I repeat, attaches itself to certain *Vorstellungen* that seem to encircle her and pulsate deep in her being. Therefore we should not consider these bodily symptoms to have emerged in childhood but as the delayed effect of sexualized, fetishistic projections that are in turn linked to the later negrophobic anxiety of Mlle B.

To understand more precisely how these states are linked temporally, we should note that the effects of these obsessive thoughts are *nachträglich*: they express nothing but the deferred action of a repetition (of reminiscence by repressed thoughts, of sexual ideas which are then deflected into negrophobic desires and discourse, etc.). At the same time, they serve to include and exclude: they allow Mlle B. to hear the illicit nature of her desire via scenes in which she *imagines* herself encircled by Negroes, but they also exclude the intelligible, or expressible, obscene limits—or silence what bears directly on their transmission: here the rhythm of the drive compelling, through sexual anxiety, her body's symptoms, and the various media through which it speaks, the radio bombarding Mlle B. with its violently primitive beats; the mother demeaned and excluded by these circles; and the inescapably terrifying sounds through which the *réel* gathers consistence through black metonyms. The substance of this anxiety is not the radio per se, but the history of persecution that Mlle B. remembers (i.e., the persecutory taunts of her siblings who teased her for her reaction to the music); certainly, these games and the power of the tam-tam are direct expressions of a rivalry and thus a plea for the ear of the father, whose recourse is to his music, but this is a music associated with night terrors, and one that brings to light, into view, an extremity between pleasure and persecution that relies on an explicit logic of race. That said, the music is not the only thing that arouses, for it is the means through which the circles take shape, as both the trace of an unconscious memory and the image of an erotic desire obscured by anxiety and shame.

How is one to sort out all these echoes (historical, unconscious, analytical) in Fanon's reading of the case? We already know that Mlle B. was admitted to Saint-Ylie suffering from neurotic spasms and tics, over which she had no control. These convulsions caused her to utter incomprehensible sounds and "loud, inarticulate cries," which only worsened, we are told, when she was alone.[11] Since the persecution of Mlle B. does not cease when she is alone, but in fact grows stronger, this must be because, in the self-image that she presents to herself, in which she recognizes a circuitous relation to the black as other, she hears or sees only an alienated self-relation from which she tries to flee and that corresponds to a sense of something missing in the very depths of her being. Nothing separates this being-affected from a feeling of being persecuted by others, by their sounds and speech (except, of course, that what is heard or seen are hallucinations); nothing separates this anxiety of a listening traversed by blackness from the giddy feeling of being traversed by the father's enjoyment (except that in her therapy it is only her awkwardness and supplication that is offered to the analyst for assessment, not judgment).

Fanon does not address the relation between transference and speech, or the differing layers of spoken as against remembered sound. Nor does he (yet) discuss the pertinence of radio, as medium and apparatus, to the conflicts on display (in particular those almost hallucinatory modes of signification and transmission by which the radio, heard by the patient whether as a child or as a woman, takes on an uncanny *presence*, whose medium is linked to sexually coded expressions—savage, bestial, dreadful, friendly, and attacking—that are attached not to the reality of what is being played but to a kind of hallucinated perception, whose terror thereby acquires a horrifying dimension when heard in the dark). Indeed, that hallucination obliges Fanon to note the presence of something that is simultaneously transmissible and immanent, but also impenetrable, so intensely is it heard. In fact, it is important to note that it is African drums that allow the circles to appear as a defense against desire. The drums do not represent the circles (as, say, metaphors), but, on the contrary, allow them to emerge (as a kind of unconscious *Darstellung*) in Mlle B.'s dream. This is also made plain in the session notes, for there we are told that it is through the drums that the Negroes and the circles come to stand in for her parents' desire and her own.

Suffice it to say, all these elements are pertinent here, starting with the tam-tams that become joined to the voice of analytic reason, as the sound of childish memory resonates in the words and images of Mlle B.'s inarticulate speech. It would be tempting to say that Fanon does not notice this because he interprets Mlle B.'s illness as the coincidence of a memory with a fantasized sequence of projections: nothing is more stereotypically pu-erile than this code of *black orgiastic excess*, but after analyzing his reading it is clear that he is just as much concerned with the circles (as hallucina-tions) as he is with a listening that archives racial tropes and, by extension, forecloses reality by anti-black communications.

There are numerous reasons why Fanon should be intrigued by this case: fear of the Negro, hallucinated sexual anxiety, the drive or pulsion of which the Negro is the imaginary signifier, a mind so disposed to negro-phobia that it seems to clearly see or hear blackness, the radio as both sym-bol and event. Whatever the reason, it is not the imago of the Negro that makes the *colon* into a fetishist, but her obedience to a phantasm; it is not the phantasm or imago that is traumatic, but the interpellation it later calls forth and that is unconsciously displaced as such. Whether that passion or obedience is moved by love, or compelled by fear, or moved (as is more common) by hatred and fear commingled, Fanon insists that the myth of the Negro necessarily extends to all aspects of life in the colony and that people submit to it whether they choose to or not.

Accordingly, we should not immediately infer that Mlle B. is a racial fetishist out of sexual perversity rather than out of cultural obedience. Hence, Fanon's interest is in how the imago of the Negro arouses an affect that has no connection to any actual experience but that appears only after Mlle B. has been exposed to the genital-libidinal stereotype of the Negro.

To begin to appreciate this structure, let us imagine for a moment a classical psychoanalytic reading of the episode: at the beginning of the chapter on "The Negro and Psychopathology," Fanon cites Freud as say-ing that a repressed idea often comes back to memory "in a disguise that makes it impossible to recognize . . . the repressed thought is replaced in consciousness by another that acts as its surrogate, its *Ersatz*."[12] Is negro-phobia then (since it arises from a fetishistic substitution) merely a de-graded, surrogate ersatz for something more originary? Yes, at the level of a prior, disguised event, as the word "ersatz" implies. Thus the negrophobic representation is not the true manifestation of the idea causing Mlle B.'s symptoms, for the representation of the original affect has been repressed and lies in the unconscious. It is in order to keep both affect and idea out-side of consciousness at all costs that Mlle B. then resorts to an exceptional strategy: whether she hears music or dances with Negroes or undergoes an erotic initiation or not, it is the void circling the father's demand (enjoy!) that compels her to enter the circles of negrophobic desire, which she experiences as so many broken-up pieces of the real, a knowledge that she performs as hysterical incoherence. Negrophobia is the recognition of this fetishistic ploy, but it is also a symptom of the repressed relation between cultural imposition and the entirely reactionary character of its ersatz form.

At the same time, Fanon offers numerous arguments as to why this language of ersatz is itself caught in a fetishistic logic of displacement that has to be disguised, or annulled. *Negrophobia is ersatz not because it is a degraded copy of reality, but because its representation rivals reality, and precisely because it does not stand for something else.* If we look back at Mlle B.'s case history, we can see how Fanon's discussion of ersatz and negrophobia connects with a discussion of fetishism in another way as well. Negrophobia is what allows the broken circles of demand and desire to be mended, and to be enjoyed, thereby reintegrating paternal and imperial authority with the manipulations of the ego, but without having to reveal what blackness represents to Mlle B. in her imaginary fears. In seeking to read the circles as a defense against hallucination, in trying to decipher how they appear without the Negroes, Fanon thus attempts to read these signifiers as the clearest example of a negrophobia that denies, excludes, or distorts. What do the circles signify? Why are they most affecting when *alone*? We have thus come back to the question of why the circles remain obscurely resistant to meaning, even though Mlle B. is able, with a stroke of her magic wand, to transform them from iron into something "shining and beautiful," to transform the repressed wish into sounds of the real and African drumming into a European waltz.[13] As threshold, instrument, or veil, depending on the dream topography, the basic function of the circles is to distinguish what is persecutory and shockingly virile from what is fine and shiningly white. And yet, since this moment of magical transformation needs underwriting by pleasure and enjoyment, it is also underwritten by the need to defend the self from the sexual reality to which it is presumed to refer, here synonymous with racially phobic metonyms. Thus it is that the circles can neither be referentially grounded nor escape referentiality, even though they seem to stand in for the racist authority of a referential ersatz, underlined by Fanon as the true object of his analysis. Fanon is for us the theorist of this *Darstellung*, which is divorced from representational logic and from actual subjects. Negrophobic anxiety thus does not speak of anything definable but signifies the power to be affected without anything being necessarily represented, a power that Fanon describes as akin to the effect of an unconscious intrusion by cultural hatred. *In the very logic of negrophobogenesis*, such a presentation, generally described by Fanon as phobogenic, presents the pure affectability of an anxiety that signifies by way of a signifier that is not its own. It follows that at no time are we dealing with a question of deciphering or decoding, but with that of an upsurge, or shock, that never ceases to be seductive.

To fill out the blurred outlines—the mnemic, conceptual, symbolic, and linguistic meanings associated with the unconscious ersatz—is not what Fanon is trying to do, even when he says that an "imaginary fear of Negroes" is key to the various *Vorstellungen* of Mlle B.'s narrative.[14] Fanon's analysis is not about the repression of these ideas, nor about their avowal through the defiles of the body, but about how certain negrophobic ideas come to be passed down and felt without being attached to any actual representation. If we peruse the opening of "The Negro and Psychopathology," we see that everything that Mlle B. reveals about the effects of racial fetishism, either in words or images, or by both these means together—so much so that it seemed to her that she was clearly hearing the tam-tams or seeing Negroes—is also part of Fanon's understanding of a shift in racist discourse, since it involves a displacement from the fear of something missing to that of an *Ersatz*. As previously discussed, Fanon's interest is in how the phenomenal state of being affected, of being on guard, minus any conscious awareness of why, can potentially produce intolerable feelings of guilt under specific conditions of life in the colony. And what is the fateful role of negrophobic culture in this rapport between the somatic and the psychical at work in the structure of the drive? Clearly, here the effect of the drives, the drive to be racially affected, is present, because racist effects are not unconsciously felt but make themselves felt, precisely, as racist.

By the same token (but indirectly, for it is not clear from the chapter what his observer role is here), Fanon too is listening in on Mlle B.'s sessions, reproducing her speech in his clinical narration, and so doubling the originary effect of the tam-tam and its hypnotic sonority, as if in a certain way the most pertinent sound here might not be that of music but that of analytic speech, or the sounds of countertransference. For, of all the sounds heard, it is the voice of the therapist that guides Mlle B. and that also encircles her as she gives expression to these aural fixations and anxieties. Indeed, she is told repeatedly, in an imperative mode that I will talk about in a moment, to go closer to the circles and to bring them back, as if being present in the presence of such *Vorstellungen* could make them more graspable as representations. I would even suggest that the voice of the therapist here is substituting not only for the black speech of the tam-tams but for the colonial authority of the father, who is clearly connected to this music that seduces and terrifies, or at least those feelings of dread and anxiety that at once produce and are produced by the music by which blackness makes itself felt virtually, that is to say, as a series of pulsating rhythms. For in the various imperative modes or figures of speech by which Fanon presents (*darstellen*) Mlle B.'s case, he too is obliged to express (*darstellen*) the fetish-sounds by which the tam-tams can be heard, as if by echoing the form of its address and destination Fanon's narrative of Mlle B. could then also lead to more analytic meaning. Fanon indicates clearly that in Mlle B. we have a case of "authentic alienation": on the one hand, the setting in motion here of a relation between negrophobia, as an affective state (*Darstellung*), and the case history, as bearing witness to its truth (*Darstellung*), places all the narrative burden on finding a final meaning in negrophobia. On the other hand, the case history cannot be represented or articulated outside of its theatricalization of anxiety, that is, the concern that in its resistance to reading there is no final meaning (either in memory or music), just a pure affectability without signification. For all these reasons, Mlle B.'s case history, in its event and structure, presents a configuration of memory, fantasy, history, and transference that could be compared to Fanon's other work on race and psychoanalysis.

The key moment for me is when Fanon appears to substitute himself for the imaginary Negroes, and in a way that circles back on itself, but via the most circuitous path. For example, towards the end of his narrative, he tells us that "my presence on her ward made no perceptible difference [*modification visible*] to her [Mlle B.'s] mental state."[15] It is as though any explicit attempt to say what the circles represent for Mlle B. can only be negatively revealed by this thinly veiled allusion to the fact that Fanon also happens to be black! The rhetoric of this kind of strategic repression is certainly of interest here, and seems to reintroduce the question of how racism ought to be read psychoanalytically when negrophobia enters into the very structure of the symptom. In any case, blackness for Fanon is never easily readable as a perceptible difference. Indeed, he wants to insist that the negrophobic signifier produces its effects without its anti-black meaning needing to be revealed. Thus, it is neither the character of Mlle B.'s mental debility, nor the contents of her disaffection, but the form through which her renunciation becomes constitutive that decides how "a fear aggravated by determining circumstance" takes on a racist form of fetishistic displacement.[16] Here we should note that the circles act like signifiers to the extent that their function does not require Mlle B. to actually see Negroes, including Fanon, although Fanon also admits that in her disturbed state, she "uttered sounds . . . but it was never possible to understand what she was saying."[17] For reasons that remain enigmatic, or at least not clear to me, Fanon never seems to doubt that these sounds, which curiously resemble an indecipherable code, are never other than an attempt to say something, or to make expressible that which is resistant to interpretation, in opposition to the Negro music that presumably only needs to be heard for an identification to come into play, for fantasy to make an appearance, and whose connection to negrophobia "was easily discernable."[18] Or it is not clear to me why Fanon should see no accord between the imaginary, symbolic quality of the music and the indecipherability of these sounds, or conversely, why he should contrast the excitations easily discernable as anxiety with an utterance whose obscurity is no longer even acting as a screen for anxiety but one that directly reveals it to Mlle B. What I do not understand, in brief, is why Mlle B. entering into an imaginary circle continues to cause Fanon interpretive trouble, as it were, when what truly disturbs are signifiers as obscure as they are impenetrable.

I need not press this point further, for what is at stake here is how Fanon views the dual relationship between ersatz and phobia. But I will demonstrate more precisely and more fully how the two come together, for it is at the moment when the mind finds itself most *alone* that it anxiously turns to projection and phobia. To understand why, we will need to go back to those passages in which Mlle B. finds herself most isolated, and where she is most frightened, but where she nevertheless "wanted to go [close to the tam-tams] all alone."[19] In these perverse wanderings we see, moreover, that the tam-tams are her true destination, and that as soon as the circles draw close Mlle B. tells us that she "wanted to break them," which she does with a stick, a wand, and her bare hands.[20] Why this destination (towards the most intolerable) and why this violence (towards what would defend her)? We will take another look at these passages in due course, but for the moment let us recall the fact that it is when Mlle B. is most *alone* (Fanon's italics) that she succumbs to hysteria, and it is also when the circles appear *alone* (once again Fanon's italics) that there seems to be no defense against their assertoric force and the ersatz reactions that they give rise to.

It is astounding how readily Fanon sees this, even though he uses the session notes to illustrate something altogether different. Mlle B. has no defense against the sounds that seem to be negatively affecting her, even when that effect is deflectively interwoven with signifiers that cause her to obsessively *see* black men and women. For similar reasons, the circles are read as the mind's defenses against hallucination, but only in so far as these mechanisms are able to ignore the predetermined contexts of racist thought and reading. The place where these contexts come together points to what occurred during Mlle B.'s adolescence, but Fanon also never neglects to mention that it is at this age that "the savage-cannibal-Negro" also makes its appearance.[21] Such imagos cannot be ignored, for whether at the school desk or in the playground, they are soon learned, even if unwittingly. That is, the negrophobic message of culture has always already been sent, and *wherever there are Negroes it can be heard or read*, even though its meaning pre-exists the subject. This is where the father's role in the notes becomes decisive, as Fanon shows, for he is the locus of transmission. And yet Fanon also notes, in several places, that despite Mlle B. having to be told, or instructed, to approach the circles by her therapist, it is she who wants to break them up, reshape them, pass through them, etc. To understand the circles as defenses rather than an attempt to represent what *breaks out of* the stereotypical forms of negrophobia is thus to lose sight of precisely why this encounter with the tam-tams is both affective and inarticulate, precisely because it renders tangible the fraught appeal of those ever circling negrophobias.

By contrast, were it true that the circles were merely defenses against the most feared aspect of the Negro (genital sexuality), then why is it that these circles come to signify the point where this myth is unveiled (made meaningful) by a subject that finds itself entirely exposed by its own negrophobia? To that end we can say: the Negro's disappearance from the mise-en-scène of representation means that blackness still persists in the representable aspect of the symptom, albeit beyond any easily discernable frame. No doubt it is because the circles can both appear and not appear with the Negroes that they can defend against what appears to be both Negro and not Negro, and only because what is Negro is precisely the relation to an appearance that, according to Fanon, constitutes the essence of negrophobia as such: as *Darstellung*, the imago of the Negro is always that which maintains itself in relation to its own dissemination, its own lack, or *n'est pas*, but this incapacity can *arrive only as appearance*, and with respect to which no object is actual, and so, as we have seen, potentially blackens all social relations *as such*. The primary force of the circles is thus, paradoxically, to present what has been cut out and taken away from them, the better to enjoy or take pleasure in what remains inaccessible to representation—the abyss, the nothing—with blackness acting as *the* fetish term for covering this void or gap in representation, like a cadence that sensuously pulsates over nothingness. It is a question not of the circles having an abyssal structure in themselves, but of how they present the abyss to Mlle B., with all the attendant anxieties and pleasures. And while it is impossible, of course, to know what these inarticulate sounds and tics of Mlle B. actually mean, what clearly matters to Fanon is analyzing the various ways in which the imago of the Negro is less about meaning or actual trauma than it is about the ways in which it manifests a vertiginous loss of self that is inevitably traumatic *and* seductive.

Our conclusion from this has to be that the effect of the tam-tams does not ensue from the repressed fantasy of a trauma, but it does follow from the effect of a certain implantation in the ear, that is, by virtue of a sound that is at first the expression of an erotic loss of self, but a sound that then echoes a need to objectify this libidinal excitation as a negrophobia, as Mlle B.'s symptoms abundantly confirm. This also very clearly emerges from the fact that the circles are where everything is suspended and where she moves toward her desire. Hence the circles are not representations of the fantasies and fears that found them but obey another order of affect that is not one of memory or representation, but that nonetheless signifies something to Mlle B., even if that message is not something she understands or can make any sense of *until afterwards.*

Consequently, another hypothesis suggests itself that would be exactly the opposite of the one proposed by Fanon: Mlle B. is affected by the circles after their disappearance not because they are disguised or repressed representations, but because the tam-tams echo an experience that is without object, reference, or destination, which means that it cannot be remembered or forgotten but must be inarticulately performed or acted out whenever she is alone. Fanon tells us that the circles are where the abyss makes its entry, but in distorted form: Mlle B.'s aural anxiety, whose meaning cannot easily be put into words, expresses the most subtle mise-en-scène of dream and fantasy, but the abyss into which she falls is only intensified by her feelings of isolation and interpolation. Hence, the *repercussions of that anguish are themselves repercussive,* in so far as they lead to a splitting (the bursting apart of the circles) constitutive of a persecutory neurosis, in which the paternal signifier is split between an imaginary (black) meaning and its perverse (ersatz) articulation. Behind the circles there is not an originary, repressed scene for which blackness acts as a surrogate, or fetishistic representative, but a darkly percussive affect that is irreducible to articulation. At each moment of their movement what appears, before Mlle B., is this loss without object. The central (or most radical) implication of these remarks is also reminiscent, I suggest, of the following comment by Freud in "The Psychoneuroses of Defense" (a text to which Fanon alludes): "The separation of the sexual idea from its affect and the attachment of the latter to another, suitable but not incompatible idea—these are processes which occur without consciousness. Their existence can only be presumed, but cannot be proved by any clinico-psychological analysis."[22]

If I insist on this relation, it is because the circles and the tam-tams, in their syncopation, are always dividing and multiplying according to untranslatable idioms (of disturbing proximity and irresistible force), whereas the words spoken, regardless of what is actually said to Mlle B. or its meaning, are either reassuring (of a representable reality) or inarticulately untranslatable (as a kind of unrepresentable real), as if in her cries there was something else being heard that could not be made present, something that closes in on meaning but that could only be established by the latter's elision, and that only emerges later, after the black men have disappeared behind the circles.

From all this it is plain that the image of the tam-tams, in its connotation, thus corresponds to a body of displacements—historical, cultural, psychical—all of which follow the order of a certain rhythm, or pulsion, that is both indefinable and irreducible. It is this displacement that I want to further outline, not with regard to the phantasms that seem to resound, but via the vertigo that tempts Mlle B. to fall, where what is effectively reverberating is a void (in which the fear of blackness exceeds representation), and one very precisely located in the very precise space of a *fetishistic encounter between phantasm and voice.* I shall straightaway give a name to this sound spilling out, as it were, from the dream and from which, I believe, this voidance (its resonance) is effectively masked by the circling fetishes of desire. (For similar reasons, this circulation around the object that never touches its center suggests that the object can never be reached because of its enigmatic nature, which is why blackness plays the role of envoy here, or tribal emissary, standing in for an idea that awaits a response that can be heard and felt but which had no signification for Mlle B. as a child.) What terrifies, of course, is deeply ambiguous: the circling sounds might get too close to the phantasm, making what is silent both audible and visible, but if these circles fail to protect Mlle B. from directly confronting the horror of the black object, they might also render visible the grounds of the fetish by which the imago of the Negro is being *heard*, in the dark, late at night.

Again, Mlle B.'s negrophobia is a fantasy to which she is subjected (and subjects herself), not through childish reminiscence but through its shadowy double—the emotive modes of a broadcast through which she vainly searches for the lost object; it is because this sound has no mediation that its *signifiance* is all the more disembodied and its enunciation uncannily amplified by hallucination. These circles are perhaps, precisely and less paradoxically than they seem, the inner truth of an enjoyment whose inner syncopation cannot itself be heard, but can only be performed through the distorting fetishism (of blackness), and this is its echoing *signifiance* from which there is no respite.

Thus we can see, in these radio broadcasts, all the features by which racism turns into a style of compulsive listening (Fanon calls it a hallucinosis), the tenacious form of its fetishism, the perverse fantasy through which it circles: in short, everything that is in the service of closing the gap between reality and fantasy, everything that bears directly on the ideological, oedipal alibis by which the *colon* sees him- or herself as a precarious (in the sense of exposed) object fallen into a black abyss. The violence of this "music" is the echo of an entirely phantasmatic beat, the space where fetishes germinate from within the wild swamps and voluptuous sounds of jungle signifiers, by which whiteness becomes effectively heard in its difference and identity, but only by succumbing to the ceaseless waves by which blackness resounds. For nothing can defend us from the deleterious rhythms of such *jouissance*. After such an experience, is it any wonder that shudders of passion should occur with the mere appearance of these circles, acting as the representative double of those abstract, disjointed movements by which the white self expires in African sound?

All of which shows that it is not very accurate to talk of blackness as a repressed stimulus to anxiety of the subject—the image of the black, more than ever, continues to be informed by a negrophobic structure. In fact, it is not even the presence of blackness that counts, for neither its corporeality nor its presence seems pertinent (a fetish may only comprise a single signified, thanks to repression, and it is this signified that is put in relation with the fetish). What are the functions of the black imago with regard to the (twofold) signified of fetishism and delusion? There appear to be two:

loss and *commemoration*. In order to demonstrate them, let us conclude by taking a look at what Fanon has to say on racial fetishism more generally, beginning first with the analyses begun in *Black Skin, White Masks*. Here is the key passage on the fetishism of representation in which the phobic object is *itself* the real fetish, rather than what makes it representable:

The choice of the phobic object is . . . *overdetermined* [*surdéterminé*]. This object does not come at random out of the void of nothingness; in some situation it has previously evoked an affect in the patient. His phobia is the latent presence of this affect at the root of his world; there is an organization that has been given a form. For the object, naturally, need not be there, it is enough that somewhere it *exist*: it is a possibility. This object is endowed with evil intentions and with all the attributes of a malefic power. In the phobic, affect has a priority that defies all rational thinking. As we can see, the phobic is a person who is governed by the laws of rational prelogic and affective prelogic: methods of thinking and feeling that go back to the age at which he experienced the event that impaired his security.[23]

Why is the phobic object *surdéterminé*? To explain this *overdetermination*, Fanon again takes the example of a childish object whose affect is then organized into a fantasized form. In fact, if we go back to the case of Mlle B., we saw there an example of how a painful past event makes itself felt and then acquires form through the belated truths of negrophobia. We also saw how, despite this reading, the rhythm of the tam-tams produced an anxiety owing to their excitation, their power and energy, but it was an anxiety that had no signification for Mlle B.; she was unable to make sense of it the first time she felt it. Is it by chance that a black object is chosen and then manifests itself as a representation to be defended against? Fanon's answer is unequivocal: the *presence* of the black object, in reality, is not necessary for it to have a malefic affect; it has no purpose other than to show and show itself as a possibility.

What Fanon is describing here is a kind of reciprocal and insurmountable exchange between affect and traumatic idea that need not have a reference in reality to be effective. It is no less evident that phobia awakens not so much a dissimulation of the subject as a splintering or dispersal of identity, one that is the consequence of the void (the nothingness that is Fanon's example here) deconstituting the subject's psychical reality. What is vital to Fanon is that the myth of the Negro that organizes negrophobic identity appears to be *needed*: the imposition of a form on the nothingness lying at the seat of anxiety is not sufficient to render that anxiety tangible, or representable, but it is enough to bring into being its possibility as an appearance, whose form can then act as a reflection of the self rather than its radical destitution (witness in this respect Fanon's emphasis on phobia as an attempt to give the void form as a representational possibility). Let us say that in the colony, negrophobia reveals obsessive ideas displaced along the lines of several associations and split between various *Vorstellungen*: the *nègre* is evil, filthy, dirty, cannibalistic, etc. Such would be the reason why the black object is overdetermined. I have already said that Fanon's reading of the circles points in this more structural direction, and that despite his ostensible emphasis on the history and vicissitudes of past events. A glance at Freud's text on fetishism suggests that the relation between the truth of castration concealed by the fetish-veil and this veil itself is always ambiguous, and precisely whenever the relation between affect and object-choice reveals an uncertainty between drive and object, libido and helpless other-directed dependence.

And, it would seem, it is exactly in this sense that Fanon picks up on the role of anxiety in the forming of racial phobias, the alibi that underpins the denial, the phantasm that is also the site of a specular condensation and a disavowal of knowledge. Fanon insists that in the investments and displacements of negrophobia, which of course combine fear and desire, the dominant motif is a fetishistic commitment to the other's *jouissance*. Thus, in Chapter Seven of *Black Skin, White Masks*, explaining how, on the basis of stereotypes condensing the black to a genital object, the white subject finds itself impelled, forced to lose all bearing, subjected to a *jouissance* threatening to engulf it, Fanon says this:

When one reads this passage [Michel Cornot's *Martinique* (1948) in which is written: "The black man's sword is a sword. When he has thrust it into your wife, she has really felt something."] and lets oneself go, that is, when one abandons oneself to the movement of images, one no longer perceives the negro, but a member: the negro is eclipsed. He is made a member. He *is* a penis.[24]

Here begins a key sequence from affect to obsessional idea, which then comes to be stereotypically regarded as the true manifestation of that idea. The enigmatic, and most disturbing, aspect of this passage is how the connection between idea and affect turns on the feelings associated with a black man's penis, whose erotic appeal need not be actually felt for its unconscious representation to be felt as exemplary, in the end, of what it really means to *feel* something, beyond reserve, constraint, status, or pleasure.

Fanon finds dozens of examples of this fetishistic substitution, in whose movement the black object represents a tantalizing series of libidinal-

ontological possibilities, a stand-in for the *jouissance* whose proxy and meaning it stereotypically is. Which is why he also says that the *nègre* does not so
much represent a choice of subject as a choice of object: the sexual myth of
the black penis does not add or subtract anything ideologically, for its significance is simply that of a presentation (*Darstellung*) that expresses nothing except the process, the striving and effort of *Darstellung* itself, i.e., as an
active power of presencing: the *nègre is* a penis. In this rhetorical example of
hypotyposis, Fanon distinguishes between blackness and the fetishistic belief that renders it the very image of copulative being, in which the copula is
less a question of truth or metaphor than of a literal condensation of being
into sex, and one whose meaning is as much metaphysical as it is social.

If it is true that the phobic object forms itself *out of* the stereotype (with
the ambiguity that that implies—the stereotype as the material from which
desire is built, and the stereotype as the disfiguring of desire by culture),
only to find the stereotype returning to haunt this fantasy of the black object at its root—then it is reasonable to suppose that the stereotype, the
one that returns to the ego its own murderous-shameful attachment, is in
fact *standing for* a fear of disintegration that is the originary trace of the
other within us. And if the contingency and violence of the stereotype is
already occupied by the returning violence of the ego, Fanon makes it clear
that the ego's neurosis just *is* where the stereotype returns—and the stereotype just *is* the real occupying the ego. The enemy attacking the ego from
within and against which it seeks to indemnify itself using phobia is, then,
the ego, for whom the contingency and violence of the other is intolerable
precisely because it originates in its own fetishistic attachments.

We must therefore distinguish the determination of the fetish-as-
stereotype from the fantasies that sustain it, which derive pleasure from
the mortification so consecrated, but which leave us undisturbed in our
everyday relationships, allowing us to explore our relations to feelings of
insecurity, but only in the absence of any crisis of self-relation or dissolution. The fetish is our way of enjoying—or consuming—our own acts of
sublation. And this concealed unconcealment is both enjoyed and, in the
end, necessarily repeated.[25] We are fetishists not in our relation to forms
of appearance, but in relation to what is always missing from appearance,
which we metaphorically assume to be masked. We act *as if* this absence is
inscribed on the surface of appearance but its meaning lies elsewhere. Racial fetishism, in other words, points to an illusion at work in social reality
itself: people are racial fetishists in how they act, and not necessarily in how

they think. If the fetish is a defense against uncertainty, a defense crucial to the belief that it is possible to draw a veil over the (misrecognized) implications of castration, this is because psychically it represents a cultural disciplining of (egoic) enjoyment through (racial) splitting and displacement. Politically, fetishism leaves us unfree within our representations, but frees us from the presuppositions and outcomes (the compensations and the punishments) of mutual exposure to ourselves and others.

Herein lies the drama of racial fetishism—the factor that exasperates it is a precarity resistant to facts or knowledge. The same must also be said of negrophobia, if the preceding analysis of it is correct, i.e., the fantasy that is itself defined by the fantasy that something is missing, a deprivation that will have to be maliciously acted out against those assumed to have it, or who have stopped us from accessing it in the past (immigrants and blacks), and who will therefore have to be punished or obliterated on that object's behalf. We may now assert this unreservedly: such fantasy is resistant, prelogical, and profoundly malicious. But if, as Fanon shows, negrophobia has been incorporated into all aspects of social life, we also need to understand the social honor of its worship, the pleasures it solicits, and then the adorations that shape and create it, of which we shall speak at greater length below.

II. STEREOTYPE-AS-FETISH

Depending on the ideational representations with which they are connected, racial stereotypes can, as already indicated, cover a range of fetishistic representatives. In *The Wretched of the Earth*, for example, Fanon writes: "you are rich because you are white, you are white because you are rich."[26] The complicity revealed here between race and capital suggests that race is a fundamental element of the fetish-character of social life, as Fanon himself suggests: "This is why Marxist analysis should always be slightly stretched every time we have to do with the colonial problem."[27] Slightly stretched? To Marx's emphasis on the "fetish of capital," which sees in the objective form of the commodity an embodied social relation but one displaced onto its object-like [*gegenständlich*] form, Fanon opposes the obverse effect whereby the commodity produced through work, as capital, is first rendered possible through a racialized chain of chiasmic equivalence: you are rich because you are white, you are white because you are rich.[28]

From this chiasmic relation, Fanon inverts Marx's own inversion [*Vertauschung*] of the fetish-character of the commodity-form as the "mystical," "phantasmagoric" form possessed by the social character of labor.[29] Instead of objects veiled by the social conditions of production, in brief, Fanon suggests that race is the fetish by which money as a value-form appears as the equivalence between whiteness and wealth. What gives racism its fetish-character stems, therefore, from how whiteness sets the limits and boundaries of expropriated labor in the form of capital; instead of leading to "natural" forms of objectification and alienation, it causes racism to appear solely as the form-positing, value-positing, equalizing work of value; instead of the social form of exchange value, it is the fungibility of whiteness that vouchsafes all other forms their commensurability as exchange values; and, above all, instead of veiling objects with commodity-language, it is racial historical life that is inverted in the money-form and its symbolism of a life worthy of life as against one *without* value. In other words, the mystical language of commodities is misrecognized because it is inverted, but this inversion is due to the racialized incarnation of material, social life, in which racism veils or inverts the historically determined production of labor.

In both instances, whiteness equals money, and the whiter one is, the more one can be credited with having money and the greater one's surplus value, but in the case where exchange value is exacted, whiteness is also taken to represent the producedness that produces itself as non-transferable value, so transforming itself into the transcendental equivalence of the money-form, while at the same time positing itself as both the abstract and speculative equivalence of capital. Whence Fanon's singular conclusion, that race relations are the true secret of exchange relations, an interpretation that leads him to argue that the secret of the commodity is equivalent to the relation between whiteness and the money-form, where what appears to be equal only appears as a chiasmic equality (in the categories of commodity and capital) whereby whiteness is the pure form of fungible life and all the other "races" natural commodities to be used up and disposed of at will.In this rhetoric of double illusion, in which the emphasis is not on how capital relations are naturalized under the guise of immediacy but, instead, on how money and race both come to exhibit a language of capital accumulation, our conclusion is that whilst the value of labor does not ensue from a direct ratio of racial worth, it nevertheless does follow that the effect of racism in the colony, that is, the co-exchangeability of whiteness and wealth, is circumscribed by a language of fetishistic inversion, as Fanon's example abundantly proves.

Money, preeminently in the form of racial capital, not only begets whiteness, as credit, it simultaneously produces blackness as a state of debt that is valueless in itself, and so never redeemable. Thus, without any logical contradiction, we can conceive of a political economy that relies exclusively on whiteness as a kind of transcendental value, and one that represents, regardless of the kinds of labor, the formal determinant of raced wealth. In Fanon's example, whiteness is envisaged as having the right and power to give itself surplus value, and never more so than in the world of capital accumulation and wealth, as if the appearance of being white were enough to confer on individuals (regardless of their class, race or gender) the *appearance* of wealth. I have already said that what defines racial fetishism is not what it veils but the speculative character of its veiling, with people acting as if, despite all evidence to the contrary, the language of difference were objectively a language of nature securely preserved for ever. But, as Fanon points out, in the rendering of the language of exchange through the figures and tropes of race, what appears in inverted form (what Marx in particular calls the inversion of labor and commodity) must first be expressed through a language of racial fetishism, as if race were the language and soul of the commodity and whiteness its constitutive value-form.

The durability of racial sovereignty in the colony, as *The Wretched of the Earth* very clearly teaches, depends chiefly upon the language of fetishism, but it is not so easy to ascertain why commodity-language is so consistently racialized in the colony. As a way of approaching this distinction, let us therefore return to the trope that seems almost synonymous with racial fetishism: the stereotype. You are rich because you are white, you are white because you are rich: the language of racial capital not only speaks through the figure of chiasmus, but its thought-form is governed by an equivalence that imprints the time of labor with the historical character of racial value and imprints the relations amongst producers and consumers with the stereotypical character of an essential truth.

But why are people inclined to give stereotypical speech social validity as objective truth? Fanon's answer is both semiotic and psychopolitical. Anyone with any experience of the terrors and anxieties of difference can be seduced by the language of stereotypes, which offers both the rule by which others are to be judged and the promise of rule by which the alien and unknown can be made representable and so ruled over; indeed, to the extent that a person knows that everything summed up and judged in this way is imaginary, this does not prevent him or her from believing in the stereotypical truth of certain representations, and precisely because they offer the pleasure of both producing and knowing difference as such, and regardless of whether this "knowledge" is a mystification or a secret. The racial stereotype seduces not because it defends a secret, but because it represents, in fantasized form, the power of a disavowed sameness, whose image is indifferent to the contradictions offered it by experience and social reality. The stereotype is thus both direct and indirect: metaphorically, it designates difference via a structure of political antagonism (the other is always *essentially* other); literally, it sums up collective opinions in an absolute, totalizing antinomy (by making present, and conventional, concepts by which the other can be judged and condemned: *Ah, everything would be different if only they weren't so different*). Without that part of the other, say, identified as the point of exclusion, the greater to effect a sense of inner coherence and rightness, the values and standards that we imagine define us cannot be made effectively universal or sovereign. Like the rhetoric of chiasmic equivalence it produces and is, the stereotype allows us to substitute facetious truths for irresolute anxieties and to disavow the precariousness of modern social life for the claims and pleasures of ill will. It is through the stereotype that one's legitimacy in the world is given; but it is *as* a stereotype that one is white and rich. From this point of view, racist ideology is already immanent to the inverse fiction of the commodity form, and the stereotype is the mythic form of its projection.

It might be objected at this point that Fanon's reading of racial capital is, if anything, too abstract or totalizing, that he loses sight of how this transcendental fetishistic racism acquires economic or political power or affects material development or social change. This could be called a fetishistic trope within Fanon's reading of culture, although that is of course its symptom. Nothing at first indicates that Fanon's work is any more arrested, fixated, or fetishistic than the speculative concept of fetishism itself. Yet, for many Marxist critics, Fanon's interpretation of racial capital remains too psychoanalytical and phenomenological, that is, Fanon is too quick to interpret race as historically presupposed by the social and political preconditions of modern subjectivity. An example of this critique is Cedric Robinson's 1993 essay, "The appropriation of Frantz Fanon," which accuses Fanon of concealing his own petit-bourgeois affiliations behind a psychological analysis of black alienation.[30] Robinson contrasts the "petit-bourgeois stink" of Fanon's early work, "concealed by a psychologistic discourse," to the anti-bourgeois critique of the later work.[31] He insists that Fanon's specific class identity is the true secret of his analysis of racial mis-recognition, but at the same time he leaves no doubt that this secret has never appeared other than in the mystifying and alienated form of psycho-analysis. He propagates an ontology of authentic critique but objects that it has heretofore only been possible to know Fanonism as an ontology of disavowal and hence only as pseudology and class delusion. But doesn't this language of concealment itself conceal what is most troubling about Fanon's critique of Marxian theoretical fetishism? Isn't this focus on class biography itself wholly psychological in presenting Fanon's upbringing as the cause (and not the consequence) of class identity, and one that presumably remains undisguised by the fetishistic value-form of race? In attempting to invert an inversion—"that Fanon in his revolutionary work mistook a racial subject for his own class"—it seems that Robinson can only disavow the reciprocal interrelation of its terms.[32] Robinson's reading is, unquestionably, a powerful attack on what he views as a certain postmodern return to Fanon, and is fairly typical of a tendency in Fanonian criticism that uses biography to divide up Fanon's oeuvre into a supposedly prepolitical, petit-bourgeois period and a later, more revolutionary period, with the latter often chastised as not Marxist enough.[33]

There is no need to survey all of these criticisms here, as the general complaint against Fanon seems to be that he uses race merely to invert the antinomies of modern life rather than speculatively renegotiate them. Instead of seeing the stereotype as the ideological mask of power and capital, Fanon undoes his more psychoanalytic-dialectic insights by insisting that whiteness, as the general transcendental equivalent of the money-form, is also the universal measure for how wealth is historically determined as a fetish object. In any case, Fanon's reading of the stereotype mirrors that of his reading of racial capital: in both the *cause* appears inversely as the *consequence*, and the secret of the commodity-form is nothing more than a racial mask that conceals nothing behind it. The things that are being confused here are Fanon's method of exposition and his actual reading of fetishistic illusion. The problem is not, in my view, one of insufficient dialectics, or an inability to grasp the real that escapes all appearance even though it can only be known *qua* appearance. Rather, what has been systematically misread is the subtlety of Fanon's point: namely that race continues to be misrecognized as both a transcendental form—of power and economy, civil society and institutions—*and* the singular incarnation of how subjects whiten themselves as fetish objects (the misrecognitions defining that decidability always found on the side of identity).

To anticipate my wider argument: Fanon scholars have tended to misread his relation to Marxism and psychoanalysis precisely because in his reading of the stereotype Fanon presents a situation of racial ideology that causes a major upheaval in Marxian notions of class consciousness, which assume that it is the relations of production that prompt men to act, to which they are blind, rather than accepting that these relations, in the colony, afford nothing more than a fetishistic misrecognition of whiteness as the universal equivalent of real and abstract value, as Fanon notes. But here we should sharpen the point of what Fanon means by the inversion of economic life by species-being, or bio-politics. Fanon stands up to the orthodox Marxian reductionism of race to class by the various European communist parties of his time, with his emphasis throughout on the racial hegemony that pertains to all aspects of life in the colony. Commenting at length on why the native bourgeoisie and proletariat are imperfect counterparts to their European equivalents, on whom they remain parasitic and dependent, Fanon judges the forces of neocolonialism to be racially fetishistic in the way that whiteness is identified—in its institutional form and representation—as the only legitimate form of existence, which is why the use of certain Marxian categories remains false and "useless" for addressing the internal nature of colonialism. And while noting that these categories remain ambiguous in terms of their political reality, Fanon judges that most invocations of Marx in decolonialism remain unduly fetishistic in their theoretical critique. This fetishism mirrors that of the native bourgeoisie who, however nativist or nationalist their politics, remain slavishly imitative in their attitudes to European concepts, so historically typifying the not-yet-attained, wholly wretched, petrified state of the colonial *Dasein*. In other words, what makes the native bourgeoisie and proletariat overwhelmingly a hindrance to the future national consciousness and its epochal new speech is a fetishism at the level of belief, which prevents them from joining the people and realizing their potential as the *anti-mimetic reinvention* of social life, an invention that challenges the language of neocolonial mimicry and its psychopolitical immiseration. What is radical about the wretched is not their economic role but their challenge to the creation of racial life as value. Even if the rural lumpenproletariat are alienated and dispossessed, they are not so simply as laborers, says Fanon, but as the *Dasein* whose fate is one of a violent singularity. This critique of the primacy of the proletariat, which has often been misread as a vitalism, has troubled many Marxist critics, though they often fail to recall how this presentation of the wretched, as already noted, proceeds along the lines of an anti-fetishistic analysis of life, value, history, and conflict. This would seem to indicate that the unmasking of Fanon's error is itself, like the fetish, at once an assertion and a denial, and one that remains in thrall to illusion and untruth, but one misrecognized as such. The real task then is not to decide whether the production of material life is the sole determinant of racial inequality, but to grasp how the racially exploitative relations of colonialism compel people to identify wealth by race, yet all the while presuming that this limit to the money-form does not exist. Consequently, the inescapable conclusion that "in the colonies the economic sub-structure is also a super-structure. The cause is the consequence; you are rich because you are white, white because you are rich," does not simply mean that race determines class, but that both are deranged through fetishistic consciousness, which is why Marx must be slightly stretched instead of ignored or subordinated.[34]

Let me simplify this quite complex issue for the sake of brevity. What does Fanon say of the stereotype? He tells us that the stereotype is always the seeming reprise of a timeless enunciation: "that's the way they are," but by means of a reflexive, cultural awareness. If that's the way they always are, that is because people deceive themselves and others concerning their relation to others in their subjective life. The stereotype, like the fetish, allows these relations to be performed as if they were naturally generated relations rather than phantasmagoric projections of social alienation. In these inversions and substitutions there is a kind of "mummification" and "harden[ing]" of the psyche and cultural life. In the stereotype-as-fetish, thought itself becomes petrified, and it is hard to decide what is truth and what is deception, what is real and what is fantasy. Truth has been disguised by the typical, the typical is the facetious disguise of truth, and what has been lost sight of is the road or pathway that leads from "individual thinking" to "the framework of a culture."[35]

This last deviation—from rigidified thought to the rigidities of culture—is a perfect description of the stereotype as a logic of illusion: a logic that, by means of fetishistic projection, ends up not segregating the different from the same but performing what is in fact the amortization of cultural life: the loss of a future-formative language brought about by the subject's entombment in an empty, history-less, commodified present. The stereotype thus enacts, in its own temporality, the loss of animation that it situates in the imaginary representations of what is missing or visibly absent from others.

Because of these various confusions in the concepts of commodified life and racial fetishism, critics of Fanon have been drawn to and yet remain reticent before those texts that affirm decolonialism as a tabula rasa that refuses the traditional rhetoric of class consciousness. The phrase "the cause is the consequence" deserves further inquiry in this regard, for it affects how Fanon reads fetishism with reference to both the Freudian and Marxian traditions. Although we do not have the space here to do an extensive reading of these traditions, I think Fanon's distinct contribution can be shown plainly enough by taking a brief look at two pivotal readings of his work on fetishism and violence. The question that offers the most to think about is how decolonialism unveils the fetishistic logic that imposes itself on all aspects of institutional life in the colony. If it is as white that the bourgeois promise of wealth and respectability presents itself as the only constant and historical value, how is it possible to attain an attitude that is not merely anti-white but, in the most critical and dialectical sense, permits the *colonisé* to invert the convertibility of whiteness into value in its capital and political functions? It is only the rural lumpenproletariat, Fanon says, that permits us, in respect to labor time and value, to take a decisive position re whiteness as the social promise of honor and wealth. All other social groups are either caught up in the deluded transcendence of the white money-form or buy into the supernatural quality of a nativist spiritual economy, in which the value of spirit possession speaks of a different, but more primal, ecstatic economy of surplus value and transfiguration. Fanon even ventures to say that this black economy of spirit is on the same side as whiteness as commodity, rather than deconstructing it, in that it continues to uphold the magical superstructure as the cause, rather than the alienated consequence, of social life in the colony. To say that the magic economy is still on the side of fetishism is thus to say at least two things with regards to both the sexual and the commodity fetish:

1. Unlike Freud, who sometimes implies that the fetish arises in response to a *perceived* deficit, in Fanon's discussion the racial fetish cannot be determined according to the categories of cause and effect, for its structure is *nachträglich*, as explained previously. It is a mistake to view cultural imposition (that is, the affect of colonial racism) as cause or effect, for its structure follows that of a phobic prelogic; indeed, it is for

this reason that Fanon's reading of the stereotype-as-fetish appeals in fact to the unconscious affect of a cultural fantasy that is pre-oedipal. The stereotype attests to a provenance that can never be causally grounded in a rationalist conception, for it testifies to a distinct impress or *causa* that proceeds *nachträglich*, or as a repetition after the event, after the violence or authority of the colonial state, as Fanon's example of the dreamlife of the Malagasy amply proves. If the stereotype can be found at the navel of the dream, then the unconscious itself can potentially be possessed by the violent work of culture, at least when the events and details at work include war, mass murder, and torture. There is one thing for certain: in the dreams of the *colonisé*, the dreamwork has been interrupted and dislocated by the real, by *"phantasmes réels"* (real fantasies).[36] This would seem to indicate that negrophobia is not a transformation of latent, unconscious content, but the ideological dream-work of the stereotype. As Vicky Lebeau asks, "Is this really an interruption of psychoanalysis, or is it to move psychoanalysis along a new track, towards the real fantasies which erupt in sleep to mirror the world in which they find their time and place?"[37]

We should note especially, here, that the importance of Fanon's theory of real fantasy for his analysis of the fetish-as-stereotype has yet to be fully grasped. Let me suggest that it is precisely Fanon's refusal to lose sight of real fantasy, whether as surplus or as limit (and it is important to remember that Fanon begins from the idea of a double illusion: stereotypes both give form to the world and manifest the experiential antinomies of modern consciousness), that he relates to a distinctly marked relationship to guilt and indebtedness. "I know that I am guilty, but I do not know of what," he writes. The stereotype, Fanon suggests, culminates in an imago that is experienced immanently, but that imago faithfully corresponds to how modern subjects find themselves caught up in a real phantasmatic world. "And so it is not I who make a meaning for myself, but it is the meaning that is already there, pre-existing, waiting for me."[38] In other words, this story of a self discovered in the afterlife of ideology inevitably becomes the story of the self's own fetishistic self-relation ("my bad nigger's misery, my bad nigger's teeth, my bad nigger's hunger"[39]). What to say about this, if not that the modern raced subject is haunted by meanings that are both spectral and hegemonic, meanings in which he is never innocent but the guilty embodiment of a hegemonic struggle? A struggle that is not over something hidden or camouflaged, but over how feelings of a fantasized lack themselves reflect the work of ideology?

Against, therefore, the concept of the fetish suggesting a lack free from fetishism, a lack that is not as it were castrated, the Fanonian fetish refers to how civil society and the state both reflect a world in which blackness is singularly lacking. Thus, black guilt arises not in response to a having had, but from a never having that spectrally precedes it and to which it remains permanently indebted. That blacks can seemingly become complicit with the history of being fetish objects is thus tied to a pre-oedipal sense of a deficiency, which, Fanon says, has the same affect as the deficitary sense that blackness *is* lacking or missing something, hence the example of the *not* or *n'est pas*, and the guilt incurred because of it. (I will explain this more fully in Chapter Seven, "The Condemned.")

There may be something to gain, therefore, by returning to the idea of the stereotype as the "royal road" to the cultural unconscious, for this journey is always a detour, not from appearance to essence, but from the racism of civil society to political life and institutions in which the black is always the form of *not* being, the inheritor of a genealogically enforced deficiency that is not-yet.

2. With these few words on guilt can be found a clue to Fanon's late thinking on the political, or at least the precise moment, if we can identify it in the posthumously published *The Wretched of the Earth*, at which "violence," as a tentative name for the decolonial subject as such, breaks or ruptures the fetishistic perspective within which colonialism has always, constitutively, attempted to think and control native insurgency, and the ways in which that break or rupture leaves traces in contemporary texts (which continue to struggle with Fanon's call for a liberated, non-fetishistic form of thinking).

If colonial racism works through a system based on indebting—your guilt is the reason that you are (b)lack—the effect of decolonial violence is to affirm and give meaning to an initiative tabula rasa where the black deficit of being falls away. Decolonial violence thus embodies a force that is neither owing nor conserving and that goes beyond the debt economy where all surplus value aptly becomes white. Hence, decolonial violence is not a struggle for recognition nor reformation, be it social democratic or socialist, but a movement to invent the economic and psychopolitical structures of the colony. For this reason, the violence that transforms the laws and commands of the racist state (which as we have shown consists solely in a racist form of indebting) thereby allows both the *colon* and the *colonisé* to confront each other as subjects free of debt. Whence, notes

Fanon, the infusing power of the revolutionary demand for a tabula rasa without mediation: "the replacing of a certain 'species' of men by another 'species' of men . . . [in] a total, complete, and absolute substitution."[40] It is a demand that intervenes in a general state of disorder, and one that in the pursuit of liberation acts without guarantees. There is no state of pre-paredness here or mass mobilization of opinion: the people's radical deci-sion involves a refusal (of the traditional political forms of mobilization) and a risk (to existence) as they struggle to abolish the colonial system by turning its violence against itself. That is, even if colonial civil war results in a collapse of state and civil society, it is not this that makes violence nec-essary; pitched against the forces of the state, law-founding violence is the population's only vehicle as it battles for survival. Further, the only way the people can bring to an end the racial debt economy—the guilt of depen-dence, the cult of racial piety—is to challenge the guilt relations of racial capital by becoming the enemy who is guiltless, and thus an enemy who sees no distinction between civil war and an expenditure that is without value. For this reason liberation is identified with those subjects whom Fanon calls the "wretched": since they come from extreme forms of indebt-edness without, however, the promise of redemption, and are located nei-ther within the system nor outside it but at its outer- and innermost limit, Fanon is of the opinion that they have the least to lose. As such, their vio-lence is not violent (in the political, teleological sense of the word), but the bringing into being of justice, since it alone defines the people's wish to go beyond the violence it (stereotypically) represents. Even so, the fact of the matter is that the wretched emerge at those points where the system of white self-accreditation is most exposed to its ruination. For the wretched neither hope to be white nor feel guilt over being black, and as will be clear from what I am about to say, wretchedness defines a state from which no salvation is expected, or prayed for, and unveils nothing but the credit and debts by which whiteness determines surplus value.

Here we should note that this reading of violence has itself been sub-ject to many violent readings. The scandal seems to lie in the way Fanon undebts himself by offering an account of violence that relies neither on reason or consent, nor on the traditions of thinking liberation as a strate-gic question of means and ends. Equally, some of the most violent repu-diations of Fanon's theory have come from those unable, or unwilling, to see how he thinks violence outside of the political orthodoxy of Western democracy. It follows that the concern with Fanonian violence remains profoundly suspicious of its claim to be a ruination of the deficit through which blackness annihilates itself. Critics such as Hannah Arendt (herself no particular friend of Fanon, precisely on the grounds of her refusal to re-think the political in terms of violence—we might say in fact that Arendt, like Fanon's Marxist critics, sees a certain turning away from the political at this point) accuse Fanon of nihilism (making no mention of the racial guilt economy), whence perhaps the attraction of looking to Arendt for evidence of why Fanonian violence continues to *trouble* the teleology of the political.

In Arendt's *On Violence*, Fanon is condemned for going too far in his "glorification" of violence and for not going far enough in his defense of politics as the legitimate sphere of social antagonism.[41] In a reading that ex-pounds "power" as the legitimate condition of the political and "violence" as its illegitimate cousin, Arendt describes Fanon's views as pre-political, instrumentalist, and anti-democratic. Leaving aside, for the moment, the violence of Arendt's own opening exclusion (of violence from the politi-cal), she starts from the view that violence is the resort of the powerless and, as such, represents the lowest common denominator of political ac-tion. Even if violence becomes intrinsic to the operation of power—as in the systematic use of torture in Algeria—Arendt is careful to distinguish the violence that sustains power from the violence that erupts in force (the "'mad fury' that turned dreams into nightmares for everybody").[42] Arendt consequently condemns Fanonism as a nihilistic example of modern anti-political thought.

The vehemence with which Arendt dismisses Fanon and those whom she views as his successors—i.e. the black student protest movements of the 1960s, which she singles out for particular censure—leads her to conclude that black (but not exclusively) armed struggle has very limited political validity. This is why, on the occasions where she discusses *black* political vi-olence, all black freedom struggles are equally condemned as *non-political* (which seems to mean nonwhite here); Arendt is therefore unable to ac-knowledge Fanon's distinction between a violence that reproduces racism as capital and the fugitive, less determinate violence that ruins law and the whole administration of the state precisely because it begins in the ruin-ation of black guilt and indebtedness. That is, despite her failure to grasp Fanon's thinking on violence as thought, or as the radical reinvention of the relation between democracy and violence I believe it to be, Arendt, far from erasing violence from the political, renders it immanently facetious to modern racial statehood, thereby putting the very separation of means and ends under erasure.

A closer look at *The Wretched of the Earth* will make this point clearer. In *The Wretched of the Earth*, violence is figured through the "wretched" (Fanon calls them "the gangrene ever present at the heart of colonial domination"[43]), who are invoked as something more than a pure opposite to power (Hegel's "rabble," Marx's *lazzaroni*) and something less than the embodiment of the revolutionary end of history as regulative Idea.[44] As the "sign of [colonialism's] irrevocable decay," the wretched represent the establishment of a radical element that makes possible the anti-colonist revolution.[45] Crucially, they do not exist as a pure heterogeneity to the system, but denote a ruination and decay at the heart of the colony. This moment of ruination is, for the colonizers, a kind of waking dream or nightmare, in so far as they are terrified and astonished to learn that what they regarded as bare essential life has grasped its non-being as a value in itself and precisely because of its secret ontological, political-economic valuelessness. Having taken control of the "ways of life and thought of the native" and realigned everyday life with "violence in its natural state," the severity of colonial rule prospered by fostering the illusion of native life as regressive, property-less, and passively indebted. Indeed, there was no reason to question the stereotype. The shock inflicted by the resistance of the wretched therefore acts like a fissure in the time of the political and its racist culture, and one promising to be all-consuming.[46] Fanon describes this shock as a baptism in which the realm of means and ends no longer has a referent (of debt or guilt) or end (in salvation), but proceeds through a generalized sense of disorder that cannot be represented as always already contracted (to the institutions and forms of law and the state).

We might therefore ask why Fanon's grasp of the wretched as a politically heterogeneous movement that exposes the racially repressed forms of capital is never addressed by Arendt. Indeed, by proceeding as if the separation of means and ends implied by the democratic need to reserve a nonphenomenal relation to the other (as being, as citizen) were universal, Arendt cannot grasp this subject who is *not yet*: the wretched who are suspended between life and death, universal and particular, rabble and proletariat, heterogeneity and self-differentiation. What goes missing in *On Violence* therefore is any sophisticated reading of how violence, *qua* states of emergency and historical crises in capital, ontologically grounds the wretched. Consequently, Arendt fails to grasp how that emergence comes to define a new transition or inner fissure of the state. As such, Fanon's exposition is dismissed as a dogmatic metaphysics of violence that, like Achilles's lance, "heal[s] the wound it has inflicted."[47] Thus, in the nature of its method and its movement, violence is supposedly Fanon's fetish.

A number of consequences flow from the tenor of this critique, and they all relate to the wretched as a new form of fidelity that literally rends the colonial phantasm, a rending that, we have already noted above, also sees the emergence of a new psychopolitics (what Fanon calls a "new humanism"). Here we should recall that Fanon's interest in psychoneuroses (at the Blida-Joinville and Charles-Nicolle hospitals) led him to see how the hypertrophy of colonial life was structured through and through by feelings of guilt or something akin to despair. The fact that the decolonial struggle didn't automatically animate the inanimate, the dead, or the petrified led Fanon to re-envision, perhaps for the first time in his clinical career, how the symptoms and affects produced by resistances at a time of total war activated a hard kernel of *jouissance* at the center of human being. So that this may be better understood, I will provide examples of this work in the following chapter, on "Desire and Law." Here I will restrict myself to a few general remarks. Firstly, the violence of revolutionary insurrection did not necessarily liberate people from feelings of being utterly guilty. Even if people chose to follow the politics of liberation for ethical or ideological reasons, they did not possess the ability to overcome the feelings of guilt emerging out of a sense of immanent ruination. For no sooner had they consulted Fanon than they underwent an "absolute depersonalization," defined by a sense of non-being that is itself preferred to the non-guilt by which they believed they could act as if nothing had happened. Fanon's analyses of these patients—guilty for not having felt guilt, including the right to murder and torture, and yet feeling nothing—reveal a concern with why the promise of liberation does not diminish the despair of non-being but on the contrary increases it, and at the expense of ego and identity. In the case of torture, perpetrators and victims were equally ignorant of why they were punished, as it were, for not possessing the right to punish; both the tortured and the torturers felt that they were under the domination of an ineffable guilt and that nothing could distinguish them in their desire for retribution. If a racial fetish was used to mask these feelings of equivalence and indebtedness, the wish to be liberated was never more vengeful than when the self tried to free itself from the fetishistic form of these racial obligations. But the fact that all believed that they could be liberated from guilt rendered them more, not less, subject to feeling guilty. For Fanon, what distinguishes these patients is not their political allegiances but how guilt is used for judgment and execution and how, through revolution, guilt is tasked with retribution and forgiveness. Or, as he wrote in "Colonial War and Mental Disorders," the final chapter of *The Wretched of the Earth*: "Total liberation is that which concerns all sectors of the personality. . . . When the nation stirs as a whole, the new man is not an *a posteriori* product of that nation; rather, he coexists with it and triumphs with it."[48]

Secondly, in comparing the wretched to a "total" capacity for representation otherwise denied by the colonial regime, Fanon's *The Wretched of the Earth* reveals how the colonial subject is trapped between an ability to think violence and the inability to resolve its dilemma without violence. What Fanon calls "absolute violence" thus sets aside the legitimacy of means and ends—the processes Arendt associates with the political—and reaches instead towards a politics of invention. To the extent that decolonization exposes and reverses French sovereign power, it remains inherently unstable and contradictory—pulled into two opposite directions at once. To the degree that the native population belongs to a world overshadowed by myths, dreams, and possession, its new energy could either regress or be recruited to new forms of mystical authority or capital-spiritual indebtedness. Inversely, to the degree that the colonial bourgeoisie substitutes its authority for the anxiety of retribution, the wretched could succumb to the temptations of an old repression. It is key, as Fanon recognizes, that, ethically and politically, there needs to be a new culture of judgment beyond the debt economies of (spiritual-nativist) capital. If radical democracy is to emerge, the wretched must be rethought by opposing the historical diremptions of civil society and the nation-state and by cultivating their heterogeneity beyond the Manichean logic of race. If there is something the wretched are not, it is a neocolonial measure for mastery. Fanon compares them to the lumpenproletariat, but this term is not entirely accurate either. Once the Algerian civil war had erupted, historic events in the city and countryside soon overtook such conceptions. To capture the revolutionary situation, Fanon speaks of an "authentic birth in a pure state": he is careful to say, however, that this birth may, without guarantees and at the cost of losing inner consistency, produce a new sociology and aesthetic culture, a new eschatology and politics.[49] But there is always risk, and the outcome cannot be known in advance.

And indeed this would help us make sense of what happens when the wretched insist that a new kind of heterogeneity is instated between statist violence and the reorganization of the political—but whose residue is not that of the fetish (with its petrification of cultural life). Hence Fanon's view of the revolution as an "intense dramatization" in which there is no preparedness and no self-interested calculation.[50] The desire to leave behind the fetishism of self-identity here merges with the discovery of a national self-consciousness.

At this point we should also consider, finally, why revolutionary violence for Fanon is not a vitalism. In "Spectral Nationality," Pheng Cheah describes Fanon's position as a vitalism seeking to reanimate the "techno-phantomatic object" of the state via the people.[51] Violence is what separates the *Dasein* of this petrified state from the ideal of national consciousness, and so provides the *means* to resuscitate the people after the reign of "dead capital": "The state can be inspirited by the nation-people precisely because it is the work of the people that has become estranged or alienated from the people during the process of externalization or objection."[52] Again in keeping with Fanon, this imaging of the state as a corpselike exteriority that, by analogy, requires reanimation by the people overlooks how the inert and apparent is not merely the phenomenal guise of some repressed vitalism somehow immanent to the people, but the fetishistic inversion of racial capital. By contrast, if the nation-people is meant to animate what is undead, or transfuse what is recognized as abortively living, what gets lost here is how nation and people are both inspirited by the wretched—the acausal force that cannot be sublated or appeased, and whose deficit is neither indebted nor fetishistic (and so neither a means to in-spiritation nor the effect of a techno-exorcism of the nation-state). For this reason, in the wake of national liberation, on whose outcome depends the whole postcolonial future of the people, it becomes impossible to tell whether the wretched will continue to support the revolution or decide to oppose it. But again, if the colonial state is corpselike, then the wretched must be recognized as that gangrenous presence already inhabiting the possibility of any future nationhood as a ruination-to-come, and one whose consequence is historically undecidable. For the singular character of the wretched is to corrode all conceptions of colonial power, whether disguised as nativist right, bourgeois sovereignty, or a contract to be redeemed against the postcolonial future.

Cheah's focus on spirit, among other things, reminds us that in the chapter on violence it is not only the state that is haunted by "maleficent spirits."[53] The people, too, are "the depository of maleficent powers."[54] This means, in consequence, that the state cannot be distinguished from the people in terms of spirit possession, or in terms of what is living or dead, or in terms of demonic exorcism. Cheah speaks with the confidence of one who knows what is said to return, to haunt; that is, he speaks as someone who knows that they are no longer caught in illusion. However, who's to say that such insight is anything more than the illusion of having uncovered illusion? Who's to say that the contaminations of spirit—nativist, nationalist—are any more deluded than Western democracy?

Perhaps this is why Fanon does not oppose national consciousness to the nation-state but insists on "a permanent confrontation on the phantasmatic plane."[55] Fanon recognizes, in short, that nationalism is often confused with phantasmagoric projections. But his reading is concerned with what is no longer recognizable or reconcilable as nationalism. The phrase "maleficent spirits/powers" draws attention to how traditional authority entrances by placing the subject at the mercy of forces that only it can designate; likewise, modern nations are demonically ambiguous in sucking the blood of the people in the name of protecting it. The story Fanon tells again and again is not one whereby instrumentalism subsumes or erases the uncanny traces of the state, for instrumentalism can only be recognized in the failure of this erasure. *The Wretched of the Earth* acknowledges that the universalism of the state can only be completed by the part that has no part, the part that has been set aside, excluded, but nonetheless exploited, but is for all that no less universal. The colonial dilemma is not the nation-people possessed by the nation's ghost but the (dead, universal) nation misrecognized as particular and living. Fanon's diagnosis of this dilemma was politically optimistic, but he was no romantic. The ghost always returns; it returns doubly in the violence towards the other-as-fetish that in effect becomes ghost to the notion of ghost.

If fetishism is the characteristic figure of Fanonian discourse, assuring triumph even as it inaugurates loss, then it is not surprising that questions of perverse enjoyment inhere in Fanon's rhetorical analyses of colonial subjects. In fetishism there is no way of distinguishing between the loss that comes to be preserved as a memorial and the exultant self-identity that confirms itself through this partial transformation. This is why the fetish is never to blame for our experience of loss, it is always the encounter with

others that derails us. Yet Fanon's deconstruction of the fetishism of racial capital has too often been read as his own failure to overcome this indebted attitude towards injury and loss. What this says about Fanonism is
more complicated. The reversal of the stereotype through violence that we
noted in Fanon's *The Wretched of the Earth* would be no reversal at all, but
a restatement of the racial precarity in which, despite Fanon's disclaimer,
there is precisely a link between violence and disavowal, between stereotype and black life-and-social-death. If the stereotype is structured like a
fetish, and if the fetish articulates a primal defense against exposure to the
other, then the theory of fetishism itself—summed up in the figure of the
stereotype—comes to look like the fantastically intricate history of endless elaborations and displacements of negrophobia! The question Fanon is
asking, then, is what happens when the fetish-as-stereotype is speaking *as*
black, a blackness whose violence arises out of—and is addressed to—the
annulling, annihilating, guiltiness conferred on it by whiteness. How does
one decide when this is emotional and political collusion, as against a deluded form of racial loyalty and love?

It is no wonder that the distinction between violence and fetishism
should become so problematic in critical readings of Fanon. It is also no
wonder that the debate about his fetishism should refuse to settle on a single
absence—the wretchedness whose weakness is also its strength. Whether or
not there has ever been something that could be expressly delegated as black
revolutionary violence, everyone participating in the debate has had to
come to terms with Fanon's theory of violence. That theory has been equally
derided for its nihilism, its petit-bourgeois romanticism, and its naïve vitalism: why is it that, generally speaking, critics resort to fetishistic thinking
in order to refuse the anti-fetishistic movement of Fanon's own texts? Does
not this agreement bespeak a refusal to recognize what Fanon himself states
(as narrated throughout this chapter) to be the key obligation of whiteness,
that is, to make blackness the infinitely indebted form of its permanently
accruing value? On one level, then, how we read Fanon has become literally interrupted by the (white) stereotype we have of him. The rhetorical,
psychoanalytical, and political complexities of his texts are profoundly implicated in one another as metaphors and metonymies through which we
reconcile him to the myth that his texts are always already indebted *as* black
texts. We have seen examples of this above. This fetishistic operation, however, culminates strangely in a phantom-like monument to the texts themselves. The Fanonian fetish is subsequently read as if it were the ghost and

symptom of fetishism itself, a fetishism oddly removed from theoretical reason, which subsequently disappears in the truer, less violent, presentation of the theory whose ersatz substitute it is. The difficulty would seem to reside in the attempt to achieve a full elaboration of any discursive position on Fanonism other than that of its phantasmatic disappearance as fetish—*that* is an intolerance of the other that we can neither fulfill nor disobey.

6

Desire and Law

Racial guilt, as we analyzed it in the last chapter, has to do with the demand that blackness, by right and in fact, should not exist as black but should grasp, or encounter, itself as a *flaw* or deficit [*tare*] that is necessarily guilty and in debt for being nonwhite. For "the Black [*le Noir*] no longer has to be black [*noir*], but must be it in the face of the White [*en face du Blanc*]"; in this explicit covenant the black must not only conform *de jure* to white symbolic law, he is required to feel guilt in his conformity, for conformance to whiteness is in fact forbidden him, since he can only conform to this duty by annulling himself as black, which is in fact impossible.[1] The law that prescribes blackness as flaw thus also makes it *de facto* impossible to identify with that law, hence the unfathomable feeling of guilt: "I am guilty," writes Fanon, "I do not know of what, but I know that I am no good."[2]

Moreover, such a form of guilt-inducing rancor has a primary effect on how one interacts with others, leading Fanon to revise Hegel's notion of *Füranderesein*, or existence-for-another [*l'être pour l'autre*], so as to say, much more importantly, that the black has no "ontological resistance" to the self-constraining imperatives of anti-blackness, for it is in fact through renunciation that blackness is enjoined to distance and so condemn itself, certain of its essential flaw.[3] Yet the demand that blackness condemn itself the better to express this flaw, whose meaning and cause thereby escapes it, nevertheless has numerous repercussions for black ethical life that are at least well worth noticing, and that Fanon describes as a moral conscience that is "not certain of itself" and in whose renunciation (which cannot be borne) there is a racially guilty form of knowledge: again, "I am guilty. I do not know of what, but I know that I am no good."[4]

The difficulty of knowing what one is guilty of comes from the fact that this feeling does not directly concern anything that one has actually done, which is why, of course, escaping it is impossible. The reason for this is obvious. Since guilt constitutes moral incertitude, at least in those colonial societies where one is compelled to live one's inferiority, the demand that orders and prohibits blacks from being anything less than inferior is necessarily aporetic, for one is obliged to disobey this demand by obeying it, by seeking a white plenitude without, after all, being *de facto* white. At the same time, accordingly, the desire to *be* white can only confirm a failure of attainment: that it is indeed impossible to conform to it, impossible not to conform without conforming to it, to the point where being black is, inescapably, to be by right and by fact indebted to what one is *not*, for it is impossible, consequently, to be black without being enjoined to renounce being black in favor of the onto-stereotypical truths of anti-blackness. How, effectively, could one ever be free of guilt and be black, since negrophobia gives the order to annul oneself, given that this very injunction enjoins blacks to maintain what is by right a state of permanent indebtedness? Blackness is therefore possessed of a command that cannot be borne, a command that simultaneously makes the desire to know rest on an incomprehensible desire to be at fault.

I. OEDIPUS AS COLONUS

This is likewise confirmed by the following: "in the French Antilles 97 per cent of the families cannot produce one Oedipal neurosis."[5] Aside from confirming once again Fanon's ambivalent relation to psychoanalysis—in his 1986 foreword to *Black Skin, White Masks*, Homi K. Bhabha calls the claim "provocative"—the idea that Oedipus is elsewhere, and that every expression of desire in the colony testifies to this, is certainly a daring claim, and one that comes down to saying that *black desire has no legitimacy* in the colony, that Oedipus has not been renounced, and that no one knows the horror (the law) of castration, and they are thus without the means for the remorse necessary to accede to culture. It follows that if Oedipus, in its classical version, cannot be produced in the colony, then the black can have no certitude that s/he is part of the symbolic life of culture, or that what is owed can ever be paid off, so as to allow the assumption of the socio-symbolic law of culture; and, conversely, there can be no prohibition against an act or desire deemed oedipal, for the commanded renunciation (of desire) has not been attained. In any case, it is as a consequence of Oedipus, in its classical version, that desire in its dispute with authority learns that it may not aspire to certain objects, and that this is judged beneficial for the preservation of the life and legitimacy of culture, including the forms by which we recognize moral law. This is why, if Oedipus goes missing, desire can never be present to itself as anything more than remorse, as if the demand for renunciation were too demanding to bear and prohibition had not yet entered into discourse. In any case, I would hesitate to read Fanon's remark too literally, for what is at stake here is how black desire comes to be ruined—enclosed, petrified—by white symbolic law, in which the possibility of renunciation gives way to something much more perverse. It follows that another version of Oedipus has emerged to take the historical place of the classic version: let us call it *Oedipus colonus*, in whose origin and possibility it is not the mythological primal father who is repressed, but the father of genealogical legitimacy.

It follows that this model allows us to conceive of a paternity that is rivalrous, possessive, and murderously authoritarian and that offers no symbolic efficacy beyond the moment in which it threatens to seize, castrate, or possess; and if, as a consequence, blacks do not obey this decadent, perverse authority, it will, without exception, inflict harm through force. Accordingly, no one is permitted what the white master regards as his by right, and his decrees do not even sustain the pretense of a claim to symbolic sacrifice. The net result is an image of the *colonisé* as permanently, perversely indebted, that is, s/he cannot attain the possibility of symbolic renunciation and so, consequently, s/he can be repeatedly, literally sacrificed in so far as his/her interminable remorse is without resolution. It would seem that the encounter with this remorse without end is when the black child's "real apprenticeship begins," and it is doubtless from the same encounter that "reality proves to be extremely resistant."[6] Citing Sartre's *Anti-Semite and Jew*, Fanon suggests that "the later the discovery, the more violent the shock."[7] Furthermore, if we are willing to accept Fanon's refusal of the presence of oedipal neuroses in the colony, certain other things come into focus:

1. First, as I said above, Fanon inverts Freud to say that the substitution of racial for paternal law is what defines the (sovereign) right to oedipal intimacy, whence the compulsion to decry blackness as a valueless form of (sensuous) expenditure, and the need to govern

and rule as if whiteness were a kind of transcendental authority and represented a symbolic law *by right* of law and desire.

2. If the avowal of black guilt is what founds the whiteness of law, it should also be noted, in keeping with Fanon's interpretation of Oedipus *as* colonus, that sovereign power in the colony has no cultural legitimacy outside of the imperative command to identify with whiteness by persecuting those in debt to it; on the other hand, this means that the social contract is based on a model of racial sacrifice whose legitimacy belongs solely to those who are symbolically white. And how does one know one is white? By being free, in principle, of the self-reproach that is simultaneously the ambivalent expression of a moral conscience as revealed through the consciousness of guilt [*Schuldbewusstein*], which Fanon, following Freud closely here, takes to be evidence of an obsessional neurosis. Also worthy of note is the fact that whilst whites hold sovereign power, they can only experience that sovereignty by administering and safeguarding whiteness as a right via a law that announces itself as already transgressed, or perverted by, blackness. This is why blackness is needed—to make the whiteness of law representable as such. By which we finally see how the business of leadership in the colony is perverted into an arbitrary manifestation of racist commandments without right, legitimacy, or foundation.

Now that all this has been established, it is time to see how much Fanon's thinking on the psychopolitical is guided by questions of desire and law, taking into account this notion of an ontological incertitude, which likewise falls victim to a humiliation without destination or end.

Furthermore, such a discussion will allow us to consider once more the complex relationship of Fanon's thought to that of (Freudian) psychoanalysis. The difficulty in demonstrating this (despite all that has been written above) comes from the fact that a certain number of critics do not consider Fanon's thought of psychoanalytic interest (they find no psychoanalytic interpretation within it), and so either reject it as inadequate or remain indifferent to it, since they argue, at least in regard to real fantasy, that Fanon "confus[es] the level of reality and fantasy to a disastrous extent."[8] Those who accuse Fanon of being insufficiently analytical inevitably point to the idea that psychic conflict is culturally "predestined," which they say confuses how people act with what they unconsciously desire; and they often try to persuade us that Fanon's interpretation of desire is entirely sociological ("sociogenesis becomes the sole determinant"[9]).

The critical question that the notion of real fantasy makes possible (the phantasmatic pressure of the real on culture; the cultural stereotype that preempts the unconscious work of fantasy and desire) is thus foreclosed by this opposition between fantasy and reality that Fanon supposedly confuses—a particularly patronizing expression, at least given that the opposition between psychic and political conflict is what allows these critics to devote themselves to an interpretation of colonialism as a purely psychical fact. For there is no doubt that they assume, due to this conflict, that people's desires have to be prompted to become political and, conversely, that to lose sight of this difference whenever political urgency is uppermost is to misinterpret what desire is, and likewise that the true interpretation of what makes desire political can in no way be made sense of. From this it is evident that Fanon's error is to "represent psychic conflict as largely an effect of colonialism," which is why he is wholly unable to see beyond the dualism that puts the European "in the category of sameness and the colonized in a position of otherness."[10] (But does not the very opposition between category and position unwittingly repeat that dualism? And is not the claim to overcome the naïveté of Fanon's oppositionalism itself blind to its own oppositional positioning of that opposition, precisely in its claim to have overcome it?)

The problem posed then is this: Fanon presents the psyche as a continuation of the violence and authority of the colonial state; they are made to intersect, to unite in the production of anti-black social relations (and the discourse of psychoanalysis is included within these relations of production as part of the economy of the subject, hence Fanon's substitution of a psychoanalysis of racism for that of a sociogenic analysis of anti-blackness). On the one hand, the question is how negrophobia speaks unconsciously in the cultural discourse of the colony; on the other, how blackness occupies the place of the unconscious in the discourse of culture. The subtlety of this shift from unconscious negrophobia to the negrophobic unconscious of culture is not tautological, and yet it has been obstinately evaluated as such, with Fanon reproached for an exceedingly narrow, voluntaristic "psychology" of the subject. From this point of view, recourse to social violence means losing sight of the far more troubling existence of psychic violence, or Fanon is "too quick" (the phrase is Homi Bhabha's[11]) to explain what remains "ill resolved" in the ill-resolved conflicts (*conflits mal liquidés*) of the *colon* and *colonisé*.[12] Recourse to incomplete resolution is justified, only as a sign or symptom of unresolved psychoanalytical conflicts. Negrophobia is from this point of view merely another metaphor for psychic conflict.

The problem with these readings, which I believe fail to read Fanon attentively, is that they are too quick to prescribe the political as if its meaning were quite clearly understood by all, and so are unable to grasp at the same time the psychopolitical nuances of Fanon's thought as having anything more to say than that mental illness is a form of social alienation, and that politics is the reparative answer to such alienation. But if, in opposition to psychoanalysis, or a certain reading of psychoanalysis, the question of alienation is more attentive to the sociohistorical, it also falls short of the critical question of *socialthérapie* as evoked by Fanon. For in reality it is evident from the manner and method of his *socialthérapie* that Fanon, as a practicing psychiatrist, retained absolutely the right to analyze racism as a group rather than an individual idea, and one in which no distinction is made between ego and culture, enmity and sociopolitical structure, as is evident throughout his work.

Doubtless psychoanalysis can only consider psychical erring as a universal structure. It prescribes that we judge enmity as universal, that is to say irreparable to man, and so ineradicable. Fanon does not contradict this, but he *does* nuance it. He says—and his example here is the work of Octave Mannoni—that Freudian psychoanalysis shares the same dogmatic presupposition, namely, that enmity is oedipal in nature, and that in oedipality desire transgresses law, a presupposition that forgets how the ego's sovereign mastery speaks first through the structures of racism, transmitting negrophobic answers in the form of unconscious affects and compelling itself to act on them. This is why, in his interpretation of psychoneuroses, Fanon's concern is with how the sovereignty of the ego, in its degraded ersatz-stereotypical form, which speaks unconsciously the negrophobic discourse of culture, repeats the racist fantasy of the colonial state, and why its desire cannot escape the most intense kind of hatred, which negrophobic hatred tends to be.

We have many examples of such hatred throughout his oeuvre. Let us go back to the Martinican philosopher who is about to discover his "true face" in France or, conversely, about to lose the white face he has been wearing as a mask, which he believed to be his own for all that. This face is not to be thought of as an object that was delusorily put on but as what is most common to his world, and that conceals his most intimate desire under the aspect of a secret shared by all. Consequently, there is no way, not even for an instant, of separating mask from persona, or the life performed from the life lived as performance; rather, the mask is honorific, it permits him to say "*I*." Nevertheless, there is no escaping the duplicity involved, nor the guilt in having to put on the mask in the first place, and that plainly shows that the ego is nothing more than dissimulation. When it becomes clear that the symbolic efficacy of the mask is no longer his true face, due to his being obliged to recognize himself in the mirror of racism as *nègre*, it is also clear that this delegated face is also a mask. Why? Because there is nothing to see behind this masked self? Just imagine: I look in the mirror and I see a mask, but the reflection looking back is already masked by its own mask, namely the shame—of being black—that masks its own guilty dissimulation. The philosopher's response to this disquiet is not cowardice or duplicity, then, but a kind of inescapable dereliction that evidently shows how guilt redoubles the shame of exposure. He is a martyr to this shame that he uses to cover up his affliction. And this martyrdom is itself *masked*, is covered over by what it covers: surprise, despair, refusal, abandonment. For in this exchange of faces he now possesses merely another mask, and one that appears through self-ruination, that is, one performed through disavowal and repression, and that is now the occasion of shame and self-disgust. To say that the *colonisé* is an actor, however, is also to say that he is a spectator who does not yet know the role he is playing, but this is a role that only he can play, beyond which no other persona is conceivable. This is also clear from Fanon's remarks on *that within*, where it is stated that *to know oneself as black is to know that one is never not wearing a white mask*, and where the ego is the effect of a mask, which we believe we have acceded to freely, and owing to which we make no distinction between the self we imagine not seeing and the self to which we remain blind despite performing. Significantly, Fanon chooses the military metaphor of a garrison to illustrate how racist misrecognition turns desire and recognition into confederates, founding and fortifying themselves through various deceptions, appointing the racial other as a judge over all inner territory, attacking any resemblance to the *semblable* that is its own illusory comparison, and generally being in conflict over the white fetish that hides the blackness disfiguring this imitation of being.[13] Fanon also says that the philosopher is already on guard (*soit sur ses gardes*) before his arrival in France, as if in anticipation of some rebuke or violation, or some defacement *against which he has no defense*, that produces an internal rupture or schism, that is, the radical contestation of who he is, or who he believed himself to be. Why?

The lesson to be drawn here is not the shock of French racism, but the moment when the subject realizes that racism is already part of the *I*'s identification with itself and, as such, is already *too* familiar, already part of the self's most intimate-disavowed fantasy. There is no escape from the shame that occurs when the subject discovers that remorse without end is once again the occasion for how he engages the world. When I discussed the notion of *Ersatz* in the previous chapter, I mentioned how the notion of a substitute that was degraded owing to the division between original and copy already presumed a gap between the subject's most intimate fantasy and the symbolic-imaginary imagos of his or her social being. For the negrophobia that one actively assumes in exchange for accepting the submission and allegiance of one's destitution does not spare either the black or white-identified *colonisé* from having their identity transgressed and exposed, for this gap between social reality and fantasy cannot be closed.

That said, in the discussion of the ersatz we did not mention that it was specifically attached to another term, *Erlebnis*, meaning lived experience, or an event of which one is cognizant, a term that Fanon borrows from the phenomenological tradition as represented by Sartre, Heidegger, and Merleau-Ponty. And yet with respect to this word, which occurs in reference to Freud on the time of trauma, Fanon is questioning, in a modest and preliminary way, the very meaning of psychical event as defined by phenomenology and that as such deserves a specific analysis. For in response to Freud's emphasis that the repressed idea "is on watch constantly for an opportunity to make itself known" but in ways that are always temporally distorted or masked, Fanon has no hesitation in saying that "these *Erlebnisse* are repressed in the unconscious," likewise they stand guard over any intolerable idea that happens to break through into consciousness.[14] In truth, he goes on to say, using the philosopher's anxiety as his example, that these *Erlebnisse* do not have to be an event to take on a neurotic structure of enmity and sacrifice, for in the midst of a negrophobic culture every wish and desire is already prefigured by the racial honor that determines all identifications and emotional ties. *In negrophobia what is awaited is already known and what reveals itself is the anguish of such repetition.*

This much resembles the situation of negrophobia—apart from the still unanswered question: why does Fanon evoke the notion of *Erlebnis* to think through that which has no knowable or determinable certainty as an event (of consciousness)? Our example of the philosopher's anxiety confirms what we said just now about how the feeling of being on guard occurs despite any experience of racial hostility. For the subject who is not yet black, who is asked to choose his true face (who does not yet know himself) as black, negrophobic knowledge lays bare the failure of renunciation. Quite literally identifying himself with the *nègre* by repudiating it, he thereby becomes more *nègre* (more other to himself) through repudiation, for he now stands on the other side of white moral law. We could even venture to say, or conjecture, that the more he identifies with what he barely knows, the more negrophobic his desire, and the more black he becomes in his desire to refuse this knowledge. Confronted by his own proper-improper whiteness, and his own proper-improper blackness, the knowledge that permits him to choose mask on mask thus duly makes him suspicious of what awaits him. Whence the retrospective fear of the *nègre*, its contagion and its interminable indebtedness, and the suspicion that every decision *not* to be *nègre* is already a symptom of an obsessional neurosis.

Blackness once again only appears, or presents itself, in its petrified dispossession, *or* it only appears without ever appearing, except in its guilt and expiation. For undoubtedly, the philosopher's feeling of anxiety was already respectful of the void by which he persisted, but that only appeared to him *nachträglich*, as already lost, impossible, transgressed, abolished by blackness; and this is how negrophobia conserves and founds itself as right and law—in the violence that destroys or pollutes it. At this point one could make an appeal to the history and politics of the colonial epoch. But Fanon's example of guardedness does not require us to settle the point historically. It suffices that structurally, blackness cannot conform to this expiation, and precisely because the *colonisés* cannot identify with the whiteness in them (in them more than them, as Lacan might say). Thus they can only respect blackness, as I have shown, as an imposed mask, or stain, that humiliates them—guilt being the effect of a law that humiliates all black egotistical presumption and self-esteem, because it comes from a place beyond our desires, beyond our being more generally. And finally, the command that we obey this law, even though it is entirely clear that it announces itself to us as our annihilation, means condemning the *colonisé* to a fate of the purest mythological violence. Another way of saying this is: whiteness is never given in itself, as Fanon testifies, it is only given in the guilty and abject affect of a blackness that is uncertain of itself, an incertitude to which no law can respond or correspond, except in guilt, obligation, or debt: whiteness obligates, it compels black guilt, and it is thus in guilt that we feel its imperative command to make blackness the flaw through which this abjection is felt, suffered, and tarried with as the anguish of a failed renunciation. Hence we should not doubt that the decision to choose not to be black is ever treated as anything less than a forced choice by Fanon, though this is not always clear from the history of his reading by psychoanalytic critics.

To this should be added that all of Fanon's thinking on *Erlebnis* (or black lived experience) is united by the fact that it is grounded in a law that dirempts it, and that is rightly considered by him to be further split between abjection and undecidability. Fanon shares with Lacan the presupposition that desire *is* law and that there is no way round this irreducibility. And there is no way out of the antinomy when a contradiction emerges between narcissism and authority, say, or transgression and desire. Hence to understand this antinomy correctly, and to understand how Oedipus takes place in the colony, it is essential to know the beliefs of those who desire not to be black and to distinguish these beliefs from what blackness represents to them. For otherwise we shall confuse these beliefs and desires with the colonial version of Oedipus and the laws of anti-blackness by which that version becomes evident. But this is not the sole reason why it is necessary to know these beliefs and these desires structured by racist misrecognition. We must also know them so that we will not confuse black desire with the imaginary visions and fantasies of Oedipus *as* colonus. Thus we may ask, by way of a counterargument, why the myth in its classical version is not itself mythic in its opposition between desire and law. By grounding universal prohibition in the murder of an original, castrating master-father, who is himself the image of a primitive potentate, Freud makes the universal nature of oedipal prohibition consequent to feelings of remorse that are effectively the outcome of a singular paternal devotion. Whether one understands such remorse mythically, structurally (as an ethnographic *fiction*, or as an ideological vehicle for explaining how primitive *jouissance* accedes to law), or as Freud's most rigorous attempt to preserve paternity by disavowing the universality of castration (for the *Urvater* is not himself castrated), it is very easy to forget the uncertain oscillation in this fable between desire, the exception, and law. It is not enough to speak of the obscurity veiled by Freud's own ideological commitments. There are entirely other reasons why Fanon has nothing to express but skepticism towards Freud's obsessional insistence on Oedipus, and on the other hand, why he needs to question the insurmountable consequence of a demand for symbolic paternity that everywhere fails to appear in the colony. Fanon starts out from the impossibility of Oedipus and ends with the impotent, fallible, tyrannical master of white patriarchy, for which no mythic meaning or explanation is needed. In a world of permanent anti-black prohibition, it is not that black desire transgresses law, or exposes the universal deception of race *qua* law and tirelessly bears witness to this fact by rejecting blackness as a flaw that needs remedying. This is only half the story. In Fanon's rereading of Oedipus as colonus, black desire is not opposed to law but is made black by law, for in the colony negrophobia is written into the very possibility of desire itself. Without doubt this is why the desire not to *be nègre* leads to the permanent consolidation of the whiteness hidden within, and, in that sense, Fanon is right to say that desire's relation to law is to affirm blackness as the accursed part, for what it knows of itself is performed without knowledge, and why any political demand (to be black) in the colony is effectively defeated and absent until the law makes the desire to know oneself the truth of black castration—and not only symbolically but literally, as in the example of anti-black violence.

It is also this desire to know, without which blackness would sink into mere personation, and into blissful support of the existing order, that transforms the feeling of guardedness into an internal and explicit sense that something has been lost, prohibited, forbidden. We may even say that it is not until the black discovers and develops a sense of himself as castrated that the *colonisé* is able to arrive at his destination or fate, where the form of his self-questioning leads to the direct realization that the master's truth is no longer the bar to the real of *jouissance* and history. If that moment ever comes, it is only possible because the mythic law of black prohibition will have transformed itself into a (poetic, inventive) desire to enter into history. For whatever is contrary to racist prohibition is contrary to the myth of the law's racial authority, and what is contrary to racist myth entails the structure of a tabula rasa, and accordingly the real of a new desire to be and know. Nevertheless, although he seems to dismiss the universality of the Oedipus complex, from the tradition of psychiatry Fanon retains the sense that the psyche is inscribed by historicity (a term that we know he takes from Jaspers's early work on general psychology). Inversely, it is true that what he says further on about neuroses is not always compatible with what he says about desire and law. In any case, the Fanonian critique of psychoanalysis does claim to exceed its model of alienation, which no longer arises simply from ill-resolved conflict and the internal anxieties of those conflicts. It belongs to what he calls, in a rather singular sense, the sociogeny of the colonial encounter, which is expressly linked to colonial war.

We must now see by what means this sociogeny was indicated by the principles of Fanon's *socialthérapie*, and how this too was clearly indicated by the effect of real fantasies on the minds of the *colonisés* during a time of war. Anyone willing to pay any attention to these clinical writings will immediately see that the hardest thing is to induce these patients to think about the phantasms that hold them in check like a foreign power holding sway over a colony. Thus, in his famous response to Octave Mannoni's *Psychologie de la colonisation*, Fanon dismisses Mannoni's use of Oedipus—justifying the place of the *colon* and the promise of allegiance owed him by the *colonisé*—as an ideological alibi for the extreme violence practiced by the French in suppressing decolonial revolution. When Fanon turns to the dreamlife of the Malagasy, he holds, for the same reason, that the dreamwork, in the context of this war, is not simply the inversion of an ethnic inheritance but a transposition already transgressed by real punishments and hatreds that are utterly distinct (as scenes of trauma) but absolutely contrary to that of metaphoric (oedipal) translation. And so in Chapter Four of *Black Skin, White Masks*, on "The So-Called Dependency Complex of Colonized Peoples," we read:

We know from other sources that one of the torturers in the Tananarive police headquarters was a Senegalese. Therefore, since we know this, since we know what the archetype of the Senegalese can represent for the Malagasy, the discoveries of Freud are of no use to us here. What must be done is to restore this dream *to its proper time*, and this time is the period during which eighty thousand natives were killed—that is to say, one of every fifty persons in the population; and *to its proper place*, and this place is an island of four million people, at the center of which no real relationship can be established, where dissension breaks out in every direction, where the only masters are lies and demagogy. One must concede that in some circumstances the *socius* is more important than the individual. . . .

The rifle of the Senegalese soldier is not a penis but a genuine rifle, model Lebel 1916. The black bull and the robber are not *lolos*—"reincarnated souls"—but actually the irruption of real fantasies in sleep. What does this stereotype, this central theme of the dreams, represent if not a return to the right road?[15]

It follows from this passage, first, that there are circumstances in which a dream is not the symptomatic expression of an oedipal prohibition, which constitutes its fathomable theme, but the imposition of the real-as-fantasy, and one that puts into crisis the dreamwork as such. There is no need to recount here all the ethnographic material by which Mannoni seeks to support his hypothesis—that the dreams of the Malagasy "faithfully reflect their overriding need for security and protection"[16]—for this analogical speculation is precisely what gets interrupted by the stereotype, by the trauma of war, that already makes the desire for security and protection part of a vicious circle. Secondly, in the event of total war there may be instances in which desire is restrained less by symbolic prohibition than by literal catastrophe, in whose obstinate reference both unconscious and cultural forms of fantasy meet, for in this way everyone knows who tortures and what rifles are being used, and the real is not so much the effect of guilt but the effect quite literally of mass murder. Finally, Fanon's reproach to Mannoni has its malice, for it reverses point by point the importance Mannoni attaches to precolonial culture, regarded, in Fanon's reading of colonialism, as an ideological displacement of the war as a *materially racist socioeconomic event*. Though arguing from a Marxian-psychoanalytic point of view, Fanon's theory of the dream tries to displace—without absolutely breaking with—the place of oedipal prohibition as origin: on the one hand, he rejects the temptation to read the violence of war, that is, the violence of the real, as in conformity with the processes of the dream-work; on the other, he is opposed to any notion of fantasy that is seen as simply replaying—admittedly traumatically, in extremely withdrawn, abolished form—the guilt of a paternal symptom, since the Malagasy are assumed to be acting under the authority of a symbol to which they give their proper consent and allegiance, a symbolic authority before which, in short, the prohibition is ethnologically, and not racially, determined. There is in certain dreams the opposite case: against all analogy, here the real (or the fantasy that constitutes it) holds power absolutely, and the dream-work carries out the command of its sole authority, even if still in the form of a dream, for the real makes of the dream-work something literally *eventful*, the event whose time and place is the same time and place as that of war and torture. It is this imperative, this situating, that materially overrides the oedipal obligation to dream *as if one were communicating a (distorted) desire* (of the guilty oedipal prohibition that defines the subject of psychoanalysis), rather than representing the horrors of warfare and torture.

Hence, at its most fundamental level, Fanon's wish to restore the dream-work to its proper time and place is not a search for the "meaning and conventional temporality" of the cure, but is more attentive to the way historical violence threatens psychic life itself.[17] Whence his interest in time *and* place—for the violence of colonial war cannot be represented without the violence of representation itself, or the representation that is already violent. Colonial civil war may have a proper time and place, those are Fanon's words, but at the same time it is in its actual occurrence an experience of radical impropriety, and in this sense there is nothing proper about it at all, even when it naturalizes its violence as a response to the counter-violence threatening its order and thus its rightful violence, which is also to say its authority. The proper time and place for decolonial violence is neither psychical nor political, but the point at which each seeks to maintain its rightful border. To the extent that this border makes us see clearly the exercise of their forceful separation by war, it also makes us see how the horrors of colonial war intrude upon inner experience. This seems like a tautology. But it is not a tautology; it raises the wider issue of the phenomenal structure of violence internal to the colony, its law, its decrees, and its logic, which is Manichean.

II. "THE TORTURER IS THE BLACK MAN"[18]

Now let us pass to another historical example, to see what it teaches about the psyche in colonial history. The telling example here would be that of the psyche under occupation. In Vichy-occupied Martinique, writes Fanon, the right to sovereignty guaranteed to the overseas departments who are therefore, besides other colonial outposts, part of French sovereign territory is coextensive with a systemic racism that challenges the belief in a shared republican universalism. Certain people may have thought that since they were legally French, the racist violence of the state could not be aimed at them. After the outbreak of war, violence would come from outside the colony, from foreign powers, and would consist of an interruption, suspending the natural teleology by which the colony saw itself as part of the republic and its traditions, and so eliminating the colony from them. That is why the fascist behavior of the occupying French forces in Martinique was experienced as the island's "first metaphysical experience."[19]

As a man who left Vichy-occupied Martinique to join the allied powers, Fanon describes this blow as metaphysical because it shattered a certain order of belief in the colony. But if this violence was shattering, it also set the conditions for the resumption and emergence of an anti-colonial resistance that sought to change the order of things.[20] And so there is violence against violence. In arguing the right to be black, the concept or watchword of the movement that came to be known as negritude did manifest a real fantasy. Fanon describes the impact of negritude as nothing less than a "metamorphosis" that required the *colonisé* to undergo "an axiological activity in reverse, a valorization of what he had rejected."[21] Negritude was not only a *letting go* (of the fear of a black nation); it also resolved the *colonisé* to take hold of blackness by possessing it as a new kind of knowledge and composition. The Vichy state could hardly stand by and tolerate this position. It deemed the new position ungrateful and then claimed that there was a misunderstanding, a misinterpretation of the state's intention, and that being French the people of the colonies were protected. The state could then condemn negritude as anti-republican and, if it persisted, as an insurrection. Such a situation did not in fact happen in Martinique, despite the fact that the Vichy regime of Admiral Robert was conceived as the exercise of a racist violence in the name of the republic. Racist violence was not external to the Vichy regime. It constituted it from within. The fascism here does not consist in a racist anti-blackness, but in defending the republic against the violence of negritude! Fanon understood Vichy as immanent to French universalism (as did Césaire). For as we have already shown, the lie of the compact was already evident in the example of a man who is already on guard before he steps off the boat in France, a migrant who knows that he can act and move freely, but who also can never be absolutely sure that the natural light of French reason will not degenerate into vile racist abuse.

Thus what the colonial regime really fears is not violence (the state being violence in its pure state) but the shattering of the fundamental, founding relation, that is, the real fantasy able to justify, to legitimate, or to dictate the "natural" relation of imperialism to colonial rule and so to prevent the fantasy of a non-racial universalism from becoming reality. The violence that belongs to the state is thus itself founded on a phantasmatic insecurity within its sense of symbolic order. Only this violence calls for and makes possible the unveiling of state violence in its raw state, which determines it as something other than a political or hegemonic struggle over force and as a defense of natural sovereignty. For a founding instance of violence (in the Benjaminian sense) to be possible, one must first recognize the fantasy of a violence that feels itself to be under threat and precarious. In this history or parable of violence, that which causes violence to be unleashed is the fantasy of violence external to the colony, to its order and origin. The phantasmatic reality of such violence thus comes up against its limit in the revolutionary violence of anti-colonialism, which is not so much the founding of a new law but the breaking of the phantasm of a compact in the colony. The revolutionary situation in any colony, according to Fanon, is not founded on the recourse to a new law or the necessity of new decrees and dispensations but on the *refusal* that undermines it from within, and always does so through violence. Always, which is to say even when there has not been bloody repression, or real traumatism, the people are capable of learning that social dishonor is not a commandment or eternal truth. And only violence can free them from servitude to this "law," which has been inscribed deeply in their hearts and consciences.

In these situations said to found law or state, the category of the tabula rasa all too well describes that moment when the order of things is changing from top to bottom. It consists, precisely, in a moment of radical reimagining. These moments are terrifying moments. Because of the sufferings, crimes, and tortures that rarely fail to accompany them, no doubt, but just as much because they are in themselves, and in their very essence, indecipherable to what passes for knowledge. That is what Fanon is calling the tabula rasa, as previously mentioned. As he presents it, this violence is certainly legible, indeed intelligible, since it is not alien to the violence of the colonial state, no more than violence is alien to the racist forms of right and law in the colony. The tabula rasa is what both founds and suspends law. This moment of suspense, this founding or revolutionary upheaval, is where the *colonisés* let go their prohibitions and fears of injury and seek out a new law that is also an instance of non-law. And it is also through the history of rupture that desire frees itself from servitude to colonial law. This moment always takes place and never takes place as such. It is the moment in which the state remains suspended over a void, or over an abyss, suspended in a pure moment of anguish. The negritude subject that Fanon talks about is capable of learning from this situation, which is both ordinary and terrible, for aware that he has yet to retain symbolic recognition, he cannot resist this moment of tabula rasa—and precisely because it is transcendent in the very measure that it is he who safeguards it, as *that within*, in the very order of his being. Here we come across a paradox: the inaccessible legibility of the white Other behind the mask before which and prior to which the black attributes pity, jealousy, anger, lust, etc. only appears transcendent and thus redemptive to the extent that, within him, the black depends on him, on the guarding act by which he maintains him: the tabula rasa is transcendent, violent, and nonviolent in a similar way, because it depends on the one who is already on guard against it—and so on the one who preserves it, or produces it, founds it, authorizes it as absolutely immanent but who finds that its presence always escapes him. The tabula rasa is transcendent and legislative, and so always about to be inscribed, always promised because it is immanent, finite, and so always about to be written.

The successful arrival of the *colonisés* as a nation is therefore similar to the guarded arrival of the emigrant in France, insofar as the successfully adapted ego (in the sense that one is said to fit in) will produce *après coup* what it was destined in advance to produce, namely the awareness of an occupying force that produces, among other effects, a discourse of radical resolve and contestation. Examples of this resolution are not lacking, whether it is a question of what happens in the metropolis or in the colony, whether it happens at a checkpoint or in the bedroom, at a seminar or in the clinic. This radical rupture results from the very exposure of the works of law to the faithful assent of a violent desire whereby, undoubtedly, one may understand the return of the wretched. In sum, the tabula rasa signifies a moment of existential-symbolic violence, a psychopolitical violence at the heart of social being and meaning, and one that turns the world upside down.

Now let us pass to the second point, running through Fanon's account, to see what it tells us about decolonial war. The first thing that strikes us is the fact that the tabula rasa introduces something new into existence that remains unreadable in regards to the present life of the colony. Hence, it entails what Fanon will go on to call an invention introduced into existence. I will explain what this means more fully in Part Two.

And so these Fanonian oppositions seem to me to call more than ever for the clinical to be linked to the political. For it is Fanon's purpose, not to reduce the clinical to the political, but to show the ways in which the very violence of the state must envelop the violence of the psyche, in precisely its desire for conservation, to be guarded, etc. when that guarding is what both founds and promises the most interruptive instant of self-constitution. Thus it inscribes the possibility of occupation at the heart of self-conservation. With this, there is no more a pure violence of the state, and so a pure external force, than there is a purely internal violence to the subject. Being on guard in its turn refounds what threatens, so that it can conserve what it claims to defend against. Thus there can be no more rigorous opposition between occupation and being on guard, only what I call (and here Fanon uses various words) *the crises of their encounter*, with all the paradoxes that this may lead to. It is in thinking about this border zone at the very heart of state and psyche that I single out this sentence of Fanon's which I hope to come back to later as one of the main interests of this book: there is, he says, a gangrene at the heart of the colony. There is something gangrenous in the colony, which condemns it or ruins it in advance. The colony/subject is condemned, ruined, in ruins, ruinous, in the very moment at which subjects are produced as *colonisés* and as *colons*.

If there is something of occupation and defense in every desire in the colony, there is also war and strife. War is another example of this contradiction internal to the subject. This warlike violence is within the sphere of law and of the subject. Here the rupture of relation is the relation. Desire *is* the law. There are many case histories illustrating this signification in *The Wretched of the Earth*. To discuss the psychic violence of the Algerian war, Fanon's main focus is on instances of reactionary psychosis. Here we are dealing with a double bind or a contradiction that can be schematized as follows. On one hand, it appears that the "wounds" left by colonial war are not representations but a series of identifiable (vengeful) revenants that cannot be renounced, that appear at the height of anguish, and that return as a malady of war. Is this a case of the psychologically dead pursued by the dead? Fanon concludes *The Wretched of the Earth* with the observation that "these notes on psychiatry will be found ill-timed and singularly out of place in such a book."[22] If there is something of untimeliness and out-of-placeness in this interpretation of colonialism, there is also something timely and in place in this very insistence on the psychic costs of war. For there is something of the untimeliness of these disorders, and thus of the situation and timing of their cure, that makes us see how these disorders remain pivotal to colonialism as such.

For Fanon, colonial war forces the people it dominates to ask: in reality, who am I? There is something violent in the very structure of the question, which produces "sensitivity" in the population. To discuss this sensitivity, Fanon refers to how violence is naturalized and how "this indocile nature [of the population] is finally tamed."[23] If, during the first period of colonization, there is no resistance, Fanon says that in time "the sum total of harmful nervous stimuli overstep a certain threshold," leading to greater mental hospitalizations.[24] In a period of total war, other mental disorders come to the fore. The novelty of the symptoms forces Fanon to revise the usual methodologies: "We avoid all arguments over semiology, nosology or therapeutics."[25] In order to comprehend the co-implication of resistance (psychotic and militaristic) and the enigmatic effects of total war, Fanon abandoned the usual ways of representing phantasmagoria resulting from delusion.

In his important concluding chapter, "Colonial War and Mental Disorders," Fanon considers four series of disorders. Series one straightaway provides accounts of patients suffering from reactionary psychoses, which causes them to invent enemies or to hallucinate their frightening semblances. The nature of colonial war, which is present everywhere and nowhere, means that the patient can no longer discern between French and Arab, friend and enemy, and everything is tinged with an ignoble, ignominious, disgusting ambiguity. In sum, the past life, which is to say the life before war, is in ruins; one could almost say that the former life *a posteriori* has become something rotten that structures the patient's discourse. Instead of seeing these ruins as repressed displacement activity, Fanon finds that the former self is neither purely repressed nor purely present. At most, the ego becomes a sign of a spectral or generalized vertigo in the wake of an attack whose wounds do not heal and remain splattered with blood. And he says as much, so much so that the event of this chapter in *Wretched of the Earth* consists of this strange exposition: before our eyes appear subjects who suspect that they are being slandered by everyone they meet, or who sense that they are being pursued by enemies that are inescapable but never seen. With each case history the misery and disorientation only deepen, as we see patient after patient relive the trauma that ruins them. They exhibit and archive the very movement of an obscene persecution that consequently immobilizes them, in relation to which their language and limbs are deprived of sense, their lives in pieces, at once shaped by torture and desirous of torture, and enclosed in a misery that singularly warns us of the psychic costs of total war. Fanon's cases do not escape the violence they relate. These subjects are ruined by their inability to free themselves from what possesses them, and precisely because what possesses them is everywhere and no longer there. But about these narratives there will be more to say.

What threatens the rigor of the distinction between these undiagnosed disorders is at bottom resistance. At one point Fanon says, "though it may appear unscientific, in our opinion time alone can bring some improvement to the disrupted personality" (of the colonial subject).[26] Time as both what causes and what cures? What resists and what improves? The vertigo that repeats itself is not then therapeutic, but a misfortune that fundamentally conserves itself. Right away then there are certain disruptions against which the personality has no defense, and which transform the very foundation of the ego. Rigorously speaking, this disruption produces effects irreducibly permanent in their specificity, in the sense that Fanon will mean in the late 1950s, following an analogous schema concerning the fatal ways in which the colonized fails to escape this very feeling of annihilation.

In the course of a meditation on time, which includes along the way an analysis of dates, vertigo, and anguish, Fanon thus comes to distinguish between psychosis and the psychosis of total war, between the moral guilt of the French that exempts them from torture and the vertigo that "haunts the whole of existence" of the resistance fighter, which profoundly modifies his acts *a posteriori*. The vertigo that haunts resistance, this feeling that is not a moral repudiation of the terroristic act, "raises the question of responsibility within the revolutionary framework."[27] Fanon explores this question in several case histories covering the period from 1954 to 1959, in hospital centers and private clinics or the health divisions of the FLN. These cases (which I will come to in a moment) suggest that there is something about the *threshold* between the psychical and the somatic, between war on the outside and a war internal to the organism, that manifests itself as the purest untimeliness when the subject is exposed to a violence that is absolute, that is to say when it touches on a mass attack against the ego. Here Fanon does not need to evoke the great analytical arguments about psychosis that before him suggested, in the same way, that psychosis is always a dispute at the border, or of "border-line case[s]."[28] If colonialism manifests the distress of such disturbing renunciations, to abolish the system is not to touch upon these disturbances, it is possibly to disavow their consequences (as some of the French left do). And that is to confirm, says Fanon, that there is indeed something decayed at the heart of the colony. The personality bears witness, it must bear witness, to the fact that colonialism is an enigma contrary to mental health. But what today bears witness in an even more haunted way to this fact is the mixing of the two forms of violence (psychical and political), in the modern form of vertigo. It is this mixture that is haunting, as if psychical resistance was the point of inaction (though Fanon does not put it this way in commenting on the spectral meaning of moral-existential vertigo). This absence of a frontier between resistance and liberation, this communication between violence and disturbance, is, as Fanon says, part of the malignant legacy of colonialism.

Let us turn to the legacy itself, to its content and objects. At one point a victim of torture has to be persuaded that his encounter with the man who tortured him (also a patient) was "an illusion."[29] All the exemplary figures in the first series are haunted by the violent consequences of such acts to the extent to which they remain enclosed by them, and to the extent to which their symptoms are singular metonymies of them. Thus there are discontinuous signs or images that refer back to signifiers without meaning, as if, in such cases, all psychic life could only be "read" or "understood" as ciphers without identifiable codes. Let us take the example of the French policeman who tortures, who mixes up this phantom-like violence with his relations to others and becomes all the more violent for this confusion. He tells Fanon that he was not like this in his former life. But what if the war and torture have brought out what is really in him? Is this what he is seeking treatment for? Perhaps this "understanding" of his psychic image and of the victims over which he lords and whom he disavows, whom he has to punish brutally because of their provocation (including his wife and small children), is his true desire? Fanon recognizes a need to go on torturing "without any prickings of conscience" as the true state of this man's problem.[30] He therefore locates the desire to torture and punish as the realization of an innermost wish of which the war has allowed this man to acquire knowledge, as the pathway to the most ardent passion even though this knowledge provides neither peace nor calm in spite of his treatment.

As such, it is evident from this case—and those in series two on the atmosphere of total war—that mental illness must be seen as part of the total persecutory atmosphere, even when there is no actual event that causes nervous illness, just a general feeling of disquiet and fear of being attacked. Fanon presents several illustrations of this feeling, for example that of a "certain sort of uneasiness" that precedes aural hallucinations.[31] While recognizing that these disturbances are hallucinatory, however invasive their reality, Fanon argues that all testify to a degeneration of the real into intense states of anxiety. Let us stay with this point for a moment. Fanon is often read as if he does not add to a psychoanalytic theory of anxiety. But the profound logic of this anxiety (alongside that of negrophobia) seems incontestable to me, even if Fanon does not theorize it in this way. The violence of colonial war becomes hallucinatory and spectral because it haunts everything: every intimacy, and every social relation; even there where it is not, there is no defense against the screams heard or imagined, the accusations coming from those murdered, tortured, or both. There is a vertiginous malignancy to these hallucinations, both in the sense of depth and in the sense of a life being lost, precisely, by means of these disturbances to the life as lived (impossibly, without morality or politics, justice or judgment). The atmosphere of uncanny violence knows no boundaries—this anxiety is both grounded and free-floating, turning friend into enemy, lover into victim, and the dead into revenants seeking vengeance. Algerians, both settler and native, bear witness to this. These disturbances manifest an "atmosphere of permanent insecurity."[32] And further on, Fanon notes how the circumstances of colonial war "maintain and feed these pathological links."[33]

The third series goes on to consider how the spirit of torture is most explicit when, after brutal mass attacks against the body and person of the *colonisé*, there is a sense of outrage and injustice. This sense bears witness in the colony to the greatest feeling of resistance, but also of euphoria and moral indignation. Why? "For these patients, there is no just cause" and "force is the only thing that counts."[34] For these patients violence is justness and justice violence, or violence is justice's essence, its idea, its spirit and revelation. The police headquarters where torture was carried out lead to the inviolable association of the police with torture, where torture is exercised indiscriminately, routinely, not in the name of law or truth but in the sense of extracting "information." Here Fanon indicates an analysis of police brutality that is oddly analogous to the principles of psychiatry. So the psychiatrist, on the one hand, uses chemicals to "liberate" the patient from a conflict. The doctor "intervenes to liberate the patient from this 'foreign body.'"[35] But this method is "difficult to control" and can lead to a worsening of the condition, when new symptoms emerge. This makes the psychiatrist, on the other hand, implicit in a subversive war where their role is to overcome the resistance of their patients/patriots. In total war, whatever form torture takes, psychiatry often proves to be what it ought not to be in spirit, part of a clandestine, surreptitious war against the colonized. The consequences or implications are twofold:

1. psychiatry is a degeneration of cure into interrogation and of symptom into the violence of the state;

2. torture leads to an inability to tell apart what is true from what is false: "Everything is true and everything is false at the same time," especially the therapies of psychiatry.[36] This means that the patient is on guard about what is being said, and in his or her replies is careful to keep hidden what is most intimate to him or her. It is only after they find themselves shattered, void of meaning and of will, that the psychiatric work begins.

And so Fanon's argument, which then develops into a critique of the language of cure, seems to be running the language of racism into that of a therapeutic intervention, or resistance, but in the sense of a (disavowed) return to a form of bad faith and a return that is now in crisis, suspended. A critique of therapy as a critique of torture is very much a critique of a violence that has no borders or that cannot be psychically controlled: it is to put into question, too, an analytic perspective that fails to see its own complicity in the malignancy by which a culture enters into the decay and practice of torture. The analogy between psychiatry and state violence does not need to be spelled out. Fanon illustrates the connection by an analysis of brainwashing that links psychiatry directly to torture interrogation techniques. And it is still a question of reaction and resistance.

Fanon goes on, in one of the cases, to touch on the most explicit example of brainwashing: that of intellectuals. Fanon refers to the way in which these prisoners are led to "play a part," which he then relates to the popularity, in the United States, of psychosocial models of social adaptation. The basic question would be: how does one distinguish between being asked to play a part through which one conforms and playing a part that forces one to realize one's conformity (as in the use of psychodrama at Blida-Joinville)? As a technique, all psychodrama is meant to preserve the ego—otherwise it would lose its value. There is no psychiatry without this "game of collaboration."[37] The result: every therapeutic contract, every clinical method, is founded on collaboration. Here an elliptical transposition by Fanon is decisive, as is often the case. The collaboration that persuades the intellectual need not be violent in order to be successful. But the promise of violence, even if not immediately present, is replaced—supplemented—by the techniques (Fanon uses the word "manoeuvres") of the psychiatrist.[38] And it is in this manoeuvering, in the brainwashing that replaces violence (or its immediacy), it is in this representable war of persuasion that psychiatry enters the game of collaboration. It leads to a kind of "antithetic" thinking, which was briefly mentioned above, in which the true is likely to be false and the false true (and where the relation between signifier and signified no longer corresponds to that of convention, but to codes without messages, as it were, whose signs open the mind to a chaotic euphoria). Fanon refers to this antithetic thinking—a phrase that is taken from Freud—as "the most painful sequel that we encountered in this war."[39] It is the sequence from interrogation to representation through which intellectuals are won over. For non-intellectuals, violence returns in the form of a "thorough breaking-in," supplemented by enforced brain-washing and coercion, so that people confess in order to avoid the worst kinds of physical torment. In face of the psychiatric interrogation, Fanon finds that the "fruit of the 'psychological action'" (persuasion, seduction, adaptation) is used in the service of colonialism.[40]

Now we must introduce a distinction that, once again, Fanon invokes to give a more precise sense of his clinical work and the different mode of thinking it inscribes. We just saw, in sum, that in its origin and its end, in its foundation and its resistance, colonialism is inseparable from violence, mediate or immediate, present or represented. In the fourth series, Fanon now turns his attention from the pathology of torture to the "pathology of atmosphere."[41] This atmosphere is how he introduces the question of psychosomatic disorders. Fanon writes that he prefers Pavlov's term "cortico-visceral," for it puts the brain *back in its place* as "the matrix where, precisely, the psychism is elaborated."[42] The psychosomatism, he tells us, is where the organism adapts itself to the conflict it is faced with, "the disorder being at the same time a symptom and a cure."[43] With this he indicates plainly enough that what he understands by atmosphere is a kind of destabilizing, complicating, or derailing of the sensorium, of intentionality, of the juridical or moral person, etc., and of all that follows from these, such as an antithetical line of reasoning wherein law, morality, and politics are transformed into a kind of magical thinking, as it were, that cannot be entirely separated from conflicts internal to the subject and the conflict of war. In these cortico-visceral disorders the conflict is resolved by "economical means" (is this also how he intends to intervene and so change the relation between symptom and cure?).[44] An economy of violence and non-violence is thus part of the conflict and its therapeutic resolution. (I hasten to add, briefly, that the atmosphere [of war] produces not only distorted imaginings and pathologies in the sensorium, but also enigmas that imprint themselves on the ability to tell apart symptom and cure, or how they are literally *denoted* and symbolically *connoted* in thought.)

Does this mean that we have to abandon the modes and methods of psychoanalysis to grasp this interrelationship? Things are far from that simple. Other therapeutic techniques such as relaxation and suggestion are also questioned as insufficient in getting at what is specific, or singular, to colonial total war. This would be, for example, the distinction between the singular muscular contraction of the native and the theory of congenital degeneration beloved by the School of Algiers. This contracture is the "expression," in muscular form, of the native's "refusal" with regard to co-lonial authority, a contracture that instead of strengthening the organism renders it impassive and strangely immobile, and that aims at the elimina-tion of conflict altogether.[45] Fanon says, without any elaboration, that this occurs mainly in men. Here is his description, which I cite at some length:

The cause of the difficulty [being unable to go upstairs, walk quickly, or run] lies in a characteristic rigidity which inevitably reminds us of the impairing of cer-tain regions of the brain (central grey nuclei). It is an extended rigidity and walk-ing is performed with small steps. The passive flexion of the lower limbs is almost impossible. No relaxation can be achieved. The patient seems to be made all of a piece, subjected as he is to a sudden contraction and incapable of the slightest vol-untary relaxation. The face is rigid but expresses a marked degree of bewilderment.

The patient does not seem able to "release his nervous tension." He is con-stantly tense, waiting between life and death. Thus one such patient said to us: "You see, I'm already stiff like a dead man."[46]

Another distinction seems even more to the point and is added in a foot-note: "It is hardly necessary to add that there is no question here of hys-terical contraction."[47] Rigidity, in brief, is not the hysterical conversion of a representation into a bodily symptom, but is precisely of the order of a *mortifying manifestation* that is, inevitably, a kind of death, or life-death. Once again it is very much a question of a renunciation that petrifies, but also the advent of racialization in the context of torture where the subject finds itself between life and death, or between immobility and a feeling that there is no way out. This rigidity does not consist in signs, considered as a means of communication as re-presentation, but arises from "the ker-nel of despair which has hardened the native's being."[48]

Fanon intends to prove that violent resistance is one way of eliminat-ing this rigidity when the self is overcome by the perverse atmosphere of colonial war, as we mentioned above. Decolonial resistance not only "con-secrates" the people's rights; it also gives them "consistence, coherence and homogeneity."[49] In brief, when the civic sphere has succumbed to mass tor-ture and restraint, only decolonial violence can redeem civil life by offering the mind a way out. Fanon's argument has been surprising, even scandalous to some political theorists and psychoanalytical critics. But his point is not simply politico-therapeutic, but also ethical. A generalized depersonaliza-tion of a population is attested to not only in a loss of cohesion, but in the kinds of antithetical thinking referred to above where there is no distinction between truth and deception, and the moral law loses faith in itself, not just for moral reasons but because rightness and justice have succumbed to absolute violence (Fanon had already made this point in 1952). It is not a matter of limiting the worst violence with another violence. What Fanon seems to be saying is that armed conflict drives out the falsehoods that literally "mutilate" the population—and that prevent the people from glimpsing a new humanism, or stature of man; or again, armed resistance is a way of refusing those relations of degradation in which, in a manner analogous to collaboration, the *colonisé* persists in his pathology through his shattered body. Non-cooperation is nonviolent in this case because it is situated beyond all order of right and so beyond the rightful violence of the racist state. We shall see in a moment how this non-collaboration is not without affinity to a pure form of resistance.

Here Fanon proposes an analogy that we should consider in more detail, particularly because it brings into view this enigmatic concept of a silence that is also a form of mental resistance to torture. What would happen if a mass refusal linked to resistance were to find itself in an insoluble conflict with the colonial regime? And in such a way that words like respect, dignity, and honor would have their meaning restored? Neither a violent refusal nor a passive resistance, undecidably, such a refusal would not even be a just means or a justified end. Indeed, it would be nothing less than a challenge to the very order of things that precedes it and surrounds it with power. It is at this moment in the text that Fanon introduces the notion of an inherent criminality (a word of constant concern). Here it will be noticed that this term is used to question the "scientific arguments" that created it, including psychiatry. This criminality, which raises all the problems of collaboration already discussed in Chapter Four ("Historicity and Guilt"), is the experience of a singular and disturbing revelation. More accurately, it reveals a fundamental incompatibility between what it means for the self to be condemned to truth and what it means for the self to decide the moment of its truth even to the point of madness or death. It is certainly not by chance that this disjunction between sovereignty and truth necessarily leads to a criminalization of subject populations. Where is one to go after this ineluctable criminality?

Such a question opens, first, upon one of Fanon's most systemic critiques of colonial psychiatry, in which the native is seen to be prone to suicidal melancholy, here an illness of the moral conscience, in which one finds "aggressivity in its purest form."[50] It seems at first that incarceration is needed in order to combat the hereditary violence of the native. This picture sums up the ideology of the School of Algiers and concerns nothing less than a certain violence of thought that presents itself as the representative of reason, law, and the state. It is not to be sure Poirot's or Carothers's thought that Fanon mistrusts, but the racial politics of their thought that, if not hidden, are none the less disavowed. This is what the racialization of science amounts to; this is where the impasse of the native's cortico-visceral nature leads. This could be developed on the basis of other Fanon texts on medicine, notably, "La socialthérapie dans un service d'hommes musulmans: difficulties méthodologiques," and especially the little-read essay, of 1957, "Le phénomène de l'agitation en milieu psychiatrique: considérations générales, signification psychopathologique," written only a few years before *The Wretched of the Earth*.[51] Both put into question the notion that the essence of the Algerian is regressive, that is to say hereditary and degenerative. This critique of the theory was political as well: the conception of liberation in these texts was seen as an integral part of the psychotherapeutic work of the clinic, with the hospital viewed as a meeting place of complex *socii* divested of all sense of punishment. Such a divestiture did arouse resistances, as previously mentioned, but for *socialthérapie* to be effective, Fanon believed that the refusal of incarceration for all but the most desperate cases was indeed wholly essential, for only then could the value of openness go beyond the platitude of a liberal idea to that of a genuine encounter at the level of the group, so allowing each individual the wherewithal to confront the imaginary order sustaining and preserving its resistances. The idea was not to remove these resistances through the removal of conflict but to make patients see how psychic liberation and resistance were also political questions, including the therapeutic organization of the clinic itself, which in its very nature (its discourse) was already violent in its conception of madness, the point being less to dispense with or remove this violence than to see it for what it is without being blinded by neurotic forms of conflict.

Beyond this simple analogy, Fanon wants to conceive of war as the greater violence that is no longer tied to private passion, or to what is conceived of as individual neurosis, but as an "occupying power" that channels all murderous acts.[52] The universalization of aggressivity during the insurgency is the self's very liberating possibility; it is analytically what transforms melancholia, say, into resistance. But in this case what is not explained is why total war is not in contradiction with resistance itself, that is, with the subject who refuses to risk himself; what is the point of saying that resistance is always a question of justice? It would seem that what emerges in the anti-colonial moment is an act that decomposes me, that introduces me to the weight of a real beyond illusion. This sudden reference to a real beyond both self and world, beyond a sort of conservation, is nothing other than a reference to the irreducible singularity of the revolution as the point where desire is no longer vertiginous, but reinvigorated. This is the war of national liberation. And the audacious thought, as idealistic as it is pitiless, of what I shall call here a resistance that is without conservation (this is not one of Fanon's expressions) is just as valid for the man who has nothing to lose as for the man for whom "Every date is a victory: not the result of work, but a victory felt as a triumph of life."[53]

To explain this triumph of life, Fanon again takes the example of criminality as if it were a normal analogy for life in the colony (or as if the life of the masses were incompatible with the laws that constrain it). In fact, he says that to steal is not "the negation of the property of others, nor the transgression of a law, nor lack of respect": rather "these [thefts] are attempts at murder."[54] All this is plainly consistent with the view that colonialism is not just an abrogation, but a form of ontological interrogation with which there can be no compromise. The explosion of murderous violence, or desire, during the war of liberation is not due to drive or degeneration but to an atmosphere that has no object other than to show itself in its fever-inducing brilliance. "Here we discover the kernel of that hatred of self which is characteristic of racial conflicts in segregated societies."[55] Once again the analogy is not between liberation and conservation, but between racialization and the politics of war. What matters to Fanon is how the manifestation of violence is not a political means or end but the manifestation of a pathological consistency where the real of colonialism is traversed.

Here begins the last paragraph of "Colonial War and Mental Disorders," which raises so many questions about Fanon's relationship to psychoanalysis. I will come back to this in due course. But for now let me stress what Fanon calls on the one hand the ethico-political demand of revolution, on the other hand the obligation of veracity and its exemplary signature; what, finally, he calls the "total liberation" of a thinking, a praxis, that knows that there is no justice, no responsibility except in the total liberation of "all sectors of the personality."[56]

In the decolonial moment, man is no longer *a posteriori*, that is to say doomed to repeat his alienation, rather he consists, he "coexists with [the nation], and triumphs with it." The appeal here is not to a retributive or distributive justice, but to the dark chaos of the tabula rasa, which Fanon evokes as a "dialectic requirement."[57] In the violence founding a new nation, the essence of the people is revealed as virulent excess, but this revelation can be both formative and precarious, since it is not preceded or regulated by any anterior, superior, or transcendent right. This founding violence is not properly destructive, since, for example, it respects life in the moment in which it is necessarily murderous. But this allusion to murder, as we shall see, is here a discriminatory index for identifying the foundation of a nation as a sovereign moment that distinguishes it from the violence of colonialism. Fanon offers multiple examples of murder as a screen (for vengeance) and as a genuine liberation (the phrase "proper time and place" recurs several times), which in its fundamental occurrence is, as Fanon himself suggests, always untimely and out of place. At the original revolutionary moment, there is no proper time and place, but only a generalized state of impropriety, which is what is most proper about its desire and its law. We have thus demonstrated:

(1) that it is impossible to separate colonial sovereignty from a perverse articulation of desire;

(2) that this perversity affects every social relation in the colony, and that this colonial phantasm arrogates to itself the license to do what it pleases, for in the colony symbolic law is no way contrary to the most extreme forms of pleasure and punishment;

(3) that resistance to this phantasm constitutes, for the *colonisés*, their first metaphysical experience;

(4) and finally, why violent resistance to the sovereignty of the colonial state is not only of destructive significance, but also comes to represent an expenditure that is no longer conserving. Through violence the *colonisés* transform the nature of the antagonism, for they are no longer fearful or motivated simply by revenge. As a consequence, they can recognize a triumphant transformation of their former petrified selves. However, such transformation comes with a cost—that is to say symptoms that can be utterly destructive of the personality. In the last years of his life, the vast majority of Fanon's clinical caseload was focused on these symptoms, which he attempted to cure for the good of the future postcolony.

7

The Condemned

The presentation offered in the previous chapter, on the mental effects of the Algerian civil war and the various complexes produced by the conflict, confirms my argument that colonial war had a profound effect on Fanon's clinical practice, and yet in many respects those effects were mostly theoretical. Anyone who reads those case histories will see Fanon struggling to define what it means to live a truly liberated life when one ceases to be treated as a human being, and when one's life can be disposed of as a mere petrified remnant that others can do with what they please. The decolonial struggle could not liberate such persons from what was making them ill, nor prevent them from loving and hating in ways that made them suffer their obsessions all the more. Fanon's clinical work brought him very close to these subjects. These people, who had answered the call of the FLN and transferred their allegiance in such a way that they did not fear the settlers who had right and power over them, were often at greater risk from their own psyches than from their enemies. That the practices of the French military authorities had a direct impact on these mental crises is clear from what has been said above. I showed in Chapter Six ("Desire and Law") that, in the war zones and the cities, people—both those who fought and those who did not—fell victim to a range of dissociative disorders. For these subjects, unable to tell apart semblance from truth, punishment seemed like a kindness, and a kind remark the most egregious, fatal offence, proof of the dead's need of revenge. If the revolutionary struggle could restore sanity to those who could be so thoroughly stripped of their identity that they could undertake nothing without putting others at risk, Fanon's clinical experience suggested that the violence of this dissociation could often be irrevocable. However, I believe that politically, he did not always accept that. It is in response to this ecstatic revolutionary movement toward liberation, where the whole relationship to the colony is reinvented, where every social relation enters into crisis and disorder (hence totally unlike political conflict and the legal form of its violence), where the space and time of the new nation produces both ascesis *and* excess (in which one can read meaning and that which is without sense), that the socially dead are meant to rejoin the ranks of the living. Such a view is more dialectical than it appears, in that it compels the distinction between the differing forms of violence adopted by the *colon* and *colonisé* and their changing relationship to the disorder from which a tabula rasa emerges. That this position does not quite agree with the clinical insights of the last chapter of *The Wretched of the Earth* is clear, I think. Hence we must admit that this chapter revises many aspects of Fanon's political thought, which therefore arrives at a new concept of freedom and pathology.

To understand more precisely how far that concept extends, we should note that liberation does not merely consist in freeing people from their symptoms, but also involves the use of the struggle itself to forge a new group idea within the space of the clinic. It is not a question of posing a world gone mad as the cause of mass unreason, but of asking why the promise of freedom traumatizes those bereft of it (although they actively desire it). In short, within the very limits of language by which the new nation's speech is given, the need is to work at patiently tracing out a new psychopolitical form that is the new space of a *pathology* (the very essence of liberation as Fanon defines it); a pathology that would not destroy everything but that begins with a profound revolution in racial-imperial law (and the passions and fears that sustain it). The necessities of revolution call forth obligations that necessarily have to be fulfilled, imperatives of knowledge, method, and ideological reinvention—everything that comes last, and is now first. But there are numerous reasons why someone who decides to carry out those obligations may not be liberated by them: fear of revenge, dread that one is acting at the bidding of another, desire for punishment, the suspicion that everyone is simultaneously a stranger and enemy, or the feeling that one's existence is not real and that, for the same reason, the only real thing is one's secret desire to be a traitor. Whatever the reason, these case histories imply that the decision to join the decolonial struggle was never simply a decision for some, and simultaneously that the war for liberation formed part of an inner conflict that was both permanent and irresolvable. That conflict led

Fanon to ask the following question: how could these subjects free themselves from the shame and murderousness of their own desires? It was a problem uniquely present to Fanon's clinical work. For nowhere else did he come across subjects with a stronger will to endure than these Algerian subjects, whose desire for liberation held an intense fascination for him, with an equal portion of majesty and misery, and for which each citizen became the perpetual owner of their accursed share.

Apart from these reversals, whose impact stems from the emergence of psychoses, there is another aspect to this state of general disorder, a very important factor unique to them that must have discouraged Fanon from thinking about liberation or ever conceiving a desire to reinvent the colony. This is consideration of the question with which we began this book: why do people choose passivity rather than the life and strength of what could actively liberate them? It is not the question that Fanon felt needed to be asked of the FLN, but of those *colonisés* who refused to comply with the struggle or submit to it: whether their refusal was elicited by love, forced by fear, or came from some other motive, these subjects posed a challenge to him, one that mingled the therapeutic and the political. It is with these subjects that the early chapters of *The Wretched of the Earth* is mostly concerned, and mostly as an opposition between native and revolutionary culture.

This also very clearly emerges from the fact that at the outset of the conflict, the FLN was engaged in an ideological war of persuasion. They needed to understand why people refused their cause, or embraced it only half-heartedly, without conviction or resolution. Fanon's various answers to this question showed a native population under complete duress, whose collusion with the status quo was less a question of hegemony than of external constraint that was also a shock to the mind. Consequently, those forces that exerted the greatest pressure on the hearts and minds of the colonized had to be identified. We have already addressed the effects of torture in this context, including a system of detention and disappearances. Other significant factors helped to maintain the citizens in their passivity, as well as to obviate the civil war and remove causes of conflict. For example, no one was free to go from the native zone to that of the settler, each being subject to constant checks and arbitrary refusal and/or detention. The sense of one's racial separateness from that of citizen was almost categorical, an awareness constantly reinforced by a rancorous atmosphere through which the militarized zones viewed each other and vice versa. But the most potent factor was the strong discipline of obedience in which they—the *colonisés*—were brought up. Here Fanon targets the role of indigenous culture in passages that have provoked the ire of the defenders of native culture, who conceive native tradition from the perspective of an authentic resistance to colonialism. For them, a sentence like the one following, from Fanon's essay "On Violence," is scandalous:

Here we grasp the full significance of the all too familiar "head-in-the-sand" behavior at a collective level, as if this collective immersion in a fratricidal bloodbath suffices to mask the obstacle and postpone the inevitable alternative, the inevitable emergence of the armed struggle against colonialism. . . . [And more specifically,] in scaring me, the atmosphere of myths and magic operates like an undeniable reality. In terrifying me, it incorporates me into the traditions and history of my land and ethnic group, but at the same time I am reassured and granted a civil status, an identification. The secret sphere in underdeveloped countries is a collective sphere that falls exclusively within the realm of magic.[1]

With regard to these traditions, too readily thought to contribute the very armature of resistance, Fanon sees a magical series of compensations and punishments by which the *colonisés* spiritually indebt themselves. They (the *colonisés*) could not urinate, spit, or go out in the dark as and when they pleased, but could only do so at certain times and at certain places, and only by following certain kinds of magical ritual at a particular time; again, they could only dance and sing in certain permissive circles at a particular time; their libido and ego without exception were subject to a continual, ritualized "pantomime" where "everything is permitted" but via a continuous practice of obedience (on this issue of magic ritual and ceremonies Fanon is adamant: "It is evident that everything is reduced to a permanent confrontation at the level of phantasy"[2]). Consequently, every aspect of native social life is prescribed according to a specific prescript of the law (of spirit). Another key factor seems to have been that at certain times of the year the *colonisés* were under obligation to devote themselves to "organized séances of possession and dispossession."[3] For Fanon such rituals played a "key regulating role in ensuring the stability of the colonial world"; it is thus through the phenomenon of spirit possession that the resentment, and violence, provoked by the crisis in the colony "are transformed, and spirited away."[4] By contrast, to the *colonisés* wholly accustomed to these rituals, the life of spirit must have appeared to be a profound freedom rather than subjugation, for "the magical, supernatural powers" whom they most feared, and whose rule over them they very much dreaded, "prove[d] to be surprisingly ego-boosting," and precisely because such fear also promised the greatest psychological award.[5] And while it is impossible, of course, to know at which point faith turns into delusion, the problem is that the colonized are still subject to a sovereign power, which has various ways to ensure that they believe, love, hate, etc., what they are told to. Fanon's conclusion from this was that the peoples' complicity with such supernatural power did not result from the command to desire what was forbidden, but was, by virtue of everyday practices, experienced as a duty to obey only what was prescribed. Thus, without any logical contradiction, we can conceive of men who loved, ate, slept, danced, and so on, not because they were free to do so, but owing to the power of a supernatural command alone.

But why, then, do they turn away from what is admittedly a feared and seductively phantasmatic power to that of a secular leadership in the midst of a war, and one that carries the risk of death and madness? Fanon's response is to simply suggest that the usurpation by the real makes even fantasy impossible. The colonized do not necessarily convert to the FLN out of ideal conviction, therefore, or because freedom remained the great and arduous task of their existence, or because there remained insufficient strength in the colonized to bear their dire situation without the compensations of magic and religion, but more because of the character of colonialism and the obstinacy of racist superstition, which impinged on their most intimate experience.

On top of this, Fanon explicitly suggests that the outbreak of civil war forces nativism itself to change (it becomes a magical, genealogical sign united to a sense of tragic belatedness). Although we can envisage why people want to hold on to native tradition during times of crisis and change, such tradition will still never be so great as the power to decide what is native or what is purely originally construed to be so, with respect to which nativism is merely the desire, both in and after the fact, for an authentic *image* prior to colonialism. As I have already said, this partly explains why Fanon is so scathing of the reverence for nativist culture by bourgeois intellectuals who scrupulously keep up the unique cult of those rituals as the "oldest, inner essence" of the nation, a reification that preserves their psycho-affective equilibrium in the absence of combat.[6] Even though this essence has, from the first, been distorted, disfigured, or destroyed by colonialism, these intellectuals seek to rehabilitate native culture as a sacred icon, both of what came first and of what can be preserved as such (as a sign of pure traditionality), that is no less than an attempt to legitimize the nationalist struggle as a supernatural struggle. The people may feel far less reverence for these traditions kept as remnants of a life prior to colonialism, but such skepticism matters little to the "secret hope" of the colonized intellectual, since only s/he can see the "magnificent and shining era" that redeems the spiritual vocation of the people as a nation.[7] Popular cultural nationalist movements hardly pose a threat here, since they pursue a reading of culture at the level of an *African* nativism rather than at the level of the nation-state. They had to try whatever they were commanded by the authority of this precolonial era or via the colonial structures that promoted native culture as a way of avoiding a genuine antagonism between the *colon* and *colonisé*. Suffice it to say, Fanon rejects these nationalist-nativist sentiments and the bourgeois elements that go with them, for reasons already discussed. I have now, I think, explained briefly but clearly the essential elements of these conserving, passive forces, preventing decolonial revolution.

Fanon had already mapped out all these worries and concerns in the section "By Way of a Conclusion" to *Black Skin, White Masks*; it remains now to inquire what he said there and how it affected his future work. So far we have addressed Fanon's clinical work as praxis, psychodrama, and as *social-thérapie*. However, in the concluding chapter of *Black Skin, White Masks*, which has as its epigraph a quote from Marx's *The Eighteenth Brumaire*, exhorting revolutionaries to draw their poetry from the content of the present rather than from the tragic expression of the past, Fanon raises the first of many questions concerning what I am here calling the pathology of nativist freedom. The link between this final chapter and the final chapter of *The Wretched of the Earth* is not one that is often made. However, as I will point out, both chapters turn on the explicit connection between passivity and consent, and both examine the history and vicissitudes by which the nativist subject opts for greater security by avoiding the greater risk of exposing his or her own desire to the present struggles of the masses.

Since the problems of history have come up frequently—viz. Freud, Sartre, trauma, repetition, etc.—let us start there. Now although the cultural conflict over the language (and concept) of nativism is somewhat distant from Fanon's critical outlook in "By Way of a Conclusion," it is still very much to the point. The schema or concept of black modernity, as the overcoming of a certain non-awareness of black civilization via its nativist negation, is the means by which Fanon conducts his examination of a new black historical consciousness (of time), and how this allows for the establishment of a new cultural spirit that claims to overcome or renew the diremptions of blackness (identified by Hegel, but also by so many ca-nonic texts of white modernity), which posits the black as the *not-yet* his-torical, not-yet conceptual part of the critical-negative work of spirit. In the relation between white philosophy and blackness, the international movement known as negritude played a symptomatic and often paradox-ical role in Fanon's thinking. Negritude is judged as still too tradition-ally Hegelian—in the sense that the development of a black consciousness is shown to be the overcoming of a white consciousness by recombining what has been separated: i.e., the (black) nativist essence alienated from it-self by (white) technico-theoretical reason, but now rejoined through the spiritual-historical form of negritude. It is traditionally Hegelian, or more accurately Bergsonian, in so far as the concept of historical time has its true abode in racial spirituality as somehow a pre-technical *Dasein*, or as the sign of historical evolution more generally.[8]

If we compare the critical, dialectical, racially essentialist (because un-critically romantic) concept of negritude advanced by people like Césaire (with caveats) and Senghor with Fanon's concluding text, then at first sight, Fanon's text appears deeply critical, albeit in a way that may well ap-pear as regressive. The first impression you receive of Fanon's text is that of an anti-historicist emphasis on non-racial identity, which would be very remote from the romantic genealogy of negritude, in which precolonial Africa is held up as the spiritual origin of black modernity. Indeed, as you read "By Way of a Conclusion," you will have been struck by Fanon's em-phasis on a new phrasing of modern blackness, continuing Marx's reflec-tions in *The Eighteenth Brumaire*, that the past is always charged with the time of the now, which interrupts the continuum of history. The reference here is to a new genealogical concept of blackness that is opposed to nihil-ism in the sense that Fanon gives it, but nonetheless turns on the meaning of freedom as a pathological deception not of blackness but of time. The problem of the reception of Fanon often centers on this problem of time, but only infrequently on decolonialism as a figure for the end of blackness as a pathological event.

We can now ask the simplest question: what does pathology have to do, in the most immediate sense possible, with blackness? Although this ques-tion might seem unnecessary, or redundant, it seems that, in the sense of Fanon's concluding remarks to *Black Skin, White Masks*, interpreters have found it very difficult to justify or excuse what Fanon means by this word "pathology," so much so that Fanon's diagnosis is taken to be more pathological than the symptom of what he is in fact analyzing. This is an odd situation, because Fred Moten and Jared Sexton,[9] the two commentators whose readings I will be using as my examples here, are in fact very powerful readers of Fanon, who should be able to tell the difference between what Fanon means when he says that the black abnormalizes himself and the claim that blackness is pathological (which is what Moten, who demands a naïve reading of Fanon, thinks he is saying). There are, to some extent, obvious empirical answers one can give to correct these assessments. But the very asymmetry between remedy and diagnosis deserves further interpretation. Let us begin by engaging with what Fanon actually says. There are four key interrelated elements to his argument: the first establishes black pathology through a discussion of black nihilism, the second draws out the implications of black *ressentiment*, the third develops some of the more philosophical implications of what it means to *be* black (which I address via a more extensive discussion of Moten and Sexton), and the fourth deals with the aporias of this consent in the form of the *n'est pas*.

All concern, without explicitly saying so, the following question: what does it mean for someone to *choose* to be black, not out of loyalty, virtue, or conviction, but rather as a form of unconscious consent? Anyone who has read Fanon will know that this question is not easy to ascertain or answer, and one that will require an effort of reading. As an example, consider the black neurotics in Fanon's first book who, rather like the paranoiacs at the end of *The Wretched of the Earth*, are wholly and wretchedly oppressed by their own desire, who *know* that everyone is whispering bad things about them to the extent that they have access to their secretly guarded inner truth and so know that they are race traitors, a truth that remains largely unthought but that they perform, necessarily and repeatedly, and by which they essentially condemn themselves, in what seems like a second betrayal. Notably envious of those who, they imagine, have never had to bear such a burden, but hostile and hateful towards those who would relieve them of it or, worse, declare themselves to delight in it, these subjects are the same subjects who recoil at the idea of being *nègre*.

There is no need to pursue this analogy here, as I have already discussed this connection between feelings of guilt and the suspicion that prompts anger, rage, and resentment in a mind in crisis. The task here, to anticipate my argument, is to ask why people feel compelled to inhibit what could liberate them from their present, unbearable situation, a problem that gives us another opportunity to ask: who would prefer to be *nègre*?

I. HISTORY; THE FUTURE PERFECT

The first part of the argument is relatively straightforward. In common with Sartre, Sorel, Nietzsche, and others, Fanon assigns a slavish attitude to the past, one that is so overwhelmed and oppressed by the present, especially with respect to life in the colony, that it can only present a miserable picture of the colonial present, in which only the precolonial is seen as proper (or primary). Fanon, more simply, says: "the black man, however sincere, is a slave to the past"; and "I do not want to sing the past to the detriment of my present and my future."[10]

One of the reasons for which Fanon takes the idea of negritude to task—namely, the manner in which it ties blackness to an absence not of sense but of historical sensibility—is due to what Fanon presents as the intellectual failure of the native bourgeoisie (who in many aspects substitutes a poetry of the past for the political struggles of the present). To become the expression of the future, negritude must give up this search for a lost cultural past whose greatness has been hidden or masked by colonialism and whose external ruination necessarily leads to a dead, ossified present judged to be secondary and derivative with respect to what is deemed properly, essentially, and intimately black. If one can think of negritude as it is described by Fanon as an identification with what can only be possessed as the loss of what was originally essential, then one can see why Fanon criticizes negritude for having established contact with blackness as a lost inheritance, wherein the only certitude of what it means to be black is thus lost from the beginning. In Senghor there are statements in that direction.[11] But closer to home, an example of someone who cannot, by definition, bear the shock of being *nègre*, who can never rest easy with the idea that blackness is nothing but *nègre*, including what he himself is, is the native bourgeois intellectual, whom Fanon reads with a great deal of antipathy and whose substitution of a black secular historicism for that of the antagonisms of the present is seen as part of a complex historical dialectic. Since race is the highest historical concept for the negritude intellectual, which then dovetails with the religious, spiritual concept of its vocation, it follows that the colonial present can only be thought, not in terms of hope or transvaluation, but from the purview of despair, or of nihilism, in which every black existent is talked about in the same terms of loss, failure, and deviation.

The question then becomes why this slavish attitude is for Fanon exemplary of a bourgeois delusion. The question also becomes one of how the black bourgeoisie-intelligentsia differs from the wretched, and here Fanon is categorical in asserting that the bourgeoisie is radically unlike, differs essentially from both the lumpenproletariat and the radical black artist-thinker. This is a curious thing to say, because one assumes (and obviously it is the case) that some of the qualities that Fanon so admires in Césaire are similar to those qualities necessary for a radically new black poetics (as Fanon's reading of *Cahier d'un retour au pays natal* demonstrates). It suffices in this respect that there is a tension in Fanon's reading of negritude as an aesthetic and as a representation of blackness. If the former is the degraded petit-bourgeois form of an unhappy consciousness, the latter is valued for offering glimpses into a blackness proper to its age, seen here as the form most appropriate to racial capitalist dehumanization. The tension does not mean that the aesthetic and the poetry are therefore founded on the same beliefs. The sensibility that defines bourgeois racial attitudes to black art subtracts the artistic effect of form from the social history that produces it. Black art can be valued because its form reestablishes the link to the nativist original from which, in principle, the contaminations of the present have been excluded. As such, the evolution of blackness as representation is disregarded in favor of the inner freedom that the artistic ideal of blackness as spirit calls for. That absorption bears witness, as Fanon emphasizes, to an *aesthetic* nihilism in the present. The assertion is so striking, so shocking in a way, that here again the critics are not sure whether to affirm or deny it. Fanon fully accepts (according to Sexton)

the definition of himself as pathological as it is imposed by a world that knows *itself* through that imposition, rather than remaining in a reactive stance that insists on the (temporal, moral, etc.) heterogeneity between a self and an imago originating in culture. Though it may appear counterintuitive, or rather because it is counterintuitive, this acceptance or affirmation is active; it is a willing or willingness, in other words, to pay whatever social costs accrue to being black, to inhabiting blackness, to living a black social life under the shadow of social death.[12]

Moten, meanwhile, writes:

A set of impossible questions ought to ensue from what may well be Fanon's pathological insistence on the pathological: Can resistance come from such a location? Or perhaps more precisely and more to the point, can there be an escape from that location; can the personhood that defines that location also escape that position? What survives the kind of escape that ought never to leave the survivor intact? If and when something emerges from such a place, can it be anything other than pathological? But how can the struggle for liberation of the pathological be aligned with the eradication of the pathological? . . . It is crucial, however, that this set of questions that Fanon ought to have asked are never really posed.[13]

Here we should note that although Moten and Sexton are ostensibly writing about Fanon, the matter of their dispute is informed by another debate that both constantly refer to, which turns on what it means to read blackness optimistically or pessimistically, and the onto-political consequences that follow. Now the fact that Fanon has been chosen to exercise this debate, including the fundamental ways in which blackness can be thought in relation to anti-blackness, and hence the entire meaning of black social life and black social death, is no coincidence. The sole difference between these two readings is how, consequently, Fanon is used to think blackness as a *political* possibility, whereas in the case of my reading, what matters is how both readings reveal how their versions of Fanon are ruled by a certain economy of representations, in which, for example, the strategically justified claim to offer a reading of Fanon involves further questions of interpretation and history for which Fanon is the substitute or stand-in, a substitution that makes Fanonism itself part of an undecidable series of displacements. However, this undecidability does not diminish the importance of these two readings but on the contrary increases it. The point here is not just to play Moten *against* Sexton, but to show how both, at strategically important moments, depend on the words of Fanon to understand black optimism and pessimism, and black optimism *as* pessimism, and in ways that render both neither decidable nor identifiable from a reading of Fanon alone. But the fact that in so doing both readings leave open the possibility of an optimistic or pessimistic reading (of blackness), which cannot be decided by a reading of Fanon's texts, reveals what I will call an aporia within the opposition in which both optimism and pessimism become in some important sense less, rather than more, decidable as opposed terms.

The passages above confirm this point about how an optimistic reading risks becoming pessimistic in face of the evidence of black pathology, and how a pessimistic reading thereby constitutes an optimistic affirmation of that pathology. There is nothing here that requires us to settle one in favor of the other, and nothing, I suggest, that allows us to be certain that optimism does not affirm its own disavowal, or that pessimism does not disavow its own affirmation. Hence we should not doubt that fidelity to the one becomes *at once and in a similar way* the true interpretation of the other. This is, firstly, because both of the above passages pertain directly, without mediation, to the issue of what it means to free oneself from that which shames you when what shames you is the shame of being (black), that is, when blackness is already shame and any attempt to escape it is already a particular instance of black pathology. What adds some pathos to these particular passages is the agonism that defines both the desire to escape and the resignation that understands escape as the active affirmation of that from which one necessarily flees, but only towards oneself. How can one escape the pathological concept of blackness, to use Moten's terms, if blackness *is* nothing other than pathology? Sexton's essay, "The Social Life of Social Death: On Afro-Pessimism and Black Optimism," first published in 2011, was written as a direct response to Moten's essay, "The Case of Blackness," first published in 2008. The essential difficulty of both texts derives from the authority of their convictions and, therefore, in a certain manner, their politics. Both essays turn on the question of what it means to make black history into a transcendent, onto-political event without escaping it, while knowing that blackness is the thing that always escapes, or is fugitive to its historical representation but in a positive rather than a nihilistic sense. For reasons that we shall soon see, both essays chiefly consist in a reading of what for Fanon is a particular instance of black pathology, the fact that the black is a stranger to himself, and what makes the essential difference between this fact and lived experience, is the misrecognitions by which the black necessarily identifies his estrangement. At any rate, to understand this para-ontological difference (Moten) we will need to understand why for Fanon there is a sharp distinction between history and time.

As regards the question of identification and liberation Fanon is absolutely unambiguous:

Here is my life caught in the noose of existence. Here is my freedom, which sends me back to my own reflection. No, I have not the right to be black.

And:

The density of History determines none of my acts.

 I am my own foundation.

 And it is by going beyond the historical and instrumental given that I initiate my cycle of freedom.[14]

As one comes upon them in "By Way of a Conclusion," such statements are so surprising, go so much against what Fanon is expected to say, that sometimes it is difficult to grasp what he is indeed saying. An example of this is the two passages above. If, on the one hand, Sexton sees acceptance where Fanon presents repeated refusal, of a willingness (to be black) where Fanon asserts that he has no *right* to be black (for acceptance and affirmation are merely symptomatic inversions of refusal and negation); and, on the other, Moten sees a nihilist response to the pathological that can never quite escape its concept, whereas Fanon, in line with what we have hitherto explained, asserts that any (theoretical) desire to escape the contingent or indeterminate relation between black experience and liberation is itself caught in the *noose* of pathology, and one that bears witness to a passive (instrumental-historicist) attitude to liberation, that is because, ultimately, Fanon's thinking, per its reading of temporality and contingency, is often *too* easy to follow or comprehend. Or, since the simplicity of the text is never *simple*, any reading that forgets this, per definition, fails.

The question then becomes why the question of black freedom is pursued vis-à-vis time: Fanon suggests that a racial-oriented freedom is a compromised freedom, for the more one looks towards the direction of a black past, the more one risks losing the future glimpsed to reification. This is why he rejects what he calls the slavish attitude toward the past of native bourgeois intellectuals, their motive being to enhance their own "psycho-existential" security rather than to become a platform for resistance (Moten) or active affirmation (Sexton). These nativists evidently believed that tradition gave them a sense of identity and belonging that made them feel majestic and dignified and so allowed them to readily submit to being ruled over in the present. Thus, the fact that such a tradition does not exist, or never did exist, and so in practice lies beyond any faithful restoration, persuaded Fanon that such derivation was in fact imaginary, or substituted what was in fact a pathological need for historico-political possibility. Indeed, as Fanon's response indicates, this attitude, in its very claim to be a vision of cultural fidelity, immediately becomes trapped in a vicious circle: the more one "exalts the past at the expense of my present and of my future," the more distant the life lived in the present becomes and the more closed the future (as nothing but a repetition of that illustrious past, a future perfect).[15] The appeal of a past that has never been present is, for Fanon, one of the more familiar, if corrupt, appeals of cultural nationalism. In "By Way of a Conclusion," he continues by objecting to the very idea that he has a right to blackness, as if a right could secure the identification so eagerly sought, rather than confirm the fundamental passivity of this attitude toward the antagonisms of the present, whose wretchedness still deserves honor and respect, rather than erasure. Any view of the past that treats it as transcendent is here dismissed as unworthy of the present political task of transformation. In the same way, what constitutes the appeal to historic precedence in Fanon's analysis is that such an appeal makes everything seem already past, and the subject a prisoner of that past (to take up an expression from his conclusion). Consider what Fanon says about the sugar plantation worker, or a member of the Vietminh: "they are not hoping that their sacrifice will bring about the reappearance of a past. It is for the sake of the present and of the future that they are willing to die."[16] For the victim of racial-capital exploitation, historical knowledge is an irrelevance, for the notion of a glorified pre-imperial past cannot convert the wretchedness of being excluded from the world into an act that would transform it. What the radical attitude to the past changes, more profoundly, is not its transcendence but how it is conceived as the expression of an alienated interiority, with regard to which Fanon sees an incertitude that is both idealistic and passive.

Although I shall not here attempt to follow Fanon's discussion of black cultural nationalism (negritude) through his writing, it is clear that the passage I have quoted is not (for good reasons) his last word: from the discussions of Césaire's *Cahier d'un retour au pays natal* in *Black Skin, White Masks*, to the discussion of René Depestre and Keita Fodeba in *The Wretched of the Earth*, Fanon has in fact been writing about the future of black critical thought, without making any concessions to the overall metaphysics of negritude. So although he rejects any notion of the past as transcendent, and even more as an exercise in progressivist teleology, Fanon's critique of negritude as a discourse of time is not historical in any simple or strict way. If in a fundamental way negritude appears here, in Fanon's text, as a nihilism, one of the key ways it does so is in its imitation and reproduction of the concept of race as the ground of human being, in the same way as the white discourse of modernity.

Here Fanon makes a pointed reference to an essay by Günther Anders, "The Pathology of Freedom," in which the contemporary problem of nihilism is related to problems of time and of historical experience.[17] Nihilism, says Anders, is a desire to possess and "render the world congruent with oneself," a thirst for power that is traced back to the disappointment at having to share one's existence with other beings—a point that also concerns Fanon, who cites it in his analysis of the colonial desire for power, for representation, to have the *all* that one is not.[18] If colonialism is not, strictly speaking, a nihilism (given what Anders calls a desire to escape the pain of contingency), it nonetheless can be taken to illustrate what Anders calls a *refuge* from the *threat* of the contingent.[19]

Fanon states this clearly enough, and adds in various asides that experience is not only a perpetual repetition, or suspense, between immiseration and usurpation, at least in so far as the future is always already contained in the past, for the subject has to learn that he has his *own* past, a past in whose relation to the self Fanon deduces a universal human *duty*, a necessity to act, and to take responsibility for, a transformation of self and world. And so he concludes *Black Skin, White Masks* with an appeal to the one who introduces invention into existence, who is ceaselessly open to this task that relates him to the world, a task that is neither predictable nor foreseeable, still less experienced (as memory), and which within the self becomes something non-contingent or, as Anders has it, even if the world appears contingent to the one who wants to transform it, "it is beyond all contingency that it is *him* who has the will to transform it."[20] This type of attitude is, along with a new sense of social worldliness (*soziale Weltlichkeit*), a persistent theme of what Fanon describes (and we will see more examples of this in Part Two) as a leap that is neither conserving nor pathological in nature and in which, like the Kierkegaardian tightrope walker whom he resembles, the black is thus able to cross, without ever arriving on the other side, the abyss between nothingness and infinity. The thought that traverses this abyss is worldly in a specific sense: it contests the nihilism that incessantly throws blackness into nothingness and contests the infinite promise of a universal humanism (which blackness cannot fail to reach without renouncing itself). Those who identify humanistically and those who identify nihilistically may both suffer strangeness to the world, but only the one who leaps can take charge of his identification without consecrating the compensations of either. This is why the Fanonian situation, described by Sexton as an affirmation made in the full awareness of despair, is less an example of *amor fati* than one of endless transvaluation, at least in so far as Fanon can say that in the world through which he travels "I am endlessly creating myself."[21]

II. ACTION AND REACTION (NIETZSCHE)

These explicit references to affirmation, and specifically to Nietzsche, are critical for our understanding of Fanon's "By Way of a Conclusion." And, although I do not wholly agree with Sexton that such affirmation is necessarily pathological, what he invokes here as the *cost* of being black is clearly important, and relates to Fanon's second manoeuver: namely, what it means to consent to what is demanded of me when what is demanded offers me the status and name of *nègre*. Whence the following reference to Nietzsche, at the end of the chapter on "The Negro and Recognition," where Fanon writes:

Man's behavior is not only reactional. And there is always *ressentiment* in a *reaction*. Nietzsche had already pointed that out in *The Will to Power*.

To educate man to be *actional*, preserving in all his relations his respect for the basic values that constitute a human world, is the prime task of him who, having taken thought, prepares to act.[22]

With these few dense sentences Fanon tries to convince us that it is man's fundamental responsibility to educate—in his concluding remarks to *Black Skin, White Masks*, he repeatedly uses the word "duty"—not only on the side of a reaction, but on the side of an action whose task is worldly transformation. The reference to Nietzsche's *Will to Power*, which condenses many of the problems discussed above, is also part of a complex thinking of black *ressentiment* that is also in some sense crucial for Fanon's thought, and for reasons that I will try to explain.

Just as there is throughout Fanon's clinical work a major concern with the border between the somatic and the psychical, so, homologically, a major concern is the point at which the active becomes passive and vice versa: there is a direct Nietzschean reference here, as can be seen in the language used, that can also be seen in the following excerpt from *The Genealogy of Morals*, where Nietzsche writes: "The whole inner world, originally stretched thinly as though between two layers of skin, was expanded and extended itself and gained breadth, depth and height in proportion to the degree that the external discharge of man's instincts was obstructed."[23] Against this feeling of expanse, according to which every experience is an economy of force that is either passive or active, Fanon will stress that lived experience for the *colonisé* is not so outward-driven. The inner life of the colonized, as we saw earlier, is one in which preservation involves the exclusion of anything that threatens the imaginary compensations of whiteness, be it on the side of negation or on the side of disavowal, an exclusion most clearly in evidence in lactification, but one that in fact defines blackness as either the *absence* of color (a nothing) or as a specular *intrusion* (an excess). However, rather than discharge conflict outwards, the *colonisé* re-interiorizes it as the sign of its social inferiority, creating feelings of shame and guilt. And so Fanon presents *le vécu noir* as a capacity to be affected that is ceaselessly open to the forces that destructure it, and that modify it, a capacity that is neither active nor passive, but the reactive affect of negrophobic encounters. In Fanon's reading of Jaspers, Ey, and Merleau Ponty, this inner insufficiency can thus only be known through what inhibits or obstructs it rather than through its movement or consecration; similarly, there can be no passivity without activity not because their relation is chiasmic, still less because they lack strength or intensity, but because black lived experience is the trace of an interrupted movement without surcease. It is therefore legitimate to point out that even in the subject educated to be actional there is always a relation to passivity that never ceases to accompany its decision to be itself, holding up to it the mirror of its own insufficiency—does not the *ressentiment* in each reaction mean, particularly for the one who acts, that any decision to be sovereign (or to be actively black in Sexton's terms) is already compromised by the slavish need to will this future appearance of itself as sovereign? If willing is the attitude that transforms what it means to live in an anti-black world, does not the language of *choosing oneself* as black not reproduce the very conditions of black abjection? And clearly if "the first action of the black man is a *reaction,*" how are we to understand this act that begins by inhibiting itself?[24]

Finally, willing change has to do with the question of why one acts; even if, as I have suggested, the desire to act is in principle formed by an unconscious consent to be acted upon (whose necessity already goes beyond the intellectual impasses of liberation), then how does one distinguish the desire to be black from its *ressentiment*? This also means that the role of will is not an *identity* to which activity and passivity are then attached as vehicles of expression. Fanon conceives of their relation in a more dialectical sense, as we have just explained it, as can be seen in the following citations from Nietzsche. For Nietzsche, experience is always a process of passive self-preservation and conquest (compare Fanon: "it is always a question of annihilation or triumph"[25]): "What do active and passive mean? Is it not becoming master and being defeated? And subject and object?"[26] And: "What is 'passive'? Resisting and reacting. Being hindered in one's forward-reacting movement: then an act of resistance and reaction. . . . What is 'active'? Reaching out for power."[27] Although such sentences are often read—like Fanon's above—as descriptions of two separate processes, what matters is the narrative that links them, for neither activity nor passivity is active or passive in itself; it is only in relation that they take on meaning and so produce themselves. For not only are they simultaneously object and subject to one another, they are also what resists and so hinders the other. In that sense activity and passivity are merely the derived form of a mediation that precedes them. I want to put a particular emphasis on this point because it is through these opposing drives that the very notion of an inside and outside, or subject and object, comes into being. A passive relationship to the past—to being black—cannot be absolutely affirmed without its correlation to an active willing to bring that past back to presence, and consequently situate it as a present meaning. Or again, when it comes to subject and object, it is only through the resistance of the colonized (object) that the colonizer (subject) discovers itself, but as an *I* that thereby only becomes accessible to itself as an object of resistance. Conversely, the colonized object, by virtue of its own resistance, becomes subject because this thing that it is not and with which it nevertheless has to be identified (object), makes it realize what it essentially means to be a stranger to oneself (subject and object). In fact, the problem is not to resolve these limit situations as resistant or passive, or to introspect them and their effects, it is to describe the cultural code (negrophobia) by which object and subject are signified throughout the process of their worldly encounter.

Thus, each time Fanon refers to black skin as represented and reports details of an *écart* or dehiscence in the experiencing, which he knows perfectly well is also the very possibility of black becoming, there occurs, by way of complex metaphor, a sense that another layer of skin has been superimposed or joined that allows black skin to be racially represented. At times, Fanon describes that imposition as an external foreign body that usurps or divides an already divided corporeal schema, and at others as an envelope that is essentially permeable, leaking outwardly what it has preserved and defended as a white inner surface that is hemorrhaging from the inside outwards and permanently altering the skin's black appearance. Likewise, what distinguishes the black corporeal schema is this chiasmus between an outer barrier that has been imposed and an inner layer that has been made permeable by internal hemorrhaging. There are other things that one can say here, but I will omit them so as to get on to the third topic I want to deal with. I will just note that the black bodily schema is the sign of an interrupted chiasma, for there would be no sense in giving blackness immediacy outside of its cultural cognition/perception. *Black skin skins itself*, so to speak: nothing is immediate or locatable as black; there is a gap or a flaw (barely perceptible) within the individual, which allows the drives to be redirected to that externality (imago) within the self, which is close to what Nietzsche refers to as the gap between two skins, allowing for a passive conquest that is actively grasped as externally imposed and thereby allowing for an imaginary aggression against oneself, which is the main theme of *Black Skin, White Masks*. That aggression comes simultaneously from within and without, which means that this skin is formed by what invades it, but also deformed by the effort to preserve this foreignness as a protection from exposure to its own occurrence. The social death that supervenes on the psyche is to this extent simultaneously a drive to make the ego the contact point for the projection that ruins it, or a state in which being fatally open to exposure is the locus of an already seeping poison coming from within. Fanon uses the phrase "sacrificial dedication" to describe this reversible, autoimmune self-relation, in several striking formulations.

There is, for example, the persistent image of the black as impotently slavish because he was formerly a slave (and one that once again has disconcerting implications for Fanon's understanding of freedom and liberation): "The former slave, who can find in his memory no trace of the struggle for liberty or of that anguish of liberty of which Kierkegaard speaks, sits unmoved before the young white man singing and dancing on the tightrope of existence."[28] On a tightrope between nothingness and infinity (these horizons that keep withdrawing from his grasp, that do not move him or stir him to act): for Fanon, the former slave therefore acts in a way that disavows, but never escapes, the suffering that is born from its own insufficiency: the *ressentiment* that guarantees and reinforces it, the impotent pretense (before whiteness) through which liberty is denied a world. Or, better put: this impassivity only confirms what is here an extreme indifference to liberation, that is impossible to quantify as either active or passive, and about which it is impossible to know whether it is attached to or repulsed by the enslavement that only it preserves. This holds that the truth (or desire) of blackness emanates not from absolutes (or objects of satisfaction) but along horizons that offer neither redemption nor salvation, in the sense that the more one discovers oneself to be unfree, or non-self-determined, the less one feels the need to act, or to experience the anguish of what could endow one with liberty. These horizons or abysses are given names—*ressentiment*, reaction—in which there is an exchange between presence and absence, between the concept and knowledge of *le vécu noir* and the equivalent forms of its "truth": the horizon (before which the former slave sits unmoved) is then simply the expression of a disaffection, and one through which the moral-political subject absents itself. That is why Fanon calls *la "chose" colonisée* a reaction, because of its refusal of anything that falls under the rule of liberty, including what it itself is: because it falls under the curse of a disaffection, it does not even know its non-existence and does not even try to escape its slavishness, for it has no concern to do so.

III. FANON—AN AFRO-PESSIMIST?

If blackness cannot know itself as black without the risk of annihilating itself, how are we to construe it? One possible answer is that of racial guilt. After some dense epigrammatic comments on time, history, responsibility, praxis, and freedom, which give some further precision to the question of bare black life, Fanon's third argument, on guilt, develops some of these questions further. His point about guilt, which we already noted in Chapter Six ("Desire and Law"), is straightforward and trenchant: namely that to freely determine oneself as black is not simply to disavow how blackness was originally, slavishly, imposed, but it is to know how one has been obligated—existentially, politically, ontologically—by that imposition. Even if the black chooses what Fanon describes as invention, it cannot be presumed that such a decision will be definitive of a new internal psychic freedom. *In precisely the same way*, it is not necessary to be black to be knowingly or actively so. Hence the reason for Fanon's rather startling claim that blackness is not a right upon which one can lay claim to existence. There is no way that one can liberate oneself from the intolerable social costs of blackness if one remains bound to it as a compact, or as something to which one remains illusorily attached; rather than seeing it as a right (and therefore predetermined in the sense of a contract), to be free to decide whether to retain that right or give it up and transfer it to some other humanism is not to reinvent it in Fanon's sense, but rather to remain transcendentally obligated to it. The substitution of right for enslavement is *still* slavish in so far as the freedom proposed keeps one formally bound, and thus *not* substantially free. This is why some of the best black readers of Fanon are very poor judges of the blackness of his thought. From the Fanonian perspective of misrecognition, any position that fails to see the reciprocal implication of imposition and misrecognition is already delusory. Accordingly, what Fanon calls the great Negro myth, or the "*Fraud* [*Ruse*] of a black world," is quite naturally viewed with some suspicion.[29] Here too the critics seem, with some unanimity, unable to see the implications of this suspicion. It is not so much that they do not want to see it, but rather that they do not know what to do with a claim that condemns blackness, or at least the illusory confirmation of a black world. This condemnation does not of course claim that blackness has no chance of a world, or indeed that it is not *the very possibility* of the world. But if one believes that this world only exists as a possibility (a thought forever enclosed by anti-blackness), then any claim to know it must be fraudulent. This is also why the suggestion that Fanon condemns blackness to a pessimistic *explanation* on the grounds that he is unable to see or imagine the lived reality of black *experience* (Moten) (and therefore can only affirm its inter-diction) itself misrecognizes what, for Fanon, is the more urgent question: whether resistance (in keeping with the modernist tradition from which we inherit it) is not entirely consistent with a slavish interpretation of black existence?

Without hesitation, it can be said that blackness is not consistent with the notion of conscious consent, and not merely because the latter fails to broach the entire question of the unconscious by which blackness submits to the law of its own abjection. What must be said in any case is that if blackness must escape all the methods of analysis, explanation, reading, or interpretation that have produced it as a *racial* revelation, it must also escape all those logics that want to make it recognizable and consistent as a *post-racial* evasion (humanism, the discourses and politics of liberation, recognition, sacrifice, eschatology, and so on). This undertaking (of reinvention) cannot be thought of merely as a way out, or even as a "fugitive movement" *more internal* to the meaning of a black liberated life restored to a more faithful, optimistic translation, which Moten argues is "necessarily unaccounted for in Fanon" and precisely because of the "inadequacy" of black existence to being in general.[30] To reinvent blackness in terms of its fragility—and consequently grasp its constitutive "homelessness" in the world—is certainly part of what needs to be done, but what Fanon means by invention has implications well beyond Moten's explicit concerns in "The Case of Blackness," and indeed well beyond the purview of blackness itself considered as a life stolen from the world.[31] So what, then, is being unaccounted for? The claim here runs as follows: any undertaking to reinvent black existence, including and especially the language of impurity or flaw, has to conceive it as a weakness, giving it a movement that has to be always "retrospectively and retroactively *located*," but that never reaches being as such.[32] This errancy of movement is neither what blackness *is*, nor what it is pathologically construed to be, but it is what appears as the history of black social life, or what Moten calls the fugitive logic of that life. As such, in so far as Fanon disavows that logic, he cannot think black social life.

Moten says this in the clearest of terms, but what nonetheless remains unclear to me is why this inadequacy should *represent* Fanon's disavowal of black social life, which is taken to stand for an ambivalent relation to "the supposedly pathological" (Moten reads the last chapter of *The Wretched of the Earth* as a sign of that ambivalence).[33] Taking those case histories as his example, Moten argues that they do indeed show a duty to resist (abjection) that makes duty as such impossible: "But this duty, imposed by an erstwhile subject who clearly is supposed to know, overlooks (or, perhaps more precisely, looks away from) that vast range of nonreactive disruptions of rule that are, in early and late Fanon, both indexed and disqualified."[34]

If Fanon were indeed merely to turn away from the kinds of disruption that Moten describes, how could he also assume what Moten calls a "preconscious duty to resist," which needs to be pointed out and even denounced because it "sabotages" the very development of the revolutionary political consciousness it prescribes?[35] A duty to resist, which does not pertain strictly to what Fanon says (he refers to a duty "to have the slightest effort literally dragged out of him [the *colonisé*]"), can, it seems, only affirm the conscious decision to *become* political as a pathological one, what Moten calls "the assertion of a kind of political criminality" as against the "crime" of complicity.[36] Why is decolonial resistance intrinsically a duty, when there always remains the possibility of its pathological "non-arrival"?[37] And why assume that Fanon has to turn away from that which consists essentially—for him—in an experience that must be either complicit or criminal? This is where I have some trouble with Moten's reading, because the word "duty" is neither volitional nor voluntarist in the concluding chapters of either *Black Skin, White Masks* or *The Wretched of the Earth*; duty is not to be understood in a moral-juridical, nor existential sense, but refers to how the *colonisés* are compelled to act in ways that are specifically unknown to them, with respect to which these subjects are profoundly unaware—but unaware in ways that might always *seem* actively chosen, and whose effect, as such, is never simply chosen, and never simply reactive or pathological. In the first place, neither the *colon* nor the *colonisé* can avoid complicity with the political-unconscious atmosphere that animates every aspect of life in the colony. As long as they comply, the doors of existence will be open to them, but every private entrance will be closed to the real. Further, if the subject takes refuge in an imaginary solitude, to the exclusion of the bonds necessary for their condemnation as black, as long as they remain suspended, each day more intimately whiter, there really is no way out from this duty to resist the world whose darkness everywhere descends. That decolonial war put an end to these mirages became all the more important to Fanon's clinical research. It became possible, in brief, to link this complicity to a profoundly racist truth to which these subjects remained bound. In order that the treatment of such subjects could be effected without any suspicion of fraud or moral condemnation, no agreement was made with these patients as to what their duty was, and certainly not before they had experienced the work of exposing their desire to the clinical group as a metonym of the socius. According to Fanon's *socialthérapie*, the cultural dimension of the symptom was always present, but it is how that presence gets lodged in the skin of the symptom, so to speak, that was decisive for how the patient encountered the languages and structures of the clinic. Psychic reinvention, as Fanon conceives it, is certainly not to be imposed, since it consists in the rigorous separation, and acting out of the separation, of what shatters from what conserves, of the therapeutic from the language of liberation, which it neither resembles, nor depends on, nor fundamentally has anything to do with. Believing that Fanon somehow, unaccountably, conflated the two, or subjected the therapeutic to the political, is to present the latter as the non-pathological truth of the former, which is precisely opposite to the final chapter of *The Wretched of the Earth*.

As Fanon puts it: "Here is my life caught in the noose of existence. Here is my freedom, which sends me back to my own reflection. . . . And it is by going beyond the historical and instrumental given that I initiate my cycle of freedom." This noose in which black existence appears to be captured is not merely a constriction, but more importantly, nor can it be fled from or escaped. It is only by means of being seized by such a stricture—at the point where one is about to fall into nothingness—that the condition for achieving that higher, more complex form of freedom opens one's reflection to a new kind of vertigo. Noosely invoked here as the figure for what surrounds black internal life, what could it possibly mean to see in the image of a lynching the image of a fall reversed from that of expiation to that of freedom? Is it precisely here that a more optimistic reading might be glimpsed in Fanon's pessimism? In a way, the entire debate between Moten and Sexton concerning the meaning of the word *black-*

ness is summarized here in this figure of "escape" that, in some way, can never be escaped, and that makes it difficult to tell whether it is an execution desired or a freedom attained through self-murder. This would also mean, clinically speaking, that the point of group analysis is not to offer respite from feelings of dissociation but to reveal to the subject the obstacles to awareness by which they remain bound to negrophobia. Or rather, it is the way in which the symptom is knotted to existence that must be held onto in clinical practice, rather than prematurely severed or brought to an end. I think that it is impossible to understand Fanon's language here without taking into account this characterization of black expiation. Yet this fall, in its tautness, is indisputably part of the historical idiom of blackness, on the grounds that this noose is not merely an *image* of black being, but part of a history in whose determination blackness can only envisage itself as a fatal freedom, a lynching that never ceases to be the *telos* of its world. And in the sense that blackness never stops being lynched in its image, or lynched as image, as Fanon says, this is why its vertiginous movement is always a drop toward the void. Anticipating here a key political insight of afro-pessimism, Fanon sees in the noose the privileged sign of what it means to be black in the world, whose *reaction*—understood in the Nietzschean sense—marks a strange fruit as devoid of life as a stone. In the wake of such images, who would not feel the weight of a constriction of, on Fanon's reading, the possibility of any black identity or positivity whatsoever? Without realizing it, then, Moten's definition of what he believes can be circumscribed as "the viciously constrained movement" of Fanon's thought (between duty and resistance) brings us closer to the pessimistic foundations of what any black liberation could conceivably be.[38]

There are some afro-pessimistic readings of Fanon, by Sexton, Wilderson, et al., and possibly my own, that see Fanon not as a disavower of freedom, but as an avower of how blackness is itself always freely disavowed as the price of its entry into the world. They are not purely, as Moten says of Fanon, refusers of black social life, but they are readers of Fanonism as the expression of why blackness is unlivable in an anti-black world. Today, I think that it is important to say that they are beyond optimism because they are also beyond black nihilism. This, unquestionably, is why our purpose here is not to read optimism pessimistically, nor to make pessimism the rebuke of optimism, but to read and reread the ways by which one reproduces the logic of the other at precisely those moments when either a pessimistic or optimistic reading of black social life is insufficient. To that extent, as Sexton says, "the affirmation of blackness, which is to say an affirmation of pathological being, is a refusal to distance oneself from blackness in a valorization of minor differences that bring one closer to health, to life, or to sociality."[39] What such sentences reveal—and here Sexton and Moten coincide—is the way that affirmation in Fanon is invariably read as a pathological affirmation. Moten is very explicit about this; he calls it "Fanon's pathological insistence on the pathological," whereas Sexton says that Fanon "fully accepts the definition of himself as pathological." Why they say this is somewhat obscure. If, for example, Fanon says that the black child abnormalizes itself before any actual racist encounter, the verb entails an incorporation that consumes itself as it were, for the child has *already kept its promise* to the world by canceling out its future as a *black* subject. Otherwise, what is its chance in a negrophobic world? Blackness is, then, not so much an affirmation as the forced exercise of its own denegation, and this is why it can only confirm itself as what it is not, and disarticulate itself as a ruined work. This is why it is not the promise that is pathological, but its injurious affirmation. A point that then gets read by Moten, notwithstanding Fanon's stress on misrecognition, as if Fanon essentially was proposing that *no one in their right minds would choose to be nègre*, which again is not wrong, but misses the philosophically interesting point—for what is at stake here is the question of freedom, or what it could possibly mean to freely choose to be black when the decision necessarily means to embrace the world that condemns you. And to choose it knowing, but without being able to foresee, that such a decision will result in a pathological feeling of vertigo. I think that it is this more difficult and demanding situation that Sexton derives from Fanon in his talk of an affirmation that is chosen *despite* it being literally at the end of a rope. No wonder then that Sexton, in his response to this reading, feels moved to point out that it is not the black who chooses to be pathological, but the world that makes the choice self-annihilating.

Moten presents his reading of Fanon as one in which optimism "is tied to the commerce between the lived experience of the black and the fact of blackness."[40] To the extent to which that life "escapes enframing" by those theories wholly given over to comprehending it, blackness is fugitive, and that is why Moten regards that fugitivity as essentially linked to a state of dispute and contestation (this is what Moten, via Heidegger, calls the *Sache*, or case, of blackness).[41] But if blackness always *escapes* from its presupposition, this presumably does not mean that it ever escapes the logic of this "commerce" between what is grasped (as fact) and what is only ever grasped as ungraspable. It is for the same reason, too, namely the incertitude of knowing, that Sexton opens his account of afro-pessimism with the following question: "What is the nature of a form of being that presents a problem for the thought of being itself? More precisely, what is the nature of a human being whose human being is put into question radically and by definition, a human being whose being human raises the question of human being at all?"[42] Since such a being can only be a problem "for any thought about being whatsoever," thus assuming and confirming that blackness is ungraspable at the level of ontology, Sexton's language is not one of revelation, but one of a radical (a word that Moten also uses) attempt to think what it means to live black life when to live that life is to live your own death in a sense, thereby confirming the social death that is the social life of blackness: what would it mean to affirm that life, that death, as the true meaning of blackness?

Between these two readings of Fanon may be perceived two differing attitudes to the ways in which blackness is revealed and reveals itself to the world. But they also reveal, due to the fact that blackness can never ever be the thing that it is presumed to be, that blackness must remain fugitive even to the concept of fugitivity if it is to be grasped (as "black") and, conversely, that any thought worthy of the name "black" must free itself from its continual misapprehension. Likewise, the true interpretation of what blackness is cannot be decided by any appeal to problems of method or of concept, for its being is nowhere: *n'est pas*. This distinction is a rigorous one, and leads to a decidedly Fanonian form of questioning. And yet both readings also want to reveal what blackness is as a fact of being, which sits uneasily with the idea that blackness remains necessarily unknown to any thought whatsoever, and precisely because it remains unthought outside the forces that shatter it. This disquiet follows from the need to make blackness reflect a demand that is either optimistic or pessimistic, an evocation that produces a slippage that leaves black thought intact. This is why I think that Fanonism remains obscure to both readings—and the complicities that link them undefined. Sexton says very clearly that afro-pessimism "posits a political ontology dividing the Slave from the world of Human in a constitutive way"; this divide does not necessarily refer to any lived experience, but nor does the argument rely on any kind of historical context in its reference to racial slavery.[43] Perhaps this is why afro-pessimism "has been misconstrued as a negation of the agency of black performance, or even a denial of black social life."[44] The response to such an accusation is unambiguous: "Blackness is not the pathogen in afro-pessimism," Sexton writes, "the world is."[45] From this it is evident that the theory has been confused for that of the anti-black world where, undoubtedly, the true politics of afro-pessimism lies. That accusation is restated by Moten with considerable rhetorical force, and yet when speaking of the "refusal of blackness" it is Fanon who is repeatedly accused (and thereby refused), so much so that the word "disavowal" itself comes to take on a disavowed structure, by means of which it is clear that the text itself becomes an example of what it exemplifies.[46] The text about the disavowal of blackness is itself a black disavowal, and the refusal of blackness that it mentions inhabits its own structure as a refusal of Fanon's black thought. That thought is unthinkably black, it is unthinkable because it refuses the logic by which fugitivity is *known*, and it is intensely black, for what it names as *n'est pas* cannot even be rendered, in a sense, as fugitive at all. This is why I necessarily believe that Fanonism begins at the point where both optimism and pessimism become *impossible*, as I hope to show in what follows.

Here the differences between the two readings take on some importance. But as I will go on to show, those differences cannot finally be maintained, for what can be analyzed as optimism can only be affirmed by its pessimistic reading. Likewise, it becomes impossible to maintain a pessimistic opposition to optimism, for then the optimistic opposition between pathogen and the world would be undone. And yet if it becomes impossible to maintain the opposition between pessimism and optimism, then it necessarily follows that this impasse should lead to the abandonment of any optimistic or pessimistic concept of Fanonism itself, in favor of a more generalizable structure. And more generally, just as Fanon's thinking about disavowal re-describes optimism as invention, so he compels us to rethink the pessimistic truths of anti-blackness and the politics by which it is traditionally held and rendered. Of the differences between the situation of the afro-pessimist and that of the afro-optimist, the first that comes to mind is that both have some relation to what Fanon calls the *mort à bout touchant* or death-in-life, the symbolic death that is not purely within the realm of language and whose meaning is neither present nor simply historical. Sexton, writing very much with the afterlife of slavery in mind, and who presents his text as an "interrogation of power in its most intimate dimension," goes on to imagine what kind of politics is possible in wake of this historical "theft that creates the crime and its alibi at once."[47] For Moten, what is most radical about blackness is the exchange between experience and fact, whose instability is located in the thought of its existence.[48] There are phenomenological assumptions here, and Moten has a long passage that refers to Heidegger[49]: both writers strongly deny that black lived experience is reducible to the way in which its political meaning has been historically produced or understood. The problem is that, whereas Moten and Sexton grapple with that history as never quite past, and so as having a kind of uncanny validity, Fanon's interest is in how blackness comes to be articulated as a kind of guilty liason whose meaning is always there before me, like a noose, or stricture, that I receive as a language and as a law, and one that is therefore *constraining*. He implies that this commandment is not opposed to the present, and at no point simply happens as the present, but nor is it a priori transcendent to black existence, in so far as the latter is thereby known historically. The way in which blackness comes to be identified as a political aesthetic, in the modern epoch, also comes to equate it, almost by definition, with the memory and identification of a particular historical suffering. For this reason, blackness exceeds not only the doctrines and decrees of this genealogy, but also the piety by which traditional historical conceptions continue to conceive of that modernity. But the equating of blackness with historical knowledge centered on the present no matter how uncanny— which Moten and Sexton both do—is put into question by Fanon. In Fanon's own discourse, blackness is always the trace of a desire that is *nachträglich*, and so is variously present even to the meaning-effects of its own uncanniness. For this reason this state could be called belated, since it is not even bound to the articulations that would seek to blacken it by representing it, and this belatedness affects even the way in which Fanon thinks about blackness as a thing or object. Indeed, his concluding remarks are first and foremost a reflection on why blackness cannot resolve itself as phenomenological knowledge, or as a being discovering itself in the world amidst other objects. And this is why it ceases, the moment that it has done its historical work as either criminal or belated. This is the first point of difference.

Now let us pass to the second, running through both texts, to see what it teaches about the social life of blackness. The first thing that strikes us about Moten's text is the story it narrates about the "appositional encounter" between black life and politics, which seems to mean that black social life represents the possibility of (rather than the discrepancy between) escape and invention, that is, a "politics of impure or impurifying facticity."[50] Even though there is the suggestion that this impurity can be purely formal, and in ways that are independent of sense and meaning, black lived experience is necessarily brought back to "the possibilities embedded in a social life."[51] Similarly, Sexton sees afro-pessimism's intervention and interlocution in how blackness can be "rendered available to thought or even become knowledge."[52] Both thereby assume that blackness has an impurity that can be rendered, and so included, in a representational politics. But as we have already shown, this is not Fanon's emphasis; Fanon, in his sharp distinction between that which eludes and that which is the inconceivable residue of knowledge, presents a blackness that is always driven to reproduce itself belatedly, like a slave, in the racial representations of culture, and one that is *n'est pas*, whose crime—and consequently transgression— is to elude both consciousness and knowledge. Hence, the refusal of any experience that agrees fully with racial common sense, and thus the rejection of any belief that *righting* the "wrong" of blackness could be secured by making blackness a right (to representation) in the present. I will come back to the question of experience below, but I wanted to raise the question of representation here in terms of a discrepancy that may be mutually exclusive. What I mean is that Moten's view of black life reveals a fundamental discrepancy between a celebratory and a nihilistic view of black experience; this is what we showed above—that the aesthetics and form of black art do not depend on knowing what a work means but also concern the way in which the work expresses meaning and value. Fanon describes this as a situation that requires black art to offer consolation for a loss that was never lost as such, but is always endlessly graspable as a separation in the present. The racial metaphysics of negritude always render blackness as in some sense present, but always lost as presence, or only apparently present. That is the nihilism of the optimist, that blackness has to represent something for it to be present, that it has to convey a power that necessarily precedes the social death of its advent, otherwise it will remain haunted by impotence and ruination.

The relationship of the pessimist to Fanon's original texts is even more fraught because of this, which I believe comes down to a demand that blackness be a death that endures beyond sacrifice or tragedy. I see in this demand a relationship between allegory and irony, wherein the problem of knowledge or the desire for understanding, or the need to make a coherent statement, is entirely postponed, or at least rendered aberrant in the very attempt at reading. It follows that the most pessimistic reading, and the most optimistic, must both engage with the elusiveness of Fanon's texts without confusing pessimistic uncertainty with the optimistic deceptions of knowledge. In this context, Sexton asks the following question: "Can there be a knowledge of a grammar (of suffering), of a structure (of vulnerability)? If so, is it available to articulation, can it be said, or is it an unbearable, unspeakable knowledge?"[53] I cannot be absolutely sure that knowledge is the right word here, rather than non-knowledge, which has its own set of connotations (*incompletion, insufficiency*) that do not agree with the stress on knowledge. Moten's various emphases on blackness as a kind of fleeting irruption are closer here to Fanon's language, because on this basis the figure that comes to the fore is that of a disorder, or disruption, best understood in terms of the difficult relationship between the hermeneutics and poetics of invention. Invention is a relation of discourse to language, not a relation to an extralinguistic meaning that could be copied, paraphrased, or imitated. It will be better therefore to adduce this disorder not according to a case law brought before an assembly (*Sachen*), but in terms of the instability immanent to the meaning of blackness itself, where the case is understood etymologically in the sense of contingency and of fall (*lapsus*), that is to say, the shock of contingency through which the case of blackness is found, invented, without the presupposition of a judgment (of affirmation), or the need to name an example (which cannot just be an example) of pathology.

In contrast, Sexton's concern is perhaps less poetic, but more politico-philosophical. He wants to argue that blackness has an essential relation to social death even when read optimistically, and this consecution is not to be simply celebrated or simply deplored. And, more crucially, that social death is the law of blackness as law (as case), but knowing that this "law" is derived in the first instance by the kinds of social processes at work in black social life. In the case of Fanon, blackness's relation to law cannot act as an example of law's self-relation, in that blackness is not reducible to either the "simple interdiction nor bare transgression" of law: whether this be figured in terms of pathology or denigration, it is clearly a situation of a duty that proceeds without right, if only in that blackness is obligated by law to renounce itself as the very possibility of its jurisdiction.[54] This difference thereby shows the second difference.

This point is best understood in terms of what Fanon means by *mort à bout touchant*, as is evident from the text in which it appears, *Studies in a Dying Colonialism*. In the essay on "Medicine and Colonialism," Fanon suggests that "the colonized, like all the people in underdeveloped countries and all the dispossessed everywhere, do not see life as blossoming and fruition but as a permanent struggle against *atmospheric* death": this omnipresent death, this *mort à bout touchant*, "tends to make of life an incomplete death," in which small and large acts of resistance are not so much a "refusal of life" as an all-too-human response to this "close and contagious death."[55] Thus, a *resistance* to colonialism is both instituted and marked by this incomplete life-death. By refusing Western medicine, by making Western therapy into a clandestine struggle over life *and* death, the colonized know that it is through the promise of the cure that the *law of colonialism reaffirms itself*. Thus the patient *vanishes* or releases himself from the passive objectivity of colonial pathology; and while this confirms the Western view of the colonized as feckless, for Fanon these acts are the site of the coalescence of a struggle in which life and death are openly or implicitly in conflict: i.e., by shutting himself up alone with his disease, fastened to it, coiled up in its fascination and pain, its emptiness and voluptuousness, the colonized produces social death as the symptom of an overwhelmed body, in whose dispossessed life and incomplete death the rottenness of Western pathology is revealed as a discourse of cure without ultimate justification or legitimation, a cure (or case) within which the rule of law and propriety is sustained by force and violence. There is then something rotten in this encounter between medical efficacy and the racialized body that infuses the cure with an element of violence and compulsion.

It is therefore surprising to read that this situation is one in which Fanon shows his "ongoing ambivalence toward the supposedly pathological."[56] Moten's mildly parodic sketch of this case history in which anticolonial resistance is both symptom and cure could well be read as a refusal to read what Fanon himself says about the contagion of social death in the colony. There has been a great deal of discussion, and long before the advent of afro-pessimism, of the different points of view that Fanon adopts to affirm the lived social death of the colonized. A way of connecting this death to his psychotherapeutics, or more broadly to his analysis of the colonial body, would be to consider what he says about that body's contraction and/or mortification; in other words, to see the truth of that body in its subsequent alienation, or rigidity, to make this body reveal itself as a form of resistance (not even necessarily a conscious one) to the signifieds of colonialism. The atmosphere of certain-uncertainty defining this body affords an example: the sheer material facticity of that atmosphere is secreted in the body (both clandestinely and literally), which is subsequently blown apart, distended, and reassembled; this body becomes virtually multiple insofar as it is injured and irreal, obsessed and petrified, a body that would assume its affirmation in so far as its injury becomes an unspeakable piece of the real, simultaneously performing delirious disorder and a conserving desire as it undergoes torture, petrification, and the seeming infinitude of total war. It is therefore not easy to see why Moten should describe this multiply injured body as a dialectical reversal (of political consciousness and cure), rather than what Fanon describes as its structural vocation: that is, not to decode (the case), but to *overcode* or *overwrite* both law and criminality, resistance and complicity with the advent—whether perverse or paranoiac, imaginary or neurotic—of decolonial war. In Moten's account this structure is read as a political prescription (to resist) that is always positioned as a natural will to resistance. It is a reading that is at once maybe too psychological and too normative, all the more so in that it seems to disregard what Fanon refers to as the indescribable, or inassimilable: the shock or accentuation of the revolutionary moment that is both destructive and decomposing. So Fanonism now becomes a text whose political prescriptions are contradicted by its psychotherapeutic demands, in so far as the liberatory narrative of revolution inevitably forecloses the now normative notion of the cure. The problem with this reading is that the notion of resistance is projected as a *telos* rather than grasped as an advent that exceeds all such narratives. This is too pessimistic a reading: unless we conceive of the incomplete death that seizes—*this* life, *this* body—as the very thing that refuses to be exhausted by categories of resistance or pathology, we will fail to read, in short, what Fanon means by the permanent hemorrhaging of this black body which ultimately no art or politics can stem, precisely because in the movement of its history there are few categories that wish to touch it without being made dirty or hysterical.

Fanon further goes on to say, in his concluding remarks, that blackness is explicitly not a problem of being, but a being whose morality and politics cannot be self-determined: the anaphora "I do not have the right" is not just repeated in a grammatical sense, but is a way of putting into question any correspondence between race and right, as if one were the culmination of the other. Not content with this, Fanon repeatedly uses the phrase "I am [not]": all this is plainly consistent with a refusal of any onto-juridical understanding of the case (of blackness), and its relationship to life, its meaning and concept. If blackness is in some fundamental way incompatible with the desire for social life, what, in Fanon's text, does blackness resemble? One of the things it resembles would be philosophy, in that it is critical, in the same way that philosophy is critical, of any simple notion of liberation, of any philosophical discourse that sees freedom as a regulative Idea (existentially, phenomenologically, ontologically) somehow abstracted from the situation. Philosophy is not a judge of the world as we know it, but it has another relationship to that world. Critical philosophy, and the reference would be to Anders again, will be critical in the same way that blackness is critical of any notion of reparation that could deliver it from the contingency that it itself is. This is why Fanon writes that his freedom "sends back to me my own reflection," for to be free essentially means to be a stranger (*étranger*) to oneself.[57]

Accordingly, we must not forget that sentence where Fanon refuses the ruse of a black world. The meaning of the word "ruse" (meaning ploy, subterfuge, machination) states clearly enough to whom this text is not addressed. What is being named here as a deceit, or as the disjuncture between the world and blackness, is the totalizing power of racist dissimulation and the fake resemblance of humanity to a world that has now come to convey, or represent, a murderous humanitarianism. With this Fanon indicates plainly enough why the history of blackness should not be understood as a ruse for apprehending the present, and assuredly why historical suffering should not be taken to express either an optimistic or pessimistic meaning. Fanon is writing for those to come, as against those for whom there has been or will always be a black world: he is writing for what I venture to call the future proper as against the future perfect, at least in so far as the future perfect has always already been contained in the past. Fanon calls this type of attitude that foresees the future as a necessary repetition of the past, as slavish. Against this gesture, according to which everything that will be said has already been said, Fanon will stress the future present, to what is radically open and unpredictable, less a will be or will have been, but a not yet that breaks absolutely with any teleology and can therefore only present itself as *a duty without a right*. For this world that is not yet must be willed, and not simply reasoned into being. For the act to be an advent, it must not only be absolutely violent to what came before, it has to be strictly unreadable to those who seek to make sense out of it as a revelation of knowledge (and this is also why the tabula rasa is neither a messianic nor spiritual concept, nor a symbol to be understood in analogy with law).

IV. THE *N'EST PAS*

The further argument for not retaining Fanon as either a pessimistic or optimistic thinker is as follows: he implies that, in order to loosen the noose of black existence, one must resist the constant tendency to sever it, or even to escape it; the point rather is to let the matter fall, so as to dispense with anything that would seek to preserve blackness as a symbol always tied to its strangulated meaning. Arguably one of the most difficult things to grasp is those passages where Fanon says that what makes blackness black is not to be understood by analogy with any genealogy or identity, or anything that resembles an object or force. We are to think of blackness not as the obverse of thing or representation, nor are we to understand it from the perspective of the "can" or "should," the "will be" or "I am." If we want to understand the thing that blackness is, we should understand that blackness is *not*. For Fanon, "[*le nègre*] is not [*n'est pas*]. Anymore than the white man."[58] In the same way, the relationship between this *n'est pas* and blackness is not to be understood by analogy with negation (in the manner of, say, Freud or Hegel), rather we are to understand blackness from the perspective of a non-negated negativity. To understand this *n'est pas* would be the burden of any reading of Fanon's texts, whether optimistic or pessimistic.

The *nègre* is *n'est pas*, yet this *n'est pas* is not a metaphor. No wonder that critics have had difficulty. Indeed, too many readings of Fanon want to say what this "*n'est pas*" is, to explain it away on the basis of what it resembles, or represents, to reconstitute it as a totality. It seems necessary to be able to locate blackness in terms of what negates it, or, more precisely, to be able to attach predicates to it to make it recognizable (it seems to be characteristic of these readings to assume at least the possibility that blackness can be incorporated as a thing, or else as an identity or subject whose demands can be met and its referent duly agreed on). If only Fanon would come clean as to what this "is" is, then it would be easier to decide what it is not, and so appropriate or denounce it. All these readings resemble each other in the fact that they try to negate what is always already negated. Or they reveal, through their failure to understand what this *not* is, what for Fanon is already an essential failure in the history of critical philosophy: to say what blackness is in a way that is entirely freed from racism. Moten talks about blackness as a thing, for example, to which predicates of disorder and deformation can be attached, even though he will at some point insist on its "inadequacy" to the "calculation of being in general."[59] Or in Sexton, who refers to the inescapability of black social death, we read: "In this we might create a transvaluation of pathology itself, something like an embrace of pathology without pathos."[60] I do not know precisely the reason for this word "embrace": a pathology without pathos does not escape the claim that this is what blackness is in so far as it too can be rendered as a pathological thing or presentation—and it is clearly neither simply an affirmation nor a negation of blackness to say that we would have to presuppose the sense of this apathetic blackness in order to understand notions of its transvaluation. For Sexton, this apathy comes into being "where thought breaks down, at its limit."[61] Or, "must one always think blackness to think antiblackness"?[62] What such a question leaves out (and in leaving it out is doubtless true to the anti-pathos it describes) is any notion that blackness has no locatable referent or unequivocal name, but is something that escapes all attributes, including the unity of an ontic-ontological fugitivity or again the hypostatized name of "absolute dereliction."[63]

Here again when Fanon says that the *nègre* is *n'est pas*, the scenario leaves unresolved, or unspecified, what blackness *is*, in the name of trying to get at what seems to be a less identifiable, more aporetic, hesitation or movement. To represent this hesitation as optimism or pessimism is simply to reduce its meaning to a desire rather than engage with Fanon's refusal to represent or name. Is Fanon, in this refusal of the preeminence of the question of what blackness is, in fact repeating the apathetic violence of blackness towards its "pathology"? Is this a misrecognition *before* the *méconnaisance* (of blackness) as described by Fanon? Would this question, which I cannot presume to answer here, send us back to what Sexton describes as "one of the most polemical dimensions of afro-pessimism as a project: namely, that black life is not social, or rather that black life is *lived* in social death," a sort of originary life-death or death-in-life: a sort of double emphasis in exactly the sense that Fanon later calls, much more laconically, but perhaps more problematically, *"mort à bout touchant"*?[64] This *n'est pas* (of blackness), to the extent that it is not a possible object of knowledge or judgment, does refer us to what, in *Black Skin, White Masks*, Fanon calls the abyss.[65] This abyss that is before any earth or world, tribunal or judgment, before the determination of "the whole possibility of and desire for a world," before even the indubitability of law or object, is obviously linked to the *n'est pas* and consequently begins, always violently, where *le vécu noir* undergoes the shock of a sudden shift or a reversal in its phenomenal existence.[66] At the same time, however, this utterly naked de-clivity is not something that can be known, or rendered, or proposition-ally named *as such*: for the non-thing that blackness is evades being judged, and should never be confused with the predicates of racism. Indeed, one could argue, apropos of Frank Wilderson, in *Red, White, and Black*, that this "great black hole" is a priori excluded from the logos of human being, and this is why it always remains other with respect to itself.[67] The thing that blackness *is* not—and accordingly, our relation to it—is the mark of a rupture that is both exterior and *radically* intimate, an abyss that is situated at the limit of judgment, thought, and desire: a monstrance without center or end. The uncanny position of this rupture is confirmed. These notions arc not rhetorical: when Fanon refers to "the unidentifiable, the unassimi-lable" there is an attempt to locate what is situated very specifically at the limit of the human: blackness is defined not by its exorbitance, nor by its inhibition, but by the way that it is always imaginarily misrecognized as a limit work rather than what, on the contrary, makes it so singular and dis-turbing as the unnameable event of an infinite postponement.

Throughout Fanon's work there are many forms of blackness as both object and thing, and they all imply a concomitant expulsion of blackness from the graph of desire. They range from what may seem to be merely fe-tishistic investments to what is explicitly connected to accounts of an atro-phic disappearance or lytic rigidification of desire (used by, for example, subjects whose object relations cannot be found in reality, but only refound in a kind of phantasmatic real, or real fantasy). To understand this work is also to understand Fanon's radical questioning of analysis and psycho-therapy. The assumption that guides this analysis is very similar to Freud's reading of *Verneinung*, but for Fanon (and in ways that recall Lacan) black-ness must be understood not as a metonym of a lost object, nor as the ma-terial mark of a deprivation, but as the structure of a never-having-had. In particular, we must not confuse this structure with either loss or lack; what matters is our *relation* to its impossibility, a relation that must here be un-derstood more grammatically than logically: in the history, texts, and lega-cies of anti-black racism there is always an imaginary misrecognition of an object that has no ontological resistance to its signifying predicates, and one whose libidinal reproduction only exists when caught up in language. For Fanon, critical-therapeutic activity is thus essentially an activity of re-invented judgment, respecting the case in its singularity, finding the ap-propriate rule always only after the event. This peculiar temporality, much more than any periodizing hypothesis, is what constitutes the lived life of blackness (which is anything but escape or theft).

This still involves a certain number of worrying presuppositions, notably that the two poles of blackness and whiteness are occupied by a kind of caesura or ellipsis, or a kind of dead end unspecified as such: "the *nègre* is not. Anymore than the white man." The scenario I want to look at is one in which what Moten calls Fanon's "pathological insistence on the pathological" is something that might be called a psychopolitics of atrophy, or possibly petrified life (as for example in the case histories that close *The Wretched of the Earth*), in which the colonial body is caught up in something like hysteria, obsessional neurosis, and psychosis.[68] Even if (as is largely the case here) that petrification is used as a metonym for colonial culture, the atrophy presupposed is only detectable as the heterogeneous movement of an originary division from which being and nothingness emerge. Conversely, that atrophy or lysis, in its very complication and its irrationality, obeys neither law nor representation but a mysterious commandment that comes to the black subject from his or her own history—perhaps even from his or her own body? And here, perhaps unavoidably, we would need to return to those pages in *Black Skin, White Masks* in which Fanon describes a black-white being who is on guard against his white-black self beginning with the very identity of the body that is and is not black, that is and is not dead.

We might say, as a matter of fact, that any reading of Fanon, today, begins effectively (and not by the utterance of a naïve hope) with the inescapability of this *mort à bout touchant*, with the always violent shock of its decrepitude, a lysis where the solidarity of self and language breaks down, neither of them permitting a diagnosis of internal renewal, however multiple and dialectical. The *n'est pas* that seems to be underlying the notion of black social life and death must not, however, be overestimated; it is part of an epistemological break, which compels us to revise the key reference points of Marxism, Freudianism, and phenomenology for how we conceive of the Fanonian object. As I see it, the word *object* must here be understood as a limit work or fragmentation: it does not refer to a series of ontological displacements or dislocations, but to the radically symbolic work of racialization; it exists only when caught up in the discourse of racialization (or rather it is *n'est pas* for the very reason that it signifies a kind of explosion, or dissemination; the abyssal aftermath of a black hole in words, meanings, and structures). Let us now trace in more detail how the black subject is traversed by this object: this object that is *n'est pas*.

Having already defined the problem of the *n'est pas* in Chapter Two ("The Clinic as Praxis"), I will discuss the psychopolitical implications of the term as Fanon elaborated them. It seems to me necessary to remind those who accuse Fanon of a fundamental pathology to return to the category of wretchedness, which Fanon places at the heart of the subject who is *n'est pas*. Inasmuch as decolonial revolution (understood as such) implies a remarkable reinvention of sovereignty, Fanon's notion of wretchedness compels us to conceive of revolutionary liberation no longer in terms of a sovereign decision or desire but as the very exercise of a suspicion of, or a discomfort with, the traditional discourse or literature of sovereignty. We can even, with a certain temerity, give this suspicion an historical dimension, as a refusal of any sovereign claim to master blackness or assume responsibility for it, which in its grandiose form prescribes decolonialism itself as a therapeutic result and cathartic demand. The disavowed reading of Fanon's text (of which afro-optimism is the latest example) would be one then that claims this mastery in a way unknown to itself. It raises the political question of reading—of how we should take responsibility for the interventions of Fanon's own text—but fails to interrogate the blindnesses of its own pious optimism. As such, it falls victim to its own pessimistic thinking of possibility, presenting Fanon's statements on invention as if they fell into a naïve optimistic outlook rather than the attempt to describe a new politics of affirmation. Again, afro-pessimism is closer to Fanon here in so far as it claims that black social death only becomes intelligible when seen against the background of the issues and questions generated by states of institutional and political states of emergency. The wretched are neither a foundation nor anti-foundation, but the figure of a dislocation at the heart of modern sovereignty. Only thus do they come into being. What manifests itself as the law's inner decay in the colony is the fact that rule of law is, in the final analysis, incomprehensible without the wretchedness that ruins it, without which law's ultimate justification or legitimation would not exist sovereignly. For this reason, afro-pessimism can be seen as a particularly refined instance of black optimism, and one that also reveals immediately why it is simultaneously an illustration of the "case" that, according to Moten in his reading of Fanon, is necessarily difficult and hard to grasp.

This new conjunction of wretchedness and non-sovereignty, which I have just mentioned, might provisionally be called, for lack of a better name, an *antinomy*, since it implies that there is a form of death in life whose everyday struggle expresses a *décalage* or cleavage between sovereign life and black being. Now, this death in life that is *n'est pas* cannot be identified with humanism, even in a new form; or in any case, humanism is far from exhausting it. It involves a perspective of an altogether different scope, whose object cannot be constituted as a simple accident of form but by the very relation between blackness and knowledge. This perspective does not imply a lack of interest in humanity, but, on the contrary, a continual return to the racial "truths," however archaic, in which whiteness is the only proper form of human being. Certain of these truths still have a power of provocation, in respect to a certain idea of language and culture, and for this reason, we must not fail to consider them. What follows will be taken up in more detail in Part Two.

1. One of the common misreadings of Fanon's theory of violence is to read it as an Hegelian struggle or, at least, as positing the struggle between colonizer and colonized as a version of the fight for prestige between master and slave: violence therefore has a progressive purpose in making the colonized the subject of a recognition rather than the thing (*chose*) that is not recognized.[69] Hence, violence is humanized as a fundamental category of human being. I am not saying that this reading is wrong, and certain aspects of it could be read into *Black Skin, White Masks*; but in *The Wretched of the Earth* decolonial violence is far from its Hegelian origin and refers to a struggle that is not *to* the death, but is *with* and *from* death, a struggle that seeks to go beyond the death in life that, however dialectical, no philosophical anthropology has yet grasped, and that reveals a certain aporia within the language of sovereignty.

Decolonial violence, which I have just said is not a dialectic, is engaged in a detoxification that is radically reinventive, since it implies that decolonialism cannot be identified with a politics, even in a progressive form, but with a language yet to be written. It leads to a tabula rasa, bringing a judgment into play, but one without jurisdiction. This violence receives extremely various contours and expressions, but one thing seems certain: the moment of invention is an event without sense or content; consequently, its appearance always exceeds the representational forms of the political. As a tabula rasa, violence has nothing to do with either right nor justice: in a sense it only takes place as a case, but this is a case that falls without order or meaning, through which the colonized is only able to express itself disarticulately. As such, it marks the absence of person and of law, and is an advent without jurisdiction. If this is criminality, at least in its decision and pathos, it concerns itself with the blackness that falls, in principle, always outside of law. Or, more precisely, decolonial violence plunges the subject into an abyss whose meaning (Fanon uses the word "measure") is always unprecedented. *N'est pas.*

2. A second principle, especially important with regard to how we read Fanon's psychopolitics, is that blackness cannot be considered an unambivalent form of *pleasure*. In his reading of how nativism inures itself to colonial repression, where every cultural value is the product of a collective punishment, pleasure (religious, pagan, aesthetic) comes to have the following resonance: there is something frenetic, ghostly, hysterical about it. Fanon writes: "This magical superstructure which permeates native society fulfills certain well-defined functions in the dynamism of the libido," and "we perceive that all is settled by a permanent confrontation on the phantasmic plane."[70] Here law itself becomes magical; in its erotic jurisdiction the subject is not so much presented as inhibited, precisely by the ecstasies that terrify and at the same reassure it and that remedy the "pure force" of colonialism by an erotism that delimits itself within the limiting force of colonialism.[71] As such, the real violence of the colony becomes indiscernible from the magical superstructure of nativism (its foundation as libido, as terrifying figuration), which it claims as a more archaic form of its own jurisdiction. Defined as law, pleasure—which might be called an eros of subjugation to be distinguished from that of masochism—signifies the institution of an "avoidance" that is itself disavowed, and represents a dissociation that is essentially turned in upon itself.

3. Moreover, from a methodological point of view, Fanon's writing on black art accustoms us to a form of libidinal economy that, at the level of psyche and culture, both "protects and permits."[72] The economy hitherto that sees art as sublimation, which must immediately be seen as a *work* (of translation), is here deciphered as an "open book" and at the same time as a *de facto* abandonment to a world of dangerous and dogmatic fictions.[73] Fanon's analyses suggest, on the one hand, that we distinguish levels of dislocation and describe the distinctive elements by which black art is able to establish a completely new form beyond judicial reason; and on the other, he asks us to recognize that, unlike nativist and colonialist practices, these

forms make possible something else, as "the imagination is let loose outside the bounds of the colonial order."[74] As Sexton has observed, it is the discovery of this passage that gives Fanon's reflections on "life and death, pessimism and optimism, subject and object, thing and case, blacks and blackness, and so on" the tone of an affirmation written, it seems to me, from a position that is both within and without, within *as* without the political life of blackness.[75]

4. There remains to be discussed one last Fanonian notion, which may illuminate the figure of blackness at its very center, since it concerns the motif of slavery. In the chapter on recognition in *Black Skin, White Masks*, Fanon refers to a governing system of "fictions" that prevents the black from encountering the world as object: the subject that seeks to know itself through its history, whether in the aspects of master or of slave, must confront the object so as to lose it and so gain its personhood, not so much in the objectivity of the given as in the form of ethical social life. Hence, it is possible to see in Fanon's commentaries on Adler and Hegel a blackness that is itself a fiction, that exists only through and as fiction, whose fictioning conforms to different levels of alienated life: political, economic, and ontological. This unity of the fictitious and the repressed authorizes Fanon's rereading of phenomenology and psychopathology: blackness can only in sum recognize itself as a fiction, which is why it turns away from the Other and from any dialectical resolution of itself as a labor that produces and sublates. It is in terms of this impasse that blackness figures the very being of the case that bars it from having both form and content. The black cannot put blackness to work—at least in the way that slavery is thought in metaphysics—for its "governing fiction" involves the resolution of figures, that is metaphors, or signs, that are absolutely self-referential and contained to the exclusion of anything else, figures and fictions whose action can increasingly be defined as a refusal of a *black* logic of the subject.[76] It is in this perspective that blackness is only ever going to be the subject of a limitation that is the limit of its own fictioning, and first of all insofar as the mirror whose whiteness it masks befalls it as a *n'est pas*.

CONCLUSION

This opening discussion of psychopolitics and war has been highly relevant to the purpose I had in view, namely to connect Fanon's work as a psychiatrist, or as a thinker of *socialthérapie*, to his politics elaborated in the context of decolonial war. In the light of this, we are now compelled to ask what can be ascertained about Fanon's cultural theory in general. What that theory teaches us about the social life of blackness, or the imagining of its concept, I shall explain in Part Two, where I propose to discuss key themes and tropes as well as key intellectual figures.

Homo Nègre

Prologue

I showed in Part One that it is because blackness is shattered in its existence, by intrusions produced through imposition, that it is seized with anguish. It is the fact that I misrecognize myself, sacrifice myself to a delusion, stupefied by my reflection, that I know nothing of who I am; only then do I discover the world in its cruelty. I also showed that all sense of obligation is rendered null or void, in the colonial encounter, because the *colonisé* is not able to be Other to the white. Indeed, the *colonisé* is all the more obligated because of this failure or flaw. When Fanon says that the black has not encountered itself in others, he means two already confusing things. 1. The black famously has no ontological resistance to the hatreds that compel him and are, so to speak, inscribed upon him. And in this sense it is impossible for him to experience himself without the illusion of an object lost, or sacrificed. 2. Blackness, then, is the vertiginous experience of its own impossibility, or its experience is that of an impasse, or aporia, that remains hidden, unknown, inauthentic. As will, desire, a demand for recognition, etc., blackness therefore cannot *be*, namely, its ipseity is that of a sea without terminus, a tragedy without resolution, and so it cannot be accounted for except as *irreal* (a word that Fanon takes from Sartre's early work on the psychology of the ego), and its self-certainty denotes a perpetual deferral or waiting. Blackness is *not*, in brief, because it cannot be *determined* as ever having been, even negatively, because it has no Other to ensure it. Fanon addressed this question as an existential problem in his early work, but also as a clinical question. The recourse to *socialthérapie* was an attempt to show how the bonds between people are formed through negrophobia, and in a way that is entirely consistent with an imaginary affirmation of colonial authority. For this reason we reach the same conclusion here as we did in the first part of this book: that the *colonisé* is haunted by its own incertitude, which is why it is "overwhelmed by sin, riddled with guilt."[1] In this second part of the book I will discuss the implications of this haunted insecurity via three motifs: invention, existence, and the abyssal.

Invention

> "I created a people, and I was unable to create men."
>
> JEAN-JACQUES ROUSSEAU, *Du Contrat social, Oeuvres complètes*, 3: 500

We have previously said that the individual and collective feeling of being on guard was part of the same structure of feeling boxed in, literally hemmed in by one's own guardedness, as if the blackness concealed or hidden by its white mask could only be embraced as a kind of coded secret (at least under its mythical appearance of power and right), as if being on guard was part of an always faithful fidelity to keeping guard, and so retaining within the self an authority that is never otherwise than rightful. For Fanon the last thing such guardedness wants is to be exposed as *nègre*. That is why it can be said paradoxically that blackness (in the ideological sense of the term) is a matter of revealing that which guards, or that which causes one to keep guard, to inhibit oneself; a blackness that would invent as much as discover itself beyond its own condemnation, as a poetic unveiling. But if blackness is never present to itself, or is irrevocably displaced far from itself, then what makes it black, so to speak, can never be reached. Fanon approaches this aporia in terms of the difference between invention and unveiling. If unveiling is the promise of revelation, then invention follows a completely different path of disclosure, and is less the promise of an adequation between meaning and authenticity than a disintegrative movement, a leap, that never reaches its mark. This is also why its path is a passage through illusion, but only as the promise of illusion's afterlife, which it neither depends on nor believes in, thereby making it in my judgment the blackest leap of all.

I. INVENTION IS NOT A HUMANISM

"I should constantly remind myself," writes Fanon, "that the real leap consists in introducing invention into existence."[1] And just before this sentence: "I am not a prisoner of History [*l'Histoire*]. I should not seek there for the meaning of my destiny."[2] In all of Fanon's writings I know of no passage that sums up, to the same extent, the enigma of his thought. The point of these gestures seems to be that invention, so often invoked as though it were *eo ipso* something historical, is here the figure for a kind of radical untimeliness that entails a leap, and this leap cannot be anticipated, nor can it be prepared for, nor can it be traced back to a prior historical moment to be interrogated as such. To leap, then, is more than a rhetorical figure; indeed, we need to see it as the very conceptuality that Fanon puts into play here, as the difference between the historically possible that has not yet become history and the hope that history makes impossible and in whose wake only remnants remain. Fanon needs to remind himself of this. He needs to remind himself of the devastating consequences of invention *and* of history. (In this he is closely related to Benjamin, whose *angelus novus* is just as essentially a figure of danger and hope.[3]) Invention, because it is a radical transformation, is not reducible to economy or strategy, and therefore, we might want to say, does not represent yet another form of political calculation. Nor is it a mode for utopia, whose possibility can now be resurrected in a myth of perfectibility, when the oppressed take a dialectical leap into the "open air of history."[4] This is why invention is not reducible to any kind of teleological schema. Despite the primary role that history plays in the meaning of colonial subjection, clinging to its truth or whatever happens to be regarded as its truth can only be imprisoning, or backward-looking, for the leaper.

Although none of Fanon's texts are explicitly devoted to this configuration, the ethico-political implications of invention can be seen throughout Fanon's work, although it is less obvious what these implications might be. I want to argue that this situation is already inventive, insofar as it gives rise in Fanon's work to a singular politics of invention, and one premised on a leap that is neither a catastrophe nor a fall, an advent nor a realization, and is mostly incomprehensible to what came before. From there it is but a step to the notion that invention *is* revolution and that the true task of politics is to embrace or demand this imperious leap. Political reinvention, on this view, begins with interruption or fracture, not memory or recollection, and cannot but appear as violent to the use of traditional concepts, in politics, of negation and affirmation. Therefore, if one says—as Fanon has just said—that this invention can never be "enslaved" by the past, nor its meaning circumscribed by history, what the leap implies is a situation of radical indecision whose emergence introduces something entirely new into the world.

To do justice to Fanon's thinking, one must therefore never lose sight of invention—which, to be sure, is neither a promise nor a claim. This more explicitly radical opening can be characterized as taking place in a space between an eschatological time of black redemption (including the space given to race by Césaire or Sartre) and the present time of political conflict that struggles to avoid the "pitfalls" of spontaneity: vengeance, indiscipline, an immediacy that is both "radical and totalitarian."[5] (To say nothing of the by no means insignificant constraint of "the world in which I travel"; the task being less to increase its constraint than to refine the ways with which I can "endlessly create myself" anew in the world. In such invention I exceed division, difference, and economy.[6]) Fanon wants to register both the force of possibility or (more radically) Sartre's suspicion of historicism in the traditional figuring of black invention, and Césaire's powerful claim, in his *Cahier*, that blackness should be reconsidered first as anti-invention, prior to what he calls the purity of its failure. There is, however, a caveat: Sartre's rendering of negritude slams the door shut on black creativity and encloses it in an historicism; and in Césaire, black existence, whose meaning plunges from abyss to mythical abyss, finds a last refuge in a "'bitter brotherhood' that imprisons all of us alike."[7] The reference to Césaire seems almost as essential to Fanon as the reference to Sartre, and one way of tracking a path through Fanon's work is to follow the great chapter in *Black Skin, White Masks* devoted to Césaire's *Cahier* and Sartre's *Orphée Noir*. In this chapter on *le vécu noir*, or black lived experience, the focus is on how Sartre reduces black creativity to an historical truth or dogma and how Césaire renders black existence in terms of predetermined myths. Both positions, incidentally, are felt to be imprisoning: they cease being inventive the moment they sublate the heterogeneous and singular in fixed ontologies or concepts.

On the other hand, nothing closes off this possibility more clearly than the insistence that the main focus or concern of Fanon's work is with "humanism." It is certainly not in itself illegitimate or foolish to approach Fanon with this insistence on humanism, but this has led some commentators to assume complicity on Fanon's part with a certain "narrative" of liberation whose ending, typically, accentuates reconciliation and redemption rather than upheaval or interruption.[8] There are, however, good reasons for thinking that this configuration of liberation, and the sovereignty subsequently disappointed or confirmed through it, is a limited way of responding to Fanon's thinking on invention. The reasons for this can be stated quickly: it is misguided to expect Fanonian invention to answer to the concept of humanism and narratives of liberation just because these are just as limiting as are the narratives or concepts of history—and in so far as Fanon's constant concern has been to comprehend how the invention (of the wretched, say) exceeds the metaphysics of humanism, and how invention itself unravels the thinking of politics on which dialectical humanism is based. Nothing is further from invention than its pre-judgment.

In this way, the political demand on Fanonism to be a discourse of humanism falls foul of a structure it is probably easiest to formulate in the context of his discussions, in the late 1950s, of Europe. "If we want humanity to advance a step further, if we want to bring it up to a different level than that which Europe has shown it, then we must invent and we must make discoveries."[9] What is involved here is the sense that for decolonialism to be fulfilled, it must not "imitate" the European model, for that would be to remain under the spell of its historicity and its racist account of the human. In the final sentences of *The Wretched of the Earth*, Fanon describes this project as the working out of "new concepts" as "we try to set afoot a new man."[10] The taking of such a step is a key figure for his characterization of invention (and it should perhaps go without saying that such a step is intimately linked to the real leap), a characterization that stands in sharp distinction to European humanism, where imitation is already the figure for the erasure of invention's distinctive traits.[11]

A number of readings of Fanon appear to offer powerful ways of *reducing* the problem of invention to various humanisms, so that Fanonism might plausibly be seen as *no more than* a particular use of Sorelian language, a particular politics of *ressentiment*, or a conditioned alienated response to recognition as such, always to be finally explained *by something else* (biography, psychology, masculinism, racialism, dialectics, etc.), that something else being the excuse not to read the text in question.[12] Fanon's impatient interrogation of these discourses involves demonstrating that in every case the very concepts supposed to operate the reduction of invention to humanism are themselves blind to invention as politics. According to the group he would later describe as the wretched, whose invention has no place or identity, is "less-than" nothing, just because its exclusion comes to occupy a place that is nothing, without ethos or privilege, but a place, a *néant* that also produces an opening, a fracture in the body politic, and whose form has no form other than that of its ceaseless negativity, the problem for Fanon was how to account for the time and singularity of the wretched within the limits of politics. The wretched is not an identitarian category, nor is it a disidentitarian category (in the sense of the promise of community). It signifies that which is radically heterogeneous and yet necessary and constitutive; the wretched are a "gangrene" at the heart of the colony that cannot be absorbed or eradicated: the inassimilable. The spontaneity of these "less-than-men" brings with it fundamental changes in colonial politics, and precisely where politics appears to be petit-bourgeois, elitist, neo-Marxist, or nationalist.[13] Indeed, certain of the strategies of mass mobilization traditionally relied upon by the political parties will have to be sacrificed (that is to say, reinvented), while the transformation of politics into war in the colony, so far resolutely ecstatic and energetic, will eventually materialize in new political forms (only if the struggle permits it). Fanon's thinking on invention, it now seems reasonably clear, follows a rhythm, a grammar (which I have often called a future imperfect), a rhetoric, a movement, a path, that shuttles between what could be traditionally distinguished as sovereignty and enslavement, asserting the priority of neither and the subordination of both to a wider movement that neither is in a position to understand. All of which can be discerned in the following two articulations:

1[1]. Invention can be approached, or experienced, as a kind of *extravagant expenditure*. Which is not simply to say that it acts as a kind of surplus, or step beyond actual existence, but that it accomplishes an interruption, a new signification of existence; in short, invention itself functions as a leap, a crossing, that can either fail or succeed; thus it answers not to a preordained meaning, even a teleological one, but to a constitutive movement, an insemination, or a deformation (of politics). Taking the word literally, it may be said that invention is a *beginning*, a step, an activity of production, an inauguration. When Fanon says that experience is not performed in conformity to historical time, but involves a process of endless self-creation, what he has in mind is that moment when there is the possibility of something becoming actual, and when it seems that there is no time remaining, when one finds oneself, unexpectedly and bizarrely, called on to choose (or at least bear witness). Fanon's formulation of this moment as one of curiosity, unease, crisis, and insanity captures the sense in which possibility can either pass one by completely, or become precipitously calamitous, and in a way that is not necessarily positive or negative. It follows that invention is opposed to what Fanon calls petrification, a term that he uses (in *The Wretched of the Earth*) to describe how the *colonisé* cannot think or speak or even breathe without being reminded that the forms of their allegiance are under constant surveillance. There is never any warning as to when the slap or rifle butt will come, and even when it seems that humiliation is always the thing awaited, each day brings not only the promise of further taunts and humiliation but also the trivial, undistinguished manner in which one greets and suffers one's degradation. This pattern repeats itself everywhere throughout the colony. Petrification thus refers to a certain numbness and complacency by which the *colonisé* survive the desperation of daily life, and the delirious disbelief in which time is lived over and over again. By contrast, it is not the first act of defiance that is inventive, but only with the second does the first become significant as the act that one has chosen, and whose inauguration allows one to say that this is the first moment, the beginning. The extravagance of invention thus lies in the fact that it can be suffered as grief, fear, humiliation, and terror, as well as fidelity, faith, love, and triumph, without any hint of being archetypally either. Invention is what endures as the undecidable; it tolerates the cruelest deprivation and refuses what lovingly honors it; and its elusive quality persists from the first, singular decision to the last, weakened compromise.

2. Similarly, the subjective *infinity* of invention refers not to some idea of the ineffable (the bad infinity criticized by Hegel) but to what, from each moment on, realizes itself as a commitment that is fulfilled beyond my comprehension, but in relation to which I have very little choice, for it feels inevitable, is irrevocably felt. In those circumstances, invention is not defined by its limits but by its contiguities, or juxtapositions. Let it be supposed that the impossible causes a little ache, or conflict, a doubt that is difficult to harness, and that insinuates itself in the reciprocal demand that it be converted into a possibility. This demand is not one of calculation: more likely it is one of obligation that forces one to bear witness, and precisely where the giddiness and "almost pathological trance" following the "death of the other" (the enemy) becomes, as it were, possessed by a realization that is discomforting, revolting, and, worst of all, leads to a feeling of estrangement, wherein the product of the impossible become possible;

it follows that invention does not encourage identification, but is the exception that exceeds and jolts our desires.[14] Whence, perhaps, Fanon's insistence that the *colonisé* would rather take on the pain of invention than go back to what is certainly unbearable and perhaps, too, why invention is the very point at which life is separated from what makes it so pathetically, shamelessly enfeebled. Invention is thus dis-locative, metonymical, whereas racialization follows limited rules of enunciation that remain recuperative, fixed, metaphorical. And so, although invention is never able to stop the subject from abandoning itself *de facto* to reassuring fantasies, that is to say, those desires that lead it to project itself as a boundary or limit to experience (and so forge dangerous and delusory fictions about others), it is in the nature of invention, as Fanon repeatedly stresses, to disturb the form and meaning of such fantasy (conceived of, so to speak, as the limit work of certain racist effects). It does so by forcing the colonial subject to recognize its own racist demeanor and so reflect on its identifications in the colony. Equally, though, and by the same token, the irresistible character—or the *Trieb*—of invention will be recognized and stated by the subject itself as the infinite limit of its own self-affection. The imperative *to be* alone will be capable of making this impulse disclose what the racialized subject is lacking: the plenitude of an imaginary whiteness it can never hope to equal, possess, or represent via a figure proper to it.

To illustrate these points let us return, briefly, to the politics of racialization. In Part One, Chapter Three ("Negrophobogenesis"), we dealt with Fanon's conception of the racialized body, showing how it inevitably changes from a phantasmatic conception to a conception of a *"corps à corps."* We also showed that in *The Wretched of the Earth*, the thematics changes from petrification to a kind of tabula rasa or disassembly of the colonial subject: "the proof of success lies in a whole social structure being changed from the bottom up."[15] What is the relationship of depetrification to this image of the tabula rasa? In this moment of absolute disorder, the past life that has hardened, due to continuous persecution, is rejected; indeed, the *colonisé* no longer seeks to conserve that which inhibits it but becomes restless, animated, creative; from the top downwards its being acquires a new disposition, as its piety withers away alongside its reverence for the old order. Hence Fanon's view of the revolution as a moment of invention, in which destructive violence allows the socially dead to acquire a new symbolic form. For this radical disarticulation is the moment when all the received and contrived principles of colonialism, which had kept the people within their proper limits, become reversed or are rendered unreliable, and the existing basis of knowledge teems with errors. It is a realization that makes the *colonisé* giddy with anticipation.

My aim in this chapter is to show why this situation is also one of invention and why it puts into crisis the prevailing dogmas by which the colonized have traditionally experienced themselves, in the name of politics and religion. There seems to be no room left for humanism here except perhaps by removing it from its foundation in race as a concept (a relation also essential to its political-religious formation), so completely have racist teleologies taken over its discourse. Even though Fanon did not give up on the task, his attempt to forge a new humanism remained incomplete at the time of his death. But what he leaves us with instead is the attempt at an analysis, which some might see as misplaced, of the unforeseeable as an event that lifts time out of history and at the same time complicates the racist politics of invention.

II. INVENTION AS READING

Let us begin with a general assumption—that all of Fanon's writing answers two, intertwined imperatives: Fanonism is at once a *therapeutics*, generated and measured by Fanon's work in the clinic, and a *messianics*, driven by the violence and artifice of colonial race war during the Algerian war of independence. The two are not contraries, for both are concerned with what disturbs, or dissipates, the foundations and principles of colonial culture. Invention is the figure for this interruption; it does so by calling attention to the psychic and political limits of racialization. How? Exactly by allowing the *colonisés* to state a refusal, which they are no longer afraid to render and make heard in order to make their disobedience evident. Fanon's commentary describes this disobedience in words that reveal a new organization of the body, whose very existence (at the level of voice, facial expressions, gestures, and musculature) reveals a new order of work and energy, and a new fidelity and faith. In addition, he notes that it is the extreme urgency of civil disobedience that produces these visceral novelties and truths. In these passages he discloses, and at the same time demonstrates, that his writing is both an analysis and a phenomenology of invention, and that his early work was similar.

Black Skin, White Masks for example envisaged itself as a "mirror" in such a way that the few who could see themselves reflected in it "will have made a step forward" on the "road to disalienation."[16] That the entire book was inscribed to those readers who could "understand the problems that were encountered in its composition" is very much linked to this desire for a change in disposition, from which it follows that the writing of the book must have performed that task for Fanon, who admits that he could not have written the book earlier.[17] It is strange to come across a work that begins like this, with talk of a truth so fervid that it prevented the author from having written it "three years ago"; whose fire no longer burns but whose task for the reader will cause him or her to descend "to a level where the categories of sense and non-sense are not yet invoked."[18] There is of course a ready explanation for it. Fanon addresses his "Introduction" to those readers who lack the ability "to accomplish this descent into a real hell" and for whom an "authentic upheaval" is yet to begin.[19] *Black Skin, White Masks* may be regarded as Fanon's wish to effect such an upheaval by referring to the necessity of truths already experienced, though he might also have meant that the authentic upheaval was the writing itself. To read *Black Skin, White Masks*, then, is to take a step forward, to descend to a place where sense and non-sense have yet to be differentiated, an indeterminate place where the text situates its very *readability* as a text. As a result, Fanon addresses his book to those readers who will come to see themselves in the details of its afterimage, as it were, and be changed by the reflection. "Man is not merely a possibility of recapture or of negation," he continues, he is also "doomed to watch the dissolution of the truths he has worked out for himself one after another."[20] In grasping these truths, readers of the book will not only re-cognize them as untruths (and hence re-cognize the misrecognition of these truths), but will ultimately *see into* how they themselves sustain what appears to be true but that cannot finally be true. Until this recognition of misrecognition, the reading of *Black Skin, White Masks* will be inseparable from a repetition in which there is nothing genuinely new. In brief, there is a ceaseless restlessness by which invention comes down to us. And any thinking worthy of the name must be open to its task.

It follows from this situation not only that reading is itself a decisive step forward, but that it can be taken to exemplify the conflict between the recognizably familiar and the insight that allows us to grasp the non-permanent nature of truth. The fact that reading is not just a tranquil act of deciphering, but an upheaval that reading can never read as such, means that to read is to be *inventive*. Being inventive means being open to what falls outside of what might be taken to dictate or prescribe final truths. In this sense, any reading worthy of the name is inventive, and inventive not at all in the interests of expressing mere subjective freedom, but in the response to those occasions when meaning evades any absolute horizon of truth.

On this construal, Fanon's own apparent untimeliness (what I have been calling invention) opens the possibility of a dramatization whose relation to history is necessarily dissolute, irresponsible, suspenseful. For Fanon's work does not just reflect, in a way we might want to call political, on the relation to the untimeliness of invention in general, but also, on occasion, within that inventiveness, reflects on the untimeliness of blackness in particular, and indeed does so increasingly with respect to time and history. We have already seen some of the doubts raised in *Black Skin, White Masks* about final truths that are used to establish a certain inventive relation to textuality itself; let us now turn to those texts for an elaboration of what Fanon says about this untimeliness, and what must be understood here as its reading, in the sense of will, upheaval, and dissolution.

III. *VOLONTÉ* AND VIOLENCE

"A people are always their own invention."

JEAN-LUC NANCY, *The Creation of the World or Globalisation*, 104

In seeking a more substantial definition of what appears in Fanon's work as invention, it is well to go back to the term *volonté*, or will. It has to be remembered that invention is not necessarily a process of emancipation; that is to say, it does not directly subvert the relation between repression and freedom. What invention changes, more profoundly, is the link between time and event that, as such, is not predetermined and is not given to be read as the expression of an alienated or repressed will. It is thus useful to ask why Fanonism continues to be read as the *animation of a liberatory, emancipatory, unitary will* that has its origin in the people as a totality? It may well be that Fanonism retains something of this emancipatory agency; the politics of invention, however, endows *volonté* with a different meaning.

In 2011 Peter Hallward published his essay "Fanon and Political Will," which presents a correlation between "an emancipatory 'will of the people'" and "*volonté*" as the "guiding priority" of Fanon's work.[21] The following remarks based on Hallward's essay are not intended to refute it; we shall, however, have to insist that the fruitfulness of this reading is far removed from what Fanon had in mind when he focused on the apparently marginal motif of *taking a step*, a small forward step, in order to take the real leap of invention. Hallward's essay on Fanon is characterized by the fundamental question of why this will of the people has been "thoroughly forgotten if not repressed" by postcolonial studies and the demonstration of why any return to Fanon "worthy of the name must involve the forgetting of this forgetting."[22] The reading of Fanon, on this view, must begin with the active, critical memory of political will—a tradition that includes Hegel, Marx, Rousseau, the Jacobins, Mao, Castro, Che Guevara, Giap, and Mandela and that has been repressed or forgotten by postcolonial studies. In this way, any reading of Fanon that falls foul of this formulation of *volonté* (and its history) is subsequently discredited as an unworthy response to the "real significance" of Fanon's work.[23] One way of understanding this gesture of Hallward's is to see in it a suspicion about the dogmatism, or piety, of postcolonial cultural criticism. But isn't this language of a right to speak or write in Fanon's name, and conversely to cast doubt on the right of others to speak or write in that name, not already implicitly dogmatic, and in ways that are not quite thought through? There are good reasons for thinking that this return to Fanon is itself somewhat forgetful in the way in which it responds to the challenge and radicality of Fanon's political thought. The reasons for this can be formulated rapidly: it is misguided to expect Fanon's work to answer to the concept of an "autonomous political will" just because this is a traditional political concept, and one that forgets Fanon's constant concern to remember and comprehend that which exceeds sovereignty and politics: the leap that reinvents the foundational claims of both history and politics in so far as both rely on the racial invention of the human and of humanism as such. This forgetting seriously discredits Hallward's historiography, and I have other reservations about his thesis, which states that Fanon was on the road to Leninism (the priority and identity of that Leninism poses a question to which I shall return).

What is it that postcolonial studies has failed to think in failing to remember *volonté*? Hallward has an apparently straightforward answer: *Fanonism is a political voluntarism.*[24] The will of the people, he says, recurs throughout the posthumous collection *Toward the African Revolution*, in such phrases as "the national will of the Algerian people" and "national will of the oppressed peoples," where the emerging will of the nation is what defines the people as sovereign, but what makes possible that self-constitution is never really thought through, though Hallward will draw on Fanon's later work to argue that "solidarity with others is a matter of freely assumed commitment, rather than an automatic orientation inherited by a community."[25] It is at this point (in the insistence on a freely assumed commitment) that Hallward makes a discreet but ambitious displacement with respect to Fanon's arguments in his late work. The question of will (as a figure for the emerging nation) should not be separated from that of revolutionary spontaneity or organization: the latter refers to the place of politics in the constitution of *volonté* (a word that is significantly ambiguous: at once decision and desire, agency and act); the status and concept of spontaneity, however, is never the result of organization, nor is it to be confused with the enunciation of a general will; spontaneity re-acquires the strong sense of impulse or drive in Fanon's work, whereas *volonté* is invariably inscribed in a politics of organization or desire. As for invention, it has already been said that it is not a search for a less confined, less suffocating *self*-representation, but registers an upheaval within petrified meaning itself, in which subjects are exposed to the conflict where truth disappears into illusion.

Discussing colonial subjection, Fanon elaborates (in that context) a description of failure in the sense of *engine failures* (*le moteur a des ratés*). This phrase, which seems to imply that the psyche of the colonized has come to a halt, or at the very least that it has undergone a seizure generated by something ankylotic (understood here as petrification), seems to put into question the rhetoric of will or decision. Within these petrified individuals, the emergence of resistance is an emergence that makes the ankylosis appear as such, and in so doing, no doubt makes possible the appearance of inhibitions in a specific sense. The machinery of the colony not only generates, but also suppresses, and in a way that shows how the colonized are undermined at key points by symptoms—a word completely missing from Hallward's account—that are neither conscious nor willed, neither inner nor outer. (At several points in his later work, Fanon refers to how tradition can in effect "canalize" the "most acute aggressivity and the most impelling violence."[26]) Will (as the figure for emancipation) ushers in a new animation of the *colonisé*, but what it actually establishes overall, and particularly in Hallward's narrative, is the disclosure of a being that is no longer possessed by its own non-knowledge, as is indicated by the words signifying detoxification and exorcism. That is, the reinvention of the *colonisé* shows how *limited* is this conception of animation-as-liberation; the time of liberation as shown by new corporeal forms of resistance is not a conversion of the lytic, it assigns it a clearly defined function as a fetish, fantasy, or myth. This is why Fanon calls for a tabula rasa: the sense in which the *colonisé* now grasp themselves is the experience of a disjuncture that is both necessary and impossible, and is not therefore willed. This is the leap about which Fanon says that it is both an upheaval and a disordering, in which there is no certainty. The very fact that invention entails a still more radical undertaking than emancipation thus deprives the existential notion of freely assumed commitment of its authority at the outset. How this is done is illustrated, for example, by the turn of phrase by which Fanon introduces the book to the reader. "This book is a clinical study," he writes, of "the *state of being* a Negro."[27] "White civilization and European culture have forced an existential deviation on the Negro. I shall demonstrate elsewhere that what is often called the black soul is a white man's artifact."[28] Even here, such artifactuality is only presented in terms of the racialized code of a deviation: the colonized are the sign of a dissociation, but they cannot be simply freed from this dissociation by recourse to a more authentic self, for the colonized is this state, its own artifact; it has no other contents to discover itself anew. It is perhaps, then, surprising to find such sentences taken as the grounding of a voluntaristic outlook. Hallward has two decisions to make concerning Fanon's voluntarism, and they are quite different in their tenor and scope. The first, based on an acceptance of these descriptions, suggests that accepting voluntarism as a matter of volition or will as opposed to "compulsion," "instinct," or impulse means that political will "affirms the primacy of a conscious decision and commitment, independent of any 'deeper' (i.e. unconscious) determination, be it instinctual, historical, or technological."[29] The same sweep is applied to everything that contradicts this primacy—the clinical writings on colonial war and torture, the case histories on fetishism and negrophobia, etc. It would be interesting to know how Fanon would respond to such a description of his *socialthérapie*. Thus far, then, Hallward is imposing on Fanon an opposition that is on the one hand aimed at an explicit reduction of Fanon's *political* reading of psychoanalysis, and on the other focusing on a valorized set of terms that are used to reduce and explain, but to which they remain blind, the role of the unconscious in Fanon's analysis of the role of fantasy in colonial power relations, i.e. the ways in which subjection and mastery are both enacted and *enjoyed*. Hallward says that will is "equally opposed to mere imagination and wish," for it realizes itself only through struggle or praxis.[30] Again, if the emergence of national consciousness is an emergence that makes the will of the people appear as such, and in so doing, no doubt replaces a politics of recognition with the necessity of action, why does Fanon present that emerging through the languages of dissociation and failure, that is, in discontinuous or excessive terms that cannot be easily translated as voluntaristic? And if "colonial mind-control [Hallward's term for Fanonian "imposition"] removes even the fantasy of emancipation," are we to assume that fantasy is to be excluded from the people's will, and in ways that are necessarily without political consequences? Such statements about the psyche forget how enmity is simultaneously the symptom of a persecution and an inhibition by which the *colonisé* is inhabited from the start.

The first decision, then, already pushes Fanonian analysis towards a certain internal opposition: in the history of the colony, Hallward wants to say that impulse, dream, wish, imagination, and fantasy have all been hijacked, and that the hijacker is colonialism, backed up by force. This focus motivates Hallward's second decision, which looks even more exclusively insistent than the first. Quoting from *Black Skin, White Masks* where Fanon is critiquing colonial psychiatry to underpin his *political* response to its ideology, Hallward quickly assimilates this critique of psychiatry to the more obvious remark that given that colonialism is "rooted more in coercion than in deference . . . it is thus easier to judge and condemn," and goes on to make the point—illustrating how a certain existential heritage can skew the understanding of Fanon's acute reading of psychoanalysis—that "colonial and racist forms of oppression thereby lend themselves to *conscious and thus deliberate* or 'voluntary' resistance."[31] The voluntaristic interpretation of racism suppresses the repressed and projected elements that Fanon attributes to negrophobia in favour of a reassuring interpretation of exterior "mind-control," which readers of Fanon ought to be the first to be suspicious of. It is here that an extraordinary slippage occurs: to produce a politics of will, Fanonism has to be purified, as it were, of its ongoing concern with unconscious complicity, the emotions and signs by which the subject is submerged in racialized "life": will can only be performed when act and gesture are in unity; it cannot allow its own (psychic) deviation to be seen without compromising its own revolutionary potential.

Where is that reading to be found in Fanon's works? In the fact that the "only appropriate response to such feelings" (of angst, phobia, anxiety, etc.) is "in direct confrontation and struggle" (understood by Hallward as violence); and as the articulation of a will to self-realization as an

act in a drama.[32] The first presentation has will perform the role of catharsis in the psyche once subjected by colonialism; the second must have will
itself as the drama, in that through it the people learn to perform themselves as a people in a political "as opposed to a merely psychological"
sense.[33] This is Fanon's greatest political insight, according to Hallward,
which he later defines as "the conversion of an involuntary passivity into
a self-mastering activity," and one that postcolonial studies presumably
cannot think within its disciplinary setup. All these phrasings suggest that
volonté, in accordance with the famous mirror metaphor that Fanon uses
to open *Black Skin, White Masks*, is the *inversion* of petrification: *volonté*
consists in converting petrified culture into animation or, at least, a self-
mastering movement. To define this movement as will or sovereignty (thus
rendering continuous or foundational that which is presented as without
foundation) is to confuse invention with a politics, or a certain language
of organization: to try to find the sources of invention in sovereignty or
nationhood is to fall back in line with what *limits* it, with what defines it
as a meaning *already read*: invention thus becomes the staging of a drama
whose meanings precede it.

The peremptoriness with which these oppositions are run together
should give us pause. It is not difficult to see that this presentation of
Fanon is based on a mirage. Hallward sees a problem in a postcolonial account by (1) assuming that the description of will-as-self-mastery is Fanon's
political *definition*; (2) de-psychoanalyzing mastery; (3) assuming that the
emergence of the people's will must be thought of as the appearing of sovereignty as such; and (4) being surprised to find that *willing* for Fanon is
not what grounds but what *haunts* the subject, passive or not. These arguments only have any purchase if one is assuming that resistance is or could
be a matter of coercion or consent. But any reading of Fanon should be
sufficient to show that *no* concept of resistance can attain to the value of
self-mastery, and that this situation is psychologically ordinary. To that extent, however interesting the notion of political will may be to Fanonism,
and however pressing the question of emancipation may be to Fanon or
any other decolonial thinker, it can never arbitrarily decide this problematic of resistance, as Hallward attempts to do through his claims about
passivity and mastery, problems with which we have noted elsewhere (see
Part One, Chapter Seven, "The Condemned"). In a gesture that also informs his readings of Lenin, Hallward wants to force the whole philosophical argumentation of Fanon through the prism of political will: the fact

that he then goes on to characterize that will in terms that are very far from Fanon's own thinking on invention does not alter the fact that his first gesture commits him to a certain decisionism *about* revolution, and this leads to his confident identification of the people's will as the name for a problem that he *also* recognizes as not going beyond any traditional determination of that concept. The curious effect of this is that a compelling, and at times urgent, account of political will is presented in tandem with a set of claims about coercion, impulse, and compulsion, as though all these claims happened on the same level of the "political." The upshot of this is that Hallward—in contrast to Fanon, who shows how invention is, from the start, never simply performed as a politics—continues to think of will as the privileged form of political performance. At any rate, it is hardly possible to overlook the absence of psychoanalysis from the discussion, down to the very formulation of political will: Fanon, quite consistently, finds that a psychopolitical reading of black identity leads to "a zone of nonbeing" inaccessible to identity as such, an "utterly naked declivity" that cannot but suspend any teleology or politics.[34] And it is from this zone that a radical appeal to the future begins, but in the absence of any piety or nostalgia, method or program. This much is certain: of all of Fanon's figures for failure, this zone can never be a ground for self or propriety, and to that extent it cannot be thought of in terms of self-present mastery. What has been forgotten—and this insight affords us another avenue of access to Fanon's work—is that identity cannot be affirmed as the meaning of any ground whatsoever. Similarly, Hallward's reading of Fanonism as a voluntarism, and the animus against psychoanalysis that appears to go along with it, is curious, but sets up an uncompromising scene that is more complicated than the notion of will suggests.

This is why, in regard to Fanon, we can no longer speak of sovereignty as the founding of a subject. And yet, for Hallward: "No less than Rousseau, Fanon is confident that if the people are free to deliberate and settle on their own course of action, then sooner or later they will solve the problems they face (or in Rousseau's more emphatic terms, if the circumstances allow for a universal or general will, if a group is indeed able to sustain a single and undivided will, then such willing *will never err*). Determination of the popular will may take time, but in the end it is the only reliable way of getting things right."[35] This allusion to Rousseau is odd: if the popular will of the people never errs, why is Rousseau keen to point out that sovereignty inevitably errs in its effort to be itself, and that from the outset, it is inherently corruptible? This comes about in almost a logical way. If sovereignty remained only itself, inalienable, indivisible, it would not even be sovereign "insofar as its will would find no possibility of execution."[36] If the sovereign is a relation to itself ("to itself as to the law"), it cannot exist prior to this relation, since it is the relation that constitutes it, but it is precisely this non-coincidence that makes the will to be sovereign open to deviation or failure.[37]

In this way Hallward's text therefore errs at the very moment that the possibility of "getting things right" in the name of will is seen to sustain the comparison of Fanon and Rousseau. This is not so much the reason for, as it is the evidence of, the extent to which Hallward has a mistaken view of Fanon's relation to Rousseau. But if will is what separates the voluntary from the merely mechanical, or the natural from the artificial (to use Rousseau's terms), and all in terms of acts in a political drama, what is will if not this artifice, or mechanism, that is needed to distinguish the rightful sovereign act from the act that errs sovereignly? If this question is valid, this would mean that erring is will and will erring, and only by erring can the will of the people realize itself as will. The will of the people can only return to itself as *self*-present after a delay, or deferral; it can only *perform* itself as a people insofar as "the people" is exterior to, and comes to supplement, its own will. As soon as there is anything politically like the people's will, the people itself errs passively (since what defines it is just the suspended possibility of the sovereign constitution of itself as a people). Or, in Fanonian terms, the people's will is, in the initial moment of its constitution, neither passive nor active—nor involuntary nor voluntary—but the consecution of what limits it: the violence that is at once biological and rhetorical, ecstatic and mystical (and that leads, moreover, to the abolition of individuality); revolutionary spontaneity, in short, is what founds the difference between popular will and sovereignty. (In the chapter on "Spontaneity: Its Strength and Weakness," in *The Wretched of the Earth*, Fanon memorably argues that there is always a "time-lag, or a difference in rhythm," between the work of the party and the revolutionary spontaneity of the people.[38] Thus the political organization of the people's will is not necessarily what carries it over—theatrically, performatively—into sovereignty.) Indeed, it is difficult to distinguish the force that petrifies and channels from the force—the violence—that causes the people's will to authorize itself as a depetrification. It is precisely this passivity of the people vis-à-vis its own capacity to actively will that makes Hallward's essay feel so arbitrary. The need to isolate will from spontaneity paradoxically requires that we exclude the *revolutionary* spontaneity of will from the institution of sovereignty. What remains to be seen is how will can indeed count as a form of knowing the world or acting in it, how it can lend validity to the kinds of judgment that Hallward calls "self-mastering." Hallward's political will is nothing if not sure of itself; but how can that certainty be asserted as universally binding on a people for a people? What is it that literally precipitates a decolonial people into being, to will itself sovereign? Fanon's answer is unequivocal: revolutionary violence. But the complexity of this term is often lost sight of in the conventional readings of his work. Strangely enough, when Fanon reflects on executive power in the colony, his point of departure is not right but colonialism's inherent violence and perversity, traceable from subjects to institutions; the word "perversity" suggests that sovereignty in the colony amounts to brutish mastery from the outset, for it entails a *jouissance* that is far away from politics and law but necessarily executes itself as such. Indeed, this perverse mastery is invariably responsible for the "nightmarish" return of the wretched, persons who appear as the horrible and monstrous realization of the master's own repulsive servility. Such perversity, incidentally, lends support to Fanon's notion that colonial mastery is not sovereignty and, by virtue of its history, racial slavery is not slavery as philosophically understood. The puzzle with Hallward is that he never undertakes a reading of this despite his insistence on political will as freedom. The oddity of his account is therefore that he understands that as soon as there is will, there is possibility, whereas for Fanon racism forces on the colony an *originary* deviation that is already there at the origin of political possibility, but that only appears *afterwards*, *nachträglich*, as a kind of hallucinatory catastrophe.

Hence the turn to invention as tabula rasa in *The Wretched of the Earth*, that moment when, "without any period of transition, there is a total, complete, and absolute substitution" of one "species" of men by another, and the whole social structure is "changed from the bottom up."[39] "The extraordinary importance of this change." Fanon continues, is that it is "willed, called for, demanded."[40] Here if anywhere would have been the place to lay open basic aspects of Fanon's thinking on the revolutionary moment as will. For Fanon, the tabula rasa is a radically democratic moment fraught with both danger and hope. (Fanon was evidently not willing to be responsible for when this moment might arrive, although he was at the same time aware of a call for a reinvention, an untimeliness that is not itself yet political or sovereign.) Is a non-sovereign form of politics possible? It would be interesting to know whether Fanon conceived of the wretched as this politics, that is, as the presence exposing the void defining modern politics as such.

The question of what the tabula rasa means has been discussed from all sides since Fanon's death; it would have been logical to pause here. Of course, this would have meant taking a slightly different course on the part of the author. What Hallward forgets is that the tabula rasa is the figure of an endlessly supplementary rewriting of what is decidable and what precedes the very possibility of decision, the heteronomy of a liberated subject rather than the unifying stroke of a revolutionary act. The dynamic of the tabula rasa will thus be the dynamic of substitution—and thereby the revolutionary moment as an improper supplementarity—in general. That Hallward does not grasp this is shown by the passages in which he undertakes to interpret Fanon's work or his style. Now this moment or tabula rasa, which is no doubt the key to Fanon's thinking about politics, is in fact a rigorous consequence of the quasi-concept of the *leap*, at least as developed through the Sorelian motifs of *Wretched of the Earth* in 1963. There, Fanon famously claims that "decolonization, which sets out to change the order of the world, is, obviously, a program of complete disorder."[41] And the abyssal structure of the relation of disorder to the tabula rasa is such that the presentation of disorder has always already begun *and* never stops arriving, and that no revolution escapes this. It is just this dissimulated (ghostly) presentation of erasure that determines the analysis of revolution from what I am calling here a non-sovereign politics of invention.

This thinking about the tabula rasa has some startling consequences. For it is not enough to stress that undecidability is a condition of decision or of radical possibility (and therefore unpredictability), for the mobilization of the masses during the war of liberation nonetheless occurs, and must occur, and where it occurs it is quite determinate. Fanon will say that "the mobilization of the masses, when it arises out of the war of liberation, introduces into each man's consciousness the ideas of a common cause, of a national destiny, and of a collective history."[42] But if mobilization lifts the colonized out of the condition of being petrified on the one hand, on the other hand the same mobilization must interrupt the very thing that is its condition of possibility, the place of sovereignty itself. Radicalizing this thought about events in general in the context of liberation leads to a *reinscription* of the concept of a people, away from the concept of sovereign will to which it is traditionally bound. For if the people are the demiurge that has to invent itself in this way, then the traditional way of thinking about mass mobilization can be said to neutralize just what makes that invention an event by referring to it as a sovereign event. That said, Fanon is not always consistent on this matter. As we shall see, his faith in the urgency of insurrection sometimes centers on decision (whereas his presentation of the tabula rasa should in fact commit him to the view that the masses have to both perform and invent themselves in the event of indecision). The fact that this is what the wretched show should not be lost sight of; invention is the stage on which "the people" can be both resuscitated and shattered, and precisely because it is not easy to be freed from the contagion of petrification. So when Hallward argues that "temporality of political will is more fundamentally a matter of constancy and accumulation than it is of transformative instants or leaps," he tends to reduce the eventhood of invention by referring it to something outside of itself, and this means the people can no longer affirm itself via the uncertainty that is the structure of every decision.[43] On this view, the decision to be a people is taken by the people's ownmost sovereign decision, but they cannot be inventive if they are already taken to be some self-coincident mobilization, they can only be decisive if there is an invention that makes an exception, a liberation, sovereignly. This is why Fanon writes that the war of liberation must not be seen as "an act of heroism [i.e., something sacrificial] but as a continuous, sustained action, constantly being reinforced."[44] And why, contra Hallward, Fanon's thinking of sovereignty should not be reduced to its traditional concept of self-identity where, citing Rousseau, sovereignty, "being nothing more than the general will, can never be alienated" and "can only be represented by itself."

Hallward, describing this as Fanon's "neo-Jacobin logic," writes: "As far as the active *willing* of the popular will is concerned, there is no substitute or representative who might take the place of the people themselves"; and "the will of the people, where one exists, not only demands but incarnates an immediate and unconditional sovereignty."[45] Suffice it to say, if the people already knows itself to be self-identical it never decides about anything, and must remain indifferent even to the decision to be anything but itself, passive even to its own decision to be sovereign, and certainly not worthy of the name invention as Fanon thinks it. Getting things right may be more urgent for instituting law and justice, but this is already a bastardization of the pure revolutionary moment, which is never entirely right or timely, in so far as this moment never really happens as such without possibly erring. When one turns to Fanon, and especially those pages in *Wretched of the Earth* describing the strengths and weaknesses of spontaneity, one reads: "the people legislates, finds itself, and wills itself to sovereignty."[46] The act of legislation may give rise to the people as self-identical and self-authorizing, but this is quite different from the moment of absolute substitution and unpredictability when the "people" does not yet coincide with itself, and is yet to write or author itself as sovereign. In fact, Fanon is very insistent that the rebelliousness of the wretched is not to be limited to a political form that could re-produce it, but, in order for its spontaneity to be precisely that which resists organization (in the sense of being a copy of the colonial power, or administered as such by the party), its emerging can scarcely be a sovereign activity. Sovereignty cannot be achieved by merely willing it so, but it does involve holding in tension the paradox that the leap is both the possibility and the ruin of politics (as a sovereign decision or legislation). To leap is to find oneself in this moment of creative indecision or danger, that is to say suspended over an abyss where law is no longer acknowledged or recognizable.

Going back to the tabula rasa: here we have, as Fanon first saw in *Black Skin, White Masks*, an opening that is formless, that is not yet law or justice, but that remains, nevertheless, their horizon or condition. The tabula rasa is not so much opposed to sovereignty as already at work *in* sovereignty as its principle of failure and affirmation. It does not disappear with sovereignty but continues to haunt every structure of decision. It can only find, will, or eventize itself as a people if sovereignty holds itself short of itself, so as to invent itself; or, as Fanon puts it: in the world in which I travel, I endlessly create myself.

A further consequence has to do with violence. And here we turn to Sorel's *Reflections on Violence*, first published in 1908.[47] Unlike Arendt, who badly misreads this text and Fanon's relation to it, I think that there are some interesting convergences still to be explored between Fanon and Sorel.[48] In this brief, infamous text, designed to awaken "within every man a metaphysical fire" and committed to "liberating the spirit of invention," "it is this spirit of invention which it is, above all, necessary [argues Sorel] to arouse in the world" of his readers.[49] Violence emerges as an issue in this text because of the structure of invention: the moment when liberation remains more or less violently unstable within the bourgeois *institutions* of thought and of politics, and when invention more or less violently, but always violently, opens up the subject and the state to destabilization and collapse. Or, violence is redemptive of what Sorel calls "decadence." Without confrontation (violence) there is no revolutionary identity; the revolutionary identity of the masses requires conflict for their constitution. Violence, according to Sorel, is not only terrifying, dizzyingly sublime, and irreversible, it is also the "pure and simple manifestation of the sentiment of class struggle."[50] And so, any attempt to dilute, reduce, or even regulate that conflict can only be an instrument of decadence and a corruption of the revolutionary proletariat. Nor is this all. Between proletarian violence and the parliamentary parties there is no compatibility (they do not coexist on the same plane); the former stands apart, separate, necessarily opposed to the oppressive force of the state and the parties' reformist tendencies.

Now this proletarian violence, which is constitutively split between, on the one hand, a syndicalist demand and, on the other, the incarnation of a social "grandeur," has in fact a rigorous consequence for Sorel's thinking of sovereignty. In *Reflections*, grandeur and decadence do not have intrinsic contents of their own, but are the signifiers of an *energy* understood as an opposition between movement, force, and violence on the one hand, and decadence, incapacity, and stupefaction on the other (it is not by chance that the class struggle is seen as the restitution of energy, whereas parliamentary politics is seen as the "*dictatorship of incapacity*"[51]). Revolutionary proletarian violence (insofar as it stems from this *Trieb* or restorative life force) is thus paradoxically both destructive *and* conserving: whereas decadence is opposed to life, and drowns it in a morass of stupefaction, the function of class struggle is to induce capitalism's historical perfection and, as such, is directly linked to the workings of civilization rather than those of barbarism.[52] (Needless to say, Fanon does not share this language of energetics, nor does he reduce the work of invention to that of European civilization.)

Sorel famously claims that the revolutionary myth (of the general strike) is the expression of a "will to act" and, as such, does not reveal a latent meaning, but consists in a challenge to the symbolic itself as a representation of meaning: myth is what allows the proletariat to capture and observe itself as the image of a revolutionary process or *movement*.[53] In *Wretched*, by contrast, Fanon famously claims that the wretched are the "grangrene at the heart of the colony"; they are both the grandeur and the corruption, the grandeur that is corruption, and without one's being able to separate them except by abstraction, and the violence that they introduce into existence cannot be separated from their contents even though the latter cannot be determined or willed into the form of a "deliberate transformation" (to use Hallward's words).[54] For Sorel, any attempt by the proletariat to constitute itself as an integrated subject can only lead to decadence; for Fanon, the wretched are the part that has no part, the included exclusion, the trace of otherness as such. For Sorel, each action of the workers— whether a strike, a demonstration, or a factory occupation—should be seen, not in its own specificity or particular objectives, but as part of a chain of events in the formation of the revolutionary will. Accordingly, the general strike is totally heterogeneous with the empirical world of limited and partial struggles. The general strike is presented as a myth (of actuality): its form or function is not to be judged by its political effectiveness, nor is it compressible to mere means or ends; on the contrary, the point of its advance is the representation not of shared interests but of a kind of secular revelation that is *intuitive, immediate, spontaneous,* and whose articulation could not possibly correspond to any actual historical event. The proletarian general strike is not—or is not merely—a political event; it is a radical nonevent that is, paradoxically, the condition of all events if there is going to be a revolutionary grandeur in society. The problem with this approach is that the proletarian myth (as the metaphor of energy) is always the signifier of an encounter that is itself fundamentally mythical. In this antinomy, proletarian violence is always the mirror of its bourgeois opposite so as the better to reveal its degradation, the decadence of its inertia, and its caricature of life. The attempt to ground revolutionary spontaneity in myth thus ends in a specifically bourgeois myth of decadence and failure, and one that borrows from physiology a certain (class) energetics of passion and of life. Proletarian violence has to affirm life's *moral* limits, for if myth is the metaphor for what separates reality from the real (of revolution), what makes myth authoritative is paradoxically what abolishes its cogency as grandeur: grandeur, by definition, is always usurped by the moral emptiness of the mythic. For Fanon, the mobilization of the wretched is an event or a decision that is radically unpredictable and entails a beginning that is irreducibly violent, and one that leads to a "total, complete, and absolute substitution," or tabula rasa.[55] In this respect, his notion of violence is closer to that of Benjamin's in "Critique of Violence."[56] That is to say, its appearance is what fissures, or disturbs, the law of the racist state, and by precisely calling into doubt the fantasies and fetishes that conserve it, including the myths that are, as it were, their concrete abstraction and affirmation.

In fact, then, what is at stake in Fanon's reflections on violence is not mythic violence but the effective violence of myth in the civilization of racial images. The analysis of decolonial struggle in *Toward the African Revolution*, for example, distinguishes three levels of violence: an originary "metaphysical" appropriation of the colony (first level) is violently organized into effects of propriety (in this instance by the racial classification of being, law, and property—second level), which can then be violently disclosed (third level) at the level of hegemony. In short, violence has a hold over all *social* relations in the colony; all pleasure and knowledge is bound to it, and no language, law, memory, or desire is safe from its presence or enunciation.

But perhaps more importantly for thinking about politics, *Toward the African Revolution* establishes, apparently against what can appear a fanatic purity in Sorel, an economy of violence within anti-colonialism itself (again this flows directly from Fanon's thought of the wretched as the image of revolutionary spontaneity, and of the party bureaucracy as "what shows itself opposed to any innovation"[57]). This leads Fanon to pose (to propose) a final transformation of politics as means and ends, i.e., that of a bloody intensification, a *jouissance* of armed struggle that calls into doubt the classical determinations of politics, i.e., reformism, classism, racialism, vitalism, etc. It stems from the fact that the wretched cannot be satisfied by these political metalanguages, or at least that they call into doubt the reduction of insurrection to a politics. Whereas in Hallward's reading, the power to resist is a capacity, and revolution is the organized will to resist domination, for Fanon (and as we shall see shortly, for C. L. R. James), organization is what *both* secures and thereby ruins mass spontaneity as innovation. As a type of violence, spontaneity also suggests something like a pure, irreducible event not retrievable by any aggregration, program, history, or will; it is a wretchedness that exceeds any preconstituted identity and, as such, cannot be thought as intended or willed. This means that violence, for Fanon, is not the redemption of politics, nor is it its continuation by other means, but what organizes decolonialism—its intensifying movement—into a single signifying practice. The distance separating this vision from, say, that of Sorel is more than historical: the mythic grandeur of political violence cannot be thought other than through the teleological perspective of nonviolence. Or, in the greatest times of social division the political value of violence increases to the extent to which the coming of socialist democracy promises to reverse its need and necessity. Significantly,

Fanon's political philosophy is not wedded to this teleological scheme in which, as Geoff Bennington reminds us, "political philosophy is always the philosophy of the end of politics, or that the metaphysical concept of politics is the concept of politics *ending*."[58] In fact, Fanon's thinking of the liberatory leap disallows this teleological scheme, or at least refuses to mimic it to the extent that the intensification of violence must be understood here as a kind of *jouissance*, bound neither to its diminishing nor to its consumption (as sovereignty, or political organization). The history of political philosophy as telos or will can only see such intensification in terms of what completes it rather than what gives it expression. Fanon's texts are very much a focus on its necessary invention as an event: it asks of the reader to enter the depths, to take a step, where the reinvention of the subject can no more be willed than it can be purified of its endless contamination by what seizes and renders it (in its racialized conformity) unreadable and beyond recognition.

IV. INVENTION AS POLITICS

"If ever a leaper was well-prepared we are."

C. L. R. JAMES, *Notes on Dialectics*, 171

All this becomes more visible if we compare Fanon's thinking of the leap with C. L. R. James's extraordinary analysis of Hegel's *Logic* in *Notes On Dialectics* (1948).[59] As Fanon does in his texts, in *Notes* James also turns to the figure of the leap to think the discontinuities, disruptions, and anomalies between invention and politics (as traditionally understood), and this not by virtue of some metaphysical appeal but by the *logic* or *algebra* of resistance: like Fanon, James is concerned to ensure that revolutionary invention continues beyond the impasses of sovereignty. This short text, presented as little more than a series of "notes" on the *Science of Logic* and the history of the labor movement, shows how the "true significance" of Hegel's dialectic, by which spirit both grounds itself and is itself this movement, entails a necessary *leap*, a figure that James takes from Lenin's *Philosophical Notebooks*, written during the latter's 1914 sojourn in Zurich. In one marginal comment on the section of the *Logic* on "Quality in the Doctrine of Being," Lenin writes: "LEAP LEAP LEAP LEAP." The series of notes by James on Lenin's marginalia is significant:

The new thing LEAPS out. You do not look and see it small and growing larger. It is there, but it exists first in thought. Thought knows it is the object. You haven't to see it (though if you know it is there you can see signs and point them out). Hegel is bored to tears at people who keep looking for external signs and "the mere magnitudinal" as proof. Lenin did not fasten on this for nothing. . . . He didn't have to wait to see anything. That was there. It would LEAP up.[60]

Lenin's marginalia to Hegel becomes in James's *Notes* the platform for a series of further leaps or jumps: from philosophy to history (that is to say, from Hegel's *Logic* to a history of labor); from Marxist political philosophy to actual politics (or when does a new historical object become knowledge: when it is objectively *seen* to appear or when it gives rise to a new objective thought?); and from history to dialectics. James's language is, as usual, both blunt and extremely delicate. The new thing that leaps out does not need to be seen to be grasped; it does not need to be represented (by signs), or vouched for (by others), to attest to its existence. For genuinely new historical knowledge does not need to be empirically proven in order to signify what it is; the leap that is the sudden monadic crystallization (even if years in the forming) of historical time, which, as history, produces a new configuration as thought and a new historical logic. The point, rather, is to know how to read it, as Lenin memorably does in the *Philosophical Notebooks*. A theory that needs to *see* (in the sense of *theoria*) new objective truth, rather than grasp the instant of its emergence, is what James construes to be the weakness of most Marxist philosophy (that it can only grasp events as either on the road to knowledge or as fetishes invariably substituted for something else). James's example here is the history of the international labor movement. In making certain historical principles determinative of that movement, Marxist philosophy has led to a view of labor that fixates it as a theoretical object rather than as the object of a new theory for radical politics. This view, attributed to Trotskyism, has to be resisted, for it prevents Marxists from seeing the critical significance of state bureaucracy as labor's new organizational form, as well as the West's imperialist legacy for labor.

But there is a further complicated truth here as well: I do not think that James returns to Hegel in order to write better philosophy, but in order to think better historically, and with respect to the way new historical objects are *determined* by political judgment. So it cannot suffice to insist that James's return to Hegel—and, in particular, to the *Logic*—is purely to resolve a philosophical problem, because it is precisely on the level of Hegel's *algebra* (of the discontinuous instant) that James, along with Lenin, approaches the political question of organization (how it separates itself from, and is yet compelled by, revolutionary spontaneity; a concern that James shares with Fanon). And yet it is Hegel, or at least Lenin's reading of him, that focuses this emphasis on historical knowledge at the heart of *Notes on Dialectics*, as both a philosophical text and a philosophy of dialectical reading. That reading, which shows how often readers of the dialectic fall short of it, suggests that what is needed is a thought that can set aside the officially recognized Marxist history of labor so as not to exclude the very thing that constitutes it: the genuinely new historical thought that leaps out of each instant like lightning through a thicket, despite appearances to the contrary, and, yes, in ways that are blinding, and ecstatic.

But then, where exactly is such invention to be found? From the first references to Trotsky to the last on Stalinist state bureaucracy, James appears to suggest that Marxist political theory has become fetishistic in its method (that is, it has become arrested and regressive with respect to the past). Like all fetishisms, this blind spot in understanding has consequences for how Marxism *thinks* invention. Posed in theoretical terms, such a critique might seem a little abstract, but posed in terms of the history of labor, it presents an exquisite derision: how can a thought that is so bourgeois in its understanding of history, and that remains so closed to the unprecedented nature of labor *as* history, claim to provide a genuinely proletarian explanation of history, and one that begins not with what comes first and is henceforth precedent but with what simply happens *before* it can be seen to be historically happening (or not happening). A thought that announces itself as genuinely proletarian cannot account for anything proletarian, at least to the extent that the latter recognizes that particularities are also possibilities, if it views the history of labor as merely a mechanical series of failures and triumphs against the backdrop of a *Marxist* theory of history. The latter behaves rather like an announcer at a cricket match who announces the score over the tannoy before it has happened, and before even a ball has been struck, and in spite of the infinite field of possibilities by which a score might be realized, or not. For James, thought is not historical until it grasps the quality of what appears in the quality of what leaps out, altering thereby the thought of what came before in the successive boundary of its thinking. We know that, for each historical moment, this logic does not have to be seen to be grasped, for its possibility is already historical, even though as a leap what brings it into play cannot be construed as either an event or a nonevent for it to be of significance. For example, James wants to hang onto the fact that, throughout its history, the proletariat has resisted its determinative principle: "We have insisted upon the fact that the proletariat always breaks up the old organization by impulse, a leap: remember that."[61] (It is worth noting here that James uses the very same terms to talk about slave rebellion in *The Black Jacobins*; namely, as a kind of caesura within the various historiographies of plantation culture.) This fact has to be remembered not as a political sign to be argued over and disputed, but as labor's essential movement, which leads James to go further and suggest that the ways in which labor has fulfilled its intention historically have always involved unprecedented party political conflict: "But there comes a stage when organization and the maintenance of the organization become ends in themselves in the most perfect conflict with the essential movement of the proletariat."[62] Setting up an antinomy in this way, in the name of a speculative leap or decision, does not seem at all dialectical, but rather makes of the proletariat an example, an essential difference which, as James says, allows truly historical thought to be grasped as the thought of a difference that leaps out into a different organization. This thought is articulated around a double structure, therefore: organization can only be understood in so far as it subsumes, or suppresses, (proletarian) spontaneity; and spontaneity can only proceed *through* this suppression: in a sense, spontaneity exists in so far as it is always an impulse or *Trieb* sublated by organization. Organization is therefore a kind of boundary or limit case of spontaneity—whence its deferred (non-self-coincident) character. This also suggests why "organization as we have known it is at an end. The task is to abolish organization."[63] According to James, the implications of this have been either ignored or misunderstood by Marxist critics (such as Trotsky and Schachtman), who cannot see that organization "has served its purpose," which is why "the present eludes them," and why they can no longer read Hegel, or for that matter Lenin, for whom it is "not the finite, the fixed limited" that is real, for it is only "the Infinite which is real."[64] Now we could leave it at that, rather than argue endlessly over the meaning of dialectic. But what intrigues me here is the movement that James introduces between the falsely interpreted and the naïvely ignored and the historical thought that would grasp them and their intention as knowledge.

Let us return to the opening citation on Lenin's LEAP: it has to be said that James's tone here is defensive, argumentative, but also emphatic (note the consistent use of capitals). The point he is making concerns how cognition can know itself by first finding itself in its own objects, and that the thing grasped is not merely the result of this search but thought itself in its affirmation, in which case it does not require any external determination: "It is there, but it exists first in thought. Thought knows it is the object." At the risk of being too literal-minded, are not those capitals also the sign of an external determination, and one organizing—capitalizing—the thought being called for? The question could also be asked of the essential spontaneous movement that is seen to be the main characteristic of the proletariat. The logic that sees organization as the eventual arrest of any spontaneous movement is what preoccupies James, in the sense that he wants to think it precisely as a movement without arresting it as thought. The way he tackles the problem is to emphatically *write* that movement in a way that interrupts it; the capital letters are not objects of thought but the purely external mechanism through which the cognition of historical movement grasps itself, or, to give the whole thing a rather brutal explanation: *writing organizes the event of spontaneity.* But this is not what we are meant to think of as James's Hegelian algebra. For James, who is supremely aware of the dialectical tension between movement and arrest, organization has historically usurped spontaneity, but only because spontaneity is from the start always a little less than spontaneous, or is *driven,* by definition, by a desire to realize itself (as a theoretical object and political subject of history). Spontaneity, precisely because it is a radical manifestation, is thereby also found wanting or failing in its movement, and simply because it needs political organization to represent it in the first place and so secure it as a politics. A proletariat that remained essentially itself, as a purely instantaneous self-coincident identity, would not *even be* proletariat, insofar as its *Trieb* would find no essential movement as a politics, and it would therefore do nothing but remain an inessential appearance, a mere reflection of capitalism (a point already made earlier with regard to the sovereign). In order to be spontaneous at all, then, the proletariat has to submit to being organized, and give itself an executive arm or branch in the form of a party, but then the proletariat necessarily has to grasp that its legitimacy does not come from the party but from its own revolutionary spontaneity. "If the free activity of the proletariat is to emerge," James writes, "it can emerge only by destroying the communist parties."[65] (In this sense, then, the party is what capitalizes proletarian spontaneous movement but also what arrests it in the party's external dramatization. The fact that James can neither affirm nor escape this logic will therefore be our starting point for the insight it affords us as both the most arresting figure of *Notes* and its singular movement.) The proletariat must be freed from the organization of the party in order to be itself. Lenin's "*thought* made that leap in 1914" when he dispensed with the figure of the vanguard, but Trotsky (and Stalin) "converted it [organization] into a fetish" (via a kind of abstract form of understanding) and one that is essentially bureaucratic.[66]

Hence the phenomenon of the leap as the discontinuous relation between thought and history, a phenomenon that is part of James's rejection of Trotskyism and Stalinism and how they understand labor and time. Lenin, on the other hand, who is also a thinker of labor and time, introduces a way of writing history that is more inventive than the respective views of the other two. Which means that, if Marxism is to leap historically and philosophically, it must think through the Leninist question of labor as organized political time; for party bureaucracy is now the *philosophical* question of Marxism. I want to try and broach this question by explaining as briefly as possible its reciprocal implication as a question of reading. To the extent that Marxist philosophical history has always focused on the relation between capital and labor, James asserts that a newer version of that dialectic will now have to be accounted for by examining the limits of Marxist labor history.

A consistent argument of the *Notes* is that labor history needs to be understood in terms of Hegel's *Logic*, whose algebraic movement has been misread as a series of fixed oppositions. That algebra, whose analysis, today, is "centred on three names: Marx (and Engels), Lenin, and Trotsky," allows James to grasp the relation between these three (actually four) names and a view of the labor movement that remains "frozen" and that cannot be maintained in the face of the capitalist state and Soviet state bureaucracy. Whence the importance of Hegel's *Logic*: for James, the "aim of the *Logic*" is "how to keep out of the fixed, limited, finite categories"; which is why the emergence of a new *concept* of the proletarian party confirms that what is anticipated is also successive, and why the emergence of a new concept is always the retrospective assumption of a prior logic.[67] If a break in traditional concepts means that "we can find *ourselves* only by tearing off this trotskyist veil and seeing the leninist content"—the figure of a veil here is of some importance, as we shall see—the question remains whether James's unveiling is entirely consistent with the usual *explaining* of traditional Marxism, or in a way that transforms that content.[68] On the other hand, James's reference to "the uncharted infinite that faces *us*" seems to be wandering off in an entirely different direction, which I will try to explain in what follows.[69]

Recall James's method so far: history is thought and thought is the movement that grasps itself as history; and it is the contradiction between the two, to the extent that this contradiction is both arresting and interruptive, that allows us to know that we are indeed dealing with an immanent, revolutionary event. It is the attempt to find the right perspective on such events that leads James to read Lenin (on Hegel's *Logic*) as an illustration of an historical thought that disallows historicism by complicating the question of what makes history possible. The leap acts as an interruption precisely to the extent that it illumines the gloom that accompanies all historical possibility; such a revelation does not dissolve contradiction by trying to fix it, but plunges into it the better to grasp its further obscurity. This may also account for why the leap calls for a singular typography and a capitalization that makes it exemplary of an emphasis that arrests it. This emphasis is already located in James's philosophical attempt to rethink the relations between bureaucracy and proletariat on the one hand, and logic and history on the other, between what is clearly demarcated as the "hard knots" of history and the spontaneous proletarian movement, "whose ultimate aim is self-mobilization" (no doubt linked here to its opposite, "developing capitalist society," or capital as a form of organization), an emphasis that allows James to grasp how each term "contains and overcomes its complete penetration by its inherent antagonism, the capital relation."[70]

In *Notes*, James insists on how this dual (if interpenetrated) contradiction is from the start affected by a *third* element. That element is the future status of the party under Stalin which, James argues, has to be negated. "Unless the labour movement arrives at the abolition of the party, the state will never wither away."[71] Clearly, what is at stake is how the hard knot of these two elements (which is really a third) already contains new transitions, or discontinuities, but ones that are unrecognized as such. These transitions must themselves be grasped historically, dialectically. Crucial here is James's "method" (his word) of reading: to read dialectically is to go beyond the finite categories of thought precisely because historic events cause "violent changes" in those categories.[72] Trotsky's great error, according to James, was to "*begin* by believing that you *know* that categories change."[73] Trotsky lectured on changing categories all the time, he says, but "fixed and finite determinations held him by the throat until the end."[74] The point Trotsky forgets is that "we establish a category only to break it up. That is the point. You no sooner have it fixed than you must at once crack it wide open. In fact the chief point about a finite category is that it is not finite."[75] At another point James defines his theoretical task this way: "We have to co-relate logic and history. We have to search and find the specific categories, the specific finite and infinite. If you jump at it abstractly, then you will be betrayed as sure as day."[76] This is why James's text is riddled with a constant series of ironic exhortations to the reader (and why it sometimes addresses itself to specific readers, some of them named [Grace Lee] and some not [Constance Webb; members of the Johnson-Forest Tendency; the second person pronoun]). It is precisely to counteract any attempt to fix or limit the meaning of James's text that in each of these instances the effects of transition must be presented as a constant oscillation between paraphrase and quotation, irony and exhortation, note and marginalia, upper case and lower case, etc., without the transition itself becoming a distinct principle of determination.

In contrast to Fanon therefore, who explicitly refuses to reduce the irruptive moment to history or politics, James's *Notes* addresses the *political* demand to free spontaneity—"the free creative activity of the proletariat"—from the repressive forces of state organization that have historically capitalized it: forces that include nationalism and imperialism, Trotskyism and Stalinism, but also capitalism more generally. Indeed, it is to distinguish the international proletariat from the imperialist form of capital and the Stalinist one-party state that James articulates the leap as an "impulse" or *Trieb* always at work in the body politic. This drive cannot fail to be usurped by bourgeois politics (the era of the French and Russian revolutions and the various Internationals), and this usurpation is itself the product of a failure of Marxist political philosophy to grasp how Stalinist political bureaucracy has become "the enemy of the very thing it had been formed to develop": revolutionary spontaneous proletarian movement.[77] The essence of Leninism is to have explored this diremption between organization and spontaneity, but what James refuses to believe is that Leninism is the last word on this diremption.[78] Accordingly, Lenin's four leaps or capitals mark the appearance of a new capitalization: "*The Party and Revolution*. That is our leap," writes James: an axiom that adds two more capitals to Lenin's four and which, to put it bluntly, signals the emergence of a new historical object whose cognition casts a new light on spontaneity, discussed here in relation to its new objective form in state capitalism and bureaucracy, as well as the legacies of Stalin, Lenin, and Trotsky.[79] Bureaucracy (which is the true fate of modern party politics) thus carries within it what is really at stake in the failure to separate proletarian invention from that which limits or negates it.

The stakes of this reading can be shown schematically in the following two motifs:

1[2]. In James's presentation of labor history from 1789 to the present day, each epoch is composed of a unity of opposites that, as they evolve and develop, briefly coalesce until one element "overcomes the other, embraces it, and itself becomes the basis of…the new unity of further opposites," whereupon a "hard knot" is formed.[80] A contradiction in historical time is thus at the same time a knot, the time knot of the phenomenon, or the knot out of which the phenomenon forms itself. In the case of the First International, which began with Marx, before the various internecine struggles of the Second and Third Internationals saw a "decay" in historical and organizational perspective, the party, far from analyzing the antagonisms between labor and capital, seems, rather, to have hardened into a form of thought as a result of this decay (a true history of the labor movement can only open out on the basis of going beyond this).[81] To this extent, James's thinking about labor history seems to presuppose that it always and in spite of itself gathers leaps and discontinuities into hardened forms, and that the knottiness of those forms can only be revealed through the escalation of their disjuncture, which then becomes an object for materialist thought. One might be tempted to think that time *must* be knitted up as one of these hard knots so that it can come down to us in the form of the Marxist philosophy, and even a politics, of history. By the same token, and in a way that disturbs all the oppositions on the basis of which James is trying to think here, starting with the hard knot that forms between historical objects and their cognition, such knots can only be known after the event, at the point at which they and their inherent antagonism unravel. "Truth, in our analysis, the total emancipation of labor," James writes, "can only be achieved when it contains and overcomes its complete penetration by its inherent antagonism, the capital relation."[82]

How does a knot unravel itself? By becoming completely and insolubly knotted. Only when its essence is hardened enough can it finally be dissolved, for only at that point is it undeniably true, emancipated, objective. This amounts to saying that we can never *see* the purpose or end of a knot, for its historical weave is too dense. We can only judge it, historically, by taking a leap of thought.

2. This brings me to James's second motif: "*The Party and Revolution.* That is our leap. That is our new Universal—the abolition of the distinction between party and mass."[83] "All politics now therefore revolved

around this leap."[84] In so far as what motivates this politics is the desire to abolish the distinction between the party and the mass, the leap must be understood as what brings that abolition into being, or as what inscribes its very possibility. James's argument is mostly an historical one about how the party becomes the objectively established concept of the "the conscious-ness" of the proletariat, a role necessarily in conflict with "its being."[85] The "conflict of the proletariat is [therefore] between itself as object and itself as consciousness, its party," and the solution of this conflict is "the funda-mental abolition of this division."[86] The point is not just to erase the divi-sion but to analyze it anew, as though one were witnessing the unfolding of a logic that is both distinction (its abolition) and relation (its division) at the same time. This logic is, for James, a leap that dialectically can never be grounded or secured by dialectic, but as what divides or abolishes dialectic against itself for just this reason: to the very extent that dialectical thought is found to contract itself into a terribly hard knot that also contains every knotted historical experience in its truth hitherto, it is the experience of those limited truths that needs to be represented in their movement, haul-ing historical time after them in their journey into new possibility. Con-sequently the very impulse that drives the proletariat to establish itself as an essential movement and thereby a subject in history entails opening it-self up to its usurpation and eventual destruction as a revolutionary move-ment, which is why the party is both its chance and ruin. (These remarks on spontaneity are very similar to Fanon's. For both men, spontaneity and usurpation are one and the same movement.) In fact, if the proletariat is proletariat only insofar as it expresses an impulse or *Trieb* to fully realize itself (to discover its *notion* in Hegelian terms) in the very form of its poli-tics, it can never *be* the party because that would be the end of its histori-cal inventiveness (and even the end of Marxism as a politics), and this is why, in *Notes*, James introduces the theme of the coming end of the party. The party has to be negated because in its current form (the one-party state) it represents "the incorporation into bourgeois, capitalist society of the nearly two-hundred-year-old efforts by the labour movement to create a party to take over the state. Instead the state takes over the party."[87] Or, as he says later, in the section on "*The Leap*": "bourgeois society has taken over the specific creation of the proletariat, the political party."[88] Unlike Trotsky, however, whom James accuses of being "caught up and strangled" by outmoded categories, James argues that "the character and perspectives of the revolutionary party and of the existing revolutionary party" are now profoundly Stalinist: "We know that stalinism today is the *true* state of the labour movement."[89] The history that James relates consists, accordingly, in rejecting the Stalinist-statist model of the party in favor of a new revolutionary leap.

The leap, then, registers the difference between the political dimension of the dialectic as disputed truth and is also the means by which the dialectical truth of politics organizes the historical life of Marxism. In this instance, Stalinism is the political truth of organized bureaucracy and abolition of the party-mass distinction the hard knot that awaits it. Now, it is in precisely this regard that the leap is a question of reading before all else: for James, the leap is what makes the troubling discontinuity between dialectics and politics clear, for the leap, in its finite-infinite character, just is the discontinuous movement that allows us to examine "an object in its changes" and examine changes in "our concepts of that object," watching "how *both* change," dialectically and politically, and "doing it consciously, clearly, with knowledge and understanding."[90] This is why James can say that Marxist thought has become unavoidably bureaucratic in its method, and is thereby completely unable to see (unlike Lenin) the troubling resemblance between the party and bureaucratic organization that is the hard knot of its truth. If thought is to correspond with the leap, then the historian and the politician also have to correspond with this moment when "the concrete stage that the notion, the absolute, has reached" becomes actualized in the truth "of the Idea."[91] For, as James says, the leap is what allows us to grasp transcendence in the immanent "self-movement [*Eigenmächtigkeit*]" of its idea.[92]

Now, before turning to my final point, I should briefly like to revisit the place of Lenin in *Notes*. Leninism in James's thought occupies the same position as Hegel's *Logic*: it confirms "something *vital*" that has to do with "*the 'capitalizing' of the concept of the proletarian party*" (party in the sense of the organized labor movement).[93] The question returns us to those four capitalized words: "LEAP LEAP LEAP LEAP" (to which James adds a further two). I should like to ask, finally, whether the leap can be situated in this capitalizing movement, between these *written* boundaries that in themselves cannot be leapt beyond or capitalized, and in whose movement there is nothing more than the errant, disjunctive form of the purely linguistic, and one that can no more substitute for dialectic than it can realize the political truth of history. In terms of the dialectic explicitly associated with the distinction and the immanent relation between the actual and the transcendent, and the thought that explores the conditions by which they intersect and inhere in a new historical movement, these four capital letters do indeed leap out by calling into doubt the very dialectic that would absolutize them by organizing their purely linguistic authority as history; for, James adds, if Leninism is the most important "thought on 'organization,'" and the *Logic* is what precisely allows us to distinguish in principle the dialectical thought that becomes and so invests in itself as a thought of organization, as against the diremptive thought that is about, but does not see how its language confirms organization, as I have said, how are Lenin's four capitalizations able to provide an alternative to that organization?[94]

It is thus evident from James's reading of Hegel, however rigorous or superficial (however historical or political), that it must resort to capitalization to make visible what historically arrests it as well as indicate the emergence of a singular thought that calls out for its political emphasis. That thought is frequently encountered in the pages of *Notes* and it arises from the following motif in Lenin's *Philosophical Notebooks* on the "gradualness of emergence" that, in the *Logic*, refers to the struggle of the Understanding to conceive of "the qualitative transition of something into its Other in general and into its opposite."[95] A key concern of *Notes on Dialectics* is therefore with what it means to know a limit, and what it means to be limited by that knowledge. Let us conclude with a brief discussion as to why. Consider the following passage from *Notes* discussing the determination of quality in the *Logic*:

Quality means that a *limit* is imposed, a *barrier* between itself and its other. . . . Something "Becomes" out of nothing. It always has its limit, its barrier. And this limit, barrier, is burst through, at a certain stage to establish the other, its other.[96]

James continues:

The proletariat politically is an undistinguished body of proletarians. Something "becomes." Some of them form a party. At once the proletariat is no longer party and proletarians. It is party and non-party, or as we say, party and mass. The party creates its other, the mass.[97]

It is this deceptively simple analogy that provides the core of James's thinking about politics and that, as we have already seen, leads to his radical rethinking of the party and the mass. (It also denotes a movement—as is also evident in Fanon—where the spirit of invention emerges as a violence within the limits of political organization. The relation between invention and its institution is the key insight of the *Notes*, despite the political urgency of James's own anti-Trotskyism. For all the insistence on logic and teleology, it is the emergence of state bureaucracy that is presented as the singular, capitalizing, spiritual event that simultaneously suspends, defers, and limits the proletariat as a politically finite possibility. Indeed, if "the next stage for the proletariat is the transcendence of the old political organizations of the proletariat," that transcendence is evoked as the end of the bourgeois form of the party *at the same time* as the hardened instance of a knot whose bureaucratic form has yet to be historically understood.[98]) Let us approach this question through James's analysis of quality, his fascination with the processes of both what limits and what determines the proletariat as a mode of being, or, to use more Hegelian terms: how essence limits being, and how being limits itself as essence. Now this doubling is exemplary of a series of pairings in the *Logic*, and the relation between a boundary (*Grenze*) and a limit (*Schranke*) is one of a complex series in so far as identity is always a synthesis of what is and what is not. As soon as the proletariat constitutes itself politically, for example, it presupposes a separation from the party that now acts as its negation or limit. As the party, the proletariat can only determine itself *politically*—that is to say, limit itself—in so far as it is not the mass, but it is the party that divides and connects it, for only in this way can the party determine itself vis-à-vis its other, the mass. And yet, it is only by limiting, and being limited by, the mass, that the party constitutes itself *and* determines itself as a party (which means that, logically, the party is always beyond or outside of itself, its own limit). But how does the political constitution of the proletariat differ from the party's representation as its limit? If I am reading James correctly, the proletariat constitutes itself by dividing itself from what limits it and, within these limits, thereby secures itself, but it is not until it has fully determined itself as the party that its realization as the party is experienced as a limit. Further, it is only at this moment that the party withdraws from the mass.

This tension, according to which the concept of the proletarian party is both subordinate to the mass and superior to it, could be followed throughout *Notes on Dialectics*: the relation between Leninism and Trotskyism, labor and bureaucracy, leap and logic, party and mass, and so on could be said to derive from this undecidable oscillation in James's understanding of history and its relation to its foundational other, the leap that can only expire *as* history. Historical cognition, on this view, can only secure itself as historical through the negation of genuine historical possibility and can only stabilize itself by determining the genuinely revolutionary moment as the boundary that completes it. For this very reason, historical knowledge is nothing more than the limitation that founds it, the limit that is internal to its possibility (that is, the inevitable relapse—itself entirely empirical—of possibility into organization, but also the *Trieb* that exceeds the limits of all thought of organization), and through which it is constituted politically. It is only when history ceases to be historical and becomes a distinct moment of possibility that the new object distinguishes itself. It is history, then, that infinitely separates revolutionary spontaneity from its realization, and that subjects it to its own bureaucratic conformity. But it is the party, too, as the figure for this delimitation: a figure that cannot create its own boundary but merely delimits itself from within a limiting structure.

In this sense, *Notes on Dialectics* is decidedly ambiguous about the uneasy complicity or structural antagonism between history and spontaneity and, by implication, the political legacy of dialectical logic in revolutionary organization. It is a suspicion shared by Fanon, who writes: "In certain circumstances, the party political machine may remain intact. But as a result of the colonialist repression and of the spontaneous reaction of the people the parties find themselves out-distanced by the militants."[99] For Hallward, by contrast, "Fanon rediscovers a lesson learned by Lenin in the wake of an anti-capitalist victory in 1917: in order to sustain a truly inclusive will of the people, in order to establish the rule of genuine democracy, the people must first smash its bourgeois simulacrum."[100] As with Hallward's earlier remarks about self-mastery, missing here is any suspicion that the party could itself be that simulacrum and precisely in its delimitation of the people's will as finite and representable. The fact remains, however, that in James's analysis of the party he repeatedly distinguishes between its historical limitations and what it is politically by virtue of this limit. One reason for this may have been itself political: a sense that the party as historically understood necessarily introduces a moment of radical instability in the very notion of the proletariat, and precisely because the party makes undecidable the relation between sovereignty and what is ordinarily taken to be the people's will; indeed, the bureaucratic transformation of the party raises the question: are there even grounds for deciding (between the leap and revolutionary organization)? Since James never uses the phrase "will of the people" in *Notes*, this insistence—that the proletariat *becomes* itself by ceasing to be "the people"—is already an *interpretation* on James's part, and quite an astute one at that, with which Hegel implicitly agrees by placing the word "boundary" as the definition of how something distinguishes itself from something else, and thus forms a boundary. Hegel writes: "through the boundary something is what it is, and in the boundary it has its quality."[101] The revolutionary proletariat becomes itself by means of the party, but in itself it remains a boundary to (or on the other side of) the party as historical limit. Clearly, for James, the party is always other to the mass, and the proletariat is the boundary that allows the mass to politically determine itself (as the limit to bourgeois politics). This would mean that it is possible to conceive of a relation *between* the mass and the party in which both cease to be *limited* by the other. That is to say, the emergence of a difference that is neither the mass nor party but the constitutive contamination of each: the wretched, for example, that is not itself identifiable as a boundary or limit. This would class what James calls mass mobilization not in Leninist terms, but in terms similar to Fanon's (and despite Fanon's equally insistent argument that the wretched was *not* the proletariat). If James opposes proletarian invention to the bureaucratic state machinery of the party, it is because the proletariat ceases to be sovereign as soon as it becomes one with the party. It would appear then that the mass can only enter into the circuit of will as a *Trieb*, that is to say, as the infinite incompletion or deferral of itself, unendingly. The party is the name of this infinite inhibiting limit. But, then, according to James, it is the traditional (the old vanguardist) concept of the party that annuls the mass as boundary, thereby allowing the party to appropriate all possibility of otherness to the statist version of itself (i.e., Stalinism), and bringing the whole thing back within the bounds of the party as the only sovereign subject (Trotskyism). The party relates to everything outside of itself not as a boundary, but as something that it is *not*, the other (or enemy) that is essentially its negation as a politics.

If Fanon can be shown to be opposed to the same kind of limited meaning of the political that James is opposed to here, does that mean that they are both really saying the same thing? Both regard invention as discontinuous, as a radical overturning of that which has ossified or become a fetish. And yet this proposition does not fully articulate the differences between them, which is not simply the result of James's more Marxist, dialectical presentation. In Fanonism, invention is bound to a form of *jouissance*, that is, to a kind of radical expenditure without subject or recuperation. This also results in a different reading of limit (*Grenze*) as an affect (*Darstellung*) that goes beyond dialectic in both its logic and rhetoric. *Toward the African Rev-*

olution offers itself, and its writing, as a praxis of *disobedience* that leaves no language or position intact. James is far more exhortatory (to the reader), but also joltingly ironic. In *Notes*, James exhorts the reader to recognize the meaning of what is being said, to recognize and so transform it; in *Black Skin, White Masks*, the reader is urged to grasp that which prevents his reflection from coinciding with itself, as the trace of something else. To read is to take a step, to be inventive, but this outcome cannot be prepared for nor prescribed. For Fanon, in brief, the leap remains a question; it has no thematic content (materialist, humanist, political), and yet without it no decision is possible, or is recognizable as such. This is why its locus (to name only one) is the tabula rasa: an inscription that is always the abyss of itself, for it is written on nothing.

It is evident, finally, that in the moment at which the colonial state is renewed by the people's commitment Fanon sees an oscillation not between sovereignty and politics, but between a politics that produces vertigo and a politics that remains indebted—strategically and methodologically—to the European model, an opposition that is, ultimately, something different from invention. James's presentation of the undecidable vacillation between *Grenze* and *Schranke* is consequently a symptom of an inability to go beyond the philosophical figure of the nation-state as the end point of politics, and despite the fact that its future, or its destiny, will have been always *perverted* by the organized meaning of its historical form.

Existence

"I should constantly remind myself that the real leap consists in introducing invention into existence."

FANON, *Black Skin, White Masks, trans. Markmann,* 229

Our investigation of certain key passages in Fanon has so far turned on the question of psychopolitics—its form and innovation. To confirm our understanding of this question, I propose now to turn to those narratives that demonstrate its existential significance. Aside from those passages containing remarks on invention, there are other aspects of Fanon's oeuvre that we need to come to grips with (in this chapter I will continue the reading of sociogeny begun in Part One, Chapter Three, "Negrophobogenesis"). I will therefore briefly summarize those passages, or at least the most striking of them, before turning to these other aspects.

1. That "time" must necessarily be related to the event that interrupts it has already been mentioned in terms of the opposition between History (*l'Histoire*) and the real *leap* (le véritable *saut*) that introduces invention into existence. The time of invention is thus situated between two modes of revelation, the event that reveals the destiny (if not the history) of events, and the narrative that strives to integrate it into a teleological movement, which knows only one dimension—that of succession. (For Fanon, the point of refiguring anti-colonialism in the colony is not to represent it, at least not in the form of a progressive teleological vision, for its hopes and its dangers necessarily remain obscure, or in any case not of a mimetic nature.)

2. Accordingly, everything that imprisons the capacity for infinite realization, everything that presents the past as criterion, as is the case with

historical judgment, is felt to be incommensurable with that refiguration, not akin to the ceaseless work of invention. The argument seems to be that colonialism has not only immured native life but has immured the meaning of history as well, and if the narratives, codes, genres, and genealogies of colonialism have tended to block the potentiality of the colonized, they seem equally to have blocked the affirmation of *l'Histoire*. Or perhaps, paradoxically, it is because the meaning of "my" destiny is not itself historical that it can never escape the concept of history that imprisons it, which is also to do with the way colonialism seized upon what were seen to be "inherited" differences to begin with.

3. In his need to challenge the canonical narratives of European *Man* (the problem of secular or anthropological humanism and the institution of colonialism) or in his need to sustain life beyond that of the colony's ethno-bourgeois economy (the problem of poverty and debt and the legal-political definitions of sovereignty and self-propriety), Fanon thus ends where he begins: with a call for the reinvention of European humanism. After all, what brings race into being as an historical concept is the European invention of Man, which also gave birth to its multiple others, whose relationship to history is necessarily one of a relegated past. So perhaps, for Fanon, in the colony, history as a discipline became, quite precisely, *racist*: a narrative whose redoubtable but all the more easily identified representations are the clearest example of a discursive machinery of power. Although I shall not here attempt to follow Fanon's discussion of history through his writing, it is clear that the reference to history in *Black Skin, White Masks*—or its carceral logic—thus turns on the difference between, on the one hand, a confined, institutional meaning in which power is violently exercised on colonial subjects, and on the other, a space of endless self-creation, in which self and world can be reinvented, and in which, implicitly at least, history, for the subject, can be given another meaning, a *future* in which time, reference, and reality can acquire new values.

I. WYNTER ON FANON

So far my main concern in this second part of the book has been with a relation of invention that is radical, elaborate, and difficult; a relation that one should not presume to be historical, and by this I mean that its inventiveness—at times terrible and majestic—has significance but no historical certainty. The time of invention, of the now, breaks off from the time of history. Yet clear though the lines of demarcation are, it is alarm-

ingly easy to confuse them. After all, invention is itself a historical problem, and history is itself, ideologically and politically, invented. Still, if to
witness the judgments of European history was always to incur the charge
that one was not yet sufficiently historical, then to sense the need to escape
from history was already to know that one's debt to such narratives had to
be acquitted. When the Jamaican writer and critic Sylvia Wynter, contem-
plating the above remarks by Fanon, insists on their importance for her
own thinking about humanism and history, and her own idea about the
tasks of black cultural criticism, she writes:

> Now, here is where the conception of the genre of the human and of the governing
> sociogenic principle [a principle she adapts from *Black Skin, White Masks*] comes
> in. For it would be the code, the law of the code, the principle, which functions
> as the ground of the history that will be narrated and existentially lived. So the
> ground of our mode of being human will itself be the a priori or ground of the his-
> tory to which it gives rise. But the paradox here, of course, is that it cannot itself
> be historicized within the terms of the ethnohistory to which it will give rise: that
> code/mode must remain, as you say, unhistoricizable. As ours now remains for us.[1]
>
> And my point here [she continues,] is that if we are to be able to reimagine the
> human in the terms of a new history whose narrative will enable us to co-identify
> ourselves each with the other, whatever our local ethnos/ethnoi, we would have to
> begin by taking our present history, as narrated by historians, as empirical data for
> the study of a specific cultural coding of a history whose narration has, together
> with other such disciplinary narrations, given rise to the existential reality of our
> present Western world system.[2]

Now, in so far as what cannot be historicized is the codes or genres
that make History itself "historical," history is in some senses the least
historical of discourses. It also seems reasonable to suppose that these
codes are separate from narrative in order to be meaningful as history.
It is a version of this limitation that allows Wynter to claim that these
codes preclude their subsequent reappearance as the referent of the historical version of themselves. Or still again: if invention is what frees us
from History, and thus permits a new breakthrough in our conception
of the human, it is because such epistemic shifts presuppose the work of
various codes, which we can only experience *as* history. You cannot his-
toricize the principle that demands that history is not itself historical (a
claim whose "paradoxical" reasoning Wynter argues is a priori). It is this
principle that requires its transcendental or transhistorical status if it is
to ground anything like an ontology: in Wynter's reading of Fanon, this

principle is also the claim for a "new science," and what Fanon's sociogeny finds in the last instance is a new history of the human, as a new object for theory. The human has to be saved from the European version of *Man*, which stands four-square behind the bourgeois notion of race as the biological essence of life (suffice it to say, this critique of the "Western World System" is already wary of how history comes to *narrate* culture, and in a way that makes it not easy to see how science is itself not a "disciplinary narration" responsible for the ways in which race has come to be read as an origin somehow heterogeneous to the movement of history). This provokes what seems to me to be an important conclusion, namely that for Wynter invention is located not in the natural sciences, least of all in biology, but in the empirical study of human consciousness, which, unlike History, has an indispensable opacity to it (referred to here as a priori codes) that is not at all a narrative, or anything like a *telos*. The price of our deliverance from history (either as ethnocultural code or as narrative genre) is not a new submission to the norms, protocols, and regulations of a counterhistory, in which invention is reduced to the internal regulation of new symbolic codes of representation. If invention is confined to the historical, then endless self-creation can only be extended as a servile representation—a mimetic mode of what was experientially felt to be imprisoning, and so always already trapped inside a predefined meaning of what counts as history.

Against this gesture, invention in *Black Skin, White Masks* forces upon Fanon's representation of humanism the necessity of a certain readjustment. However, there is no invention without a leap. And there is no leap without unsettling the borders of self and history. Yet if that leap is to unsettle all horizons endlessly, Fanon also insists that "for the black man there is only one destiny. And it is white" (a phrase that he repeats verbatim at the close of *Black Skin, White Masks*).[3] This can easily make the introduction of invention seem like yet another *telos* or humanism, *in opposition* to history and domination: Fanon's writing does not always avoid giving this impression, but in the notion of invention outlined above such an oppositional model cannot be sustained—in the affirmation of invention as a moment of uncertainty, or radical undecidability, there is an affirmation not only of an ethics, but of a politics as the infinitely irreducible future that cannot be anticipated, or known in advance, even though it always happens *now*, a happening that cannot be easily subsumed under humanism or teleology. Broadly speaking, this is where Fanon and Wynter diverge. For Wynter, invention is more or less an event of epistemic *breakthrough*, or at any rate a kind of rupture to be reinserted into a new narrative of the human, the coding of which can be grasped, in turn, as contrary to the "disciplinary narrations" of the West.[4] "Breakthrough" is thus conceived as heterogeneous to narrative, but this rupture can only appear *out of order* to the narratives it interrupts, and so bound to those narratives as content. Further, that breakthrough is meaningful—to humanity, to history—only when a breakthrough is adduced to have reordered codes that cannot themselves be historicized (does this not make breakthrough itself the origin of the historical?). Without breakthrough, in brief, there would be no history. And Wynter can only register that fact from the illusory privilege of historical continuity. A certain number of points follow from this. Wynter's statements about breakthrough are themselves far from discontinuous, and her theory of historical rupture remains a philosophical abstraction of history, since by taking a stance against disciplinary narration, she can only impose universal philosophical order on historical texts (or, paradoxically, she can only attack History by making it subject to codes that she cannot do without, nor address as specifically "historical"). Rather than going beyond disciplinary narratives, then, Wynter's notion of epistemic breakthrough can only preserve the latter's heterogeneity via a kind of transcendental optimism, which continues to think inventivity in teleological terms (as a moment wherein the "human" and the "historical" can be reconciled).[5] As such, the strange kinds of repetition, interruption, and arrest that Fanon is trying to bring out in his notion of the leap are lost sight of, seemingly disposed of as the promise of a new epistemic breakthrough.

So although invention is opposed to history in a sense, and the limiting of time to that of teleology in a sense, its meaning is not an horizon (of a potential presence) and still less an exercise in utopianism: for whereas both of these contain implicit reference to grounds and predictions, Fanon's references to invention are more akin to a kind of "stricture" (or endless deferral and complication) without being historical in any simple or strict way.[6] Thus, the white destiny of blackness, often thought to be a sign of Fanon's contradictory universalism, can be shown to be related to his refusal of History as the ground of any concept of race whatsoever, in so far as any attempt to claim an *escape* from racism necessarily involves a teleological appeal to a post-racial future that compromises the escape the moment it is claimed. One way of understanding this complication of fate and identity is in terms of recognizing the limits of the colonial episteme (this is Wynter's focus), if only because it is predicated on the idea of reducing human life to biological necessity, wherein the racial Other is labeled and expelled as pre-human. The distinctive gesture of European historicity— that of constraint—only makes sense here, at the end of the day, when those who are other are deemed to be without meaning or time. Though historically those put outside of time are circumscribed as pre-human, this literally non-evolved life only restates the difficulty of locating it substantially (rather than allegorically, or metaphorically), since how does one tell the story of what falls outside of time? The ultimate unlocalizability of such beings, on the one hand, permits them to be in time but not yet in history (like an end point that can never amount to an ending). On the other hand, this absolute beforeness presupposes a trait or tendency whose persistence has to be endlessly reinvented as history for race to take on the appearance of a natural telos *within* time. As Fanon writes: "Below the corporeal schema I had sketched a historico-racial schema . . . [it was] the other, the white man, who had woven me out of a thousand details, anecdotes, stories."[7] This essential relationship between historical and biological time, or the pre- and the properly human, is also what Wynter calls the fundamental epistemic conception of modernity in which knowledge, *techne*, and legislation unite in an anxiety about *reproduction*: "[T]he way an order must know itself is in the adaptive terms that it needs to secure its own reproduction. So what this means is that normally the subjects of the order can never know the order as it really *is*. Rather, they must know is as it *needs to be known*, in order to secure its own existence," but it would perhaps also be the case that such "adaptation" could never capture what really "is," since all orders rely on the phantasmatic projection of their own mystical foundation, even those like colonialism that seem to present themselves as the beginning of history.[8] And the nature of that imaginary continues to haunt black being and time, the immense geopolitical reach of its filiations being matched by the long temporal duration of Western notions of freedom and sovereignty. Fanon's comments on how history performs the work of this imaginary is a necessary, political act of questioning the epistemic nature of Western humanism, for the power organized under the name of Man is repeatedly demonstrated to be all too effective. Like the *negros* and *indios* that are its first symbols, this power insinuates itself by virtue of its quasi-historical allegory. To violent acts of penetration it adds modes of persuasion, and instead of being densely consolidated into a force prepared to encounter a certain resistance, it is so finely self-inventive—sublimated, we should say, thinking of how culture "whitens"—that every native it needs to "save" is already testimony to how many welcome their damnation. Unlike, say, the power that keeps order in Foucault's early work, this power does not distinguish between hegemony and domination (though, as the case of colonial education reminds us, it does dispose of native imaginaries for those cultures it occupies). Rather, it relies on being voluntarily assumed by its subjects, who, terrorized by it, seduced by it, addicted to it, internalize the requirements for maintaining its hold. No one wants to be or be seen as the *nègre*. What racial history produces, or threatens to produce, is an organization of power that, ceasing entirely to be a humanism, has become violence itself: a system of control that can be all-encompassing because it cannot be compassed in turn by *subjects*.

Writing in the 1950s, Fanon would not be the last critic of colonialism to notice how narratives of beings outside of time, on which racist humanism turns, are worked into every aspect of belief and being in the colony. Yet though we see nothing but the effects of domination, everywhere present in the colony, affecting everyone, everywhere, regardless of class, gender, or color, we never come close to seeing what Wynter describes as the experience of "*our reality* was not real to us," as though this "reality" were somehow hidden or disguised by illusions that allowed the disposition and deployment of hegemonic targets and techniques.[9] She continues: "while it is we humans who ourselves produce our social orders, and are in reality its authors and its agents, we also produce, at the same time, the mechanisms of occultation which serve to keep this fact opaque to ourselves."[10] This claim comes dangerously close to saying that reality is real to us because we invest in illusion. It is all too easy to suspect some idealism in the assumption that reality is an occulted state beyond current illusions, or certain epistemic claims. Fanon's aim is not to denounce racism as an illusion or an error: or at least not in this way, which cannot account for the tenacity of how unreality is experienced and lived. Indeed, he offers slightly different descriptions, in which the real is imaginary (and vice versa): thus, "White civilization and European culture have forced an existential deviation on the Negro. I shall demonstrate elsewhere that what is often called the black soul is a white man's artifact": here recognition of deviation may demolish certain foundations and strategies, but only at the level of artifactuality.[11] What is the reality of illusion for Fanon? Reality emerges out of our experience of illusion, but illusion persists by means of reality, which is why this deviation from reality never appears as such and also why illusions take on the sense of destiny. (I think that this is what Wynter is trying to get at in her construal of a real behind illusion, but, unlike Fanon, for whom the real is always veiled or masked, Wynter presupposes that the real can somehow be *known*. Indeed, she defines the task of black cultural criticism as the "making conscious" of the "non-conscious" laws or codes defining "our genres of being human."[12]) It would follow that Fanon's stress on the need for an entirely other order of inventiveness, for the (impossible) reinvention of the other as such, cannot be seen as an *historical* opposition to colonial historiography (and thereby to *l'Histoire*), despite his angry denunciations of colonialism's teleological thrust: if the aim is to escape history's imprisoning, that escape will not be achieved by epistemic critique, but rather by contesting colonialism in a more general description of its language of time. The interminable process of interpretation to which competing histories give rise, literally maddening to those who bring to it the demand that it issue in final truths and objective fact, is abandoned by Fanon rather than adjudicated. If history thus names a disciplinary organization of meaning and power that is total but not totalizable, total *because* it is not totalizable, then what is most radically the matter with history is not that there may be no way out of *their* referential reality (a dilemma belonging to the problematic of irreality in Wynter's analysis) but, more aporetically, that the binarisms of us and them, white/black, become meaningless and the ideological effects they ground impossible as history. If it is the destiny of blackness to become white, it is not because blacks and whites are destined to be the same, the same that is in their relation to reality and illusion, but the same in so far as each is, on the contrary, irremediably other, an alterity whose inventiveness or creativity essentially takes on that form. And clearly the writing of that alterity has to do with a future that is not always already contained by the past, a future that will not (always) have been: but a writing of what I venture to call Fanon's future imperfect; a moment of inventiveness whose introduction necessarily never arrives and does not stop arriving, and whose destination cannot be foreseen, or anticipated, but only repeatedly traveled, and is therefore not future at all.

Furthermore, the nature of colonialism necessarily affects the nature of the resistance to it. Almost inevitably, Fanon has some quite complicated and interesting things to say about when resistance is, precisely, resistant, and when it falls into mere expediency that makes resistance as such impossible. Fanon's thinking on this topic is, from the first, remarkably consistent. For example, he questions why, given the total social reticula-

tion of colonialism (in places like the Caribbean), the colonial bourgeoisie should find its corresponding oppositional practice in the equally total
cultural affirmation of a negritude (or "blackism").[13] The appeal of such affirmation is, primarily, that of a kind of archaeological faith in a *black* presence, or past, underpinned by a metaphysical belief in race purity, which is
also understood as cultural destiny: "And it is with rage in his mouth and
abandon in his heart that he [the poet/philosopher of negritude] buries
himself in the vast black abyss. We shall see that this attitude, so heroically
absolute, renounces the present and the future in the name of a mystical
past."[14] This mystical past is "past" only in the sense that it is taken to precede the colonial *present*, whose effects on identity in general are seen as
a loss—or interruption—of an original presence or plenitude (the "black
abyss") that is then projected (or, rather, retro-jected) absolutely as a way of
grasping and naming the redemptive presence that is now lost. Given the
elision of black agency from European accounts of modernity (who can
only imagine blackness as the sign of absence), stopping short of any subjective assumption of this absence, negritude mirrors perfectly the racialism
whose origin is the birth of *Man*. The wish, moreover, for a black origin
may be considered a need to replace one myth of modernity, with Europe
at the foundation, with another. It is as though an apocalyptic teleology
were the only conceivable way to put an end to history's meaning as myth,
symbolic inversion the only means to abridge its elaborate racial allegory,
and a black myth of myth the only response to its incarceration of meaning. One of the least welcome implications of an all-inclusive racialism,
such as colonialism is implied to be, is that even opposition to it, limited to
the specular forms of reflection and inversion, merely intensifies our attachment to the perceptual grid constructed by its practices. It is this archaeoteleological schema that Fanon's thought on invention is meant to question.

To say so much, of course, is to treat resistance to colonialism, if not
more radically, then certainly more single-mindedly than Fanon is ever
willing to do. For while a major effort of Fanon's work is to establish colonialism as an all-pervasive system of domination, another is to refute the
fact of this system and recontain its history within a larger spatial conception of culture that would once again permit a new humanism, along with
all the ideological effects attaching to it. If negritude, for instance, illustrates the apocalyptically anti-colonial trends of retribution that are the
only adequate responses to cultural imposition, it can also be seen to re-
instate precisely those social and political constraints that colonialism, as

a total order, also presents as the outcome of a natural order (and, as such, not invented). For in so far as negritude is mythic, as in the idea of race as a mystical essence, then it cannot release black self-invention from the mythic origin of Man in European humanism. In response to this attitude towards time, Fanon writes, as already noted: "I will not make myself the man of any past. I do not want to exalt the past at the expense of my present and my future."[15] The form of the argument here is that as a discourse bound to colonial racial truths, black anti-colonialism has to presuppose the validity of those truths in its recourse to a different kind of black discourse (as such, its so-called narrative of liberation, oriented teleologically by the origin to be refound and unveiled, in its attempt to legitimate itself as a counterhistorical knowledge, fails to liberate itself from the Eurocentric '*l'Histoire*'). Alternatively, in so far as Fanon wants the end of colonialism to foreshadow the birth of a new humanism, this humanism, let us not forget, is not just the promise of new institutions and a new politics of culture; the essence of this humanism, for Fanon, is the task of an endless self-creation, without status, rule, or protocol: "In the world through which I travel, I am endlessly creating myself," he writes. This invention, in fact, may even exceed the work of cultural criticism as Wynter conceives of it, in so far as it evades all logics of representation that have, in thought, tried to capture it, and also refuses to be bound by the conventional or contractual terms of "method": "I shall be derelict. I leave methods to the botanists and mathematicians. There is a point at which methods devour themselves."[16] I shall return to this notion of dereliction, and its opposition to that of science, a little later.

These reservations are most tellingly inscribed in *Black Skin, White Masks* as a black response to History, once again centering on the question of destiny, its meaning as possibility and revelation. Against the omnipresence of colonialism, according to which the Negro is "the biological," "the genital," the "predestined depositary," and the "phobogenic" object of culture, Fanon will stress certain acts of decision.[17] "In order to terminate this neurotic situation," he writes, "in which I am compelled to choose an unhealthy, conflictual solution, fed on fantasies, hostile, inhuman in short, I have only one solution: to rise above this absurd drama that others have staged around me, to reject the two terms that are equally unacceptable, and, through one human being, to reach out for the universal."[18] What could this possibly mean at the level of culture? In her work on Caribbean expressive culture—such as Rastafarianism, ska, or reggae—Wynter finds this reaching in the people of the *liminal,* that is, those who, by their excluded social position, find themselves having to reinvent themselves in the margins of culture; indeed, they constitute an excluded space within the institutional, social spaces of the nation-state and, as such, both in their economic and symbolic position, they constitute something of what Fanon called the wretched. (In a 2000 interview with David Scott, Wynter says that the term is a translation of Fanon's *"les damnés.*")[19] The liminal, whose labor in the production of the politico-economic ends of man makes them incorporated and alienated at the same time, cannot afford to look forward on the basis of a mythical past, and they therefore occupy the *present* in a way that breaks with the very value of history in the colony. As such, they open up the political dimension of invention in part because, being an "entirely different form of sovereignty," they live a reality that is not mediated by the dominant imaginary.[20] Wynter refers to the "explosive moment of a breakthrough to a new [popular] imaginary," a moment made possible by earlier national struggles that these populist movements reactivate.[21] Yet it is also possible to argue, as did Fanon and Wynter in their differing early responses to Marx, that the liminal not only exposes the deficiency of Marxian categories but also highlights a different experience of being and time, one that remains nonexistent even to the ontological sovereignty supposedly handed down by productive labor. The masks imputed to the colonial bourgeoisie, which hide the notion of a lost time behind non-fungible claims of race, cannot be extended to the liminal who remain precisely useless as such: their narratives disrupt capital's racial hegemony and its reliance on time-as-exchange. It is, of course, Fanon's 1952 text that opens up the possibility of this explanation in its reluctance to commit itself either to a dialectics of history (e.g. a Marxian ontology of labor) or to a psychoanalytic reading of culture:

If there is an inferiority complex, it is the outcome of a double process:
- primarily, economic;
- subsequently, the internalization—or, better, the epidermalization—of this inferiority.

Reacting against the constitutionalist tendency of the late nineteenth century, Freud insisted that the individual factor be taken into account through psychoanalysis. He substituted for a phylogenetic theory the ontogenetic perspective. It will be seen that the black man's alienation is not an individual question. Beside phylogeny and ontogeny stands sociogeny. In one sense, conforming to the view of Leconte and Damey, let us say that this is a question of a sociodiagnostic.[22]

Wynter's reading of Fanon proposes that the key to the early work lies in the term "sociogeny." And what is at stake in this term between phylogeny and ontogeny, culture and the individual, is the role of race in bioeconomic accounts of the human. In "Towards the Sociogenic Principle: Fanon, Identity, the Puzzle of Conscious Experience, and What It Is Like to Be 'Black,'" a dense, difficult essay first published in 2001, Wynter sets out her case.[23]

According to Wynter, sociogeny is not an attempt, rapidly proposed here by Fanon, to rethink the relation between symptom and culture, but an effort to think about how the human *qua* human comes to be structured as such, as a recognizably "biological definition of what it means to *be*, and therefore of what it is *like to be*, human"—a definition whose presuppositions Fanon is contesting.[24] It follows that a shared likeness among members of a "race" is not essentially biological in nature, but nor is it accidental; Wynter's concern is with how modern culture construes individuals in recognizably racial-teleological terms, a mode of being that has become hegemonic. Sociogeny, then, at least in this initial sense, prior to its generalization as a critique of neo-Darwinism, is less a critique of biocentric thought (its *telos*, its method), than the emergence of a "new science" or "methodology" (and here the question of scientific method returns) that allows us to see the ways in which culture-specific codes appear regularly and consistently to us as "*self*-evidently evident to our consciousness."[25]

Here then is a concern with how we, as subjects, come to know "the terms of the sociogenic principle which institutes" us as subjects, terms that are non-conscious and that we experience as self-evident within our "genetic-instinctual narcissistic somatic norms."[26] These codes duly show the limits of a natural science perspective on what it means to be human, on the grounds that it is subjective experience alone that provides us with insight into what it is like to *be* symbolically encoded as white or black. And this "coercive" schema can, where necessary, override "the genetic-instinctual sense of self, at the same time as it itself comes to be subjectively *experienced as if it were instinctual*," and thereby confirms in an important sense our "common reality."[27] For Wynter, as already indicated, what is at issue is how these quasi-transcendental schemas acquire the phenomenological status of lived experience. Attacking what she sees as a central disavowal of ways of thinking and writing the human, Wynter turns to Fanon, whom she enlists in the ranks of thinkers for whom humanism is crucial to their views on race and modernity.

According to Wynter, Fanon allows us to see these (biocentric, eugenic) codes from his *liminal* position as both Self and Other, and precisely because his is a "conflicted perspective" he is able to question the self-evident orders of scientific culture and consciousness.[28] The conclusion to be drawn is that Fanon's thinking on sociogeny was influenced, if not compelled, by his actual readings of racist popular science. And this seems to be the point of Wynter's discovery, in "Towards the Sociogenic Principle," of a "new language" of consciousness beyond the grasp of physical science as such.[29] In the end then—precisely there—Fanon's sociogenic attempt to differentiate humanism from something grounded in science implicates invention once again in an oppositional resistance. As we began by observing, however, Fanon's notion of invention troubles such oppositions. We have also suggested how, in every instance, Wynter's very desire to affirm a post-racial humanism is undercut by the need to present post-racism as the re-manifestation, in consciousness, of cultural codes whose "outside" is never made clear, and whose effects "inside" us cannot be brought into consciousness (and this in a text that understands these codes in non-psychoanalytical terms). The simple methodological point here is that Wynter does not address why Fanon turns to psychoanalysis to think sociogeny beyond the causality of the natural sciences. And, consequently, she avoids asking why the time of trauma, for Fanon, goes beyond that of biological constitution as the ground of experience.

This reading, we might be tempted to say on the basis of this description, is not only not opposed to, nor really even distinct from, biocentrism, but reduces the entire problematic of invention to that of *techne* or method, and thereby (because of the periodizing and historicizing emphasis) makes sociogeny into something more like an empiricism (Fanon's critical comments on [racist] popular science and method, scattered throughout *Black Skin, White Masks*, ought to be thought here for what they differently lay out and rhetorically perform).[30] Let me first say that I do not think that Wynter's reading is simply tendentious, or inaccurate, but she does appear to be simplifying what Fanon himself says about the origin of sociogeny. Ultimately, she argues, sociogeny shows how the modern self oscillates between two seemingly naturalized sets of assumptions about what it means to be human—one deriving from the *bios* of natural selection, the other still attached to competitive struggle as the true *telos* of biological life. Thus, just as the evolutionary efficiency of Europe is understood as the natural outcome of the inherited power of race, so the success of capitalism, upheld as the form of political economy closest to that of biological life, can be shown to be an expanded development of what it means to be properly human:

> By placing human origins *totally* in evolution and natural selection, they [bourgeois intellectuals] are going to be able to map the structuring principle of their now bourgeois social structure, that of the *selected* versus *dysselected*, the *evolved* versus *non-evolved*, on the only still extra-humanly determined order of difference which was left available in the wake of the rise of the physical and, after Darwin, of the biological, sciences.[31]

All the evidence of capitalism's totalizing effects—of its productivity as an all-englobing system of power—is equivocal in such ways, as Wynter claims that this system underpins at once the classification of human hereditary variations into races and the distinction between bourgeois Man and his various Others. In the literal sense of a double discourse, what Fanon's sociogeny refers to is how (human) inferiority comes to be read in biological, solely racial-economic terms. Yet as we continue to consider the operation of this sociogeny in Fanon's text, we should be wary of prejudging it, in a certain historicizing manner, as the symptom of an epistemic bind, and in which racism obligingly explains the taken-for-granted existence of races. We need rather to be prepared to find in the source of sociogeny the very resource on which Fanon draws for this thought on black existence; in the torsion between phylogeny and ontogeny, Fanon finds a precise means of addressing and critiquing *racism as a discourse of time*; in the "failures" that are the object of his study, he presents his term as an advance on that of Freud's (a name completely missing from Wynter's account). In short, we need to ask why sociogeny needs to be invented to explain the only possible creative mode of invention: that of a subject whose destiny is marked by something other than itself, a crossing of chance and necessity that is that subject's singular invention, according to which it is only black insofar as, paradoxically, it grasps its own impossible whiteness.

II. THE SOCIOGENY OF TRAUMA

Of all the difficulties that will crop up in *Black Skin, White Masks*, not the least instructive concerns the move whereby a text dealing with colonialism begins with a call for a "liberation of the man of color from himself," and whereby the themes of power and social control are passed accordingly from the repressive functions of the state to the abyssal liberation of a self that is other to (of) itself.[32] By what kinds of logic or necessity is power thus turned over to liberation, and domination turned into self-invention? For if the liberated self provides the ground for political revolution to begin, it is certainly not because this liberation is itself easy to grasp. In one sense, its structure is so elusive that we do not even have a sense, as we should with revolutionary discourse, of what needs to be freed or, more importantly, of what might constitute the clues or cruxes of such a liberation. In another, the pathologies of colonialism can be read fully and clinically treated as *narcissistic* disturbances: in the case histories of various neuroses, in the many tales of white-black suffering and desire—in all the etiologies and ailments that accumulate over Fanon's training and experience, narcissism is primary: "A moment ago I spoke of narcissism. Indeed, I believe that only a psychoanalytical interpretation of the black problem can lay bare the anomalies of affect that are responsible for the structure of the complex. I shall attempt a complete lysis of this morbid body."[33] This belief does not prevent Fanon, a page later, from claiming that psychoanalysis is somehow depoliticized and desocialized; hence the need for sociogeny. As we shall see, Fanon's engagement with psychoanalysis offers either too little or else too much to amount to a simple case of negation. In principle, the treatment of narcissism in the text, whatever its *psychoanalytic* validity, does not maintain the term in opposition to Freud, nor does it even invert its more traditional meaning. Having published analyses of this elsewhere, let me simply state that, in so far as the colonial subject uses mirrors both to mask and to conceal that masking, Fanon's concern is with the deformations and constraints of such *seeing* and of such *knowledge* (at the level of sign, signifier, and affect). In a sense, Fanon's stress on the psychoanalytic concept of narcissism, the desire, as he puts it in the introduction, for its complete lysis, can be linked here to sociogeny in so far as the *I* or ego is always, for him, a question of the other, of others. The implication is that sociality inscribes itself in the individual, and egoic love is inhabited by the political, and that is why power is both the condition of the subject and the reason why self-love is always a question of mastery. And this certainly seems to be the implication of the stress on narcissism, on what it means to be an alienated, divided subject, a subject unable to represent itself to itself in the racist mirror of culture. (The phrase "morbid body" also raises, implicitly, the question of narcissism in relation to that of the death drive, and in ways that are necessarily difficult. For what could it mean to say that when looking into the mirror, instead of some trap and illusion, what I see staring back is the other who is me, who fascinates and enrages me, the other in whom I love and kill myself?) Besides, nothing about these anomalies is secret or hidden, unless we count the repressed elements, and this hardly brings us closer to a judgment as to why sociogeny should take us beyond Freud. All that is available is what Fanon means when he says there is a need for a new "sociodiagnostic" of black lived experience, which we have examined previously.

It would be seriously misleading, however, on the basis of this sociodiagnostic, to read sociogeny as that which, confronting the absence of a specifically *black* meaning in the psychoanalytic discourse or text, must unfold as a crude proliferation of an anti-psychoanalytic conception of blackness. For one thing, if sociogeny can be thought to give expression to such difficulties of interpretation, this is because, more than merely opposing sociogeny to psychoanalysis, Fanon goes out of his way to connect them; and no response would serve his invention of this term or the logic of its inventiveness better than to see this connection as inhering in a non-positive affirmation (of psychoanalysis) rather than belonging to a simple logic of opposition. For another, it seems willful not to see that connection occurring in what is far more obviously and actually Fanon's reading of colonialism as a psychopathology. With its phobias, fantasies, distortions, and affects, Fanon's negrophobogenesis positively adds to the psychoanalytic project of interpretation that nominally guides it. Alice Cherki correctly realizes how ridiculous it is to speak of sociogeny as anti-psychoanalytic, since the term concerns how racism is unconsciously lived, which, while fully suitable to the project that subtends Fanon's own writing (indicatively begun under the title of a "disalienation of man"), can never be wholly absent from a text that, typically, offers itself as a psychopathology of a self that is, as it were, *unlived* (the ways in which the death-work of culture is recreated—unconsciously performed—by [in] the colonial subject).[34] Moreover, to see that, in sociogeny, the process of decision and interpretation is from the start an analysis of the conflict and violence in and against which "the *imago* of the negro" emerges is also to see that Fanon makes a demand on psychoanalysis, or a certain version of psychoanalysis, to show how culture remains marked or haunted by this hatred and phobia; or, more precisely, how the imago or fantasy of the negro shows something like the "essence" of colonial culture as such, or at least something without which the pressure of a certain phobic fantasy of the negro on the real would not be so violent, and the acting out of this

"ambiguity" not so "extraordinarily neurotic."[35] Which is to say: a psychoanalysis not somehow opposed to culture, but a psychoanalysis which, in
its analysis of unconscious fantasy and colonial reality, revises Freud's late
reflections on the social bond to show how racist fantasy can not only be
fully integrated and institutionalized, but remains as a kind of traumatic—
albeit disavowed—memory in the unconscious life of the colonized. It is
a psychoanalysis, in other words, of the ways in which the unconscious is
constituted by the real that halts and interrupts it: the imagos and stereotypes by means of which the colonial subject hates and enslaves itself as a
subject, affirms its immorality or malfeasance, and fails to know itself as
anything but (a masked, white) European.

This is why Fanon never quite dispenses with psychoanalysis, despite
the appearance of having done so. I have tried to indicate how sociogeny,
as a response to Freud's seeming developmentalism and individualism,
forms the basis for Fanon's turn to narcissism. To condense the problem a
little brutally, we can say that *precisely* because, in Fanon's view, the black
is imprisoned, unable to escape the summons of its foundation, caught up
as it is in an utterly morbid fixation on the past, which is also to say the
projection of an imaginary whiteness, it can never be present to itself in its
representations, and so can only appear through its disappearance (and it
is this necessarily haunted narcissism that Fanon wants the colonial subject to be liberated from). Unable to represent himself to himself as white,
the "man of color" is also unable to represent himself as black; since he
has identified himself as white from the start, that assimilated whiteness
has made blackness narcissistically impossible to represent. Further, this
haunting is originary, just as, for Fanon, the black binds himself narcissistically to this alter, this irreal other, who is both model and rival and who,
in a very necessary way, precedes the fiction that is the condition of possibility of the black *as* subject.

Fanon also recognizes this, explicitly in *Black Skin, White Masks*, as a
problem of time: or rather, the discovery that (black) narcissism is perhaps nothing other than a morbid fixation on the past, on an alienation
that tends to repeat itself, as obsessive recollection. There is no good reason for assuming that psychoanalytic theory is not essential to this notion,
and indeed it is Freud's reading of fate and accident (or, in Lacan's terms,
tuché and *automaton*) that is worthy of note here.[36] Again, formulated very
quickly, what I shall be attempting to sketch out is how sociogeny is an
explicit engagement with Freud's notion of *Nachträglichkeit*, which Fanon

will use politically, ethically, to question the psychic effects of colonialism. It seems to me to be no accident that Fanon's formulations are always and everywhere struggling with the idea of untimeliness—exemplarily so in *Black Skin, White Masks*, and elsewhere in the repeated discussions of how, in the colony, narcissistic desire appears to be equivalent to an incorporation that destroys it, a sacrifice that only becomes manifest afterwards, that is, *nachträglich*, here registered *in the colonial subject's very untimeliness*, and so unable to recover or represent itself as an egoic presence. What would it mean for the colonial subject to discover itself in such relations? This is, I think, the sense of the "I should not seek the meaning of my destiny there [in History]" remark in *Black Skin, White Masks*, to the effect that the meaning of the future cannot by definition be a simple matter of what happened in the past, but involves a more complex articulation of time and repetition. Turning to Fanon's discussion, we will see how invention and the theme of time come together as a problem of traumatic repetition (this repetition being, in my view, crucial to the various arguments of *Black Skin, White Masks*).

We could illustrate this motif of trauma in all of Fanon's texts, with maybe the caution that "trauma" is not Fanon's term. If we had time, a study of Fanon's clinical writings (especially those written at Blida-Joinville), which pick up on the notions of neurosis and failure in *Black Skin, White Masks*, would make it clear that what counts as shock, and more especially its memorialization and re-inscription, involves, in the colony, a more radical sense of the event than is normally presupposed in studies of trauma, and one that Fanon had begun describing in 1952. When does historical catastrophe become traumatic? In Fanon's many writings on Martinique the answer seems to be: not until it is linked to something that comes after. It is the articulation of at least two "events" together that makes colonialism traumatic—that is, it is not until the imposition of the French policy of assimilation (with its attendant emancipation, racism, and faux universalism) that the collective experience of exclusion is remembered as if for the first time. It is a view that renders the time of trauma as the complex articulation of two moments and in which, to cite Lacan, "past contingencies . . . [are given] the sense of necessities to come" only after the event as it were, and in which "the realization by the subject of its history in its relation to the future" may turn out to be, retrospectively, that subject's only means of escape from the past that haunts it, and precisely because "*l'Histoire*" has mutated into a neurotic fear of the past that remains unexplorable.[37] I shall suggest that the drama and pathos involved in *Black Skin, White Masks* are not to be read as symptoms of Fanon's character or pathology, but as indications of the structure of this irrealization in general in its irreducible relation to the future, to both destination and destiny. Indeed, in his chapter on *le vécu noir*, or black lived experience, Fanon returns to Freud's notion of afterwardsness, in a slightly (but crucially) different way, to think this reorganization of both the past *and* the future, via the many ways that colonialism repeats or reproduces itself as itself, its tendency to symbolize its own immutable institution as timeless and immemorial, and always via the seemingly atavistic quality of the colonized, whence the need to endlessly police the borders of self and state. Whence, too, the neuroses of the colonial subject whose relations to the colonial order and to the past take on the form of guilt and debt—the sense that one's destiny is always belated, and so compelled to repeat the first event (which I am suggesting is just the trauma of assimilation). Or as Fanon puts it: "I am guilty. I do not know of what, but I know that I am no good."[38]

This reordering of the past, present, and future also raises further questions for Fanon's refusal both of History and of negritude. If, as Derrida rightly says, one of the paradoxes of invention is that for it to be inaugural it must be accorded a status, or recognition, and consequently this is why "[t]he first time of invention never creates an existence," for Fanon, by contrast, the introduction of invention into existence is already an act (of resistance?) even if it is not recognized as such.[39] Indeed, it would seem that what he wants to value as endless self-creation would necessarily have to escape the very concept of event, and accessorily all the attendant metaphorics of becoming and transfiguration, to be an invention worthy of the name. "In opposition to historical becoming," he writes, "there had always been the unforeseeable."[40]

Similarly, I have tried elsewhere to show in some detail how trauma in Fanon is a concern with fantasy, even as Fanon is arguably more lucid than most about the violent nature of the colony. "Has there been an ancient experience and repression in the unconscious [*Y a-t-il eu expérience ancienne et refoulement dans l'inconscient?*]?" he asks, in the chapter on "The Negro and Psychopathology." "Has there been a real traumatism [*traumatisme effectif*]? To all of this we have to answer, *no*. Well then?"[41] This "no" is of the utmost significance for Fanon's reflections on repetition and trauma—which I think are tied to his speculation concerning colonialism as an event, the violence of its founding act, whereby the colony gives rise to the "imposition of [its] culture."[42] Imposition suggests a certain kind of passivity, but Fanon suggests that what appears to be passive is also the outcome of a "sacrificial dedication permeated with sadism" that implies that the colonial subject is in the grip of intentions of which it is not (yet) aware but that will have all the force of necessity.[43] (Indeed, in this traumatic encounter with the real, in the words of Lacan, "What is repeated, in fact, is always something that occurs . . . *as if by chance*."[44] What the subject confronts, in an apparently accidental manner, is what Fanon and Lacan both call the "unassimilable": "It is what, for us, is represented in the term neurosis of destiny or neurosis of failure," writes Lacan; and for Fanon, "You come too late, much too late. There will always be a world—a white world—between you and us."[45]) To say that the subject's encounter with his *tuché* is only apparently accidental, however unpredictable it seems, is to suggest that what befalls the subject is already anticipated ("predestined" is Fanon's word), and therefore marked by a kind of after-the-eventness. In fact, Fanon's work, from the start, stresses an untimeliness that does not belong to the order of historical events, but is the origin of the earliest symbolizations by which the subject is constituted, and so both in and beyond the ego. In the kind of encounters described by Fanon, at any rate, the subject's discovery that it is hated may be an encounter with the unforeseeable—hence the shock—but there is nothing accidental about that hatred; it comes already articulated via a thousand anecdotes and stories that the subject has learnt to identify with (Fanon uses the word "devour") and therefore has a meaning (a sociogenic truth) that very quickly reveals a double bind between the unconscious and culture, or the cultural workings of the unconscious that these stories recite, reveal, and exhibit. This is what Fanon means when he says that this traumatic repetition is predestined. Or as he puts it earlier, "in one sense, if I were asked for a definition of myself, I would say that I am the one who waits."[46] The real may appear under the guise of destiny, but its true meaning or reality is always veiled (or in Fanonian terms, masked).

And here we come back to the issue of assimilation. Though the French project of assimilation was virtually annulled in the workings of its formalism (i.e. various formal freedoms combined with substantial unfreedoms), the *promise* of assimilation remains absolutely necessary for Fanon and his account of how the colonial subject is led to narcissistically sacrifice itself to culture. At the theoretical level of ideology, the promise functions to confer legitimacy on racist treatments: as all of Fanon's neurotics, in their confusion of race with identity, are capable of revealing, the social system must appeal for its authority to concepts of truth, justice, meaning, and equality, even when its actual work will be to hold these concepts in racist abeyance or to redefine and contain them as functions of its own white supremacist operations. And at the practical and therapeutic level of such operations, the promise of a healthy ego becomes the lure of an impossible narcissism extended by venalities such as "it is not enough to try to be white, but that a white totality must be achieved."[47] Here is a sentence from Fanon's chapter on "The Man of Color and the White Woman" in which these tensions come together quite clearly, and indeed explicitly go back to the problem of narcissistic morbidity: "Unable to be assimilated, unable to pass unnoticed, he [René Maran, author of *Un Homme pareil aux autres* (1947)] consoles himself by associating with the dead, or at least the absent."[48] Assimilationism forces Fanon to confront the split between adaptation on the one hand and domination on the other; it also leads him to contest how certain versions of psychoanalysis work precisely in the service of the status quo and its representation.[49] Insofar as ego and libido are never simply ontological concepts, but complex forms of institution, there is no question, says Fanon, of phylogeny or ontogeny simply being inherited, or biologically determined. This is why the task of sociogeny is defined as the apprehension of the close imbrication of narcissism and race, symptom and culture, desire and power, institution and identity.

Perhaps the most interesting effect of all produced by the promise of assimilation, however, considerably exceeds these theoretical and therapeutic frictions. If assimilation exploits the logic of a promise by perpetually maintaining it as *no more than such*, then colonialism must obviously produce a subject who is dirempted, who is as much frustration as hopefulness. Accordingly, one consequence of the system that, as it engenders debt and loyalty (debt *as* loyalty), simultaneously deprives the system of all the requirements for its accomplishment, is the desire for an identity that would not be so torn. This desire is called into being on two counts: because it cannot be grounded in status or sovereignty, and because it can only have agency insofar as it is willing to be anxious or neurotic. What such a desire effectively calls for, in short, both as a concept and as a fact, is *an invention that is not a form of non-fungible debt*. In the first place, there is the desire to free native life from the carceral effects of colonialism, in so far as life, in the colony, follows the temporal logic of a *not yet* or future anterior (as, for example, the obsessive, compulsive *effects* of an imaginary whiteness that is experienced as such after the event, *nachträglich*), as if black lived experience could only be understood retrospectively, afterwards, and never simply at the time of happening, by the obsessional neurotics or "failures" who go on to discover their "true faces" in France, a journey that is always in some sense traumatic whether in dreams, screen memories, or affects.[50] Whence, too, Fanon's famous example of an encounter on the streets of Lyon: "Look, a Negro"; and the feeling of being shattered and overwhelmed owing to the libidinal development of the colonial subject. This process of *Nachträglichkeit* (whose after-the-eventness evokes a radically unpredictable, unforeseeable play of necessity and chance) can be extremely complex for Fanon, as in his remarks on the collective response to the Vichy occupation of Martinique during World War II, or in his comments on the Martinican family's sacrificial dedication to French culture.[51] And indeed this whole setup is part of his meditation on the process of *epidermal* or *sociogenic* memorization by which the colony repeats the traumatic after-the-eventness of colonialism. This differential understanding of how culture is inscribed in the body puts paid to any stable distinction between the real and the phantasmatic, between who is inherited and who inherits. It also complicates the Nietzschean language of *ressentiment* (the desire for sovereign status) that Fanon sometimes uses to contrast with the *active* need for creative reinvention within the colony.[52] And once the simple oppositional model of a good narrative (freedom; anti-colonialism) and a bad narrative (history; colonialism) is disturbed, then the meaning of invention (as chance, accident, or *tuché*) emerges in a much more complex fashion, as a disruptive force that cannot be absorbed into the "historical, instrumental hypothesis" of a teleological narrative order or account, and whose inventivity exceeds the programmed narratives of Marxism and psychoanalysis alike.[53] This motif, elaborated and complicated, will remain central to the later work.

Psychoanalysis gives Fanon a name and a technique for thinking invention, in that highly specific sense whose ultimate meaning describes the equally specific sense of sociogeny. If the colonial system imposes everything but sacrifices nothing, then one way in which it differs from psychoanalysis is that the latter is, precisely, not a historical narrative: sufficiently open to hearing gaps and absences in meaning to allow for the emergence of a narrative and properly committed, once it has emerged, not to fully understand its "non-sense" as meaningful. In relation to a temporality so complex that it often tempts its subjects to misunderstand the present as always simply present, time in psychoanalysis realizes the possibility of a before-ness that is only comprehensible insofar as it comes after, and an afterwards-ness that is before the origin. And in the face—or afterwardsness—of a temporality where it is generally impossible to assign causality to guilt or indebtedness, where even the process of assimilation seems capricious, psy-chic time performs a drastic understanding of the effects of power as well. For unlike colonial time, time in psychoanalysis is fully prepared to affirm the efficacy and priority of delay or failure in personal agency, be it that of masks that do the work of hiding concealment or that of the missed *rendez-vous* that undoes the work of masking. Fanon was well aware of this double bind: the colonial subject waits for the other precisely because s/he is always in the position of the one who waits, the one who makes nothing happen, and precisely because "everything is anticipated" time for this subject who feels himself to be empty, non-existent, and so unable to be "historicized."[54] It is not at all surprising, therefore, that the desire to have psychoanalysis work at the level of culture first emerges for Fanon from within the com-munity of the *assimilé* themselves, in those neurotics and failures, since the partly assimilated, having an attachment to the system, are most likely to be aware of their dirempted status to the extent to which they merely con-vey a power that is theirs to admire and not to have. It is entirely suitable that those who continually desire that power of belonging—in the sense of bio-political privilege—should be the first to become aware of themselves as *failures*, so that those who are "morbidly" interred in the colonial pres-ent, for instance, are also those who are "slavishly" attached to the past.[55] At the other end of the civic hierarchy (though not during times of mass up-heaval), the damned do not shared this agonized vocation:

I do not carry innocence to the point of believing that appeals to reason or to re-spect for human dignity can alter reality. For the Negro who works on a sugar plantation in Le Robert, there is only one solution: to fight. He will embark on this struggle, and he will pursue it, not as the result of a Marxist or idealistic analy-sis but quite simply because he cannot conceive of life otherwise than in the form of a battle against exploitation, misery, and hunger.

It would never occur to me to ask these Negroes *to change their conception of history*. I am convinced, however, that without even knowing it they share my views, accustomed as they are to speaking and thinking in terms of the present. The few working-class people whom I had the chance to know in Paris never took it on themselves to pose the problem of the discovery of a Negro past. They knew they were black, but, they told me, that made no difference in anything. In which they were absolutely right.

In this connection, I should like to say something that I have found in many other writers: Intellectual alienation is a creation of middle-class society. What I call middle-class society is any society that becomes *rigidified in predetermined forms, forbidding all evolution, all gains, all progress, all discovery*. I call middle-class a closed society in which life has no taste, in which the air is tainted, in which ideas and men are corrupt. And I think that a man who takes a stand against this death is in a sense a revolutionary.[56]

What is being sketched out is the difference between the colonial bourgeoisie's attitude towards time and that of the common people; the mirror in which they recognize their difference shows two images. The first is: a neurotically alienated form of morbid rigidity without risk, or challenge, and that is not prepared, whether theoretically or practically, to suffer or act, and that, as such, confesses to a sort of passivity or weakness that is a kind of "death." This confession suggests a life that is tainted, a closed society in which men and ideas are corrupt. Here we see a neurotic relation to time itself, a time that is non-existent, for, in trying to undo what has happened (colonialism) in the name of an albeit alienated past, the colonial bourgeois forbids all discovery, and as a result of this identification with a dead other he is himself already dead. He cannot recognize himself in time—or in the time of labor—and so cannot impose himself for the world as is eludes him, he is not in it. In contrast to this nihilistic image, one reads of a weak, and yet stronger, power, for whom everything is or nothing is, for whom the question is not that of knowing whether something happened or stopped happening but of what can *happen*, and for whom being is not a question of knowledge or history but of struggle and force, one that is affirmative, that has the strength to maintain itself in the value of surprise and, as such, allows itself to be open to the unforeseeable, the unanticipatable, without logic or calculation, *telos* or narrative. The strength of invention makes those who are weak actually stronger than the strong, for when it comes to self-creation, it is the destiny of weakness to be transformed into strength. The curious result of this is that despite an obvious contrast between the good spontaneity and creativity of the proletariat and the deadening constraints of colonialism, life and death and labor and revolution are all *included* within a general economy of time. This insistence, which is perfectly consistent with all we have discussed so far, leads directly to some of the most enigmatic assertions of *Black Skin, White Masks* and, predictably enough given the importance accorded to death and discovery in Fanon's analyses, invention reappears at this point. The counterexample of the wretched may be seen as Fanon's attempt to grasp the power of the colonial system over him by turning everybody in it into either complicit or resistant. It may also be seen as the desperately fanciful effort of an otherwise lower-middle-class member of the bourgeoisie to overwrite the impersonal consequences of his destiny with dramas centered on those unlike himself (and there have been examples of this kind of crudely reductive reading).[57] In either case, it suggests precisely the sense in which those excluded from the narrative of colonial history generate a notion of agency that evades the grasp of all such narratives, including dialectics, alienation, and liberal humanism. And indeed this seems to be part of Fanon's critique of those who refuse to choose the act that could liberate them, and consequently are left with morbid repression, choosing to *live* that repression in their relation to time rather than, say, take the chance of reinvention. Or, as these relations might be generally summarized: the reinvention of the colonial proletariat is indispensable for countering the insecurity of the colonial bourgeoisie, whose precariousness finds its neurotic social validation in History, through whose meaning it never ceases to inter itself.

Yet within this perspective, one must also register the level of the failures in *Black Skin, White Masks* in terms of a will to truth and power. Anecdotally, their stories all reach a point of checkmate. The wish to be whiter, or less dark, feeds off an imaginary whiteness that is also indissociable from an imaginary blackness; and even language, Fanon suggests, is experienced as a promise and calculation wherein one's ignorance or lack of culture can be sublated by how well one rolls one's *r*'s, a pronunciation that, by itself alone and without any work of the mind, will be seen as the proof of one's reinvention or, more ironically, or disdainfully, one's superficial inventiveness. The suspicion, however, would be that "pidgin nigger" will reappear to offset the reinvention.[58] These performances and performatives, which effectively place language under the paradigm of a *gateway* to mastery, also carry "cultural" rebukes, as the pride and pathos of correct pronunciation can easily be denied the power to which their user seems to think this invention and realization (of *le langage français*) entitles him/her. "There is no forgiveness," Fanon writes, "when one who claims a superiority [in French language and culture] falls below the standard."[59] This rebuke aimed at errors in speech is a key example of the difficulties of invention itself, but also of how self-invention is always a complex negotiation of public encomium and public reprimand, private legitimation and legitimation by performativity. The profound reason for the anecdotal failure of some of these errors is that they fail, as performances of identity, as certain parts of the mask slip and the will to culture no longer has the power of the production of truth: variously the *we* who are, in fantasy, as good as *them*. Even when the stories have more to go on than the subject's—in principle forced, false, or flawless—pronunciation, they are marred by an egocentricity that confers on them the epistemologically suspect tautology of wish fulfillments; for once the heroism of invention has paid off the debt owed for facility, language goes on performing racism and, in principle at least, to both the *arrivant* and the *arriviste* (part of Fanon's notion of minoritarian invention is concerned with how the mask-wearer discovers his "true face" in mainland metropolitan culture; the masks, to which the French are indifferent, and regardless of his inventiveness, are seen to be his essence and that of blacks in general, hence the death of invention and fantasy alike). It is not enough to say that, if invention generates such aberrations and a mimicry that is social and cultural in nature, then a great deal must be lost in the performance. For that loss to be registered as a loss, in its formal incompletion, its cultural inadequacy, and its political failure, what must also be asserted is the priority assumed by social and individual legislations over the individual legitimacies and falsifications that they will ultimately reabsorb. (For examples of this phenomenon, see Part One, Chapter Four, "Historicity and Guilt.")

Even as a failure, however, the project of detection and punishment enjoys a certain efficacy. For these subjects fail in respect of cultural commands and obligations. Their weakness as individuals becomes a demonstrable strength as at least they have undertaken the work that shows how legitimation is bound up with coercion on the mainland, despite the narratives of justice and enlightenment. As a *common* experience, unmasking poses a threat to the social and institutional orders that continue to doom island culture to being a supplementary undertaking. From beginning to end, colonialism sanctions an attitude towards language that means the *arrivant* will never arrive at what Fanon calls the *logos* of the French language. The experience of difference, in which the desire for reinvention founders, itself reveals the racial dimension of the social contract in the colony. As such, the failure of arrival, in the civic space of the nation as well as in the logos of reason, gives scandal to the twin unities of colonial imaginary and French universalism that colonialism puts at the basis of family, status, assimilation. To disclose this failure, moreover, exacerbates its scandalous effects, as when the *arrivant* returns with tales of public humiliation, refusal, and violence. In a context where home and family are the chief battlegrounds against the fall into linguistic blackness, this kind of rejection on the mainland must seem ultimately destructive of the native imaginary. Born into a family, as his remarks in *Black Skin, White Masks* make particularly clear, where French is the ideal, Fanon tells us of the familial, rivalrous world in which the tension between Creole and French is an early symptom, and in which the personal arrogation of Creole (or black *parole*) to the language of niggerdom, though shocking, is perfectly proper.[60]

We begin to see why the psychoanalytic narrative of neurotic splitting has to come under the rubric of a sociogeny charged with the task both of understanding this split (between language and the social order, being and logos) and also of supplying concepts for the "failures" who provide the psychoanalytic test cases of this splitting. We begin to understand, in other words, the profound necessity of the unconscious in *Black Skin, White Masks*. (This irruption, into a story of legitimation by performance, of a neurotic splitting can of course be linked to education and to a historically bound circuit of symbolic codes, which is what Wynter insists on; but we cannot dispose of the matter so simply: there is here a political and ethical tension in the learning of language itself that it would be odd to explain away, as Wynter tries to do, in terms of biological, as against neurotic, complications. I will come back to this in the next section.) Though language, in the colony, produces a desire for civilization (or the cosmopolitan story that founds it), as that which will confer on the native the legibility of a truly cosmopolitan meaning, this desire, far from issuing in an order that can be comfortably proffered and consumed as the essence of the universal that is the nation's imaginary appearance, threatens to reduplicate difference in the yet more explicit form of social disaggregation. What keeps the production of this desire from being dangerously excessive—what in fact turns the dangerous excess back into conformity—is that history, following the same logic whereby it produces effects of meaning, produces among *its* effects the desire (in the native) for its own authoritative version and regulatory agency (of culture). Out of these meanings the subject imprisons himself to the point that, as Fanon insists, the very principle of self-invention confuses *being* civilized with the act of *speaking* French, a confusion that results in a state of arrest. "I am a Negro—but of course I do not know it, simply because I am one. When I am at home my mother sings me French love songs in which there is never a word about Negroes.

When I disobey, when I make too much noise, I am told to 'stop acting like a nigger.'"[61]

Such regulation of the self should not be seen as a purely repressive practice, involving, for instance, the coercion of the state. The *langage fran-çais* not only represses but also, profoundly, satisfies the desire to which cultural hegemony gives rise. For in addition to doing the negative work of correcting the socially undesirable consequences of local dialects, it performs the positive work of discharging for the colony as a whole the function that these dialectal differences had assumed unsuccessfully: that of providing, within the fractious space of the colony, a *national* representation of order and power and struggle. The shift in focus from dialectal class and color differences to a Martinican identity encompasses a number of concomitant shifts, which all operate in the direction of this sublation: from civil law and questions of political economy to more metaphysical questions of filiation and guilt; from neurotic splitting to the conscious urgency of an act, beyond such debilitation, of critique and/or struggle; from an obsession with an ever-displaced cosmopolitan origin represented by *le français* to a sense of the non-originary origin of all imaginary communities, including those of law and nation; from the long, slow, time of localism to the swift and productive time of the emerging nation; and finally, from the institutions of home and family that cannot justify their power to ones that, for all the above reasons, are discovered to be quite simply seduced, invested. It is as though every aspect of the failed *arrivant*—which he himself was—is dialectically redressed in Fanon's account of language, so that one might even argue, on the basis of his later claims about the importance of language and of culture to the formation of national consciousness, that the excruciating experience of the *split* produced various theoretical coups. Along these lines, one might even want to read, in Fanon's 1956 comments on the effects that a revolutionary war can have on colonial language, a sense of how disciplinary power is indeed supplemented by language, a sense that he had already explored in 1952. Yet to the extent that we stress, in Fanon's evident insistence on invention, the emergence of a new kind of leap or project, and in its elaboration (as endless possibility) beyond a traditional model of representational power or sovereignty, a new kind of force or violence beyond calculation, sense, or organization, then we need to retain the possibility that Fanon's view of invention intervenes, substantively as well as nominally, for an opening that is neither *for* the law or the system, nor founded on representation, and one that does not serve an ideological function within the state system, nor against it. Because it is not desirable as an alternative to institutional status, nor for the ideological efficacy it affords within systems of power, invention is not *a representation* of power or its containment, but a force, a violence, a leap. The shift from foundation to ceaseless invention dramatically goes beyond the usual narratives of the field and exercise of power, as well as, of course, the representational agencies that seek to contain, or contest, that power, either through affirmation or resistance. And when the "failures" pass from adulatory wonder at the power and splendor of France to the sad, resigned acknowledgment of their limits (as citizens, as subjects), the circumscription of language and power, reaching the end to which they always tended, becomes a "real" possibility of reinvention.

III. THE QUESTION OF METHOD

Language thus allows for the existence of inventions—self-transformations—that complicate the dynamic of freedom and power in their effects. Once installed in this performative realm, one could cease to internalize—as the desperate, expropriated psychology of neurosis—the lures of the colonial system; from within it, one could bear witness to the possibility of a genuine criticism of the system, one that would no longer be merely the sign of the impossibility of withdrawing from it. Shifting focus from alienation to invention, Fanon works toward the recovery of the latter elsewhere, in a two-pronged strategy whose other line of attack lies in refusal and in the various disorders and perversions by which such refusal is enabled and/or to which it attests. For in point of fact he does not specify the outside of power as irrationalism or madness, occupied by the failures of the system. Not the least evil aspect of the colonial system in this respect was that, in it, the native mind and irrationalism are blurred into one another.[62] As an apparatus of power concerned to impose, protect, and extend itself, colonialism naturally included a biopolitical function, which took on the aspect of presenting the nation as family, but it also sanctioned a eugenic recoding of native life along racial lines. In effect, the emergence of bio-economic or liberal humanism on the one hand and the biological racism on which it is based (which will seek to codify birth, blood, and descent) achieves the extrication of the subject from being into that of racial being, a disarticulation into separate domains of evolution and descent which will be knitted seamlessly together into the bureaucracy of the colony.

According to Wynter, this reorganization and bio-politics go hand in hand, whereby the struggle for existence (the extension of political economy to the economy of life itself) comes to be understood as a process of natural selection on a biological level, so that in a Darwinian, Malthusian, or even neoliberal view of human life, the founding idea of our *"experience of ourselves as human"* is that of a natural agonism in which competitive selection becomes "the master code of symbolic life and death."[63] It is this conception that grounds "the multiple and varying *genres* of the human" in the terms of which our destiny remains marked or is dictated by those instincts for survival from which we supposedly began.[64] What is more, this view of the social contract along the lines of a biosphere, whereby the strong are those who survive, or at least those who are selected, has become a matter of popular belief. When Wynter defines modernity through the secular invention of biological humanity ("since we attribute what we now invent and institute to the 'imaginary being' of evolution/natural selection as the ostensibly agent/author of the structures/roles of our contemporary bourgeois order of things"), the invention here is the production and institution of an episteme and the deference shown it in "our" contemporary milieu.[65] Whence her concern with the believing attitude to which such a conception of life leads at the level of experience. This is why she turns to adaptation and autopoesis, in opposition to struggle and scarcity, as less virulent geopolitical terms. As an example: she cites Antonio de Teruel's *Narrative Description . . . of the Kingdom of the Congo* (1664) to show how the recognition of an inescapable likeness between members of a shared biological heritage is necessarily mediated by what is seen to be liminal. And so the Congolese veneration of blackness also manifests, in the words of de Teruel, a feeling of revulsion towards white-skinned European people who are regarded as "ugly" and "monstrous."[66] In Wynter's terms, this means that identity is already in a complicated, dialectical relationship to alterity in ways that are not necessarily biological or historical. Indeed, she insists, with reference to the liminal, that "our present culture's biologically absolute notion of human identity" makes difference legible in terms of a growing naturalization of identity.[67] So: the notion of sociogeny, the experience of what it *feels like* to be human, gives Wynter an important weapon in her dispute with contemporary versions of social Darwinism; selection can be shown to be overshadowed by distinctive cultural modes of *adaptation,* or even of *autopoetic* mutations, corresponding to psycho-physical "laws" of experience. (By laws, Wynter means the categorical ways in which we invest in phenotypical form as if it were inherently teleologi-cal or in some sense the instantiation of some quasi-intention or formal es-sence, recognitions that are made possible, she tells us, by the genres and codes and institutions of language. The racial ways in which individuals are seen to be of the "same" species or profoundly alter is, then, a consequence of a conception in which a biological drive to survival is seen to underpin the individuation of all physical reality as such.)

We must not be surprised, however, if there are problems in this struc-tural-historical account of sociogeny—and perhaps an issue with precisely the link here between history and invention, institution and evolution. If it is as biological beings that we continue to experience ourselves as human, "through the mediation of culture-specific masks" or even, strangely, as verbally defined "genres" of being, why is the *experience* of being black, for Wynter, nonetheless the effect of "species-specific" narratives?[68] The raison d'être of the Western episteme according to Wynter (and in a distinctly eschatological fashion) is to construct a racist narrative of the human, where historical meaning itself is made synonymous with a more or less European philosophical *telos* of time and being (it is an ethnocentrism articulated in evolutionary terms).[69] Her claim is not that consciousness simply becomes "the expression of a mutation in the processes of evolu-tion"—it does not—but that the view of others as somehow "*discontinu-ous with evolution*" is brought into existence or, rather, is founded by a world-historical narrative schema.[70] In contrast, Fanon's sociogenic prin-ciple offers us a "new theoretical object of knowledge" with which to think modernity and difference.[71] Although Wynter presents this principle more than once, and at key moments, as essentially Fanon's, her use of it is evi-dently a radical departure from the notion set out in the introduction to *Black Skin, White Masks*.

The true puzzle of sociogeny, then, is not just related to, or contrasted with, a genetic definition of organic life; it also refers to how the experi-ence of consciousness is "non-reducible" to these (neurobiological) pro-cesses.[72] One may read the resulting ambiguity—does sociogenesis refer to an epistemic breakthrough or a new historical narrative?—in the very char-acter of Wynter's formulations. The fact that sociogeny is virtually entirely confined to the question of *experience* is already revealing of the strategy of containment whereby invention is constituted—in highly problematic terms—as an epochal rupture that allows us to go beyond the current his-tories of the human. I do not think that Fanon for one moment attempted to represent sociogeny as a psychophysical *law* (of knowledge, of the conscious mind), or even attempted to restrict the term to that of a new *telos* of the human. In Wynter's reading, however, the meaning of the term can only be adequately rendered in the sense of Fanon's challenge to the biocentric discourse of the human, and this fact, among others, makes it a genuine theoretical invention or "counter-manifesto" with respect to "our present culture's conception of the human."[73] Whereas Fanon suggests that sociogeny is to do with the aporias of narcissism, with how difference is psychically lived, fantasized, contested—with an insistence opposed to those views reducing man to a mere "mechanism"[74]—Wynter reads his speculations on racist fantasy in culture as "data" for an "objective phenomenology," which, for her, calls for "another form of scientific knowledge beyond the limits of the natural sciences."[75] Through this concept of *science*, Fanon's careful questioning of the limits between phylogeny and ontogeny, inside and outside, the psychical and the physical is, inversely, read as a call for a new scientific description that would "harness the findings of the natural sciences (including the neurosciences) to its purposes, yet able to transcend them in the terms of a new synthesis."[76] It strikes me as odd, perhaps, that an argument for humanistic reinvention should be illustrated as a new way of making the human calculable and predictable, a science that also happens to show why the "we" who know better (who have somehow become scientists of the codes of consciousness) can see more clearly why the narratives by which we "objectively construct ourselves" remain "opaque to us."[77] Yet if sociogeny is to explain what it means to be human, how it transcends (the natural sciences) and illumines that opacity is never developed beyond a narrative that already *presupposes* a certain fantasy of science.[78] (At least to the extent that our *"sense of self"* is "culturally programmed rather than genetically articulated," a "fact" that the natural sciences fail to grasp in so far as they rely on "our present culture's conception of what it is to be human," Wynter never questions the implications of relying on scientifically determined concepts such as "program" and "adaptation" to think through humanization: it is precisely such terms that make her emphasis on a new scientific History seem somewhat limited.[79] Why are these terms any less illusory or opaque than the biocentric languages of popular opinion?) On the one hand, it is not at all clear what political relevance this claim for a new science can have, and on the other the claim that there is a position beyond the continuities of race and historical consciousness could only ever be substantiated by writing another history of the human: the politically most favorable logic to be drawn would seem to be that what counts is the *efficacy* of such narratives, which are in any case no longer anything like scientific breakthroughs—but then cultural theory would have no job left to do, as the pretense of science and the subsequent knowledge of lived illusion would be meaningless. The claim to be able to discern reality and thus to ground those fantasies at least partially in sociogeny depends simply on the illusion of the cultural critic as a subject of science who is able to stand outside and above that reality and those fantasies. This is on its own terms not at all a historical or historicizing position: to rehistoricize *this* fantasy would be to see in it a story on the same level as the biocentric narrative, and to abandon any transcendental horizon and with it any notion of *telos* or epistemic breakthrough.

Wynter's strategy with respect to history and narrative seems no more satisfactory when she turns to the question of method (and, once again, in a distinctly non-Fanonian fashion). Her faith in science, which makes sociogeny itself appear as nothing but *techne* (culture, for Wynter, is technology[80]), can only evoke invention as an empiricism (and one that relies on the historical necessity of science to be recognized as such). With no ironic reservation, thus only magnifying the ambiguity, Wynter's faith in science even offers the following observation in support of this destiny: what is needed is a new study of "the *rhetoricity* of our human identity," she tells us, and a new science of the word.[81] But what can this rhetoric do if the governing codes lie beyond history? By writing history as text, Wynter moves towards a position that implies that scientific method exceeds narratives (even those of racist illusion), but science also forecloses the textuality of history (and so, presumably, that of rhetoric). Another way to bring out the ambiguity of method here is to ask: on behalf of whom or what is the biological conception of the human no longer absolute? Answers in "Towards the Sociogenic Principle," which moves by way of multiple analogies, are elusive. (Wynter acknowledges that she does not quite believe in the veridical value of the natural sciences, but she can only imagine transcending it, and perhaps unavoidably, via a narrative that presupposes the authority of science.) The odd thing is, she knows all of this, too. Wynter asks, more than once, how we, as subjects, can confront the following "paradox": how can we escape "the self-evidence of the order of consciousness that is everywhere the property of each culture's sociogenic principle, and of the mode of nature-culture symbiosis to which each principle gives rise"?[82] How, in brief, do we extricate ourselves from such prisons?

Lacking the time for more extensive development, I emphasize the terms that pinpoint Wynter's sense of what maintains the difference between inside (the self-evident nature of a consciousness that we *feel* ourselves to be) and outside (the *techne* and institutions, the sociogenic modes of being) so as to contrast it with that of Fanon. The difference on which Wynter insists allows her to say that modes of being (human; liminal) are culture-specific, where the experience of the *liminal*—as the mediated mode of negation, abnormality, deviance—is what highlights the limits of what passes for "normal," "good," "*Man*."[83] Imprisoned as we are by what we take to be "the self-evidence of the order of consciousness that is everywhere the property of each culture's sociogenic principle," it is only by encountering the liminal perspective that we can free ourselves.[84] But is the liminal perspective not also imprisoned? Is that not precisely Fanon's point? It seems to me that here, and elsewhere, Wynter needs this limit: not only in order to show the fragile, enigmatic, threatened, defensive state called "normality" but also in order to isolate the context of liminality (normality's outside), the production of which she argues is necessary for the recognition of what, in the singular, she calls normality. But already she has great difficulties with this separation, as she does in other places where the question of hegemonic order presents itself. On the one hand, there is the move back to illusory narrative: Wynter is concerned to write the narrative history of the rise of the racist concept of the human, to study its rhetoric and governing codes, and even to write the narrative history of a new concept of the human. But against this move, a newly stressed notion of discourse as a question of biopower and strategy moves against the narrativizing tendency displayed by sociogeny, and suggests that illusions be read neither as the distorted truth of the matter, nor as false consciousness allowing Wynter to stress a rhetorical approach to experience, as a scientifically inclined move designed to obtain certain textual effects. This shift moves us far from any claim for scientific method: this is perhaps why her reading of sociogeny feels so phantasmatic. The representation of the wretched in *Wretched of the Earth* permits us to answer the question (of liminal escape and incarceration) in a more complex way: to insist, as Fanon does repeatedly, that the wretched are an infection ever present at the heart of colonialism opens up their localization (where, among other things, is the infection, how has it spread, and how does the state police it?); or to suggest, when theorizing black lived experience, that there is a *defect* whose (cultural, unconscious) form is *predestined* implies a more complex play of chance and necessity, selection and destiny than that of a program of inclusion/exclusion.[85] The wretched simultaneously produce and permeate (produce as permeable) the crisis in (the state, cultural, historical) representation that incarcerates them. In a similar fashion, Fanon sees the wretched as aporetically virulent to colonial forms of sociality: their appearance is not one of dialectical mediation, nor that of a real breaking through illusion, but that of a difference in excess of any preceding continuities, and precisely because of the founding violence of colonialism, the institutional event that founds them and, as it were, gives them the chance of existence.

If, therefore, we need to say that, in its representation of colonialism and cultural life, *Black Skin, White Masks* regularly produces a difference between institutions and the heterogeneity that threatens them, we must also recognize that it no less regularly produces this difference *as a question*, in the mode of auto-immunity. The bar of separation and even opposition that it draws between the two terms is now buttressed, now breached, firm and fragile by turns. On one hand, colonial domination seems to cease precisely at the point where the state elects to erect bulwarks against its demise and overthrow. Or again: if the wretched represent a reduction of the domination of colonialism, and thus permit an existential autonomy, it is also suggested that the state, as all-encompassing violence, can at any moment abolish that autonomy. Or still again: the wretched are other, a gangrene at the heart of the colony, but they can also be the organ that polices on its behalf and thus works to preserve it. (As was so often the case, Fanon gave an early warning of problems to come in this domain. See especially *Studies in a Dying Colonialism* and *The Wretched of the Earth*.) We cannot too strongly insist that these paradoxes are not merely confusions or historical contradictions that tug and pull at a text helpless to regulate them, but rather productive ambiguities that facilitate the disposition, functioning, and promotion of certain aporetic effects, some of which we have already suggested. Neither, however, should Fanon's *Black Skin, White Masks* be denounced—or reinvented—as the ultimate science (or historical master-narrative) of these effects, as though one could allow such effects their broad epistemological resonance without also recognizing their broad cultural production and distribution. Yet if the text no more invents the equivocations we have traced than escapes them, perhaps the most pertinent reason is that it lacks the distance from them required to do either. We have seen how, in the first place, these equivocations are its own, always already borne in the play of chance and necessity in its form; and also how, in the last instance, these equivocations *come to be its own*, as if Fanon-ism reproduces in the relationship between form and content the "slightly stretched" dialectic that occurs within each of its terms.[86] This formal un-decidability is what I earlier called Fanon's future imperfect. The emphasis seems to be on failures and repetitions at the level of the psyche that are no-where subordinated to a centralizing ideology or a master narrative: "I shall be derelict. I leave methods to the botanists and mathematicians. There is a point at which methods devour themselves."[87] As such, invention has both positive and negative dimensions: if it is to preserve itself as the promise of endless creativity, it must leave all teleologies—all methods—derelict; but should it fall back into the representations of History, then it must fall back into the carceral register of ends and meanings—to abjure the one seems to be to absolve all responsibility for change to the other: "I should con-stantly remind myself that the real *leap* consists in introducing invention into existence."

In conclusion, here is an example of Fanon's own use of sociogeny in which a change in self-awareness is seen to simultaneously dispossess the subject and give it a new chance of being, and whereby a loss of security itself becomes a drive for mastery as a means of legislating against such dispossession:

The black man who has lived in France for a length of time returns radically changed. To express it in genetic terms, his phenotype undergoes a definitive, an absolute mutation. Even before he had gone away, one could tell from the almost aerial manner of his carriage that new forces had been set in motion.[88]

In a footnote, Fanon adds: "By that I mean that Negroes who return to their original environments convey the impression that they have com-pleted a cycle, that they have added to themselves something that was lack-ing. They return literally full of themselves."[89]

How does one explain the strange diremption on display here between genetics and travel, whereby the journey outwards to consumption and leisure and the promise of culture and civilization in the metropole leads to a shift in the very locus of being from being grounded—or worse, held down—to an enlivened, even actional way of being? Phenomenologically, are we not seeing the emergence here, on the surface of the body, of forces immanently absolute and at work in the deepest depths? I have tried to indicate how the study of the traumas suffered by obsessional neurotics, from Freud's concept of *Nachträglichkeit* to Niezsche's concept of *ressenti-*

ment, forms the basis for Fanon's reintegration of Freud's concept into his presentation of the temporality of colonial life. At least two features of sociogeny are taken by Fanon to be inimical to the positivist phenomenological explanations adopted above by Wynter. Firstly, there is the notion of how epidermalization is *inside* the body qua introjection and imposition. Fanon follows Freud here—and it is no coincidence that he cites *Studies in Hysteria*—in his recourse to the idea that the "pathogenic material behaves like *a foreign body*" in the psyche of the colonized.[90] There is no way of rendering this process as that of consciousness without losing sight of the ways in which the experience of past, present, and future comes to be reordered in relation to traumatic repetition. Such repetition is not conscious, nor is it seemingly experienced until after the event, nor simply remembered unless at the order of the signifier. Secondly, there is the notion that these happenings after the event are a constant theme in Fanon's thought on history, in so far as the encounter with the real (the *tuché*) sees the past retroactively reordered by future events, so that the future becomes (once again) an open question, that is, a possibility of reinvention *recognized as such*. The sense of fate or chance that informs both encounters, even as it acknowledges that colonial life has to break out of the limits of history if it is to avoid becoming a total, all-pervasive institution *like* colonialism, reinforces our perception that Fanon refused the teleology of biological constitution that keeps colonial subjects in their place. What the body of those who return from the mainland exposes, then, is the close imbrication of force and pleasure, imposition and invention, drive and culture. A change in one's relation to bourgeois imperial culture, the journey outwards generates a form of being and awareness in the same degree as it inures the self in the necessity of renouncing the entrapments that sustain it and always exceed it (the leap that is the subject's justification and its truth). In reading these anecdotes, one is made to rehearse this problematic—always teetering on the brink, but then again always entrapped—of life lived as absolute heterogeneity. In this perspective, to leap is to escape and yet remain, to continue to relate to the historical and yet never abandon the possibility of an open-ended traveling: where reaching towards the universal is to reach for oneself as other, not as the performance of some mask or illusion, but as a process of endless creation, infinitely expressed, and likewise perpetually self-engendering.

10

The Abyssal

I pass now to my final discussion of negritude. About the passages on negritude in *The Wretched of the Earth* I have nothing further to say than what has already been said in the first part of this book. For in those passages Fanon once again attacks what he sees as a futile "racialization of thought" that fails to "take account of the formation of the historical character of men."[1] This shows that Fanon rejects negritude in the same way that he rejects the French policy of assimilationism, which it unwittingly mirrors: both involve a universalism emptied of true particularity, and no doubt for the same reason, both abstract the universal from history and genealogy. But we cannot leave it at that. Fanon's relationship to negritude is divided across several works, and his emphatic rejection of its aesthetic was variously mediated by texts and events that arguably present a more complex engagement. Although I do not think that he ever wavered in his rejection of the metaphysical bond between diaspora and identity, (racial) citizenship and the nation-state, humanism and culture, his relationship to texts such as Césaire's *Cahier* attests to the emergence of a new relationship to the universal and the particular as the simultaneous rebuilding of the polis through art and regaining of black particularity through the incarnation of an abyssal (a word that I take from Césaire). The abyssal collects together at the *same time*, at least in Fanon's reading of it, an emptiness through which the illusion of totality can be momentarily glimpsed and an incarnation that can only be seen at the moment the universal illusion disappears, and precisely because the realms of the particular and the universal have become detached from one another, pulled into the black hole or void in which each is held—dazed, stupefied—by white universality.

The abyssal is what gathers the universal and particular precisely by pulling them apart, by assigning each the limited transcendental coordinate of the other, coordinates that can only be misrecognized from outside the void by which each remains unseen by, or at the furthest reach from, the other. There is a blind spot linked to these movements in which the *colonisé*'s passage to existence finds itself lost in a profound obscurity, where everything slips away. To the extent that the black experience of the world is unknown to itself, lost in abstract self-delusion, the abyssal is both the summit of what is known and a path into the unknown, and as such everything enters into its tumultuous movement. It could justifiably be claimed that the abyssal is neither the universal nor the particular, which in classical logic are opposed, nor is it simply and immediately the one reduced to the other, but it is the constellation through which each crystallizes in the other like two spheres held in the arrest of their emergence, which is consequently both an emptiness and a saturation, or an emptiness that arises in multiply saturated planes of being. I take my cue here from Césaire's famous 1956 letter to Thorez, where he writes: "I'm not burying myself in a narrow particularism. But neither do I want to lose myself in an emaciated universalism. . . . My conception of the universal is that of a universal enriched by all that is particular, a universal enriched by every particular, the deepening and coexistence of all particulars."[2]

This means that:

(1) Not only does the universal attain legibility through particular experience, that legibility constitutes a specific deepening of the universal in its ecstatic penetration of the world. Each universal is thus determined by those singular experiences that inter-sect with it, and that inter-section in turn opens up an abyssal perspective on each particular according to a relation that will be exercising us, a relation that is one of enrichment and depth, or that one could choose to say represents the abyssal depths of enrichment, which thus coincide with the abyssal birth of negritude—we will come back to this birth in due course—a relation that Césaire postulates as *neither a burial nor an emaciation but the work of an enriching saturation*, whose "invention" clears the path of those "petrified forms that obstruct it."[3] Given that there is no single point from which one can judge what are, strictly speaking, the limits of the universal or particular as they come together in a constellation, in which the singularity of one cannot be *opposed* to the exemplary generality of the other, their inter-section is not a case of arrival or of departure, but one that denotes a mutual submergence

in which neither is dissolved, but both are *reinvented*. Without this coming together, this coexistence, there is neither embodiment nor depth in which either could be recognized, neither as a particular recognized *as* particular, nor as a universal in which the horizons and depths of particularity could be established, and therefore both would become narrow, empty, emaciated forms of being. The universal and particular are thus always implicated, and only in this mutual implication can they both be indicated and recognized, but also demanded and claimed in the abyssal form of their presentation.

(2) Secondly, this neither-nor does not express a profound faith in the world as is but a desire to see its transformation, in other words it expresses a desire to see each particular reach its limits without being *subordinate* to a judgment foreign to its task: e.g. Césaire's black poetic knowledge has no other end than itself, it is not aligned with philosophical or historical judgment, likewise its refusal to submit to racist notions of common sense is necessary for the universality of its knowledge, whose truth is not exterior but inherent to black desire and faith, to appear.

(3) Thirdly, this is not a subjective claim, but a position that takes black poetic thought seriously; that sees in it, ideologically and politically, a refusal of the belief that to choose blackness is always to choose a knowledge that *has to wait* for universal recognition, or for an immediacy that is judged to lack completion and/or historical possibility. The letter to Thorez specifies that to escape this impasse, it suffices merely that blackness become what it is: the inarticulable or unimagined horizon that cannot be grasped from a universal standpoint, at the same time as it nullifies itself as merely a "black" perspective. There is no political answer to this impasse: for the intrusion of race into the very concept of the human means that there is no position to which one can commit oneself that is not already a sign of racism's interconnectedness with the history of the human. The novelty of black poetic knowledge cannot be known by either instance, for the infinite horror of its being precedes its historical meaning in the world, for what it is in the world is without form and without mode, and is seen to be an exorbitance that ruins the history of human being as an abyssal impossibility.

(4) What I understand by black poetic knowledge is thus the incarnation of an ungraspable demand that must remain oblivious even to the demand that it reveal itself as particular experience or as the innermost working of a new universal. Blackness *is* the world's aberration; from this we know that any claim it has to right must at the same time be the most

comical, shameful genuflection, for what the black desires is the recognition of a non-existent freedom as seen through a glass darkly. Since negritude is often read as an inversion of this genuflection, especially in criticism, its demand for freedom is often ambiguously read as a demand for a human recognition that retains race as its essence, with the work of art thus understood as an intellectual restatement of this position. We have perhaps to go further: it is precisely because negritude is not an inversion, but a work of creative negation (with all the nuances that this implies), that its decipherment requires that there be no racial basis for freedom. Today I would add: in such freedom the black is not only the first historical human, but always the first human to come. Just as the white world uncompromisingly founds itself as the universal difference to which every other racial nationality is understood, so blackness, as the difference that is the subordinated movement of difference per se, is needed to be the (abyssal) point through which difference emerges. And I must immediately say that the universal perspective through which whiteness is seen as a sovereign object can only appear through the exclusion of blackness to the limitless depths of particularity; for he who is black knows that he can never know himself as merely particular, but must in principle lose himself in the demand that he annihilate himself as black, and this is why he scorns the particular as a form of consolation. In a sense this is why negritude is not an identity politics, because such thought cannot grasp the ways in which blackness has been forced to grasp itself as the perpetual servitude of a primary subordination. But this is thereby also why Césaire presents blackness as a paradoxical consciousness subsumed by irony. It is also why negritude cannot simply be put to work as an anti-racist negation, for its end is neither in night nor darkness, but involves the perpetual traversing of the saturated depths that is black poetic knowledge. If blackness is the lowest incline of universality whose historical truth has been able to look into the void of what it is without being blinded, that is because it accepts its ties to an immanence that condemns it to a universal servitude not in hope or resignation, but with laughter, joy, and a lacerating irony.

With black poetic knowledge, founded on a difference that remains the undefined different, Césaire thus appeals to a human to come who is conceived as transcendent to the world as is and, at the same time, the blackest, most immanent part of the order of things, in whose exaltation there is also, despite everything, the consciousness of a sumptuous sublation that is both limitless and tangible.

It is an instance in which the universal and the particular are both carried in the stream of an immanence in which both are absorbed, integrated in the sphere of objects, but without canceling the ensemble of which both are a part; in the manner in which both differ from the world, they both introduce new planes of being that are never determinately empty, nor replete in their saturation. The choice to abandon what limits blackness is I believe the same choice as accepting what exceeds it: in the end, this is the double principle of negritude; it is through the leap, beyond servitude and injustice, that the abyssal nevertheless appears in the world as an impossible limit that is recognized as such, as what surpasses limited possibility.

The abyssal is, I believe, an important element of Fanon's response to Césaire, and yet critical opinion on it is surprisingly absent. The abyssal is really what is at stake in Césaire's "accusation of singularity" in what has come down to us as the historical image of black particularity: this accusation is how blackness acquires a particular form and, conversely, this form remains aesthetically unknown, uncertain, prior to its confrontation in whose singularity a new invention is always required. In this new commitment to blackness-as-form, what appears are not just art or ideas, but a language that signifies new "relations," clearly defined not as its being, "but its potentialities" (its tears, ironies, paroxysms, obscenities, laughter, and astonishment).[4] This potentiality is black creative thought and its expression goes beyond any organicist conception of race, even though its origin lies in the exemplary, visceral truth of the black body (its ethos and value). For that body further involves both movement and arrest, a movement wherein language is saturated by black revolutionary images, and where the genuinely creative thought of negritude emerges as the arbitrary, discontinuous, universal revelation that it is. I would like to begin by delving into that body, that is, by presenting it in terms of the very code by which it is excessive: the *corpsing* that exteriorizes and dispossesses it, that censures by way of annihilating it, that makes it obedient by not suppressing it, and by exhibiting its own enjoyment condemns it (this is its definition in anti-blackness).

I. CORPSING AND SOCIAL DEATH

How does the abyssal appear? Inevitably as a horror and a contestation, but also as an initiation that arises from the depths of a vertiginous astonishment. In Part One we began an outline of its effects in terms of a gap, or *décalage*, between obligation and delusion, between a being that is not yet aware of itself, that loses itself in its alienated performance, and a being so consumed by the poverty of its discourse that its wretchedness is unknown to it. The hallucinated subordination of black *parole* to a racial *sens* (or meaning) introduced a particular example of this division between a black impropriety of speech (presupposing a comedic failure or praxis) and a white *signifiance* of thought (not to be distinguished from an imaginary of thought, attitude, or behavior). Essentially, we saw how, from the start, the situation of the colonial subject, in so far as it speaks and to the extent that it hears itself speak *qua* its being-in-the-world, is always haunted by the *lapsus*, or error, through which the *nègre* appears, and which, at any moment, can open a fundamental division or void in any social ensemble. This *lapsus* proceeds from an imposed disarticulation that, were the *colonisé* to speak of it, it could only prove the subordination of blackness to the "chatter" that grounds its meaning. This *lapsus* before social being cannot itself be represented—*nor can it be distinguished from black thought or self-knowledge*—but through its imposition, social humiliation functions to reinforce the servitude that is its imaginary principle. That function makes blackness known in so far as it is *inarticulable*, in principle, a non-meaning that, in the end, is not to be distinguished from its subordinated character within the order of things. In this chapter we will further outline the consequences of this *lapsus* for black poetic knowledge, and its possible development as a new mode of thinking blackness and what is distinct from it.

In the first place, this *lapsus* appears as a mocking reversal of black articulation or social being. No one who peruses Césaire's writing can doubt that blackness, whose existence is repeatedly compared to something dead, is the starting point of a profound fulguration (a Césairean word that also occurs on the first page of *Black Skin, White Masks*) in which everything anti-black is burned to the point of exhaustion. However, as we showed in Part One, negritude offers not so much a concept of social death as a mythical speech of ruination and desire. The fact that blackness, in this way, condenses itself into a lightning flash that sets the anti-black world on fire, should lead us to question what the relation is between this fulguration, whose eroticism is always violent, and the life that imagines itself to be alive but is in fact socially dead, and whose existence takes on the form and force of a non-knowledge that negates itself.

Hence, we may wonder whether this state of social death is limited to a kind of ecstatic conflagration for the one burned by it, or whether this ruination itself reveals two kinds of dying, one based upon corpsing and the other upon social death. This is why, I maintain, one needs to enquire whether the abyssal is subtly graspable as a representation that dramatizes itself by making poetry out of black social death. Hence, anyone desirous of understanding Fanon's relation to negritude must go towards these abysses, if only to seek out what remains buried in their depths.

When I began writing this book I was far from knowing what I see clearly today, that these depths testify to a corpsing by which the *colonisé* empties itself to the point of diminishing the various meanings and expressions by which it is given a servile expression; on the contrary, I was obligated to see at the same time that negritude is both a melancholia of thought and a malevolent form of enjoyment that is equally prophetic and revelatory in turns. It is from this conjoined summit that I perceived both what this melancholia reveals to the poet and the lacerating disdain by which he submits and abandons himself to it, to the point of rebellion and death. It is this second aspect that seems to come to the fore in Fanon's later engagements with negritude as a process of corpsing. Furthermore, if we reread Césaire's "Letter to Thorez" in the light of this, we shall see that negritude is no stranger to corpsing, but regards it as part of what is destined for the one who is socially dead. On the other hand, Césaire, in his notion of enrichment, nonetheless communicates another step, the leap into an impossible equivocation where poetic existence meets its end in an ecstatic transfiguration and is able to annihilate the social death in itself. Only in this way does negritude have the power to transform itself from an ascesis to an inner audacity of thought, and so accomplish a more disorderly expression than that of corpsing.

In any case, we need to begin with the meaning of this corpsing and why, as drama, blackness is tasked to perform itself as socially dead. The word corpsing signifies a blunder in which, in performing a role, an actor is "put out" of his part. A role that is corpsed is one that exposes the limits of performance and, depending on the metaphor, is one that denotes the "death" of theater, as theater. A role that is corpsed, which is contrary to the usual performance of a part, is one that evidently does away with the actor's mastery (of illusion), and no more clearly than when the disjoin between persona and part is exposed. Corpsing therefore raises the more general problem of how any kind of performance can proceed or withhold itself from the possibility of blunder when trying to follow certain rules, or at least how any performance that relies on the ability to properly communicate itself to an other can do so without, conversely, also revealing that propriety as artificial and theatrical. For example, from the fact that when an actor is corpsed s/he also reveals the necessary demise of their role, or what is most proper to its performance, it follows that the possibility of blunder—like a catalyst—has a force and impetus that cannot be easily borne by the normal codes of performance, except in laughter. So too, when an actor is seen corpsing it tends to produce a kind of infectious joy at the actor's expense, at his or her inability to subdue or subordinate the corpse (and its effects) to the governance of spectacle, authority, or ego.

But the fact that something so contagious should also compel an actor to give up the role and commit him- or herself to a particular loss of character does not mean that we should lose sight of the fact that corpsing is also spectacle. And while I entirely agree that corpsing is usually determined rhetorically as a kind of excess of body over representation, I also want to insist that the whole scandal of corpsing (its impure force) lies in this spectacle of what happens when the most self-present mastery (of representation) encounters that which is both unmasterable and unrepresentable. Firstly, in so far as corpsing reveals a discord, it is not clear from the metaphor whether corpsing denotes a failure to repress or the pleasure of failed repression, a pleasure that is also a death. Hence whatever follows from the failure of performance (that is, from performance itself in so far as we understand the corpse to be expressly, if unwittingly, performed) results also, albeit unconsciously, from the pleasures of failure. Hence, the infectiousness of corpsing may quite correctly be said to follow from the spectacle of unmastering, because this spectacle depends especially on the failure of any resistance to manifest itself, in so far as the subject gives in to this failure, but not without giving up on the persona of a role as I have just defined it. Secondly, I have said that this failure does not depend on decision or will but on the unconscious nature of performance, and a general consideration of accident and contingency cannot help us at all in the formation and ordering of corpsing as event. For corpsing to be an event it must resist the very notion of event, i.e., as something ordered, for it surpasses those terms. Indeed, the moment of the corpse amounts to no more than a moment of imperfection that is fleeting, furtive, with which no future (defection) can be predicted, for it will not last. Corpsing is not just something that happens to you just like that, even if, from one moment to the next, you persevere by various artifices in the belief that it can be averted. Hence, it follows that corpsing cannot be predicted, nor is there any possible reason to make it the basis of a revelation. We are also ignorant of the actual motivations and reasons behind corpsing, that is, why orderly forms of communication and performance succumb and fail, and therefore it is better and indeed necessary, for what follows on corpsing and black social death, to regard corpsing as radically contingent.

Here we must add that if the essence of corpsing remains inaccessible to us, what it brings into being, as experience, is the knowledge that this is a disorder that no one can escape, or grasp, and that no one truly knows anything about. This explains the sadistic part played by the theater of corpsing, whose excess or pain can be enjoyed precisely because the corpsed subject does not have the power either to oppose or to avoid that which ruins and that which is opposed to ruin. In such moments, corpsing could, in truth, be seen as an excessive collapse by which the world as sovereignly enjoyed gives way to laughter and cruelty. Yet unlike, say, *that within*, corpsing seems, from the outside, to be a sign that everything is slipping away, lost in weeps and curses—corpsing is the negative aspect of a ruin through which a hole opens up in representation. The rupture that it reveals is consequently more intense: it vividly impresses itself on the eye and the imagination by enveloping what seems without disclosing the being that one is, and in this movement what also becomes present is what emerges from the shadows of being, which is not so much experienced as suffered; what passes from the inside to the effects of the outside is thus not a real leap into presence, beyond the servility of discourse or reason, but a separation that is also a social erring.

It seems to be only by a metaphor that the word "corpsing" is applied to acting and theater. What is commonly meant by corpsing is thus a moment by which an actor exceeds the limits of theater, and no longer is in command of a role. But if corpsing therefore seems to have been defined more precisely as the death of theatrical artifice, the hole wherein the mind awakens to the abyssal aspect of itself is not one that can be closed up without the subject in the end losing itself as a subject; this suggests that there is no respite from corpsing and that there is no recourse but to suffer the pain of its undoing. Which is to say: corpsing is a death where artifice forms a hole for enjoyment. In this sense, corpsing is also evident outside theater; we see it when people fail to live up to, or grasp, their social roles. Hence the derisive laughter attached to those who forget themselves, or have their pretenses exposed, or who fail to convince us of their authority. The promise of a role is meant to accord with the performance of desire, and so corpsing occurs when desire violates or threatens that promise. In this way the codes of social performance are used to discipline desire like a bridle, insofar as one's persona is taken to be more than a formal tie of social being. This is why the essence of corpsing is the violation of rules of prescribed performance under the command of social laws, and consequently those who obey the rules are said to be at one with their roles and not regarded as subjects of them. But what if one's social role is to be a failure, or the way in which one is ordered and commanded to perform a role is through one's own corpselike obliteration, would this not mean that corpsing can only occur when one refuses that spur and its contagious pleasure? Would this not be an example of a death of "death," so to speak?

If I describe corpsing as the difference between imposture and failure, the bitterness and social humiliation it imparts certainly illumines the region from which blacks discover themselves to be the butt of culture. However to make this claim (which, for other reasons, is crucial to both Césaire and Fanon) I would need to demonstrate that corpsing is certainly linked to the discourse and command of a delirious contempt or ridicule. (Why do we seem to have such contempt for that which elicits laughter at the mere sight of it?) Corpsing would then reveal, to the extent that social death can be known or confirmed as such, that to be corpsed is to be shorn of one's universal expression, as the context of social death indicates. Since corpsing is a single and abrupt renunciation, and not an historical experience, it is, strictly speaking, an instrument in the black's more general renunciation of itself in the framework of culture. This is why the essence of the theory of black social death is taken to be a rule of life that prescribes to blacks that they live under the command of death (as citizens, parents, siblings, and subjects); consequently those who obey this rule are said to live under a law of symbolic death and are regarded as subjects who are already dead. So much about social death is to do with how blacks are limited to a realm where they are ceaselessly returned to death. What interests me here is how corpsing works in scenes of black social death.

Truly he whose role is to be socially dead because of the fears and hatreds of others is acting under the behest that his social life always be lived under the threat of suffering harm, and of being corpsed the moment that he claims life; but he who lives as socially dead is given his due because he knows the true rationale of social life and understands its necessity, is acting at the behest of another who commands what it means to live (as black), and therefore is deserving of his role. I think that this is what I was pointing out as a *fatal way of being alive* in my first book, and in my second, I compared the role of black social life to that of a revenant forced to live under a law of *revendication*, a word meaning both ownership and disfiguration.[5] For black social death, as it is commonly defined, is the constant perilous exposure of life to injury, and this is why in *Haunted Life* I analyzed this as the relation between the ownership of black claims to be living and the performance of black life as a kind of epitaphic speech.

Since corpsing, accordingly, is nothing more than a rule for deciding when a role is accidentally, irreparably lost, it seems it has to be divided between proper and improper modes of performance. By propriety I mean the rule for those whose only purpose is to perform life as a kind of social death and to preserve life from their infection. By impropriety I mean the law that sees the socially dead not as a problem of truth or sensibility, but of right and jurisdiction; that is, the relation of race to corpsing is one where the subject fails to escape its socially dead conception. The fact that something has left life but nonetheless returns and survives, but can never be its former self, raises the further question of the proper limit between right and interiority, or what separates the subject of right (in law) from its persona; between these two concentric terms (the one being *inside* the other) is assumed a reciprocal guarantee, which I will now explain as briefly and clearly as I can.

Since the best part of us is our social life, it is certain that, if we want to represent ourselves as subjects of right, we should try above all things to perform this right as the only guarantor of our jurisdiction; for our social being should consist in how well we perform the role. Furthermore, since this performed claim is always already marked by the fear of its deformation, which is the other meaning of "revendication," corpsing takes away all certainty and introduces doubt, and since we are in doubt that right is merely an accidental form of our being, it follows that right and perfection depend on illegitimate foundations. Again, since nothing can be absolutely performed or guaranteed without erring, it is certain that a subject whose right to life involves and expresses a conception of life as right as its essence and perfection has a greater risk of failure and of a self-constitution without proper jurisdiction or sovereignty. Further (since knowledge of a role is no defense against its corpsing), the more we come to learn of our role (through the concept and intuition of right), the more we know that all performance is precarious; and all those rules, that is, rules of social interaction, not only depend on failure but consist in it altogether. This also follows from the fact that a subject is more perfect (and less abject) the further away he or she is from the merely mechanical nature of social obedience; and therefore that man is most human and participates most in the proper realm of desire when he frees himself from a slavish obedience to the rules, which is where he is most vulnerable to the state of being corpsed.

This then is what corpsing is, the knowledge and loss of the rules determining the subject. But what of those subjects whose rule of life is to endure life under the ownership of another, and consequently are said to live as objects and are regarded as subjects dead to law, and who live in a state of permanent threat of injury? I think this condition of the slave is what the theory of social death is meant to explain, and it therefore deservedly calls attention to itself as a black state of exception. Therefore race is the means by which corpsing comes to be a metaphor for social life, insofar as the slave fails to perform any juridical understanding of the subject as alive or sovereign, because it is perceived as having been born symbolically dead (*partus sequitur ventrem*), and therefore is reduced to an object or *res* whose prime value (if we define sovereignty as ownership) is a rule of life defined by its symbolic fungibility, which also denotes the end of life in terms of its reproducible non-existence. It is this vision of corpsing as the natural life of the inhumanly alive (under cover of a raced logic of capital) that has led to the reduction of black life to the fungible (in whose performance the owned life always arrives without a proper sense of life), and to how the fungible is then seen as the foundation of an infectious laughter that is where the trope of the dumb nigga begins (dumb in the sense of being unintelligible to law and language), thus marrying meaning with value in a way that is highly profitable and pleasurable; and because it is specifically as a corpse that blackness appears, blackness then assumes a fungible function, which many critics have well-described as a form of social death. Suffice it to say that, unlike the theatrical actor who consents to being "under" his role, it is evident that the socially dead do not arrogate to themselves the part or role they play in racial capital. Here I propose only to speak of corpsing in the context of social death in general.

Since the slave cannot easily play the role of a legal person—even when legal personality ironically refers to itself as enslaved, it maintains the illusion of itself as formerly free—it follows that as society establishes, recognizes, and assumes the racial rights of citizenship, the black subject must confront the discomforting possibility that any performance of black social life is always corpsed by the fact that racial blackness is seen to be the performance of radical indebtedness or loss. The sum of black being therefore, and its highest power, is to know itself as a mortgaged claim on the living, that is, blacks must learn not to speak or perform life, nor to desire this role. For the idea that black life can be rendered as a livable life that matters, rather than a life lived in a state of injury or permanent nonexistence, is to effectively transform it by corpsing the failed performance that blackness is. The white subject cannot understand this; it seems foolish to him because he has too meager a knowledge of what black life is, and he finds nothing in black culture that he can refer to that makes any impression on his conviction that black flesh is only a thing he can take pleasure in owning or scorning, for knowledge of what it means to be black always takes the form of the following kind of existential reasoning: if he were black he would kill himself (because he would be already dead).[6] But those who know that they possess nothing more than life's refusal will certainly judge that being and right are the most unreal realities.

Thus understood, corpsing is what follows, then, when the subject enters into a kind of abolition of all that attaches it to knowledge of sovereignty. In the same way, social death occurs when the rule of life is withdrawn from those deemed to live under the command of death. Those who, in other words, are put in the situation where they have to obey the command that demands that they live as subjects who are already dead at pain of death. We have now explained what corpsing chiefly consists in and what racial corpsing is, for in the history of human being, black existence has always been understood differently, as the sanctioned impropriety of right and being. For this too is how blackness grounds the metaphor of corpsing (as I explain above), and in this sense black life does matter, even though not as life but in its preservation as social death, as confirmed by the historic legal codes of racial slavery.

If we now consider the character of recent responses to black social death as I have just explained it:

(1) We shall see, in the preponderance of extrajudicial killing, or the literal arrest of black life, the repeated performance of an "accidental" choking in which the relation of jurisdiction to propriety is key.

(2) We shall see that it does not require belief in any kind of right to life on the part of blacks. Since black social death is inferred from the consideration of black social life alone, it is certain that the spectacle in which the black body suffers and helplessly succumbs is as much about confirming the proper role of blackness as it is about performing the sovereign power of whiteness. Belief in black social death, however perva-

sive it might be, can give us no knowledge of black life nor consequently of what it means for that life to become visible solely through its corpsing. For these murders are the expression of what Jared Sexton aptly calls "unbearable blackness," whose violent end must always be assumed; and so it is by no means the case that the belief in black social death is a necessary requirement for the violence of law to corpse the life it portends.[7] But although belief in such non-life cannot give us a knowledge of black social life, we do not deny that anti-blackness has a very useful purpose in civic life; namely, to decide who can and cannot live, where violence of law marks the limits of racial personation. The more we observe and understand the extrajudicial murder of blacks, which can best be seen as an unavoidable relation with injury or accident, the more we shall be able to see how blacks have struggled to maintain themselves beyond threat or injury, and the better we shall be able to see how black life responds to its own deadly impersonation as the performance of a corpse.

(3) We shall see that black social life is not disfigured by its corpsing. Corpsings are merely blunders, indifferent in themselves, and are infectious only by convention or by those rules that represent the performance of authority. For black life to live itself beyond a form of death requires nothing but that it perform itself differently; it requires only what carries the clearest evidence of life's affirmation. For black life to go beyond the command of a tradition that relies on its symbolic representation-as-disfiguration, it must change the understanding of what it means to be black and living; it must change the way that it is seen as an infection whose dispatch produces intense enjoyment, so to speak, of body and mind. This also implies that it is in principle impossible to make sense of black life unless we posit what makes it unlivable, even though what gets corpsed is in a certain sense what keeps on living. We need not demonstrate all this here at greater length.

(4) Finally, we see that the supreme reward of social death is to know the black law of fungibility, that is, to know that one's role can be endlessly impersonated whatever the complexity of the situation; the penalty of not knowing this is as fatal now as it ever was, and especially when the gap that opens up between the ego and its enslavement by racist codes can legally be named as *dying whilst black*.

Having made these general points, we must now ask: (1) whether Fanonism allows us to conceive of blackness as a non-epitaphic discourse; (2) what kind of writing that would entail; (3) what it would mean to make black life into a thing that matters; and (4) what this material after-life is that blackness seems to have won for itself in critical theory. I shall discuss the first two questions in the next section and the latter two in the final section. Before doing so, allow me to say one more thing: it is as a corpse that the extraordinary effect of the abyssal occurs: far from being a negation of mere mimicry, the corpse brings into being—as a breathless, dispossessed form—a collapse that is also a massive insecurity, where the socially dead disappear without however falling into nothingness, paused over a black abyss.

II. POETRY, OR THE RIGHT TO DEATH

What we should think regarding the first question is readily adduced from the movement known as afro-pessimism, which, as already noted, is distinct in its analysis of black social life and social death; that is, the life alienated from life and the life subject to permanent dishonor are in reality one and the same thing in themselves, and are only distinguished in relation to the codes of racist performance that inform them. That said, this emphasis on black symbolic death has proven to be controversial. For example, when we focus on criticisms of afro-pessimism, we see a persistent tendency to link its analysis of black life with the phenomenon of nihilism and political pathology.[8] Proponents of afro-pessimism are attacked for both an insufficiency and an excess of judgment, for being at once not black enough and all too predictably too black in their reading. I have written elsewhere on why I think this is a peculiarly tendentious reading that, perhaps unwittingly, can only repeat the disavowal of blackness that they claim afro-pessimism enacts.[9] It is as if the act of saying that blackness has no value in the humanistic canon were the same thing as saying that the value of blackness is nothing; or as if measuring blackness against its denigration were to reject, dismiss, or pervert it. On the surface, of course, these accounts may appear to be reductive and inaccurate, but they are constitutive of a crisis in the meaning of blackness. Afro-pessimism refers to the attempt made by critics to include within the history of blackness (as well as its ongoing politics) more diverse questions and approaches than those offered by traditional cultural studies and identity politics.[10] Afro-pessimism is the name chosen by these critics to attack the ways in which modern blackness has been understood. For afro-pessimist thinkers such as Jared Sexton and Frank Wilderson, among others, black life represents an ontological shift in the human. "Nothing in afro-pessimism suggests that there is no black (social) life," writes Sexton, "only that black life is not social life in the universe formed by the codes of state and civil society, of citizen and subject, of nation and culture, of people and place, of history and heritage, of all the things that colonial society has in common with the colonized, of all that capital has in common with labor—the modern world system."[11] "Violence and captivity are the grammar and ghosts of our every gesture," so says Wilderson, adding: "this is where performance meets ontology."[12] The choice of rhetoric in these two citations is no doubt interesting; both involve reference to racial slavery as a foundational event that, far from being over, is endlessly repeating; here, the social life of black social death acts as a kind of index, or grammar, that defines both the possibility *and* the limit of black speech and existence. The phrase "where performance meets ontology" suggests that black social life can only be lived or thought about as a kind of debacle that can only be performed as a corpsed remnant between the language and meaning of the human. No doubt this emphasis includes a certain, irreducible question of role and exposure, but also one of responsibility and self-critique. In afro-pessimism, however obscure its notion of social death may be, blackness is not so much claimed as performed differently so as to transform the philosophical question that blackness represents in both thought and politics.

Furthermore, if we read through afro-pessimistic texts themselves with some care, we shall see that they do not proclaim a new theory of blackness, but seek to perform it, as I said just now, in a way that embraces its dispossession: put more clearly, what makes afro-pessimism so singular a movement is its awareness that blackness can never be distinct from the dispossession that possesses it at the level of being. Wilderson clearly points this out in his seminal text, *Red, White & Black: Cinema and the Structures of U.S. Antagonisms*, in these words: afro-pessimism sets out to "deconstruct and humiliate" what necessarily follows from the inability of Western cultural-philosophical discourse to grasp blackness without corpsing it, by troubling the foundations of that discourse.[13] For Wilderson, this means that blackness remains ungraspable to those theories that seek to limit it, but also that blackness surpasses—"humiliates"—all attempts to humanize it as a "capacity" that vainly seeks to escape from the violence that founds it.[14] And this word "capacity" is meant here as "subjective transformation and recomposition."[15] From this perspective, it is clear that blackness cannot be grasped as a capaciousness whose humanistic truth is indubitable. And this is so true that I found myself agreeing wholeheartedly with Wilderson's claim: "Blackness is overdetermined by [and underwritten by?] death."[16] Blackness *is* corpsing: be it as slave or *colonisé*, the moment it appears in the West it is already lost, "exiled from the drama of value."[17] Also, this exile, so easy to dismiss as an exile from representation, and all the more admissibly so when the limits of humanity are at stake, is inseparable from the grammar through which this separation (of blackness as representation) is enunciated and maintained. Wilderson could have remained there, mourning the various ways that separation is announced, but instead he shows how in this grammar of separation blackness is never separate, and is discouraged from existing beyond its separation from the human. Here we should note that humanizing—Césaire's emaciated universal—can only mask what the corpse in the end shows is unmaskable, and what the presumed redoubt that directs the ego beyond itself, or that prolongs its role and value in civic life, or that assumes a being different from one vested in dereliction, can never assume without crisis and dispossession: the abyssal that streams through the white mask as it slips and that allows us to enjoy black social death while desperately awaiting its transfiguration. If to be white, I resign myself to submit to the law that corpses blackness as unfreedom, and in my effort to gain access to right and jurisdiction, I obscurely evoke a presence whose derision and precarity confirm my bearing, afro-pessimism teaches me that such affirmation is always composed of an internally violent comedy, whose pleasure belongs entirely to my being able to enjoy the spectacle of a death outside of my (human) being.

If, for example, we were to compare afro-pessimism to another key moment in black intellectual history—that of negritude, as set out in Césaire's famous *Cahier d'un retour au pays natal*, alongside various responses to this text—then we would see another understanding of black performance as ontology, for Césaire's poem also contains reflections on corpsing's necessity and its truth.[18] Based on contemporary accounts, Césaire's poem, no matter how initially obscure, seems to have been an ineradicable event in the *experience* of being black.[19] In this first major epic of the black experience, the caricatures of colonial life are transformed by a kind of deconstructive *questioning* of their absolute claims re historical, ethical life. The same holds true for black being itself: in the poem, the "natural" order of racial life is literally cut open by a single signifier, that of "negritude," whose status as a kind of radical autonomous act exceeds both meaning and judgment. It is to counter the racist signification of anti-blackness that the neologism "negritude" proposes a different *sens*, but one that refuses any racist concept or paraphrase. As such, it is as a signifier arising out of nothing that negritude unburies what already considers itself socially, universally dead. This signifier takes its stand, as it were, where racism grounds black being in a dead zone where black life and death mean nothing.

Negritude thus becomes the bearer of a new performative; it speaks for those who lie *beyond* petrification. Thus the poem has been seen as the outcome of a refusal that is also a resuscitation giving the socially dead new life. The enslaved dead have arrived—quite literally—from a time without us, from a past not our own, from a time that is not historical. As such, they denote the supernatural limit of what it means to be a *person*. Nameless, they arrive without sense or life; as augurs they are neither messianic nor miraculous. Because they come from a place that is literally dark—and here the middle passage is the metaphor of a primal dislocation—it has often been remarked that to try and represent or memorialize them one had to confront the discomforting possibility not of retrieval or of restoration but of having to read a text without the possibility of translation, one whose origin was seen as prior to history and language. The whole aesthetic of negritude in its achievements and promises was wholly based on the conviction (and the poetic proof) that these revenants not only allowed a grasp of the historical present, but made possible an act of authentic naming that is original and originating, and that dovetails with a sacral, religious concept of black experience and history. These revenants were not so much given as claimed; split off from any location in history or narrative identity, they nonetheless signified the language of some original, mythic text, whose narrative identity suggested both political and existential possibility. In order to make the dead speak, to reconstitute their ancestry, or to redistribute their power—in short, to bring to light those who were made racially dark—negritude must annihilate or willfully extinguish (or, more generally, self-sacrifice) the present in order to invent a radically futural language: negritude would then be a *symbolon*, both symbol and what it symbolizes, whose naming harbors the promise of a revendication. That Jean-Paul Sartre refers to all these terms in his famous essay "Orphée Noir," the preface to the 1948 poetry anthology *Anthologie de la nouvelle poésie nègre et malgache de langue française*, as does Fanon in his 1952 response to Sartre, should come as no surprise here.[20] When Sartre describes negritude as an aesthetic, it is precisely because he sees something funereal and fantastic about it, something irreducibly mythical, since it is a sign of a transcendence that is unavoidable but unknowable. The opposition between himself and Fanon, as we shall see, will turn on this question of unknowability, which Fanon will insist is also untranslatable.

The main innovation of negritude, however—and it is here that we must modify our vision of it as performance—would be its descent into language as some kind of original and founding mythic violence. This descent is not so much a search for presence as a convulsive refusal in which the racist power of certain words is exceeded and consumed. In order to purify language of anti-blackness, the poet must recover other signifiers free of abjection (with the emphasis placed on the force of certain tropes rather than on their meaning). It is specifically this trope of forceful restoration, and its phenomenological-existential vision, that is often read as the superposition of an anti-racist racism and one that is very specifically opposed to universal humanism. Whatever the validity of this doxa, the first thing negritude teaches us about blackness is not that it is an essence to be restored under the aspect of myth or natural creation, but that it is a signifier that cannot be narrated or known as such, which seems to mean that negritude is not just another poetico-juridical personation of foundation—the mystical foundation of race as law (for the negritude text, be it Césaire's *Cahier* or, more recently, M. NourbeSe Philip's *Zong!*, is always articulated around juridical-historical codes it can neither actualize nor exhaust).[21] In brief, the secret and sacral blackness that must be sought, and that underpins this hermeneutics, proves to be just as illusory as the old signs of white privilege and hierarchy. This is a case of corpsing the whole history of racial parable and many of those narratives in which blackness is absolutely bereft and absolutely excluded from the white light of reason. Recently, rereading Césaire's *Cahier*, however, I was struck by how the pivotal scene on the tram brings to light—without reference to negritude or history—a poetic theory of blackness that shows the interplay of five different codes of corpsing: the comical, the ugly, the contagious, the shameful, and the symbolic. In this encounter with a poor, ugly, comical nigger, as Césaire presents it, what makes this man into a nigger is the racist laughter that demeans him, but what disarticulates the poet is his complicity with this laughter in his role of imaginary white spectator.

He was COMICAL AND UGLY
COMICAL AND UGLY for sure
I planted a smile of complicity
My cowardly self rediscovered![22]

Laughter, complicity, cowardice—even while he is enjoying the path that leads from servility to rediscovery, something seems to have happened to this complicity—it reveals a failure, an essential failure to deliver the self, as well as black poetic language, from the comedy of a servitude unknown as such. We must infer from this encounter that the comedy that befalls the *nègre* can no longer be distinguished from the hypocrisy of the bourgeois intellectual and the ugliness that comes in its wake, whose political consequences cannot be escaped. When one has become *nègre*, one discovers how one's alienation imposes on one a particular servitude, without respite, and not from any action carried out but from one's own humiliating realization, wherein reason collapses into shame, and the revelation that one too is *nègre* is shattering because it exposes how one's enjoyment is connected to an abjection that is as indelible as it is unbearable.

It is for the same reason too, namely his gushing, even shameful, complicity, that Césaire evokes, in the final lines of the poem, the black abyss of language (*le grand trou noir*), to free himself from this comical, ugly scene. Since the poem begins with the "old négritude . . . becoming a corpse," i.e., with the deadliness inhabiting its language, it ends with a new invocation. "And the great black hole wherein I longed to drown myself / . . . that's where I now long to fish out the / baleful tongue of night in its lustral stillness."[23] If the poet once perceived the *nègre* not as life but as a social death to be rejected, at the end of the poem this same death is now embraced, and performed differently. Why would Césaire speak of the poet as sacrificing himself to the great black hole of language? On this Césaire is very precise, and offers us what amounts to an abyssal theory of negritude. What is meant by negritude, and the way in which its language means, is here radically different. If the latter has to be expiated or deformed for black lived experience to emerge, the point is not to flee from this void, for it cannot be avoided; for the *trou* is precisely the point where anti-black connotations and meanings are consumed. The effect of the abyssal is not dialectical or historical, as Sartre presumes it to be, but *inhumanizing*; and, more important, it opens onto a kind of unreadable rupture or fissure. For black self-liberation to take place, the equation of racist language with humanity is in question. What this means is that there is no racism necessarily in the way language means, for racism it must be said is not strictly a question of meaning, but one of performance and praxis.

For example, a word like *nègre* does not reveal or describe a reality but performs the belief that what is expressed corresponds completely to what is meant, and in fact embodies it, as if *nègre* were the expression of blackness's own sense. As such, the word may be grasped as a performative, in the sense to which it decrees the thing it names by separating the mythically impure from what is seen as lawful and proper, and in ways that compel obedience. When Césaire tells us that he grasped this complicity as cowardice, he is referring to the ways in which language reveals to him how black being literally loses itself, annihilates itself, in the tragicomedic negation that is corpsing. Thus he perceived how language makes us complicit with prescribed racist rules and decrees. That is why at the end of the poem, negritude emerges as a verb (rather than a noun), for it is about inaugurating possibility rather than performing dissimulation. What is being named here as negritude is the disjunction between racist words and racial meaning; the former is the reason why blackness disappears, evanesces, descends into an abyss, but the poet can no more escape nor vanquish this abyss (this *trou*), nor plot its emergence into historical meaning, than he can prevent that sense from being corpsed, lost in a comical or ugly meaning. The poet can no more empty *nègre* of its racist connotation than he can rid black lived experience of its imaginary *sens*. The irony that infuses this entire scene on the tram therefore suggests that negritude is at its blackest when it undoes any illusion of a black essence, which is, of course, the aim of all racist discourse.

I emphasize that these things must be seen as part of the history of negritude, but that they are often overlooked. Hence we can no longer see the *Cahier* as Sartre saw it, as the expression of an anti-racist claim to history, or as the dialectical resolution of both text and meaning. But nor can we see it as Fanon sometimes presents it, i.e., as nothing more than the unhappy romantic expression of a black bourgeoisie. If negritude is a dialectic in the Hegelian sense, although Sartre appears to see this in Kojevean terms, one must see that the *Cahier* traverses various personae without resolution, via a kind of restless negativity; in "Orphée noir," what Sartre calls the revolutionary nature of negritude is not so much due to its achieving that higher, more complex form of unity that is the universal, nor to its being the mouthpiece for a Marxist conception of form and its political-poetic history. For, as we showed above, the black hole consumes form, it saturates it, until what is consumed is commensurate with what is overflowing the depths. So it would be equally reductive to think that Césaire adapts this new role to suit his revolutionary, political beliefs as that he previously adapted his performances of black alienation to racist belief (i.e., the belief that black life is a life not worth living) in order to communicate this revelation as the moment when his political restoration (as black) begins. No thought could be more absurd, especially as Sartre wants also to portray the black poet as the image of Orpheus sent to rescue humanity through an act of artistic self-murder. "I shall call this poetry 'Orphic,'" Sartre writes, "because the negro's tireless descent into himself makes me think of Orpheus going to claim Eurydice from Pluto."[24] It is not enough that blackness die; it is necessary that it should affirm itself as already dead, that is, that it should die in the universal; that it should reveal itself as transitory and delusional, limited in its conception and, like Eurydice, that it should become ruinous when seen or touched: at "the moment that every black Orpheus must tightly embrace this Eurydice [his negritude], they feel her vanish from between their arms."[25] Undoubtedly, since Eurydice reveals herself to Orpheus never directly, but through intimations of love and loss, via imaginary words and visions, we can draw no other conclusion than that Orpheus's blunder is truly a corpsing event; for at the very moment he turns around to look at her, Sartre pictures him grasping negritude through its disappearance into universal words and visions.

Sartre therefore understood negritude as the desire for a self-renunciation that is also a generous surpassing. Knowing that negritude is always a game of *qui perd gagne*, in which the loser can only gain possession of himself through renunciation, means that blackness can only liberate itself by being bound to its own obliteration. Hence "it is when Negritude renounces itself that it finds itself; it is when it accepts losing that it has won."[26] In this matter Sartre suggests that black particularity is a kind of wager that privileges losing as the only chance of winning universal justice; consequently, although he gave black poetry an authority and importance as political critique, he nevertheless still taught that blackness is a performance that condemns itself, especially when its claims to justice beyond the false attributions of race can only end in death; the "twilight of his negritude . . . [in] the dawn of the universal."[27] For those who are capable of finding this dawn, he undoubtedly did see a future and not just a repetition; in this twilight both illusion and that which causes a break in illusion are what allow humanity to transcend, or repudiate, the false universalism of race. Hence he freed negritude from servitude to the law of racism and yet in this way also confirmed and stabilized that law, inscribing it deeply in black imagining. Particularly in the case of the politics of negritude, Sartre's analysis has been seen as reducing its political invention to "a certain affective attitude toward the world."[28] But instead of grasping how blackness is always the contestation of the world, Sartre failed to see how blackness is also the possibility of the world, a future that is not limited to that of sacrifice or expiation (i.e. negation), but a future saturated by the impenetrable depths of blackness (i.e. the abyssal). Insofar as the black poet fails to surpass the limits of race as a discourse or concept, racism will bring his poetry to an end. For Sartre, of course, what makes negritude revolutionary is precisely its historical, political transfiguration of art. It is in negritude's self-murder as art that its political restoration begins. This is why most readings of "Orphée noir" are really posthumous readings of the artistic and political necessity of blackness as a voice from beyond the grave.

Sartre too seems to indicate as much in certain passages where the loss of Eurydice is itself metaphorically lost *to* the dawn of a new Marxist History. While poetry names a truthful descent, only philosophy, it seems, can lead blackness to the path that opens onto a new beginning. Sartre says that the poet, as the self-sacrificing subject of negritude, cannot simply expire; he must die a *racialized* death. If he fails to die as black, his death will not be dead enough. While, to Sartre, blackness/Eurydice is necessary to this ascesis, for Sartre, black poetry is also always the posthumous work of its own demise. And though blacks will be reborn from this corpsing to enrich, poetic-like, the labored objectivity of liberty, they will still be symbolically dead in a double sense, drowning while trying to ford the gaps between alienated life and its sublime transfiguration. The recognition that black social death can only in the end be *artful* once it has been redeemed as philosophy or politics eschews what I am trying to get at here, that is to say, its abyssal undecidability. Similarly, Sartre's text does not stop at this allegory; he also wants to say that the *situation* of negritude is due to a new revolutionary attitude towards language that is anything but abyssal. For Sartre, negritude is a prophetic style of writing, a *vates* or pathic use of thought and language that consequently resolves itself in *silence*, rather than in logic or argumentation. It is because the oppressor's language is a "trap-covered ground" that black poetry, to escape this trap, must explode each word in its struggle for a complete *nudity* of French thought and language.[29] Finally, Sartre writes that, in contrast to the analytical tautness of the French language, negritude must "*de-Frenchifize*" French in order to make out of it a "solemn, sacred superlanguage," whereby, undoubtedly, language is made into a sacramental object.[30]

Let us examine these points in more detail. Essentially, negritude here means the attempt to make race into a concept, by which the poet "tears negritude out of himself in order to offer it to the world."[31] In a sense, the poet must descend into the "abyssal depths" of himself in order to contest the ways in which blackness, in the colony, is always mediated by white culture and language. We are talking here about blackness not as an identity, but as the product of an inner division, from whose inherent contradiction negritude delivers us: "it is because he was already exiled from himself that he discovered this need to reveal himself."[32]

In the first place, this division prevents the black from grasping his negritude; it rises up between him and it as he turns around to look back on it, and in turning back he can only lose it to a white mediation. But in order to grasp it he has to transcend this mediation and situate it in a new language. Sartre describes how the syntax and vocabulary of French are inhospitable to black consciousness. Why? It is not because French is foreign to the *colonisé*, far from it, but that when he speaks in French he is aware of a difference "that separates what he says from what he would like to say," and that it is this awareness that obliges him to establish a different relationship between words and black being.[33] This is why negritude has to take the form of poetry and not prose, for it is only through the poetic operation of the word that language (French) is forced to signify the impossibility or failure of a black particularity, or *le vécu,* which is why negritude thus represents a desire to express the inarticulable revealed by this gap between *sens* and *signification* (as Sartre defines them). Now, Sartre also designates this gap—between French and the meaning of black experience—as a "disappearance of the word" in silence; or by saying that the negritude poet "must *make silence with language*": by destroying language the poet makes words express the silence of being.[34] Yet this is a silence that never ceases to sacrifice itself, such that negritude itself becomes a metaphor of sacrificial violence. And since French lacks the terms and concepts to define negritude, since "negritude is silence," it is as a sacrificial becoming that negritude obtains to a "dialectical law of successive transformations."[35]

Sartre singles out Césaire as the poet whose work is closest to this Orphic thematic: he is the one who "probes the depths of the abyss."[36] He does this through surrealism, through an erotic intoxication, in which words are not used to describe, or designate, but are torn apart, made delirious, and so detached from the sense in which French lexis and morphology designates a world. But this too is why French is a *trap* into which negritude might fall, or in which it might lose itself. The abyss into which black writing might venture, or that it should avoid, is thus equated with a consciousness that has not yet risen in revolt, insofar as such revolt occurs at the level of the alienated means of French expression rather than take up arms against the very force and law of its emergence *as* black, a destiny from which Sartre continues to derive its essence and limitation. For herein what is refused is transformed into a radical sociopolitical object, but only on the condition that it conform to a dialectical plot of negotiation. And the more complete the refusal, the greater the density of this auspicious obliteration—Sartre refers to it as an appropriation that is both fecund and tumescent. In the end, undoubtedly to better compare negritude to the myth of Orpheus, Sartre insists that it is as a poetic fecundity, or phallic erotism, that Césaire grasps his negritude and necessarily pursues its (dis)possession, but only as an absolute that knows it is transitory, and as a nothing that can only be grasped through its disappearing. This renunciation is, from the perspective of mediation, a particular experience that is opposed to more universal means of affirmation. But by becoming a concept without historicity, and in its tragic impossibility, lacking certainty, being unable to absolutely determine itself, the blackness of this poetry remains subordinated, or subordinates itself as nothing more than a project of subordination. While for Sartre it is the prosaic world of capital that is the object of negritude's revolutionary negation, for Césaire and Fanon it is negation itself that has to be negated; and while Sartre presents Césaire as sacrificing poetry to revolution, Césaire is seeking to make revolution poetically black.

We conclude therefore that negritude for Sartre works as a negation (of racism) but remains trapped in the role of negation because, in this limited dialectic, the black poet seeks only the remediation of a "complete nudity," and so can never go beyond the sacrifice or holocaust of words (and in a way that misreads Bataille, from whom this phrase is taken), within which French words are used precisely in order to dispense with them or, at least, to ceaselessly call into question language as such.[37] Sartre's explanation of all of this is to say that literary form is merely a ruse, a mask (negritude remains a descent into the depths in order to bring back the subject as *vates*). And though we cannot miss the teleological thrust here, Sartre's narrative is curiously prophetical in noting it (curious because "*vates*," or prophecy, is precisely the word he uses to define what is revolutionary about black surrealist poetry). He does not zoom in on blackness or single it out as a situation, as he would typically do in his other work; instead he refers to negritude as a symbol of blacks *"becoming conscious"* and that the poetry allows us to see this becoming and its passing from a lived particularism to a true universal. The movement seems a bit diffuse, not pointed enough to justify the apparent point. A further, more pronounced indecisiveness may be observed when the Eurydice motif is used to reframe the politics and philosophy behind the poetry. Even as he isolates this figure at the edge of an absolute nudity, it moves back and forth with a tremor that makes the motion of going forward or back, up or down, oddly equivalent. The poet descends into an unknown region in order to drag us along in his fall. No doubt this descent is one of desired rebirth and is of value only to the person undergoing it. As soon as it falls under the sway of the dialectic, an apotheosis occurs, the pathos loses its necessity, and the poem enters into its own death, as History. "It is the matter of making negritude pass from the immediate to the mediate, a matter of *thematizing* it," Sartre writes.[38] "The black must therefore die to white culture in order to be reborn with a black soul."[39] It is not in discovering the black night of the world that negritude's self-undoing lies. Which explains the desire to look at Eurydice, the better to see our own poverty of discourse. Nor is it a question of what happens when, in anguish, we discover our complicity with non-knowledge. As an instance of this sacrifice, Césaire's poetry must, in order to recover his black soul, refuse her; he must drown in his own desire in order to be marked as a subject of rebirth, and only then will politics and art be radically transformed in their relation to the necessity of that sacrifice. That is why most readers of "Orphée noir" say that Sartre gets the myth wrong; Orpheus is meant to find Eurydice (through descent) and lose her (through ascent) precisely in order to discover poetry. In Sartre's version, Orpheus must do everything to refuse Eurydice (as symbol, as language) and so murder-rediscover himself in the name of a purer negation or eschewed negativity. Inversely, it is not until this suffering becomes historical that it reveals a certain historicity of meaning. It seems that it is only when the holocaust of racist words becomes historical that Sartre sees value in its poetic expression. This is why for Sartre, blackness will always remain an epitaphic discourse.

Now let us pass to the second point, the stylistic choices running through the *Cahier*, to see what it shows us about negritude as black writing. The first thing that strikes us is that the descent from disillusion to poetry and politics is by way of a descent into a black abyss. Sartre presents this as an example of Orphic knowledge and metaphor. Césaire tells us, moreover, that the black abyss is where symbol and what it represents do not correspond. The signifier "black" cannot simply be translated, and precisely because it signifies an anamorphic limit to received ideas about loss and liberation. Fanon's chapter on Césaire in *Black Skin, White Masks* treats this disunity in a way that is strikingly prescient of afro-pessimistic critique. First, Fanon is aware of the non-dialectical meaning of the abyss (its structural role in the poem is one of not restoration but ellipsis). Secondly, his fidelity to the language of the text is his way of stating that black life matters precisely through its resistance to the authoritative ways of its reading. To say that blackness is singular in its difference does not mean that it does not contain its own imperatives and prohibitions, but that its opacity (as a signifier) must nevertheless be maintained. What does opacity mean here, if not that the abyss is a signifier that cannot be paraphrased or translated? Is the black abyss a void or merely a plenitude that disguises itself as such? In any event, the abyss cannot void or destroy itself as a signifier, for to do so would be to erase its black materiality, to kill it dead. So that we can say that if negritude is a verb, it is very possible that its role is explorative rather than restorative, or that its logic is metonymic rather than metaphoric. Hence it is perhaps in that direction that one would need to pursue Fanon's study, to pursue his reading of the *Cahier*—its irony, not its truth. Evidently, there is a risk in so doing of weakening the identitarian claims of negritude (at the level of form and experience), but that is precisely Fanon's point. Yet in saying this, it is equally important to remember the Césairean tropes of descent that occur in *Black Skin, White Masks*. Descent invokes a movement that is not necessarily one of knowledge but one of fall or encounter. Indeed, Fanon addresses his "introduction" to those readers who lack the ability "to accomplish this descent into a real hell," and for whom an "authentic upheaval" is yet to begin.[40] He wants them to descend "to a level where the categories of sense and non-sense are not yet invoked."[41] To read *Black Skin, White Masks*, then, is to descend to an obscure indeterminacy where the text situates its readability as text; it is in this abyss that the reader will undergo a fulguration or upheaval rather than a revendication. Therefore the distinction between revenant and revendication, the nonadequation of black life to politico-juridical reason, the nonresolved character of this nonadequation, is Fanon's version of Césairean irony and indicates exactly the distance between this and a dialectical reading that reduces the problem of descent to a question of meaning or sense. In this obscurity that Césaire calls the abyssal, it must be remembered that blackness is always displaced with regard to its origin— that origin can never be reached. One is dealing here not with naïve romanticism but with a constant struggle to displace the racist meaning of certain tropes as ever adequate to the meaning of black experience. This struggle is a corpsing, an irony, a permanent parabasis if you wish, but it is not really the sign of an alienation, for there is no origin to be alienated from. Least of all is there some purity hidden by language or history, whose meaning awaits some *Aufhebung*.

It will be better, therefore, to adduce negritude as a surpassing *through the depths* (with the ambiguity that that implies—the lowliest is the plateau from which the summit is built, and descent to the lowly is the role that must be left behind through descent into the greater depths below: a leave-taking from the lowliest into the lowest) only to find the lowliest returning to haunt the universal at the dialectical summit, and where *this* descent, the one that *returns* in an apparently higher position, is in fact the most abject performance. I mean that this paradoxically dialectical reversal (in Sartre's deduction that what comes last in the natural history of blackness really comes first) implies, with Sartre, that the really first revolutionary thing is not the apparently first thing, but also suggests, against Sartre, that no more is it the apparently last thing turning out to be really the first (History as the telos and therefore the summit of the most sovereign blackness). We will see how, as if reenacting this *telos* of death and suffering, Fanon causes negritude to appear like a negation whose death is always *just beyond* death, the stage that also, then, turns out to be just *before* life, in a temporality that we can only guess at, rather than make sense of "as the minor moment of a dialectical progression."[42]

III. BLACKNESS, OR THE DEAD WOMAN

"*Black?* I felt as if the word were deflating, being emptied of its meaning."

JEAN-PAUL SARTRE, *Nausea*, 183

"man is a subject empty of errors"

AIMÉ CÉSAIRE, "Maintenir la poésie," *La poésie*, 124

We showed in the previous section that negritude enacts a new role for blackness that necessarily has nothing to do with essentialism and everything to do with an abyssal explanation, and consequently with a writing that inscribes an emptiness that is deeply saturated by its non-manifestation.

We also deduced that role from Césaire's abyssal theory of language and, so to speak, the *Cahier* as its written performance. As for black writing, let the two epigraphs above stand as two different ways in which blackness can be written. The quotation from *Nausea* reveals the extent to which blackness can be reduced to an existential formulation. For the signifier "black" to *become* empty presupposes a fullness of meaning, but what Sartre's text actually performs is the meaninglessness of such projections. In enjoining the reader to watch the meaning of blackness disappear *within* the text, and not to see it at once as the marker of its own disappearance *as* text, Sartre urges us to imagine the otherness of a world suddenly gone black. But in doing so, he absolutizes the authority of blackness as absolutely black, as the outlier to any code or reference. This is why, immediately following, the referent is not so much the word "black" but that of a world emptied (*vide*) of meaning by (black) structures of language. This also agrees with those passages from "Orphée noir" cited above: blackness is always a *dark work* for Sartre, pregnant with its own expiration, and in renouncing the nostalgia and desire to coincide with this Eurydice, black poetry can only establish its language in the void of her negation. By way of contrast, in the passage from "Maintenir la poésie" we read: "man is a subject empty (*vide*) of errors." One of the tenets of Césairean negritude seems to be that words such as "empty" are never empty as such, and can only be emptied when deemed merely rhetorical, which is in itself an error of false completeness typifying the desire to be absolutely free of emptiness or lack. In other words, if man is subject to error in so far as he tries to empty himself of lack, this error necessarily follows from trying to imagine a world of plenitude that he absolutely lacks. This ironic juxtaposition, which draws out the implications of what it might mean for a reader to respond to the *Cahier* as literally a *black* text, is also central to those scenes of reading as performance in Fanon and Sartre. Just as Sartre portrays negritude as "living like a woman who is born to die and who feels her own death even in the richest moments of her life," a "tragic beauty that can only find expression in poetry,"[43] Fanon's response to "Orphée noir" is to question this symmetry between social life and social death, or black life and suffering: "I felt that I had been robbed of my last chance," he complains.[44]

Last chance? It is a phrase taken from Césaire's anti-colonial masterpiece, *A Discourse on Colonialism* (1950), in a highly ironic passage on the opposition between a Europe devoted to racism (a Europe living under "the mortal pall of darkness") and a Europe salvaged by "the only class that still has a universal mission, because it suffers in its flesh from all the wrongs of history": the proletariat.[45] From this quotation it becomes clear that Europe's last chance can be understood in two ways: either Europe recognizes those whose anti-colonialism is allied to their Marxism, or it admits that there is no possibility of its salvation. The later *Discourse* thus necessarily concludes that anti-colonialism is a phenomenon that cannot be explained by European humanism, and that it surpasses its understanding of modernity and enlightenment. Suffice it to say that this is not the same teleology that Fanon claims exudes an all-knowing disregard for the ways in which blackness *means*. Thus the universal mission of the colonial proletariat for Césaire is not the same trope as that used in "Orphée noir," for it comes into being out of something that must be understood clearly and distinctly as a particular experience of suffering. Consequently, a universal community is only universal in so far as it is bound by those particular experiences of suffering, and is nothing more than the work of surpassing that defines the particularized agon of the colonized. I do not think that this vision is Sartre's, but it is clear that what is central to Fanon's reading of the *Cahier* is that the last chance should always come first, as the *black* implication of a poetic writing, before it is read as part of some Marxist-humanist orthodoxy and so deemed merely historical. This is especially so where it is a matter of black life that is in question as a matter of corpsing.

We showed in the previous section that Fanon's reading of the *Cahier* is loosely organized around three propositions: that blackness is in some fundamental sense meaningless; that it can be understood as a void or unexplainable difference (the term is Bataille's) that absolutely resists cognitive knowledge; and that in some necessarily aporetic way negritude is nothing more than a substantively absolute difference that resists not only the narrative mastery of dialectic, but also the prestige of the universal in white critical thought. We also deduced that negritude must itself be deemed a void (*vide*) whose emptiness is irretrievable, whether in the form of historical allegory or philosophical romanticism. It is certain, therefore, that although Fanon also sometimes criticizes negritude for being a romanticism in its belief that blackness offers an incontestably sacral or spiritual form of renewal (as in Senghor), it is also clear that his reading of the *Cahier* requires us to read otherwise. As does his critique of Sartre. Though the sway of Sartre's critique of negritude remains valid, it goes without saying that he loses sight of the relevance of such scenes as the tram scene in the *Cahier*. In his rush for the resolution of poetry in the truth of historical contradiction (which is, as already noted, the metanarrative of "Orphée noir"), Sartre suppresses how Césaire empties the discourse of negritude of any positive content: negritude is *not*, Césaire tells us, repeatedly; and even though he insists that it is not this and not that, neither a tower nor a cathedral, etc., this has not prevented critics from trying to gain custody over what this not *is*. This principle of non-knowledge that gives the *Cahier* its rhythm and lack of resolution pushes beyond the limits of knowledge precisely because it is not grounded in revelation *or* negation, prophecy or myth, by conveying an emptiness that cannot be read or filled. I propose now to show that this insight remained central to Fanon. Then, for yet greater clarity, I will show why and how Fanon, a former student of Césaire, remains a disciple of negritude in his effort to understand and work through its abyssal non-foundationalism.

Fanon teaches nothing more clearly than that the *grand trou*—its danger and militancy—should not be reduced to History or aesthetics. In his response to "Orphée noir," Fanon is concerned with the ways in which Sartre uses history to resolve and validate the meaning of the *grand trou*, and in a way that excludes the aporetic self-questioning of the *Cahier*. When we read the chapter on "The Lived Experience of the Black," in contrast, negritude is proclaimed as the effect of a certain linguistic predicament, summed up in these few points: the "*n'est pas*," or the not yet, that blackness signifies, and which I have already commented on, has no signifiable meaning, even though it continues to generate potentially fatal interpretive effects (see Part One, Chapter Seven, "The Condemned"). Equally important is the testimony of the *grand trou*: it traces a path that is without solution or synthesis; it figures a language (of blackness) that ceaselessly calls into question all origins, but is neither a holocaust nor an offering. Thus black life matters to Fanon only to the extent that it names this unknowable, utterly naked declivity, and excludes all meaning from it. In precisely this way negritude (it would be better from now on to say black *writing*) goes beyond a dialectic of interiority and substance, or secret, and ultimate meaning, and ranges instead over a kind of non-usable ascesis, one that is truly subversive since it refuses to embrace the corpse that blackens it in its meaningless exemption from reason, law, subject, or history. Other passages in Fanon's corpus testify to the same thing, but it is enough to refer to these two.

It is also evident from "The Lived Experience of the Black" that *poiesis* contributes nothing to *Aufhebung*, and that allegory is only relevant to negritude insofar as it allows us to see it for what it is, as an acute example of black romantic *irony*. Fanon makes this absolutely clear. In his reading of Césaire he demonstrates conclusively that non-sovereignty is the ambition of negritude, its texts being the affirmation of the life that is *not*, that has no existence, place, or identity, as we noted above, other than this *néant*, or void, in which the black is obliged to lose or abandon itself as to an abyssal destination that cannot be represented or known, and in whose abysses the subject encounters boundaries it cannot cross. If negritude is a battle lost as soon as it is waged, what Sartre failed to understand is that winning is not the point. On the contrary, as Fanon and Césaire repeatedly insist, negritude is a negativity emptied of content and is a mode, not of praxis but of corpsing—endlessly, ironically—the racism of representation, and not just the representation of race.

Equally, Fanon resists the urge to reread this irony as a form of teleological judgment. If he had wanted to give these poets moral instruction, he could simply have followed Sartre, who advises the poets to wait for their knowledge to catch up with what white Marxists already know, and for whom poetry is the act of an internal consent to being belated and so further proof that blackness must enter into the classic state of *ressentiment* in order to be taught the universal truths of Marxism. This is the reason why Fanon sees the spiritual reward of blackness as a falsehood of the most imaginary and abject kind; for Fanon, as I said, this obligation says more about white theory which, like a practiced magician or con artist, no sooner sees black experience than it instinctively begins correcting its posture, language, and speech. Hence, Fanon's overriding concern is not simply to bemoan the fact that Sartre's entire argument makes black Orpheus into a white philosopher—one who is wiser and more knowing—but to distinguish this reading from the actual working of the poetry. And so he writes: "And Sartre's mistake was not only to seek the source of the source but in a certain sense to block that source."[46] (Compare Sartre: "The black's secret is that the sources of his *existence* and the roots of Being are identical."[47]) Were black Orpheus to notice *this* oddity, it might be fatal to the whole enterprise of negritude. But if this source had been overlooked in his descent, and a white philosopher happened to observe it later, the only thing that would lose luster would be negritude's reputation as a discourse that returns to the essence of blackness (as to the "source"). Reset in this way, the most striking rhetorical feature of "Orphée noir" is the decision to address Eurydice as if only a white philosopher could see her without loss: the conceptual nudity of which such vision consists renders her transparent to the white philosophical gaze precisely because white theory forgets the "absolute density" that structures her non-existence and that precedes any becoming: who then is Orpheus, and who is abandoning whom to eternal night?

But let us return to our subject, and offer other passages from Fanon's reading of negritude that call into doubt racist history and, consequently, may be conceived as a refusal of an aesthetics of social death. No reader of negritude has taught this more clearly than Fanon. In the chapter of *Black Skin, White Masks* condemning Sartre, Fanon commends the *Cahier* for not having blinded itself to the corpselike nature of blackness and, in return, for not being seduced by the truth offered up by white politics or philosophy. Again, if Fanon insists that he "needed not to know" the end point of Sartre's critique, and if the reading of "Orphée noir" felt like the shattering of a "last illusion," what remains key for him is that we should not confuse the belief in negritude with the imaginary and prophetic vision of its blackness. In "Orphée noir" (as we have already mentioned), negritude is represented via the diurnal myth of Eurydice, in whose apparition the poet loses himself only to find himself both rhetorically and intellectually. Blacker than day, blacker than night, Eurydice's obscurity is inseparable from her promise, which can be seen as a kind of blinding flicker or absence of being—it is as such that Fanon encounters her in Sartre's text. On remarking on her first loss (of day to night), Fanon makes the pertinent observation that negritude itself is always waiting to find her, too; on remarking on the second loss, which requires a finer allegorical perception of poetry and philosophy, he remains uncertain of what he has *seen*, but he is sure that it was meant not to be *observed*. Her obscurity is blinding because blackness, as soon as it is seen philosophically, becomes immediately lost, unknown. For Sartre seems not to need to give her a glance, let alone a thought, in order to justify her disappearance to philosophy. On the contrary, no sooner has he completed his reading of her portent than he is overwhelmed by a fresh burst of Marxist orthodoxy: he will serve the political superego on the side of whiteness, but the black body of Eurydice is not something he is prepared to look on. "Negritude is a sad myth full of hope, born of Evil and pregnant from future Good," he says, equating pregnancy with death, "living like a woman who is born to die and who feels her own death even in the richest moments of her life."[48] When it is said that negritude is also a prophecy pregnant with its own death, one could infer from this that its purpose is expiation, or that its role is to devote itself to its own death, but what it knows of this death as death is wholly philosophical. As such, what remains to be sacrificed is the fate that is reserved for the surety by which blackness is always made servile to the work of separation.

Thus we see that revolutionary Marxism promises, as the reward for liberating (the socially dead) Eurydice, an improbable absolution "that knows it is transitory," and that condenses three different elements in Sartre's reading—the poem that is reborn as politics, the desire to become that fades into sacrificial non-existence, and the corpse putrefying because, as Sartre says, it is "unamenable to analysis": and yet, in this gratifyingly obscure allegory of philosophy, Sartre concludes that any attempt to name or conceptualize black Eurydice philosophically is bound to fail, for only poetry (as conceived posthumously by philosophy) can capture her "luminous night of unknowing."[49] All this evidently proves that, for the socially dead, the affect of being dead is both known and unknown to us, and that it follows from the ordering of black being. This, then, is what is explicitly the matter with black life; nowhere does it murder itself more than when it feels most alive, and nowhere is it more dead than when it relates to the living as a pious claim that it be allowed to come into being without the attribute of being already dead. It is no wonder then that Fanon should challenge this opinion as both symptomatic and foreclosed! Further, all these opinions of Sartre's insist that negritude is solely a mythic understanding of black experience. It now occurs to me that my own reading of "Orphée noir" in *Haunted Life* was perhaps too readily prepared to credit this myth of a black Eurydice. I may have been looking *too* closely at her and, in consequence of this fixation, found myself blinded—unseeing, dazzled—by the community of spectators who have confidently turned to philosophy to name or reveal Eurydice's meaning. In trying so hard to see her, to be the redeeming spectator, have I really done nothing but become a reader-celebrant of her loss? But no, not quite: after Fanon, who found himself walking both towards and away from her, it is clear that any reading of negritude is itself a revendication, and one that shifts the entire argument about the limits of analysis; my observation is that this is key to his reading of negritude after all. It therefore comes as no surprise that Fanon, ever resistant to teleological narratives, should also resist the symbolism of a text as always already readable precisely in so far as it is unamenable to (white) analysis.

Herein lies Fanon's different imagining of Eurydice: she is the unknowable, ungraspable moment of being that opens in us, and that could enrich each moment of black lived experience if we did not flee from her into the false consolations of racist knowledge. And to the extent that she remains inaccessible to us, unknown or unrepresented, and endlessly eludes our grasp, she can be neither annihilated, nor negated, nor possessed; indeed, if she ceased to be unknown, the world as such would not exist and would lose the density of its embodied existence. On the other hand, it is clear from her resistance to philosophy that negritude-Eurydice also prophesied this resistance: it is the effacement of her resistance that drives Fanon's response to Sartre, but she is also central to his reading of *le vécu noir*. Faced with this insistence, let us briefly retrace what Fanon says about experience, in this chapter. What does Fanon say about *l'expérience vécue noire*? To my surprise, he refers not to experience but to loss and time: he thus begins with the motif of hemorrhaging. It is as if he were saying that after the encounter with racism the being of the (white-identified) black *empties* itself (*vide*). "I *needed* not to know," he writes, implying that this new "decline" has yet to take on the formal aspect of "completeness."[50] Fanon's reading of Césaire's poetry confirms the same thing, for as we said, the abyss cannot be defined as completeness of meaning, and its language abolishes the mythic role of sacrifice as superfluous to its concealment. What is more, the poetic and linguistic emphases of this poem—those that had formed the very standard against which Sartre perceives that Césaire "realizes" the "great surrealist tradition"[51]—these too begin to hemorrhage with their irregular reading of blackness as performance: whether as myth or negativity, "natural eros" or revolutionary poetry, the *Cahier* signifies a date in the *poeticization* of being black. It is as though Fanon had craftily acknowledged this date, which, having arrived on the road of destiny the moment he came across it, could never be removed *as* poetry, and so has to disappear as racial myth.

These passages, I think, support my position re Fanon's three most innovative responses regarding Césaire, as already mentioned above. I will have more to say about these later on, but just now I am impatient to talk about the politics that Fanon's rearward glimpse towards the *Cahier* signifies on the other side, as it were, of negritude. The oblivious need not to know is just where the first discovery leaves him, resetting the terms of the journey to his negritude. Fanon starts out on that journey as a search for meaning where, as a pretext for the new discovery of negritude, negritude is to be laid out for easy perusal by Césaire's poetic epic. As he is doing this, he sees—like every other spectator—negritude as a chimera just dangling out of reach, and, like these other readers, he waits for the world to notice it too. But at nearly the same moment—in this, *not* like the negritude-philosopher—he again catches sight of negritude not as a "remarkable discovery"; indeed, this brief glimpse suffices to tell him that, since he first saw it, "this discovery was a rediscovery."[52] The "limits of my essence," he writes, have been turned into a sign of belatedness, and negritude, formerly occupying the leftmost (or hindmost) fecundity of the world, now stands exposed as the "zero" that he first imagined it to be. By virtue of this reversal, negritude confirms Sartre's reading of it as black unhappy consciousness: it is out of place and time in *two* ways now. It remains now to show how and why Fanon's disillusion with negritude nonetheless serves to preserve and maintain it as a most radical form of corpsing. I shall demonstrate this through one telling example: that of experience.

Anyone reading *Black Skin, White Masks* must, in order to understand it, confront Fanon's concept of experience. That is, one must come to terms with the personae or masks by which whites convince themselves of their whiteness by becoming unwittingly black and blacks learn to perform themselves as white through an unconscious fear of their own blackness. However, unless these experiences are understood as imaginary misrecognitions, they will, even though it might be convincing to say so, still not suffice to illustrate Fanon's understanding of the word "experience," especially where it is a matter of questioning roles that put in question, or corpse, what is often meant by the term. Often, though, a long chain of linked inferences is required to follow the intellectual argument that connects persona to phobia, phobia of what Fanon calls *that within*, a term that he takes directly from theater, where it is linked to the role played by unconscious ambivalence in the constitution of the racist subject. Furthermore, this requires great caution and perspicacity regarding Fanon's understanding of psychoanalysis in the psychodramas of racism. Critics tend to read Fanon's concept of experience as if it were just an existentialist premise of self-alienation, or inauthenticity. Consequently, when the performance of racism is at issue, not to speak of the entire question of unconscious desire, critics often lose sight of the inferences linking his arguments together, and especially the way in which he substantiates his points about experience through the definition of "*that within*." For example, when he refers to his case histories of negrophobia, that is, when he is trying to explain how certain interracial fantasies require certain personae and narratives, namely, stories of rape and black rapists, Fanon is anxious to point out that these personae and testimonies always involve a kind of unconscious corpsing through which the ego violates itself and for whom that violation can be enjoyed through the pleasures of failed repression, as can be seen in the infamous case history of "a Negro is raping me." The purpose of the fantasy, in brief, is to allow a violation in which the subject does nothing at their own discretion and everything at the command of the black other, except that the ego's obedience to orders and commands prescribed by race law is what allows both the fantasy of obedience and its sadism (and here the black is obliged to symbolize both the aggressor and the aggressed, both legislator and victim) to be continually enjoyed without consequence.

From all this it is clear that what connects *that within* to the performance of interracial desire is the psychical benefits of corpsing, and consequently it has nothing to do with the existential rhetoric of inauthenticity. Concerning that rhetoric, and its notion of authentic and inauthentic experience, it would be a mistake to understand *that within* as an example of bad faith. As I recognize it, Sartre's example of bad faith always means that people are in denial about the choices they make, and especially when their lives are bound to these decisions. Indeed, one could almost say that Sartre, insofar as he is always obliged to point out what these choices might mean, is always able to decide what living the good life consists of and, in so doing, actually proves the point by making the example of bad faith the pious sign of a critical faith but not the bad faith of his own philosophical reading, a fact related to the certainty that he knows and consequently never doubts the authenticity of this reading. Manifestly intelligible, controlled, and exempt from any symptom of self-doubt or uncertainty, Sartre's style appears nearer mastery and perfection the further it gets from experience; and we never feel better as readers of Sartre than in recognizing how each instance of authenticity is confirmed and each principle of bad faith traduced. By contrast, Fanon's style (of which I take the chapter on *le vécu noir* as a key example) is aphoristic, recessive, poetic, esoteric, and hard to see, much less sum up. Like some faintly transmitted white ectoplasm, it can only reach those unhappy few who (by dint of pathology, bad luck, elective affinity) attend to the text precisely in order to see themselves reflected there. To see themselves in close-up, I mean, for the comfort of aesthetic appreciation, since the Fanonian style, invariably linked to the various symptoms, oversights, and inelegancies that run all through the text, seems to treat no other subject but *the failure of the black to be recognized or seen* beyond the symbolism of its corpsing. Sartre's aestheticization of negritude would receive its dialectical correction in Fanon's resistance to theory's representation of black experience as always already comprehended by the "life" of a concept.

Therefore, since all of those scenes of *that within* are revealed for the benefit of showing how racism is performed and, ultimately, enjoyed, the notion has considerable repercussions for Fanon's views on experience. Let me explain this more clearly. Among the many neurotic obsessions of the patients that Fanon presents, the most important is that of sexual difference, or rather the ambivalence of white and black women towards black men, which is seen as both the greatest punishment as well as the last chance of "authentic love" (a phrase laced with deep irony). These obsessions are too coherent *as* structures not to be symptoms, but they are so deviously concealed that, once they are observed, the ostensible story is lost to view. Like Eurydice in Sartre's "Orphée noir," these negrophobic women are hidden, remarkably out of place with respect to the experiences they are used to narrate, but they must also be *seen* to be impossibly out of place, unable to yield nor teach any clear knowledge, but illumining the truth of desire precisely because of their obscurity. With this ghostly Eurydice, Fanon employs one of his favorite forms (the perverse *inform*) but empties it of its customary consequence; this figure sheds no other light but the obscure brilliance of its perverse elaboration of interracial desire.

From this I think it is clear that *that within*, which for Sartre is among the ways in which an actor comes to play a role in bad faith and takes pleasure in being dispossessed by this part, is the frame through which Fanon interrogates the limits of black existence or, more accurately, black existence *as* art. Even in the framing that finally makes such experience appear, it is not the only thing that we see. Those who have read those chapters in *Black Skin, White Masks* dealing with sexuality will have earlier observed that, in denying that he has anything to say about homosexuality, say, or black women ("I have nothing to say about her"), Fanon leaves these corpses sticking up out of the text. Now that once unruly, inauthentic desires have been fastidiously turned down, why is it that there is no evidence of authentic love to oppose this? They will further notice, along with black and white women, a third figure in need of (failed) repression: the black neurotic who can only reject the role that racism imposes on him, by abandoning himself as living, as we expressed it above, and who also possesses a drive (rather than a desire) to be socially dead. Jean Veneuse is Fanon's main example here, who is the case of someone who believes that to be black is to be dead, and who is driven to mourn this fact by calling off his love affair with a white woman (for it follows that if she loves him she is not competent to perceive clearly and distinctly the difference between life and death, or how black life sustains itself as already dead). Crossing over from desire to discourse, from loss to its memorialization, black existence becomes spectral here; and in repairing Veneuse's oversights, Fanon also comes to resemble him in making gaffes of his own, fouling up the neurotic force of *that within* that is the obvious formal ideal of *Un Homme pareil aux autres*. But with, as mentioned above, this crucial disparity: unlike Sartre, say, who never notices his oversights (the romanticism, the philosophy, even, in the end, the teleology), Fanon often seems to bestow on his own lapses a strange, secret *assent* (that requires the ambivalent refusal of negritude). To prove his doctrine that *that within* is a thoroughly neurotic structure, Fanon insists that it is impossible to draw the conclusion that Veneuse's neuroses are a symptom of his blackness, despite obviously demonstrating their derivation from experiences of black social death. Why should he simultaneously attend to feelings of being dead and yet deny the circumstances and histories from which those feelings derive? I remain unpersuaded that this is simply due to the masculinism of Fanon's own text, and much less do I believe that this is due to a blunder, or corpsing, of his reading of psychoanalysis, or a failure on Fanon's part to comprehend the classically triadic narrative structure of loss, recovery, and loss again by which Veneuse imagines himself to be the loss that loses itself, infinitely, in *Un Homme pareil aux autres*. In disclosing an essentially faulty, flimsy, transient negritude, Fanon seems to be performing a role instructively linked to a broader—and undeniably controversial—failure of judgment, since here he gets more pleasure from corpsing that demonstration than from critiquing the actual doctrine of blacks having to mourn their failure to make a claim on the living. What is less known, or studied perhaps, is how this inversion turns on a different reading of phobic neuroses in Fanon's final, posthumous work. But that is another story, which I have written about elsewhere in this book (see Part One, Chapter Six, "Desire and Law").

What can be said about this disillusion with disillusion at the level of theory? To remove blackness from racist myth is extremely useful, indeed wholly essential, not only for severing blackness from its fetish but also for understanding black social being separately from its performance. For unless we are willing to see blackness as real and not just as a phantasm, we will be unable to distinguish its imaginary role from its real historical significance. We should add, though, that when we say that an awareness of their difference is necessary, we do not mean awareness of literally how one stands apart from the other, but rather how one radically informs the other, which is one of Fanon's most important insights. For if performance is ontology, and it is impossible to know blackness without a thorough consideration of all its roles and performances, then obviously the demonstration and derivation of fantasy from the real, and vice versa, would allow us to grasp the ways in which blacks are put out of their roles not just neurotically, politically, or historically, but aporetically too. In Fanon's version of negritude, blackness is neither the coming of a plenitude nor a posthumous self-erasure, nor is it merely the reversed turn under the glimpse of theory to authenticity, not to mention the redemptive capacity of a no-win wager, which is then seen as a timely victory for those positioned precariously at the dawn of history. Again, let us state the conclusion we set out to prove, namely that, whatever the validity of Fanon's reading of the *Cahier*, he is not concerned to spell out its dialectic, nor does he wish to prove that some forms of blackness are more important than others, or that poetry is subservient to philosophy. No, the only reason he reads the *Cahier* is to explain how certain roles inevitably corpse their actants, and how certain acts, albeit completely ignorant of their being corpsed, are nevertheless salutary in offering blacks a new conception of living, beyond the common wretchedness, neuroses, and social dishonor.

However, white existential philosophy holds completely to the opposite view. Sartre thinks that a black conception of life makes no contribution to the universal *as* black, and so he spells out its dialectic and lets its ending be known, in advance. This prophesying leads him to openly assert that blackness has only one chance: to corpse itself as the body of an already dead woman, which has been cleansed and denuded for the purpose. Throughout all this, the black seems not to breathe until philosophy puts the black life of social death back into the underworld that defines him/her. And to Fanon's utter chagrin after Sartre does this, negritude, praised as an aesthetic of sacrificial generosity, finally looks acceptable. More: with negritude again banished to the edge of the frame, poetry succumbs to the same back-and-forth tremor of what Fanon calls the "nonexistent" (the aesthetic equivalent of the idea of black existence as a stutter between Nothingness and Infinity) that he accuses Sartre of plunging him back into. The symmetry suggests a tragic denouement: a sequence has been concluded, a chiasm rounded out, a glimpse that is loss itself finally seen for what it is as a judgment that is for ever, and without any way of escape, with theory in charge of bringing this black essence to life. I think it is evident to anyone who reads *Black Skin, White Masks* attentively that all this is treated as mere projection and does not rest upon the authority of black experience, and hence one need only expound it in order to refute it.

I would add just this: if we can show on the basis of these texts that black death can never be sovereignly dead, nor entirely alive (which would come to the same thing), what are we to make of this life-death? Historically we must never forget, of course, that blackness is always caught up in the catastrophe that this endless death harbors. This is death as nothing, less than nothing; as such, this death is never assumable as possibility. But if this death is perturbing, it does not perturb us more than those attempts to sublate it as a deformation that keeps on living as, for example, the perpetual fall or descent into an abyssal insignificance (the minor term defining a transcendental crossing). There is no debate to be had here, in so far as the choice must presuppose two roles: in one, the black realizes his abject complicity with illusion; in the other, he is always the victim of a murderous disillusion against which he is too stifled or feeble to defend himself. Nothing, not even his death, drives away this drive to corpse himself as both possibility and representation. Likewise, the Orphic (white) reader, though always at the frontier of that self-mortification, cannot look back on it without losing it, or providing the last redemptive act that is also its murder. I hope and trust, to that extent, that if black life matters, it cannot be as a revendication, nor as the poetical grasp of an historical meaning, nor as the breathless emergence of a politics of ascent. For such roles are not meant for the living; they depend on the idea that blacks can only perform and perfect the role of their deaths, and that they should do so forever as corpses.

Hegel (II)

In Fanon's chapter on "The Lived Experience of the Black" can be found one of the most often discussed passages in *Black Skin, White Masks*:

As long as the Black is with his own, he will not have occasion, with the exception of petty internal struggles, to experience his existence for others [*son être pour autrui*]. There is undoubtedly the moment of existence-for-another (*Füranderesein*) [*l'être pour l'autre*] that Hegel speaks of, but all ontology is rendered unrealisable in a society [of] colonised and civilised. . . . There is an impurity in the *Weltanschauung* of a colonised people, a defect [*tare*] that interdicts all ontological explication. Someone could perhaps object that this is so for every individual, but that obscures a fundamental problem. Ontology, when we admit, once and for all, that it sets existence to one side, does not permit us to understand the being of the Black. For the Black [*le Noir*] no longer has to be black [*noir*], but must be it in the face of the White [*en face du Blanc*]. Some may take it in their heads to respond to us that the situation is reciprocal [*est à double sens*]. We respond that that is false. The Black has no ontological resistance in the eyes of the White.[53]

The problem posed by this interdiction is: how can the black acquire knowledge of itself, grasp itself in its self-relation to the other, when what separates it from both other and world makes the human relations of recognition impossible? That is to say, how can the black become other when what interdicts this desire is its very interaction with others? For the moment the black appears he is hidden, shut up within the borders of a separation that excludes him from the rest of the world. Hence the figure of the corpse with which the last chapter began, and which obviously refers to how this existence-for-another (*Füranderesein*) is made unrealizable in colonial social life, whose entire representation presupposes (theatrically, as well as ontologically) a corpsing that censures it, or better murders it. Not just murders, moreover, but sacrifices the persona through which blackness is seen as death, and in a theater in which all the actors are socially dead. There is no resistance to this corpsing (hence its meaning as a kind of death), for it separates being from existence; it exhibits black existence, it allows it to be seen, but purely within the terms of a murderous enjoyment. Being (and there is then the risk in saying that blackness has no other, except the degradation that corpses it) is thus folded into an immense abyss in which it drowns in contingency. It is here that Fanon's revision of Hegel takes on an extraordinary resonance: if recognition, by Hegel's own testimony, brings prestige and exaltation, then clearly the black possesses neither; his self-relation is not mediated by his relation to an other who opposes him, but by the corpse that envelops him, conferring on him a theatrical (and not a phenomenological) appearance, and which he performs under the pretense of living. It may well be that this artifice confirms our earlier commentary on the racial fetish-mask, but there is something else being stated here that works more conclusively, since we could deduce from it that the phallic genital thing that blackness is clearly is not the same thing as the corpse, for the latter quite simply reverses the artifice that maintains the fetish by revealing the fetish-body in the throes of its annihilation. Everything that we attribute to the fetish—the pleasure and fixation, anxiety and paranoia—is taken up and restated as evidence of a singular enjoyment by the corpsed subject: and who among us would not enjoy the spectacle of a man struggling in the ash heap of his composure? Another opposition that is destroyed is that of domination and dependence—the relation of master and slave that has dominated anti-colonial discourse for the last few decades. We have already discussed the relevance of this allegory to decolonial violence (see

Part One, Chapter Seven, "The Condemned"). Corpsing adds another dimension, which is essentially to reveal the secret of Hegelian mastery, the pretense by which it conceals the very artifice of mastery—not as regards fine gesture and speech, or the public trappings of power, but the pretense by which it grasps corpsing as its own inner essence; likewise, if sovereignty is the negation of corpsing, that is because mastery is nothing more than a debased version of such lordship.

Hence, we see the reasons why slavery and mastery are jointly doubled by corpsing: in the case of mastery, corpsing reveals how one is mastered, and never master; in the case of slavery, corpsing reveals why the condition of being *black* is inter-dicted by a flaw, an impasse, which makes being as such inaccessible. Since I have just said that this flaw is also an impasse—a word that Hegel restricts to the master (and precisely because he consumes the products of mastery rather than producing them), it is my intention to discuss the above quote alongside Fanon's later chapter on "The Negro and Recognition" so as to specify why corpsing is of relevance to Fanon's reading of Hegel. Moreover, such a reading will allow me to work through the following question: what is the relation between Fanon's genealogy of mastery and the history of racial slavery? By what displacement does this genealogy determine itself as a historical correction to Hegel? Certainly not by drawing on alternative historical evidence (as though Hegel had simply got history wrong), but by presenting a phenomenology of mastery (and slavery) that *separates* itself from the forms of mastery and slavery as understood by Hegelian philosophy. On the one hand, the passage above still speaks in Hegel's language, but as it unfolds and summarizes the torment of an obscure weakness of black being, the philosophical certainty of that language is condemned as delusory. If one considers why black ontology is rendered unrealizable in the colony (or, what is the same thing, is denied recognition), it can readily be seen that this is not a purely historical question, but one that calls attention to the encounter wherein *that within* myself exposes me to a derision that is felt to be a kind of death that cannot be transfigured, or sublated, and which it would perhaps be very wise not to resist.

Furthermore, if we now turn to that later reading of Hegel, we shall discover other things deserving of notice. First, given that the corpse openly shows itself as a gap between the subject and its essence, the authority of what is usurped is not rendered permanently, nor is it preserved as negated. The reason for this is obvious. In the corpsed state, what cannot be resisted is the sheer contingency of its encounter, which is why self-certainty can never be secure or be put to work by negation. At the same time, accordingly, the profound seriousness with which Hegelian philosophy administers and safeguards itself here meets its match in a derision that is not so much sovereign as stubbornly ridiculous. Although the Hegelian philosopher is right not to be worried about seeming merely ridiculous, for in the midst of laughter he alone is possessed of the authority to see the seriousness of what lies behind all humor, in corpsing the speculative ridicule that preserves itself as philosophy is unmade absolutely, and thereby sees its authority wither away, like the dumb nigga it is. So if any reading worthy of the name must pass through the negation of its object, any attempt to lend such a ruling the same authority as that of a corpse will find its thought perverted by the counter-authority of that corpsing, both under its arrest and laughably in a state of arrest without the promise of salvation. Similarly, corpsing has no beginning and no end, it has no exergue (to the speculative life of the concept); it goes along with whomever and wherever it finds itself, for it is sheer stupidity insinuating itself, fatally, in all sense and interpretation, dragging along all in its wake. As such, the corpse cannot be transfigured, amortized, or preserved in Hegel's speculative restoration; it cannot even be exposed as a corpse without producing more laughter, and it cannot be mastered as a justifiable blunder and so "removed from the tomb of its incomprehension" without further errors.[54] It suffices in this respect to say that unlike the Hegelian corpse (the dead letter, object, fetish), which can always be restored to the life of spirit, what I am here calling the corpse castigates both the messenger and its knowledge.

Let us say that the corpse, in its theater, does not have any expressive role at all; for its blunder is the stumbling block of the half-spoken, and its denouement is the corrupted form of the half-done. Moreover, corpsing is always punctuated by the desire *not to be recognized*, which is at once the immanent pleasure of its failed concealment and the exposure of its failed negation. In this sense, it exposes itself as the failed desire to conceal itself—again, in this sense unlike the fetish—as such it cannot be self-appropriated as a speculative power that preserves the Hegelian actor-philosopher from its death. Indeed, in so far as corpsing reveals an actual and symbolic death (in the terms of our reading), it touches on that which is most intimate and also most social (the *part*—written, ethical, legal, political, civic, pedagogical—by which black propriety is made both legible and impossible, and regardless of one's negative doubt, questioning, criticism, or faith). The corpse cannot be read or staged, in brief, as either on the threshold of philosophical mastery or as the slavish version of its servile fulfillment.

Therefore, Fanon is absolutely right to point out that Hegelian mastery in the colony is colored by an impasse whose numerous failings are immediately obvious to everyone and cannot be readily put right: instead of work, masters are imitated by their slaves, exposing their masterful pretense to the ridicule of a pretense that is slavish. As for the colonial master, it has already been said that his authority is not sovereign but brutish, thus conferring on him the semblance of a mastery that has not even earned him the pretense of a recognition; it is not his face that he offers to the slave, but his lechery and arbitrary cruelty (and all the fractured projection of an unmastered libido). For Fanon the story ends even before it has begun. "Historically, the Black steeped in the essentiality of servitude was set free by his master. He did not fight for his freedom."[55]

It would be a mistake to read this as just an historical point, or as merely the inversion of the narrative by which Hegel posits the dialectical resolution of the conflict. In the conventional reading of these passages, the colonizer who is put in the place of the master clearly does not want recognition from the colonized *"but work"*; and the slave, instead of producing the work necessary for the reproduction of life, loses his relation to desire, work, and freedom, including his own and that of others—consequently, envy is substituted for interiority, imitativeness for self-discipline, slavish mastery for a mastery earned.[56] Every single commentator who tries to reconcile these blatant contradictions of the Hegelian text offers solutions that allow us to see what happens in the struggle for recognition—which is said to give form to human life and meaning, and supposedly resulting in the triumph of the slave (a triumph read by Kojève as rendering the contradictions and fates of modern consciousness in the revolutionary-democratic process)—when racism gets in the way and the slave is left in the middle of this Marxian-Hegelian fantasy. But as I mentioned above, in situating the above passage as Fanon's historical response to Hegel, these readings make it appear that what Fanon simply wants is a humanist recognition. They thereby utterly obscure the lucid simplicity of Fanon's point, which is that the Hegelian slave, and the mastery that tallies with it, are derived from an artifice whose ruse is that of a theatrical illusion. For if you add corpsing to Fanon's insight about the inessentiality of servitude, you arrive at a reading of Hegel that does indeed illumine what is concealed or opposed to mastery, but that is never absent from the dynamics of mastery. With corpsing, mastery is exposed to the void of its own contagious laughter, the source of which is a slavish attitude towards its death *as* theater. The same cannot be said, though, of the corpsed slave. For I am quite convinced that if he is steeped in his own inessentiality, that is because the inessential is his clearly defined function: to preserve the genealogy of mastery's pretense the slave must preserve the slavery of its theater (its deceit, its fragility, and insecurity). By corpsing himself the slave presents and conceals the very terms of this mediation, and this is why he is derided and laughed at by the white master; he carries the corpse within himself as the symbol of his own prostration, thus signifying in the clearest and most evident sense that blackness is nothing more than an artificial caricature of the slavishness that is its covenant with white mastery. This is why, in corpsing himself, the slave also explicitly knows that he can be put to death, for death's calamitous stupidity is his role. Hence the dialectic of lord and bondsman is thereby given a new and disturbing twist.

Also worthy of note is the fact, already indicated, that Fanon's reading of the corpse as an interdiction should not be confused with Hegel's reading of fetishism. If the fetish is a privileged figure for concealing the scene of an act to which one imagines oneself to be a spectator, doubtless because that scene corresponds too well to our vision of what *should not ever be seen*, which has in turn a sense of a prohibition whose transgression will be mortifying, the watchword of the corpse is directly opposite, for here what discombobulates is how one sees oneself represented in the seen, but it is not the seeing itself that is deadly, rather it is the failure of representation that corpses. One can draw from this the following consequence, and I have already done so more than once: the gaze is what corpses, but this gaze is one to which one is always already given to be seen and from which there is no escape, and which one discovers one already resembles despite the insufficiency, incompetence, and misfortune by which one has performed it or hosted it, and in the place where one would elevate or observe it above the *philosophical* derision that is its punch line. Corpsing, therefore, is the travesty of the dialectic; it is where identity and meaning collapse *tout court*. And the reason that I know this is that even this claim of non-mastery is at risk of being corpsed. There are also reasons, apart from this, showing that black religious fetishism is also the consequence of a defect for Hegel, not to mention the fact that it forms a limit to what appears to be the human form best fitted for the speculative task of reason.

Indications of this can be seen in Hegel's *Philosophy of History* and *Reason in History*, where black existence is consistently presented as pure anteriority. "What we properly understand by Africa, is the Unhistorical, Undeveloped Spirit, still involved in the condition of mere nature." And: "We cannot properly feel ourselves into his nature, no more than into that of a dog."[57] In the insistence on the proper—"What we properly understand"; "We cannot properly feel"—Hegel suggests a limit to the passions and forms of *sympathy*; black being is where feeling itself dissolves, or disappears, for there is no evident kinship between the human, placed here within Europe, and what is reputed to be the human's impossibly undeveloped form. Africa—synonymous with religious fetishism for Hegel—confuses artifice for spirit, and fetish for concept, and so cannot pass beyond itself into work or history. Being all *outer* and not yet *inner*, Africa not only has no consciousness of itself, and no self-related identity, it paradoxically lacks the self-alienation that is alone capable of revealing spirit through nature. Thus what Africa lacks, in its religion, is what true nature (the nature of nature) possesses: namely, the ability to negate itself and so reveal the discontinuous sign by which spirit is able to deliver or reveal itself *through* the forms of nature. "Corrupted by fetishism," African culture is thus mired in improper rituals of veneration and artifice: "The power of the dead over the living is indeed recognized, but held in no great respect; for the Negroes issue commands to their dead and cast spells upon them."[58] What could be plainer than that blackness amounts to a bad form of theater because it literally remains obedient to the object-like character of things whose authority is not based on the pretense of their universality, but is infected by the capricious need to master their debased particularity; without being assimilated to supernal truths, the worship of such authority remains devoted to an exteriority trapped in a corpselike object from which all life has withdrawn;

and African judgment, restricted to sovereignty over nature, remains arbitrary and cruel in its manifestation through spells, dances, and orgies—fetishistic forms that represent the death and sacrifice of signification itself, and a mastery whose power remains under the sign of nature.

Now, Hegel clearly divides the world up into cultures of recognition and cultures bound by disappearance; religions that inscribe themselves on the map of world-spirit (*Geist*), and religions whose capricious sensuousness, as objectified in the fetish object, only makes them venerate base material things, including the corpses of their dead kin. African religion, in other words, is not yet universal but arbitrary and finite; if spirit finds itself through sublating the fetish object, African religion, in its degraded fetishistic form, cannot sublate the sensuous into spirit, and because it remains obstinately attached to the sacred as object (it is the fetish that won't let fetishism disappear), spirit remains in bondage to a finite, material, grossly particularistic embodiment: without the disappearance of the fetish, in short, even if it is in the partially "independent . . . spiritual" form of a finitely speculative object, spirit cannot reveal itself, and remains under the sway of the fetish: its rituals, protocols, modes of speech, and instrumental significance.[59]

Before attempting to relate these passages to corpsing and the interdiction of the black, which certainly adds to this dialectic of spirit and fetish, let us take seriously for a moment this philosophical derision aimed at the black. In his response to the *Phenomenology of Spirit*, Fanon, not disagreeing with Hegel's general characterization of the fetish as materialist and finite, presents mastery and slavery as two arbitrary forms of sensuous collusion. This is what motivates him to say that the colonial master and slave interact as two desires who turn away from the object—that is to be consumed and/or produced—and towards the imaginary, arbitrary, capricious, fetishistic form of their respective rivalries; and to the extent that fetishism also fails to disappear here, what is revealed is not a materialism on the threshold of spirit, but rather a trickery, a delusion that, according to Fanon, is the true ideological meaning of race as spirit. This is why Fanon does not oppose negrophobia to fetishism in this regard, but sees in the racial fetish the reason why master and slave are locked in a battle not of prestige but of abasement, which explains the unparalleled ferocity of the battle and stems from the fact that death is not just a natural power but a sovereign license to enforce one's rule; the killing of the fetish object cannot be condemned as murder, for the intuition of its human existence is always linked to the laws and social forms that produce it as an enslaved form of being. According to the formalizable relation of blackness to the corpse, Fanon basically reproaches Hegel for confusing mastery with its racially metaphysical form (and this would also have been the case with the republican, monarchical pretense of white lordship) and with repressing the racially fetishistic form of spirit in his axiomatic reading of culture that determines whiteness as *the* teleological meaning of world history.

This is not—to repeat the point—simply an historical reproach, nor an historical claim about fetishism in Hegel. But Hegel's argument could be taken to be exemplary of how race, as an immanent fact of both species being and consciousness, permits the exclusion, both *de facto* and *de jure*, of the non-European from the ontology and progress of human citizenship, and from the civilizing work of universal culture (*Bildung*). It was precisely as a *refusal* of such metaphysical racism that negritude came into being. Fanon's reservation about negritude (despite his stated admiration) comes from the fact that its discourse remains too Hegelian in its teleology and metaphysics. Such a view implies that negritude has its inevitable counterpart in a black dialectics of meaning: so long as there is a white axiomatics of culture (national or international), the racial division of the world will be inexpiable.

Fanon's response to Sartre, who, of course, is decidedly Hegelian, has also to do with fetishism, it should be noted, and also involves an explicit disagreement over Hegel. In the chapter on black lived experience, for example, having quoted and contrasted Hegel with Sartre, Fanon gives a more explicit and argued sense of why the assimilation of the black to an historical dialectic should be resisted. Among the reasons given, Fanon accuses Sartre, in so far as he has forgotten that "negativity draws its worth from an almost substantive absoluteness," of having fetishistically determined what cannot be determined as a fetish, according to which, in principle, blackness is the finite, particularist appearance of what will give way to the universal, signified truth of class conflict, so that blackness is merely the fetishistic substitute that necessarily loses its substance, presence, and what Fanon calls its "absolute density" to the historical logic of a dialectic.[60] With respect to this loss Fanon posits another loss that he refuses to lose, and one that must be maintained against the fetishism of its disappearance: "In opposition to historical becoming, there had always been the unforeseeable. I needed to lose myself completely in negritude."[61] The distinction between a loss that is dialectically lost, and that then creates a memorial in reaction to that loss, and a loss that cannot be foreseen and therefore, according to Fanon, cannot be dialecticized as a fetishistic loss, becomes part of that abyssal perspective on blackness that I indicated earlier. Fanon here suggests that the relation between blackness and dialectical logic essentially decides that blackness is always *servile*, that it owes its authority and consequence to something else (history, spirit, etc.) and can only be recognized as the *fetish that conserves itself in so far as it is always already lost.*

The difference between Fanon and Sartre concerns less the fetishistic attitude of Sartre than the nature of blackness discussed and the use made of it in white philosophy and politics. In the opposition between the decidable and the unforeseeable, what gets lost, perhaps, is the abyssal significance of the universal and the particular, their density and mass, whose movement is both and simultaneously a movement and an arrest, or, in Fanon's words, the co-existence of "what was already there, pre-existing" and what "takes on an aspect of completeness" in the unfore-seeable "decline" of being.[62] If we try to calculate that movement as a logic, we shall produce a significantly abstract understanding of the depths of each particular, but also an extremely narrowed perspective on the completeness of the black universal. And this perhaps shows up in return as a refusal to identify blackness as anything more than the object that makes the fetish of fetishism visible, and so always de-cidedly disavowed, and to that extent never really on the threshold of being at all.

Although Fanon does not here go into this, it might be thought that corpsing, through its derisory exposure, offers a direct challenge to the resolutions of sub-lation. Although the word is not Fanon's, I believe that a study of what corpsing denotes clearly speaks to what we have already written about concerning mask, spectacle, and *that within*, where the *inner* no longer performs the *outer*. In so far as the unforeseeable is part of the pernicious work of the corpse, corpsing is nei-ther dialectizable nor decidable. Rather, the corpse is what recalls me to myself, and even if that recall lends itself to a traumatic and ridiculous shock or guffaw, this is not a dialectical description of my return to the world, nor of a return to the authority of a role, for the place one starts from, dialectically, has no end in dialectical terms, but begins with public ridicule. Where this happens, the unfore-seeable at least leaves open the possibility that one might or might not be educed and traduced for being corpsed. As I have said, it is impossible to put up with, depart from, or resist the corpse, and yet the fact that blacks are persecuted and resented for being a corpse shows how vexed the distinction can be between what is decidably black and what is unforeseeably so. This aggressive license cannot be easily checked because it attests to something that is more elementary and more indelible than an historical article of faith. The word faith here brings me back to the question of religion: let us say that blacks can be sacrificed precisely because, in their object-like character, they hide under the cloak of nature as fetishes, and are not yet regarded as part of the symbolic work of spirit. It is in this movement between the fetish and what corpses it that there is both a black epiphany of the word (to whose interpretation we have added the word corpsing) and what is, for me, an encounter with the abyssal question of negritude. It is at this point that what I call afro-pessimism must be thought as the black task of thought, in order to understand the life that gives birth to itself as a corpse, a death-in-life that is the essence of its very election, and that defines its exemplary universalism as an his-torically precipitous ruin. Here it is not so much a case of the fetish disappearing in the truth of race-as-spirit (as in negritude) as it is taking responsibility for a new form of spirit, as the discovery of a differentiation that is also the abyssal rupture of the bond between the universal and its various incarnations in nation, commu-nity, religion, race, and spirit.

Finally, the question is, is any of this still Hegelian? Werner Hamacher points out quite convincingly, I think, how in Hegel any "mortifying hermeneutic" (or any claim to murder Hegel) is always thereby turned into "an affirmation of the true life" of speculative idealism.[63] But however that may be, I have my doubts that corpsing can be sublated at all, and no doubt that this doubt itself opens this text to the taint of ridicule. One can no more dissociate oneself from being corpsed than one can prevent the rupture, or separation, and radical unbinding that remains the corpsed possibility of any thought, bond, or origin. So it is that the experience of corpsing is both livable and mortifying, mortifying because livable. So I return once more to my question: how does one play the role of dissociation, if deadly dissociation is the role that one plays—a role at once fixated and degrading in its abjection, a role whose license and authority have always been uniquely black?

CONCLUSION

This completes what I proposed to discuss in Part Two of this book. It remains only to say explicitly that the political themes and tropes written about here are the reason why Fanon's thought endures beyond the narrow perspectives wherein it was founded and, subsequently, denounced or celebrated. I have taken pains to show how the violence of that thought— forged in decolonial war—was linked to the violence that founds it. For this reason we reach the same conclusion here as we did above, in Part One: that Fanonism begins in contestation, and a new mode of opposition, and coincides with a clinical attack on colonial culture, and the obscene rigor wherein it endures, the thought that is entirely consistent with the attitude of a *racial humanity*. It was in opposition to this thought that Fanon founded his *socialthérapie*: an approach to individuals and classes that examined the link between misrecognition and disparagement. From the start, however, Fanon had another object—psychopolitical in fact—in view: to invent, theoretically, a new poetry, a new praxis of thought, capable of negating colonialism's limits in the service of revolution. Invention, the abyssal, the tabula rasa, the *n'est pas*: I have demonstrated why these key themes and tropes remain pivotal for any future thinking of Fanonism. But this whither does not yet have a meaning. It is precisely for this reason that I can say that to read Fanon is to know a thought that is not yet.

Afterword

I have finished writing this book, but this is not the book that I wanted to write. I would like to have written it in fewer words. I would like to have freed my desire from its obscurity and loosened the strictures confining it to irresponsibility and triviality. But something got in the way—something that occupied me as a *whither* that was neither present to me (as an object of thought) nor absent (as a kind of imaginary). This *whither* neither belongs in the world of what is, nor is it the fantasy of an untimely future object. It is a door that remains open, but what it opens onto is a nothing where everything converges and from which everything emanates, a nothing where desire meets the great overarching force of a destiny in whose unveiling there is neither force nor significance.

All in all, here things happen only because they may never happen, and so never stop happening; here blackness reveals itself in the constant restless movement between nothingness and infinity; and lastly perhaps, and more importantly, this future imperfect has become the key attribute of Fanonism—a *whither* that is both irremediable and unrealizable, a consequence free from mere worldly concerns precisely because it hangs at the end of a rope, in whose detachment from the merely human there is neither transcendence nor infinity and whose opening to an exemplary relinquishment is always mingled with the potentiality of *an invention that can neither be subjugated nor foresworn.*

By this I mean not only that Fanonism remains obscure to me but also that that obscurity is itself an indication of its power. We might even say that Fanonism cannot yet be thought because we are still in thrall to the history of a thought that makes *race into a destiny.* Truth to tell, this book has not been about the future of Fanonism—its value as the mystical foundation of a new politics. It is about the *violence* with which it has been read; it is the violence with which Fanonism has been thought and, at the same time, opposed, that situates the limits of Fanonism as a psychopolitical form and desire. I have not sought to go beyond this violence, nor have I sought to overturn its fantasy or disavowal. But what I have tried to do is to understand the pleasures it gives—its enjoyment and luxurious inauthenticity.

But it is this *whither* that, nevertheless, defines the obscurer moments of this book. In the end, everything begins here, and this explains why I could not produce a written version of the path that I wanted to take. By which I mean it seems to me that in depicting Fanonism, I was forced up against the pessimistic limits of a thought that left me bewildered. And conversely, in discussing the relations between blackness and being, it soon became evident that I was on a path where what was known no longer had any meaning, or limit, and that there was no way out of this experience of being abandoned to the dark night of the abyssal.

Writing *Whither Fanon?* returned me to those depths and this is why, when all is said and done, Fanonism remains for me a point of interruption as well as the gateway to a difficult, most urgent encounter.

Notes

FOREWORD

1. Frantz Fanon, *Black Skin, White Masks*, trans. Charles Lam Markmann. New York: Grove Press, 1967, 155.
2. Frantz Fanon, *The Wretched of the Earth*, trans. Constance Farrington. Harmondsworth: Penguin Books, 1967, 70, translation modified.

INTRODUCTION

A version of this chapter was previously published as "Whither Fanon": *Textual Practice* 25, no. 1 (2011): 33–69, tandfonline.com.

1. References will be made to the following English editions of works by Frantz Fanon: *Black Skin, White Masks*, trans. Charles Lam Markmann. New York: Grove Press, 1967; *Black Skin, White Masks*, trans. Richard Philcox. New York: Grove Press, 2008; *The Wretched of the Earth*, trans. Constance Farrington. London: Penguin Books, 1963; *The Wretched of the Earth*, trans. Richard Philcox. New York: Grove Press, 2004; *Toward the African Revolution: Political Essays*, trans. Haakon Chevalier. New York: Grove Books, 1988; *Studies in a Dying Colonialism*, trans. Haakon Chevalier. London: Earthscan, 1989. In some instances the translations have been modified in the interest of accuracy.
2. David Scott, *Refashioning Futures: Criticism after Postcoloniality*. Princeton, New Jersey: Princeton University Press, 1999; Achilles Mbembe, *On the Postcolony*. Berkeley: University of California Press: 2001. No attempt is made here to do justice to Nigel Gibson's interesting but somewhat wayward *Fanon. The Postcolonial Imagination*. Cambridge, Polity: 2003. Important essays by Henry Louis Gates, Jr.; Cedric Robinson; Stuart Hall; and Azzedine Haddour, all of which contain discussion of the future of Fanonism, are not discussed here.
3. Patrick M. Taylor, *The Narrative of Liberation: Perspectives on Afro-Caribbean Literature, Popular Culture and Politics*. Ithaca: Cornell University Press, 1989; see also Scott, *Refashioning Futures* for a different reading of this narrative.
4. For readings of Fanon along these lines see Hannah Arendt, *On Violence*. New York: Harcourt, Brace & World, 1970.
5. Walter Benjamin, "Critique of Violence," in *Reflections: Essays, Aphorisms, Autobiographical Writings*, trans. E. Jephcott. New York: Schocken, 1985, 277–301.

See also Jacques Derrida, "Force of Law: The 'Mystical Foundation of Authority,'" trans. Mary Quaintance. In *Deconstruction and the Possibility of Justice*, eds. Drucilla Cornell, Michael Rosenfeld, and David Gray Carlson. London: Routledge, 1992, 3–68.

6. The first commentator to elaborate Fanon's theory of violence in Benjaminian terms was Ronald Judy in his valuable essay "On the Politics of Global Language, or Unfungible Local Value," *boundary 2* 24, no. 2 (199): 101–43. Judy's understanding of violence is considerably different from mine, however, since he holds that from the tabula rasa of revolutionary violence emerges the "revolutionary expression of a new law" (124). Judy rightly observes that revolutionary violence is lawmaking, but he wants to distinguish the absolute ("fateful") violence of the tabula rasa from what he conceives of as violence as "*the* agency of historical change" (ibid.). Thus, Judy claims that "the fact that revolutionary violence requires both the features of eruption and continuity in order to be conceived of as *the* agency of historical change keeps the antinomy [between lawmaking and law-preserving violence] insoluble" (124–25). This argument is untenable, since it reintroduces the opposition between means and ends that the tabula rasa suspends: even on Judy's own account, there can be no criteria for this abrupt, interruptive disjunction between discourse and the world. On the contrary, the coming into being of the wretched puts into crisis all the inherited diremptions of civil society and the nation-state, for the simple reason that they precipitate a foundational crisis in the colony. Furthermore, the logic of the tabula rasa enables a new understanding of this fatefulness that haunts both colonial law and sovereignty. Fanon did not strive to translate or present the wretched as a new measure for mastery or community, but sought to affirm their generalized impropriety—their incommensurability to the field of onto-political thought.

7. Lewis R. Gordon, *Fanon and the Crisis of European Man: An Essay on Philosophy and the Human Sciences*. New York: Routledge, 1995; Ato Sekyi-Otu, *Fanon's Dialectic of Experience*. Cambridge, Massachusetts: Harvard University Press, 1996.

8. Fanon, *The Wretched of the Earth* trans. Farrington, 255.

9. See Homi Bhabha, *The Location of Culture*. London: Routledge, 1994.

10. Sekyi-Otu, *Fanon's Dialectic of Experience*, 3.

11. Sekyi-Otu, *Fanon's Dialectic of Experience*, 45.

12. Sekyi-Otu, *Fanon's Dialectic of Experience*, 45.

13. Sekyi-Otu, *Fanon's Dialectic of Experience*, 5.

14. Sekyi-Otu, *Fanon's Dialectic of Experience*, 4.

15. Sekyi-Otu, *Fanon's Dialectic of Experience*, 45.

16. Nigel Gibson, "Thoughts about Doing Fanonism in the 1990s," *College Literature* 26, no. 2 (Spring 1999): 113.

17. Homi Bhabha, "Remembering Fanon," *New Formations* 1 (Spring 1987): 119.

18. Sekyi-Otu, *Fanon's Dialectic of Experience*, 8.

19. Sekyi-Otu, *Fanon's Dialectic of Experience*, 6, my emphasis.

20. Sekyi-Otu, *Fanon's Dialectic of Experience*, 107.

21. Sekyi-Otu, *Fanon's Dialectic of Experience*, 4.

22. Fanon, *The Wretched of the Earth* trans. Farrington, 117. Sekyi-Otu, *Fanon's Dialectic of Experience*, 121.

23. Sekyi-Otu, *Fanon's Dialectic of Experience*, 122, 132, 153.

24. Sekyi-Otu, *Fanon's Dialectic of Experience*, 61.

25. Sekyi-Otu, *Fanon's Dialectic of Experience*, 187, 196, 158.

26. Sekyi-Otu, *Fanon's Dialectic of Experience*, 158. Fanon, *Studies in a Dying Colonialism*, 91.

27. Fanon, *Studies in a Dying Colonialism*, 73, 89.

28. Fanon, *Studies in a Dying Colonialism*, 89.

29. Judy, "Politics of Global Language," 118–19.

30. Fanon, *Studies in a Dying Colonialism*, 90, 96.

31. Fanon, *Studies in a Dying Colonialism*, 201.

32. Sekyi-Otu, *Fanon's Dialectic of Experience*, 202.

33. Gordon, *Crisis of European Man*, 8, 6.

34. Gordon, *Crisis of European Man*, 8.

35. Gordon, *Crisis of European Man*, 10.

36. Gordon, *Crisis of European Man*, 10, 35, 12.

37. Gordon, *Crisis of European Man*, 23, 29.

38. Gordon, *Crisis of European Man*, 8.

39. Fanon, *Black Skin, White Masks* trans. Markmann, 109–10, 110, translation modified.

40. Gordon, *Crisis of European Man*, 58.

41. Gordon, *Crisis of European Man*, 59, 58–59.

42. Fanon, *Black Skin, White Masks* trans. Markmann, 145, translation modified.

43. Fanon, *Black Skin, White Masks* trans. Markmann, 161.

44. Fanon, *Black Skin, White Masks* trans. Markmann, 163.

45. For a commentary on "that within" see my *Haunted Life: Visual Culture and Black Modernity*. New Brunswick: Rutgers University Press, 2007, 33–69. See also Germaine Guex, "Les conditions intellectuelles et affectives de l'œdipe," *Revue Française de Psychanalyse* 13 (1949): 273–74.

46. Lewis R. Gordon, "The Black and the Body Politic: Fanon's Existential Phenomenological Critique of Psychoanalysis." In *Fanon: A Critical Reader*, eds. Lewis R. Gordon, T. Denean Sharpley-Whiting, Renée T. White. Oxford: Blackwell, 1996, 74–85.

47. Gordon, "The Black and the Body Politic," 80.

48. Gordon, "The Black and the Body Politic," 80.

49. Jean-Paul Sartre, *Being and Nothingness: An Essay on Phenomenological Ontology*, trans. Hazel E. Barnes. New York: Philosophical Library, 1947, 167; *L'Être et le néant: Essai d'ontologie phénomènologique*. Paris: Gallimard, 1940.

50. Sartre, *Being and Nothingness*, 121.

51. Sartre, *Being and Nothingness*, 713.

52. Jean-Paul Sartre, *L'Imaginaire, psychologie phénomènologique de l'imagination.* Paris: Gallimard, 1940. Reprinted, *Collection Idées*, 1986, 58.

53. Jean-Paul Sartre, *L'Idiot de la famille, G. Flaubert de 1821 à 1857.* Paris: Gallimard, vols. I and II, 1971; *The Idiot of the Family*, trans. Carol Cosman. Chicago: University of Chicago Press, vol. I, 1981, 714.

54. Jean-Paul Sartre, *Situations IV*, 196.

55. Fanon, *Black Skin, White Masks*, trans. Markmann, 110.

56. Fanon, *Black Skin, White Masks*, trans. Markmann, 191, translation modified.

57. See my analysis of this problematic in Chapter Five, "Racial Fetishism."

58. For an interesting exception to this narrative, see Paul Gilroy, "Fanon Again," in *Darker than Blue: On the Moral Economies of Black Atlantic Culture.* Cambridge, Massachusetts: Harvard University Press, 2010. Gilroy takes Fanon to be an antiracist thinker whose disturbing insights make him "our contemporary" (155): this is clearly linked to Gilroy's argument, in "Race and the Right to be Human," that the continuing role of race in political culture calls for "acts of imagination and invention that are adequate to the depth of the postcolonial predicament he [Fanon] described." *After Empire. Melancholia or Convivial Culture?* Abingdon: Routledge, 2004, 58.

59. Scott, *Refashioning Futures*, 206.

60. Scott, *Refashioning Futures*, 201.

61. Hayden White, *Metahistory: The Historical Imagination in Nineteenth Century Europe.* Baltimore: John Hopkins University Press, 1973; cited in David Scott, *Conscripts of Modernity: The Tragedy of Colonial Enlightenment.* Durham: Duke University Press, 2004, 47. See also David Scott, "Tragedy's Time: Postemancipation Futures Past and Present," in *Rethinking Tragedy*, ed. Rita Felski. Baltimore: Johns Hopkins University Press, 2008, 199–218.

62. Scott, *Refashioning Futures*, 204–5.

63. Scott, *Refashioning Futures*, 206.

64. See Frantz Fanon and J. Azoulay, "La Sociothérapie dans un service d'hommes musulmans," *L'Information Psychiatrique* 30, no. 9 (1954): 349–61; Frantz Fanon and Charles Geronimi, "L'Hospitalisation de jour en psychiatrie. Valeur et limites," *Tunisie Médicale* 38, no. 10 (1959): 689–732; and Frantz Fanon and S. Asselah, "Le Phénomène de l'agitation en milieu psychiatrique," *Maroc Médical* 38, no. 380 (1967): 252.

65. Indeed, Scott's reading of alienation, focused exclusively on a Marxian-existentialist genealogy, overlooks the term's various meanings in psychiatry to which Fanon resorts when trying to clarify specific symptom formations in *Black Skin, White Masks*.

66. Fanon, *The Wretched of the Earth*, trans. Farrington, 202, 203.

67. Fanon, *The Wretched of the Earth*, trans. Farrington, 202.

68. Alice Cherki, *Frantz Fanon: A Portrait*, trans. Nadia Benabid. Ithaca: Cornell University Press, 2006.

69. Vicky Lebeau, "Psychopolitics: Frantz Fanon's *Black Skin, White Masks*."

In *Psycho-politics and Cultural Desires*, eds. Jan Campbell and Janet Harbord. London: UCL Press, 1998, 113–23.

70. See Françoise Vergès, "Creole Skin, Black Mask: Fanon and Disavowal," *Critical Inquiry* 23 (Spring 1997): 578–95; David Macey, "The Recall of the Real: Frantz Fanon and Psychoanalysis," *Constellations* 6, no. 1 (1999): 97–107; and Hussein Abdilahi Bulhan, *Frantz Fanon and the Psychology of Oppression*. New York: Plenum Press, 1985.

71. Scott, *Refashioning Futures*, 13.

72. Scott, *Refashioning Futures*, 29.

73. David Scott, "The Tragic Sensibility of Talad Asad." In *Powers of the Secular Modern*, eds. David Scott and Charles Hirschkind. Stanford: Stanford University Press, 2006, 134–323.

74. Scott, *Refashioning Futures*, 206.

75. Scott, *Refashioning Futures*, 206, 207.

76. Cited in Scott, *Refashioning Futures*, 205.

77. Fanon, *Black Skin, White Masks*, trans. Markmann, 229, 231.

78. The standard case would be that presented by Hannah Arendt, *On Violence*. New York: Harcourt, Brace and World, 1970; and Jean-Paul Sartre's justly infamous "Preface" to the *Wretched of the Earth*; for a reading of Sartre's "Preface" that also misreads Fanon on violence, see Judith Butler, "Violence, Nonviolence: Sartre on Fanon," in *Race after Sartre: Antiracism, Africana Existentialism, Postcolonialism*, ed. Jonathan Judaken. New York: Suny Press, 2008, 211–31. Butler, albeit more cautious than either Sartre or Arendt, repeats the tendency to read violence in Fanon as "an instrumentality in the service of invention," which leads her to ask "whether violence continues to play a role in what it means to create oneself, what it means to produce a community, what it means to achieve and sustain decolonization as a goal" (225). Butler's basic premise, which she supports by alluding to Rey Chow (and others) on the masculinism of Fanon's texts, is that the model of self-creation through anti-colonial violence remains hypermasculinist, which is false, and that there are other more universal modes of address (what she calls the "constitutive sociality" of a "you") that bypass that hypermasculinity, but how they do so is left obscure. Or, to put it another way, Fanonism is not reducible to the violence of anti-colonialism, which remains particular, racial, grounded in the male (and female) bodies of the colonized, and politically instrumentalist. However, only quite brief scrutiny is required to show that these oppositions are all wrong: violence, for Fanon, is neither positive nor negative, but marks the possibility of every relation in the colony (including ethics, politics, race, and gender), which is why violence is not opposed to the human, but inextricable from its very possibility (in his conclusion to *Wretched of the Earth*, Fanon also recommends that any new humanism should try and avoid becoming a "caricature" of European humanism, especially the latter's violent separation of humanism from war, genocidal violence, and massacring force; 252). In all his major texts, Fanon shows how violence is at work in the formation of any (racial) identity and thus

fantasmatic exclusion cannot be eliminated from any self-creation, be it an "I," "he," "she," "they," or "you." To posit such a possibility is to reduce antagonism to an imaginary thesis or delusion in which nonviolence is duly prescribed as the teleological end of politics (rather than, say, force). In other words, his appeal to a new humanism entails a thinking of irreducible violence that is not derivative of some prior or hoped-for peace, or some symptomatic alienation to be overcome by *lex talionis*. It is striking how few commentators note that the tabula rasa (like all revolutionary or undecidable moments) is more or less violent, but nonetheless necessary (in its undecidability) for the constitution of any humanism as such.

79. Achille Mbembe, *On the Postcolony*. Berkeley: University of California Press, 2001.

80. Achille Mbembe, "Prosaics of Servitude and Authoritarian Civilities," trans. Janet Roitman, *Public Culture* 5, no. 1 (Fall 1992): 139.

81. Mbembe, *On the Postcolony*, 15, 14.

82. Achille Mbembe, "De la scène coloniale chez Frantz Fanon," *Rue Descartes* 4, no. 58 (2007): 54.

83. Mbembe, "Prosaics of Servitude," 133.

84. Fanon, *Black Skin, White Masks*, trans. Markmann, 10.

85. Mbembe, "De la scène coloniale," 38.

86. Mbembe, "De la scène coloniale," 51.

87. Mbembe, "De la scène coloniale," 53.

88. Mbembe, "De la scène coloniale," 53.

89. Mbembe, "De la scène coloniale," 40.

90. Achille Mbembe, "Provisional Notes on the Postcolony," *Africa: Journal of the International African Institute* 62, no. 1 (1992): 4.

91. Mbembe, "De la scène coloniale," 44.

92. Mbembe, *On the Postcolony*, 242.

93. See Carl Schmitt, *Political Theology: Four Chapters on the Concept of Sovereignty*, trans. George Schwab. Cambridge: MIT Press, 1985.

94. In a 2008 interview with Isabel Hofmeyr, Mbembe says: "The last chapter [of *On the Postcolony*], 'God's Phallus,' was written as an allegoric dialogue with Frantz Fanon." Isabel Hofmeyr, "Writing Africa. Achille Mbembe in conversation with Isabel Hofmeyr," in *New South African Keywords*, eds. Nick Shephard and Steven Robins. Jacana: Ohio University Press, 2008, 253.

95. Mbembe, "De la scène coloniale," 25, 38.

96. Mbembe, *On the Postcolony*, 133, 167; "De la scène coloniale," 38, 39.

97. Mbembe, "De la scène coloniale," 39.

98. In the same 2008 interview with Isabel Hofmeyr, Mbembe says: "I was struck by the quasi-impossibility of revolutionary practice in the [African] continent. There are social upheavals to be sure. Once in a while, things break loose. But the latter hardly translate into an effective, positive, transformative praxis. It is almost always as if what ensues is a continuation in the void." Hofmeyr, "Writing Africa," 252.

99. Hofmeyr, "Writing Africa," 253. On this logic, see Abdul JanMohammed, *The Death-Bound Subject*. Durham: Duke University Press, 2005.

100. Hofmeyr, "Writing Africa," 253.

101. For a discussion of Fanonian ethics more generally see my "Afterword: Ice-Cold" in *Haunted Life. Visual Culture and Black Modernity*. New Brunswick: Rutgers University Press, 2007, 225–41.

PROLOGUE, PART I

1. Fanon makes use of the figure of disavowal at several key points throughout his work with respect to phobia and fetishism. See, in particular, Chapter Five, "Racial Fetishism," of the present work. For the classic account of disavowal, see Sigmund Freud, "Fetishism." In *The Standard Edition of the Complete Psychological Works of Sigmund Freud*. London: Hogarth Press, 1966–74, SE XXI, 152–7.

2. Frantz Fanon, *Black Skin, White Masks*, trans. Charles Lam Markmann. New York: Grove Press, 1967, 10.

3. Here I must point out that the word "real" needs to be understood differently from its inflection in Lacan's late works. While Fanon shares with Lacan the notion that there is always something in the subject that *escapes* it, and is therefore evidence, as shown above, of something that cannot be grasped, this does not mean an ineffable beyond of the subject but refers to a gap or hole in knowledge that cannot be grasped at the level of representation, even though the subject nevertheless remains tied to its symbolization. But whereas for Lacan the *réel* is at the foundation of the subject, in Fanon's usage the *réel* is also *imposed*, and denotes a being confronted with a violence that makes the *réel* indistinguishable from *la réalité*, and thus the experience of a certain violence of constraint, guardedness, inhibition, and indebtedness—as if what cannot be escaped is the *réel* of being constrained by the epidermal violence of culture. This is a theme that we will return to throughout this book, since it betokens not only a limit of experience but the experience of an encounter with a limit that cannot be resisted or known, and which Fanon describes as a "noose" that has the force of law and of revelation (see also Chapter Seven, "The Condemned"). In the current state of the conversations and debates around Lacan's notion of the real, one problem that ought to be raised is to what extent the ineffability of the real is bound to race. All forms of anti-blackness necessarily contain a violent expulsion of blackness as evil and contaminating, and in ways that I would say are extremely singular in their phantasmatic, coercive force. The subject living in an anti-black society is therefore forced to fall back on the ropes, or to play the classic role of a rope-a-dope in relation to such virulent violence. What would it mean, then, to secure, or imagine oneself in the grip of such a noose by which one is permanently endangered? In such encounters *la réalité* and the *réel* seem to feed off one another beyond any alibis of the subject, and this is still more clearly confirmed by Fanon's remark that the black literally has no ontological resistance to the words or visions of anti-blackness.

CHAPTER 1

1. David Macey, "The Recall of the Real: Frantz Fanon and Psychoanalysis," *Constellations* 6, no.1 (1999): 97–107.

2. Frantz Fanon and François Tosquelles, "Sur quelques cas traits par la méthode de Bini," *Congrès des médecins aliénistes et neurologistes de France et des pays de langue français*. Pau: 1953; Frantz Fanon and François Tosquelles, "Indications de la thérapeutique de Blini dans le cadre des thérapeutiques institutionnelles," *Congrès des médecins aliénistes et neurologistes de France et des pays de langue français*. Pau: 1953; Frantz Fanon and François Tosquelles, "Sur un essai de réadaptation chez une malade avec épilépsie morphéique et troubles de caractère graves," *Congrès des médecins aliénistes et neurologistes de France et des pays de langue français*. Pau: 1953.

3. Françoise Vergès, "To Cure and to Free: The Fanonian Project of 'Decolonized Psychiatry.'" In *Fanon: A Critical Reader*, eds. Lewis R. Gordon, T. Denean Sharpley-Whiting, and Renée T. White. Cambridge: Blackwell, 1996, 85–100.

4. The *École d'Alger* of psychiatry, headed by Antoine Porot, sought to develop a semiological system of Arab behavior and what it considered to be the "native mentality." That mentality was defined by its suggestibility, credulousness, hysteria, pithiatism, mental childishness, stupor, hysteria, "criminal impulsiveness," and *"crises excite-motrices"* (crises of motor excitation). See Antoine Porot, "Notes de psychiatrie musulmane," *Annales médico-psychologiques* ii (1908): 5–14; and Antoine Porot and D.C. Arrii, "L'Impulsivité criminelle chez l'indigène algérien. Ses facteurs," *Annales médico-psychologiques* ii (1932): 228–41.

5. Vergès, "To Cure and to Free," 85.

6. Frantz Fanon and C. Géronimi, "Le T.A.T. chez les femmes musulmanes. Sociologie de la perception et de l'imagination," *Congrès des Médecins aliénistes et neurologists de France et des pays de langue français, LIVe session, Bordeaux, 30 Août–4 Septembre 1956*. Paris: Masson, 1957, 718.

7. Vergès, "To Cure and to Free," 87.

8. Vergès, "To Cure and to Free," 87.

9. Cited in Vergès, "To Cure and to Free," 93.

10. Vergès, "To Cure and to Free," 93, my italics.

11. Frantz Fanon, *Toward the African Revolution: Political Essays*, trans. Haakon Chevalier. New York: Grove Press, 1964, 53.

12. Vergès, "To Cure and to Free," 95.

13. Frantz Fanon, *The Wretched of the Earth*, trans. Constance Farrington. Harmondsworth: Penguin, 1965, 202.

14. Jacques André, "Fanon entre le réel et l'inconscient," in *Memorial International Frantz Fanon*. Paris: Présence Africaine, 1984, 108–27.

15. See André, "Fanon entre le réel et l'inconscient"; Homi K. Bhabha, Foreword to Frantz Fanon, *Black Skin, White Masks*, trans. Charles Lam Markmann. London: Pluto Press, 1986; Hussein Abdilahi Bulhan, *Frantz Fanon and the Psychology of Oppression*. London: Springer, 1985; Christopher Lane, "Psychoanalysis and Colonialism Redux: Why Mannoni's 'Prospero Complex' Still Haunts Us,"

Journal of Modern Literature XXV, 3/4 (Summer 2002): 127–50; David Macey, *Frantz Fanon: A Life*. London: Granta Books, 2000; and Françoise Vergès, "Creole Skin, Black Mask: Fanon and Disavowal," *Critical Inquiry* 23 (Spring 1997): 578–95.

16. Lane, "Psychoanalysis and Colonialism Redux," 129.

17. Fanon, *Black Skin, White Masks*, 104.

18. Frantz Fanon, *Studies in a Dying Colonialism*, trans. Haakon Chevalier. London: Earthscan, 1989, 121–47.

CHAPTER 2

1. See Jacques Lacan, *Les complexes familiaux*. Dijon: Navarin Editeur, 1984; and Maurice Merleau-Ponty, *Phenomenology of Perception*, trans. Colin Smith. Atlantic Highlands, NJ: Humanities Press, 1961.

2. For an overview of these experiments, see Frantz Fanon, *Écrits sur l'aliénation et la liberté*, eds. Jean Khalfa and Robert Young. Paris: Éditions la Découverte: 2015.

3. See Jean Khalfa, "Fanon, psychiatre révolutionnaire," in Fanon, *Écrits sur l'aliénation*, 137–67.

4. Alice Cherki, *Frantz Fanon: A Portrait*, trans. Nadia Benabid. Cornell University Press, 2006, 120, 121.

5. Cherki, *Frantz Fanon*, 121.

6. Cherki, *Frantz Fanon*, 121.

7. Cherki, *Frantz Fanon*, 121.

8. Cherki, *Frantz Fanon*, 121.

9. Cherki, *Frantz Fanon*, 121.

10. Cherki, *Frantz Fanon*, 121.

CHAPTER 3

1. Frantz Fanon, *Black Skin, White Masks*, trans. Charles Lam Markmann. New York: Grove Press, 1967, 111.

2. Fanon, *Black Skin, White Masks*, 112.

3. Fanon, *Black Skin, White Masks*, 185.

4. Fanon, *Black Skin, White Masks*, 169.

5. Fanon, *Black Skin, White Masks*, 11.

6. See Jacques Lacan, *The Seminar of Jacques Lacan, Book 11, The Four Fundamental Concepts of Psychoanalysis*, trans. Alan Sheridan. New York: W. W. Norton, 1998.

7. For a summary of Freud's (and Lacan's) use of the term, see the entry for "deferred action" in Jean Laplanche and J. B. Pontalis, *The Language of Psychoanalysis*, trans. Donald Nicholson-Smith. London: The Hogarth Press, 1973, 107–9.

8. Frantz Fanon, *The Wretched of the Earth*, trans. Constance Farrington. London: Penguin Books, 1963, 2.

9. Fanon, *Black Skin, White Masks*, 134, 144.

10. Fanon, *Black Skin, White Masks*, 167, 179, 180, 151.

11. Fanon, *The Wretched of the Earth*, 27.

12. Frantz Fanon, *Toward the African Revolution: Political Essays*, trans. Haakon Chevalier. New York: Grove Books, 1988, 53.

CHAPTER 4

1. See Frantz Fanon and Jacques Azoulay, "La Socialthérapie dans un service d'hommes musulmans: difficulties méthodologiques," *Information psychiatrique* XXX, no. 9 (1954).

2. See Jacques Lacan, *Les complexes familiaux*, Dijon: Navarin Editeur, 1984.

3. Frantz Fanon and J. Lacaton, "Conduites d'aveu en Afrique du nord," *Congrès des médecins aliénistes et neurologistes de France et des pays de langue française*. Nice: 1955.

4. Frantz Fanon, *The Wretched of the Earth*, trans. Constance Farrington. London: Penguin Books, 1963, 241.

5. Frantz Fanon, *Black Skin, White Masks*, trans. Richard Philcox. New York: Grove Press, 2008, 69.

6. Fanon, *Black Skin, White Masks*, 69.

7. Karl Jaspers, *The Question of German Guilt*, trans. E. B. Ashton. New York: Dial Press, 32.

8. Fanon, *Black Skin, White Masks*, 69–70.

9. Fanon, *Black Skin, White Masks*, 70. For an excellent reading of anti-Semitism in *Black Skin, White Masks*, see Bryan Cheyette, "Frantz Fanon and the Black-Jewish Imaginary." In *Frantz Fanon's Black Skin, White Masks*, ed. M. Silverman. Manchester: Manchester UP, 2005, 74–100.

10. Jean-Paul Sartre, *Anti-Semite and Jew: An Exploration of the Etiology of Hate*. New York: Schocken, 1995. Cited in Fanon, *Black Skin, White Masks*, trans. Markmann, 182.

11. Henri Baruk, *Précis de psychiatrie*. Paris, 1950. Cited in Fanon, *Black Skin, White Masks*, trans. Markmann, 182.

12. Fanon, *Black Skin, White Masks*, 35, 36.

13. Fanon, *The Wretched of the Earth*, 202ff.

14. Fanon, *The Wretched of the Earth*, 202.

15. Fanon, *The Wretched of the Earth*, 202.

16. Fanon, *The Wretched of the Earth*, 203.

17. Fanon, *The Wretched of the Earth*, 203.

18. Fanon, *Black Skin, White Masks*, 123.

19. Lacan, *The Four Fundamental Concepts of Psychoanalysis*, trans. Alan Sheridan. New York: W. W. Norton, 1998, 84.

20. Albert Memmi, review of *Fanon* by Peter Geismar and *Frantz Fanon* by David Caute, *New York Times Book Review*, March 14 (1971): 5.

21. Fanon, *Black Skin, White Masks*, 17–18.

22. Fanon, *Black Skin, White Masks*, 18.

23. Maurice Merleau-Ponty, *Phenomenology of Perception*, trans. Colin Smith. Atlantic Highlands, NJ: Humanities Press, 1961, 390–91.

24. Francis Affergan, *Anthropologie à la Martinique*. Paris: Presses de la Fondation Nationale des Sciences Politiques, 1983, 2.

25. Fanon, *Black Skin, White Masks*, 25.

26. Fanon, *Black Skin, White Masks*, 27.

27. Fanon, *Black Skin, White Masks*, 32.

28. Fanon, *Black Skin, White Masks*, 32.

29. Fanon, *Black Skin, White Masks*, 34.

30. Fanon, *Black Skin, White Masks*, 36.

31. Brian T. Edwards, "Fanon's al-Jaza'ir, or Algeria Translated," *Parallax* 8, no. 2 (2002): 101.

32. Edwards, "Fanon's al-Jaza'ir," 101.

33. See John Mowitt, "Breaking Up Fanon's Voice." In *Frantz Fanon: Critical Perspectives*, ed. Anthony C. Alessandrini, 89–99. New York: Routledge, 1999.

34. Frantz Fanon, *Studies in a Dying Colonialism*, trans. Haakon Chevalier. London: Earthscan, 1989, 73.

35. Fanon, *Studies in a Dying Colonialism*, 73.

36. Fanon, *Studies in a Dying Colonialism*, 72.

37. Fanon, *Studies in a Dying Colonialism*, 73.

38. Fanon, *Studies in a Dying Colonialism*, 88.

39. Fanon, *Studies in a Dying Colonialism*, 71, 93, 95.

40. Fanon, *Studies in a Dying Colonialism*, 88, 71.

41. Fanon, *Studies in a Dying Colonialism*, 71.

42. Fanon, *Studies in a Dying Colonialism*, 94.

43. Fanon, *Studies in a Dying Colonialism*, 95.

44. Fanon, *Studies in a Dying Colonialism*, 87.

45. Fanon, *Studies in a Dying Colonialism*, 87.

46. Fanon, *Studies in a Dying Colonialism*, 78.

47. Fanon, *Studies in a Dying Colonialism*, 89.

48. Fanon, *Studies in a Dying Colonialism*, 95.

49. Fanon, *Studies in a Dying Colonialism*, 87.

50. Fanon, *Studies in a Dying Colonialism*, 89.

51. Fanon, *Studies in a Dying Colonialism*, 82.

52. Fanon, *Studies in a Dying Colonialism*, 82, 76.

53. Fanon, *Studies in a Dying Colonialism*, 84.

54. Fanon, *Studies in a Dying Colonialism*, 85.

55. Fanon, *Studies in a Dying Colonialism*, 36. For a discussion of "Algeria Unveiled" in relation to the Algerian War of Independence and after, see Assia Djebar, *Women of Algiers in Their Apartment*, trans. M. de Jager. Virginia: University of Virginia Press, 1992; and Nigel Gibson, *Fanon: The Postcolonial Imagination*. Oxford: Polity Press, 2003.

56. Fanon, *Studies in a Dying Colonialism*, 40.

57. Fanon, *Studies in a Dying Colonialism*, 41.

58. Fanon, *Studies in a Dying Colonialism*, 45.

59. Fanon, *Studies in a Dying Colonialism*, 44.

60. Fanon, *Studies in a Dying Colonialism*, 46.

61. Fanon, *Studies in a Dying Colonialism*, 46.

62. Fanon, *Studies in a Dying Colonialism*, 46.

63. Fanon, *Studies in a Dying Colonialism*, 47.

64. Fanon, *Studies in a Dying Colonialism*, 49.

65. Fanon, *Studies in a Dying Colonialism*, 50.

66. Fanon, *Studies in a Dying Colonialism*, 59.

67. Fanon, *Studies in a Dying Colonialism*,

68. Compare these descriptions to the following comment by Roger Callois: "*I know where I am, but I do not feel as though I'm at the spot where I find myself.* To these dispossessed souls, space seems to be a devouring force. Space pursues them, encircles them, digests them in a gigantic phagocytosis." Roger Callois, "Mimicry and Legendary Psychasthenia," *October* 31 (Winter 1984): 30.

69. Fanon, *Studies in a Dying Colonialism*, 59.

70. Gilles Pontecorvo, in the film *The Battle of Algiers*, has the unveiling scene take place before a mirror, so that what the spectator sees is something opposite to what the unveiling woman sees; in her gestures before her mirror image this opposition becomes palpable. What is at issue is that this is someone else's image being unveiled, an unveiling that is imposed in the alienness of a reflecting surface that is necessarily misrecognized by us, the filmic spectator. It is as if the unveiling is located in the diegetic space and is at the same time outside of it—an enigma that necessarily reflects without a reflection.

71. Fanon, *Studies in a Dying Colonialism*, 60.

72. Fanon, *Studies in a Dying Colonialism*, 65.

73. Fanon, *Studies in a Dying Colonialism*, 66.

74. Fanon, *Studies in a Dying Colonialism*, 65, 66.

75. Fanon, *Black Skin, White Masks*, 35.

76. Fanon, *Black Skin, White Masks*, 71.

77. Fanon, *Studies in a Dying Colonialism*, 76.

78. Fanon, *Studies in a Dying Colonialism*, 71.

79. Harold Rosenberg, "Du Jeu au je: Esquisse d'une géographie de l'action," *Les Temps Modernes* 31 (April 1948): 1729–53. The essay first appeared in English under the title: "The Stages: A Geography of Human Action," in *Possibilities* (Winter 1947–48): 46–65. All references will be to the English edition unless otherwise stated.

80. Rosenberg, "The Stages," 48.

81. Rosenberg, "The Stages," 49.

82. Rosenberg, "The Stages," 49.

83. Rosenberg, "The Stages," 50.

84. Jean-Paul Sartre, *The Transcendence of the Ego: An Existentialist Theory of Consciousness*, trans. F. Williams and R. Kirkpatrick. New York: Noonday Press, 1957.

85. Fanon, *Black Skin, White Masks*, 161.

86. Rosenberg, "The Stages," 55.

87. Rosenberg, "The Stages," 56.

88. Rosenberg, "The Stages," 58.

89. Rosenberg, "The Stages," 58.

90. Rosenberg, "The Stages," 58.

91. Fanon, *Black Skin, White Masks*, 63.

92. Rosenberg, "The Stages," 50.

93. Germaine Guex, "Les conditions intellectuelles et affectives de l'œdipe," *Revue française de psychanalyse* 13, no. 2 (1949): 257–76.

94. Fanon, *Black Skin, White Masks*, 56.

95. Cited in Fanon, *Black Skin, White Masks*, 57.

96. Fanon, *Black Skin, White Masks*, 59.

97. Guex, "Les Conditions intellectuelles et affectives," 274, 268.

98. Guex, "Les Conditions intellectuelles et affectives," 264; Fanon, *Black Skin, White Masks*, 147.

99. Fanon, *Black Skin, White Masks*, 62.

100. Fanon, *Black Skin, White Masks*, 61.

101. Rosenberg, "The Stages," 60.

102. Fanon, *Black Skin, White Masks*, 60.

103. Fanon, *Black Skin, White Masks*, 61.

104. Rosenberg, "The Stages," 64.

105. G.W.F. Hegel, *Phenomenology of Spirit*, trans. A.V. Miller. Oxford: Oxford University Press, 1977, 9.

106. Alexandre Kojève, *Introduction to the Reading of Hegel: Lectures of the "Phenomenology of Spirit,"* trans. James H. Nichols. Ithaca: Cornell University Press, 1980, 13.

107. Fanon, *Black Skin, White Masks*, 10.

108. Fanon, *Black Skin, White Masks*, 122.

CHAPTER 5

A version of this chapter was previous published as "On Racial Fetishism," which originally appeared in *Qui Parle* 18, no. 3 (2010): 215–49. Copyright 2010, Editorial Board, *Qui Parle*. All rights reserved. Republished by permission of the copyright holder and the present publisher, Duke University Press, www.dukeupress .edu.

1. Frantz Fanon, *Black Skin, White Masks*, trans. Charles Lam Markmann. New York: Grove Press, 1967, 151.

2. Frantz Fanon, *Black Skin, White Masks*, trans. Richard Philcox. New York: Grove Press, 2008, 180.

3. Fanon, *Black Skin, White Masks*, trans. Markmann, 159.

4. David Marriott, "On Decadence: Bling Bling," *e-flux Journal*, #79, February (2017). No page numbers.

5. Fanon, *Black Skin, White Masks*, trans. Markmann, 205, 208, translation modified.

6. Fanon, *Black Skin, White Masks*, trans. Markmann, 208.

7. Fanon, *Black Skin, White Masks*, trans. Markmann, 204.

8. Fanon, *Black Skin, White Masks*, trans. Markmann, 204.

9. Fanon, *Black Skin, White Masks*, trans. Markmann, 205.

10. Fanon, *Black Skin, White Masks*, trans. Markmann, 207.

11. Fanon, *Black Skin, White Masks*, trans. Markmann, 205.

12. The citation is as follows and is taken from the Clark lectures: "This trauma, it is true, has been quite expelled from the consciousness and the memory of the patient and as a result he has apparently been saved from a great mass of suffering, but the repressed desire continues to exist in the unconscious; it is on watch constantly for an opportunity to make itself known and it soon comes back into consciousness, but in a disguise that makes it impossible to recognize; in other words, the repressed thought is replaced in consciousness by another that acts as its surrogate, its *Ersatz*, and that soon surrounds itself with all those feelings of morbidity that had been supposedly averted by the repression." Freud, cited in Fanon, *Black Skin, White Masks*, trans. Markmann, 144.

13. Fanon, *Black Skin, White Masks*, trans. Markmann, 207.

14. In the discussion that follows *Vorstellung*, literally to put forward, in front of, will be used in its more general sense of representation; and *Darstellung*, literally presentation, or exhibition, will be taken to refer to an immediacy of presence in the thing presented.

15. Fanon, *Black Skin, White Masks*, trans. Markmann, 208; *Peau noire, masques blancs*, 168.

16. Fanon, *Black Skin, White Masks*, trans. Markmann, 209.

17. Fanon, *Black Skin, White Masks*, trans. Markmann, 205.

18. Fanon, *Black Skin, White Masks*, trans. Markmann, 208.

19. Fanon, *Black Skin, White Masks*, trans. Markmann, 206.

20. Fanon, *Black Skin, White Masks*, trans. Markmann, 207.

21. Fanon, *Black Skin, White Masks*, trans. Markmann, 208.

22. Sigmund Freud, "The Neuro-Psychoses of Defense," Standard Edition III, 53.

23. Fanon, *Black Skin, White Masks*, trans. Markmann, 155.

24. Fanon, *Black Skin, White Masks*, trans. Markmann, 169–70; translation modified.

25. See Homi K. Bhabha's essay "The Other Question: the Stereotype and Colonial Discourse," *The Sexual Subject: A Screen Reader in Sexuality*. London and New York: Routledge, 1992, 312–31.

26. Frantz Fanon, *The Wretched of the Earth*, trans. Constance Farrington. London: Penguin Books, 1963, 31.

27. Fanon, *The Wretched of the Earth*, 31.

28. Karl Marx, *Capital: A Critique of Political Economy*, Volume 1, trans. Ben Fowkes. New York: Vintage, 1977, 143.

29. ibid., 148.

30. Cedric Robinson, "The Appropriation of Frantz Fanon," *Race & Class* 35, no. 1 (1993): 79–91.

31. Robinson, "The Appropriation of Frantz Fanon," 82.

32. Robinson, "The Appropriation of Frantz Fanon," 80.

33. See Benita Parry, "Problems in Current Theories of Colonial Discourse," *Oxford Literary Review* 9, 1 (1987): 27–58; and Neil Lazarus, "Disavowing Decolonization: Fanon, Nationalism, and the Problem of Representation in Current Theories of Colonial Discourse," *Research in African Literatures* 24, 4 (Winter, 1993): 69–98.

34. Fanon, *The Wretched of the Earth*, 31.

35. Frantz Fanon, *Toward the African Revolution. Political Essays*, trans. Haakon Chevalier. New York: Grove Books, 1988, 34.

36. Fanon, *Black Skin, White Masks*, trans. Markmann, 106.

37. Vicky Lebeau, "Psychopolitics: Frantz Fanon's *Black Skin, White Masks.*" In *Psycho-Politics and Cultural Desires*, eds. Jan Campbell and Janet Harbord, 121. London: UCL Press, 1998.

38. Fanon, *Black Skin, White Masks*, trans. Markmann, 134.

39. Fanon, *Black Skin, White Masks*, trans. Markmann, 102.

40. Fanon, *The Wretched of the Earth*, 35.

41. Hannah Arendt, *On Violence*. New York: Harcourt, Brace & World, 1970, 12. See also Kathryn T. Gines, *Hannah Arendt and the Negro Question*. Indiana: Indiana University Press, 2014.

42. Arendt, *On Violence*, 12.

43. Fanon, *The Wretched of the Earth*, 130.

44. See Peter Stallybrass, "Marx and Heterogeneity: Thinking the Lumpenproletariat," *Representations* 31 (Summer 1990): 65–69.

45. Fanon, *The Wretched of the Earth*, 130.

46. Fanon, *The Wretched of the Earth*, 33, 48.

47. Arendt, *On Violence*, 20.

48. Fanon, *The Wretched of the Earth*, 250.

49. Frantz Fanon, *Studies in a Dying Colonialism*, trans. Haakon Chevalier. London: Earthscan, 1989, 50.

50. Fanon, *Studies in a Dying Colonialism*, 50.

51. Pheng Cheah, "Spectral Nationality: The Living On [*sur-vie*] of the Postcolonial Nation in Neocolonial Globalization," *boundary 2* 26, no.3 (Autumn 1999): 236.

52. Cheah, "Spectral Nationality," 236.

53. Fanon, *The Wretched of the Earth*, 43.
54. Fanon, *The Wretched of the Earth*, 32.
55. Fanon, *The Wretched of the Earth*, 43.

CHAPTER 6

1. Frantz Fanon, *Black Skin, White Masks*, trans. Charles Lam Markmann. New York: Grove Press, 1967, 110, translation modified.
2. Fanon, *Black Skin, White Masks*, 139.
3. Fanon, *Black Skin, White Masks*, 110.
4. Fanon, *Black Skin, White Masks*, 227. The phrase "not certain of itself" can also be seen, I think, as an allusion to Freud's Kantian-inspired views on the nature and origin of the moral conscience. In *Totem and Taboo*, attempting to provide a genealogy of guilt, Freud writes: "Conscience is the internal perception of the rejection [*Verwerfung*] of a particular wish operating within us. The stress is upon the fact that this rejection has no need to appeal to anything else for support, that it is quite 'certain of itself' [*ihrer selbst gewiss ist*]." Freud, *Totem and Taboo*, Standard Edition XIII, 68.
5. Fanon, *Black Skin, White Masks*, 152.
6. Fanon, *Black Skin, White Masks*, 149.
7. Fanon, *Black Skin, White Masks*, 150.
8. Macey, "The Recall of the Real: Frantz Fanon and Psychoanalysis," *Constellations* 6, 1 (March, 1999), 104.
9. Macey, "The Recall of the Real," 103.
10. Lane, "Psychoanalysis and Colonialism Redux: Why Mannoni's 'Prospero Complex'" Still Haunts Us," *Journal of Modern Literature* 25, 3/4 (Summer, 2002), 135, 149.
11. Homi K. Bhabha, foreword to Frantz Fanon, *Black Skin, White Masks*, trans. C.L. Markmann. London: Pluto Press, 1986, xix.
12. Fanon, *Black Skin, White Masks*, 101.
13. In the *New Introductory Lectures*, Freud writes: "the repressed is foreign territory to the ego—internal foreign territory—just as reality . . . is external foreign territory." Standard Edition XXII, 57. And in *Inhibitions, Symptoms and Anxiety*, symptoms are described as "a kind of frontier-station with a mixed garrison." Standard Edition XX, 99.
14. Freud cited in Fanon, *Black Skin, White Masks*, 144. In his commentary on *Erlebnis*, David Macey emphases its phenomenological provenance as proof of Fanon's non-psychoanalytic usage, and despite Fanon's use of the word to illustrate citations from Freud and his repeated use of the word "repressed." Macey, "The Recall of the Real," 100.
15. Fanon, *Black Skin, White Masks*, 104, 106.
16. O. Mannoni, *Prospero and Caliban: the Psychology of Colonization*, trans. P. Powesland. New York: Frederick A. Praeger, 1964, 89.

17. Lane, "Psychoanalysis and Colonialism Redux," 145.

18. Fanon, *Black Skin, White Masks*, 189.

19. Frantz Fanon, *Toward the African Revolution. Political Essays*, trans. Haakon Chevalier. New York: Grove Books, 1988, 23.

20. "Thus the West Indian, after 1945, changed his values . . . in 1945 he discovered himself to be not only black but a Negro [*nègre*], and it was in the direction of distant Africa that he was henceforth to put out his feelers." Fanon, *Toward the African Revolution*, 24–25.

21. Fanon, *Toward the African Revolution*, 24.

22. Fanon, *The Wretched of the Earth*, 200.

23. Fanon, *The Wretched of the Earth*, 201.

24. Fanon, *The Wretched of the Earth*, 201.

25. Fanon, *The Wretched of the Earth*, 201.

26. Fanon, *The Wretched of the Earth*, 212.

27. Fanon, *The Wretched of the Earth*, 203.

28. Fanon, *The Wretched of the Earth*, 203.

29. Fanon, *The Wretched of the Earth*, 214.

30. Fanon, *The Wretched of the Earth*, 217.

31. Fanon, *The Wretched of the Earth*, 220.

32. Fanon, *The Wretched of the Earth*, 224.

33. Fanon, *The Wretched of the Earth*, 225.

34. Fanon, *The Wretched of the Earth*, 228.

35. Fanon, *The Wretched of the Earth*, 229.

36. Fanon, *The Wretched of the Earth*, 230.

37. Fanon, *The Wretched of the Earth*, 231.

38. Fanon, *The Wretched of the Earth*, 232.

39. Fanon, *The Wretched of the Earth*, 233.

40. Fanon, *The Wretched of the Earth*, 233.

41. Fanon, *The Wretched of the Earth*, 234.

42. Fanon, *The Wretched of the Earth*, 234ff.

43. Fanon, *The Wretched of the Earth*, 234.

44. Fanon, *The Wretched of the Earth*, 234.

45. Fanon, *The Wretched of the Earth*, 235.

46. Fanon, *The Wretched of the Earth*, 236.

47. Fanon, *The Wretched of the Earth*, 236.

48. Fanon, *The Wretched of the Earth*, 237.

49. Fanon, *The Wretched of the Earth*, 237.

50. Fanon, *The Wretched of the Earth*, 242.

51. For a commentary on these essays, see Jean Khalfa, "Fanon, psychiatre révolutionnaire," in Fanon, *Écrits sur l'aliénation et la liberté*, eds. Jean Khalfa and Robert Young, 137–67; here 155–56, 162–63. Paris: Éditions la Découverte: 2015.

52. Fanon, *The Wretched of the Earth*, 247.

53. Fanon, *The Wretched of the Earth*, 249.

54. Fanon, *The Wretched of the Earth*, 249.

55. Fanon, *The Wretched of the Earth*, 250.

56. Fanon, *The Wretched of the Earth*, 250.

57. Fanon, *The Wretched of the Earth*, 250.

CHAPTER 7

1. Frantz Fanon, *The Wretched of the Earth*, trans. Richard Philcox. New York: Grove Press, 2004, 18.

2. Fanon, *The Wretched of the Earth*, 19.

3. Fanon, *The Wretched of the Earth*, 20.

4. Fanon, *The Wretched of the Earth*, 20.

5. Fanon, *The Wretched of the Earth*, 18.

6. Fanon, *The Wretched of the Earth*, 148.

7. Fanon, *The Wretched of the Earth*, 148.

8. See Donna Jones, *The Racial Discourses of Life Philosophy: Négritude, Vitalism, and Modernity*. New York: Columbia University Press, 2011.

9. Fred Moten, "The Case of Blackness," *Criticism* 50, no. 2 (Spring 2008): 177–218; here 178, 179; Jared Sexton, "The Social Life of Social Death: On Afro-Pessimism and Black Optimism," *In Tensions* 5 (Fall/Winter 2011): 1–47. All references are to paragraph numbers.

10. Fanon, *The Wretched of the Earth*, 200, 201.

11. See Gary Wilder, *Freedom Time: Negritude, Decolonization, and the Future of the World*. Durham: Duke University Press, 2015.

12. Sexton, "The Social Life of Social Death," 27.

13. Moten, "The Case of Blackness," 208–9.

14. Frantz Fanon, *Black Skin, White Masks*, trans. Richard Philcox. New York: Grove Press, 2008, 203, 205.

15. Fanon, *Black Skin, White Masks*, 226.

16. Fanon, *Black Skin, White Masks*, 227.

17. Günther Anders, "The Pathology of Freedom: An Essay on Non-Identification," trans. Katharine Wolfe, *Deleuze Studies* 3, no. 2 (2009): 278–310.

18. Anders, "The Pathology of Freedom," 293.

19. Anders, "The Pathology of Freedom," 294.

20. Anders, "The Pathology of Freedom," 305.

21. Fanon, *Black Skin, White Masks*, 229.

22. Fanon, *Black Skin, White Masks*, 222, translation modified.

23. Friedrich Nietzsche, *On the Genealogy of Morality*, trans, Carol Diethe. Cambridge: Cambridge University Press, 2007, 321.

24. Fanon, *Black Skin, White Masks*, 36.

25. Fanon, *Black Skin, White Masks*, 229.

26. Friedrich Nietzsche, *Sämtliche Werke: Kritische Studienausgabe*, eds. G. Colli and M. Montari. Berlin: Walter de Gryter, 1967, 12, 1885, 7 [48], 311.

27. Nietzsche, *Sämtliche Werke*, 12, 1886, 5 [64], 209.

28. Fanon, *Black Skin, White Masks*, 221.

29. Fanon, *Black Skin, White Masks*, 229, translation modified.

30. Moten, "The Case of Blackness," 179, 187.

31. Moten, "The Case of Blackness," 187.

32. Moten, "The Case of Blackness," 187.

33. Moten, "The Case of Blackness," 208.

34. Moten, "The Case of Blackness," 211.

35. Moten, "The Case of Blackness," 213.

36. Moten, "The Case of Blackness," 213.

37. Moten, "The Case of Blackness," 211.

38. Moten, "The Case of Blackness," 212.

39. Sexton, "The Social Life of Social Death," 27.

40. Sexton, "The Social Life of Social Death," 182.

41. Sexton, "The Social Life of Social Death," 182.

42. Sexton, "The Social Life of Social Death," 6–7.

43. Sexton, "The Social Life of Social Death," 23.

44. Sexton, "The Social Life of Social Death," 23.

45. Sexton, "The Social Life of Social Death," 31.

46. Moten, "The Case of Blackness," 188.

47. Sexton, "The Social Life of Social Death," 29, 30.

48. Moten, "The Case of Blackness," 179.

49. This reading of Heidegger raises another notable problem, which we can do no more than mention here: that is, how Heidegger's archaic language of the thing, and all reference to its *hearing* and *revealing* (as a case), remains tied to a metaphysical notion of race that is both its *telos* and its point of departure. See Robert Bernasconi, "Heidegger's Alleged Challenge to the Nazi Concepts of Race," in James E. Faulconer and Mark A. Wrathall, eds. *Appropriating Heidegger* (Cambridge: Cambridge University Press, 2008).

50. Moten, "The Case of Blackness," 201, 193.

51. Moten, "The Case of Blackness," 192.

52. Sexton, "The Social Life of Social Death," 34.

53. Sexton, "The Social Life of Social Death," 34.

54. Moten, "The Case of Blackness," 179.

55. Frantz Fanon, *Studies in a Dying Colonialism*, trans. Haakon Chevalier. London: Earthscan, 1989, 128.

56. Moten, "The Case of Blackness," 209.

57. Fanon, *Black Skin, White Masks*, 203.

58. Fanon, *Black Skin, White Masks*, 231.

59. Moten, "The Case of Blackness," 187. In a later essay on "Blackness and Nothingness," this tension is repeated in the insistence on the "refusal of stand-point" and the ongoing desire to define what blackness is (in its anoriginal, para-ontological fugitivity). See Fred Moten, "Blackness and Nothingness (Mysticism

in the Flesh)," *The South Atlantic Quarterly* 112, no. 4 (Fall 2013): 737–80; here 738, 739.

60. Sexton, "The Social Life of Social Death," 28.

61. Sexton, "The Social Life of Social Death," 30.

62. Sexton, "The Social Life of Social Death," 31.

63. Moten, "The Case of Blackness," 187.

64. Fanon, *Studies in a Dying Colonialism*, 128–29.

65. Fanon, *Black Skin, White Masks*, 14.

66. Fanon, *Black Skin, White Masks*, 27.

67. Frank Wilderson, *Red, White, and Black: Cinema and the Structure of US Antagonisms*. Durham: Duke University Press, 2008.

68. Moten, "The Case of Blackness," 208.

69. For an example see Achille Mbembe, *On the Postcolony*. Berkeley: University of California Press, 2001.

70. Fanon, *The Wretched of the Earth*, 43.

71. Fanon, *The Wretched of the Earth*, 43.

72. Frantz Fanon, *The Wretched of the Earth*, trans. Constance Farrington. Harmondsworth: Penguin, 1965, 44.

73. Fanon, *The Wretched of the Earth*, trans. Farrington, 44.

74. Fanon, *The Wretched of the Earth*, trans. Farrington, 53.

75. Sexton, "The Social Life of Social Death," 9.

76. Fanon, *Black Skin, White Masks*, 212.

PROLOGUE, PART 2

1. Frantz Fanon, *Toward the African Revolution. Political Essays*, trans. Haakon Chevalier. New York: Grove Books, 1988, 26.

CHAPTER 8

A version of this chapter was previously published as "No Lords A-Leaping: Fanon, C. L. R. James, and the Politics of Invention," *Humanities* 3, no. 4 (2014): 517–45. http://www.mdpi.com/2076-0787/3/4/517.

1. Frantz Fanon, *Black Skin, White Masks*, trans. Charles Lam Markmann. New York: Grove Press, 1967, 229.

2. Fanon, *Black Skin, White Masks*, 229.

3. Walter Benjamin, "Theses on the Philosophy of History." In *Illuminations*, trans. Harry Zohn. New York: Schocken Books, 1968.

4. Benjamin, "Theses," 253.

5. Frantz Fanon, *The Wretched of the Earth*, trans. Constance Farrington. London: Penguin Books, 1967, 105.

6. Fanon, *Black Skin, White Masks*, 229.

7. Fanon, *Black Skin, White Masks*, 124.

8. See Patrick Taylor, *The Narrative of Liberation: Perspectives on Afro-Caribbean Literature, Popular Culture, and Politics*. Ithaca, NY: Cornell University Press, 1989.

9. Fanon, *The Wretched of the Earth*, 315.

10. Fanon, *The Wretched of the Earth*, 316.

11. Fanon, *The Wretched of the Earth*, 313.

12. Examples would include Albert Memmi, "The Impossible Life of Frantz Fanon." *The Massachusetts Review* 14, no. 1 (Winter 1973): 9–39; Christopher Miller, *Theories of Africans: Francophone Literature and Anthropology in Literature and Culture*. Chicago: University of Chicago Press, 1993; and David Macey, *Frantz Fanon: A Biography*. London: Verso, 2012.

13. Fanon, *The Wretched of the Earth*, 104.

14. Fanon, *The Wretched of the Earth*, 111.

15. Fanon, *The Wretched of the Earth*, 27.

16. Fanon, *Black Skin, White Masks*, 14, 184.

17. Fanon, *Black Skin, White Masks*, 11.

18. Fanon, *Black Skin, White Masks*, 11.

19. Fanon, *Black Skin, White Masks*, 10

20. Fanon, *Black Skin, White Masks*, 10.

21. Peter Hallward, "Fanon and Political Will." *Cosmos and History: The Journal of Natural and Social Philosophy* 7, no. 1 (2011): 104–27; here 104, 105.

22. Hallward, "Fanon and Political Will," 105.

23. Hallward, "Fanon and Political Will," 104.

24. Hallward, "Fanon and Political Will," 105.

25. Hallward, "Fanon and Political Will," 106.

26. Fanon, *The Wretched of the Earth*, 57.

27. Fanon, *Black Skin, White Masks*, 14, 15.

28. Fanon, *Black Skin, White Masks*, 16.

29. Hallward, "Fanon and Political Will," 107.

30. Hallward, "Fanon and Political Will," 107.

31. Hallward, "Fanon and Political Will," 110, my emphasis.

32. Hallward, "Fanon and Political Will," 110.

33. Hallward, "Fanon and Political Will," 111.

34. Fanon, *Black Skin, White Masks*, 10.

35. Hallward, "Fanon and Political Will," 112, my emphasis.

36. Geoffrey Bennington, "Sovereign Stupidity and Autoimmunity," in *Derrida and the Time of the Political*, eds. Pheng Cheah and Suzanne Gherlac. Durham: Duke University Press, 2009, 97–113.

37. Jean-Luc Nancy, *The Creation of the World or Globalisation*, trans. David Pettigrew. New York: SUNY Press, 2007, 99.

38. Fanon, *The Wretched of the Earth*, 85.

39. Fanon, *The Wretched of the Earth*, 35.

40. Fanon, *The Wretched of the Earth*, 35.

41. Fanon, *The Wretched of the Earth*, 36.

42. Fanon, *The Wretched of the Earth*, 93.

43. Hallward, "Fanon and Political Will," 119.

44. Frantz Fanon, *Toward the African Revolution. Political Essays*, trans. Haakon Chevalier. New York: Grove Books, 1988, 151.

45. Hallward, "Fanon and Political Will," 120.

46. Fanon, *The Wretched of the Earth*, 132.

47. Georges Sorel, *Reflections on Violence*. Cambridge: Cambridge University Press, 2004.

48. See Hannah Arendt, *On Violence*. New York: Harcourt Brace Jovanovich, 1970.

49. Sorel, *Reflections on Violence*, 7.

50. Sorel, *Reflections on Violence*, 17.

51. Sorel, *Reflections on Violence*, 73.

52. Sorel, *Reflections on Violence*, 85.

53. Sorel, *Reflections on Violence*, 28.

54. Hallward, "Fanon and Political Will," 126.

55. Fanon, *The Wretched of the Earth*, 35.

56. Walter Benjamin, "Critique of Violence." In *Selected Writings, Volume 1, 1913–1926*. Cambridge: Harvard University Press, 1996, 236–52.

57. Fanon, *The Wretched of the Earth*, 99.

58. Geoffrey Bennington, "Derrida and Politics." In *Jacques Derrida and the Humanities: A Critical Reader*, ed. Tom Cohen. Cambridge: Cambridge University Press, 2001: 193–213; here 203.

59. C. L. R. James, *Notes on Dialectics*. Westport, CT: Lawrence Hill & Co., 1981 (first published 1948).

60. James, *Notes on Dialectics*, 100.

61. James, *Notes on Dialectics*, 117.

62. James, *Notes on Dialectics*, 117.

63. James, *Notes on Dialectics*, 117.

64. James, *Notes on Dialectics*, 117, 103, 104.

65. James, *Notes on Dialectics*, 118.

66. James, *Notes on Dialectics*, 137, 89.

67. James, *Notes on Dialectics*, 105.

68. James, *Notes on Dialectics*, 147.

69. James, *Notes on Dialectics*, 135.

70. James, *Notes on Dialectics*, 10.

71. James, *Notes on Dialectics*, 11.

72. James, *Notes on Dialectics*, 17.

73. James, *Notes on Dialectics*, 18.

74. James, *Notes on Dialectics*, 18.

75. James, *Notes on Dialectics*, 47.

76. James, *Notes on Dialectics*, 183.

77. James, *Notes on Dialectics*, 116.

78. James, *Notes on Dialectics*, 116.
79. James, *Notes on Dialectics*, 180.
80. James, *Notes on Dialectics*, 9.
81. James, *Notes on Dialectics*, 9.
82. James, *Notes on Dialectics*, 10.
83. James, *Notes on Dialectics*, 180.
84. James, *Notes on Dialectics*, 142.
85. James, *Notes on Dialectics*, 59.
86. James, *Notes on Dialectics*, 61.
87. James, *Notes on Dialectics*, 11.
88. James, *Notes on Dialectics*, 179.
89. James, *Notes on Dialectics*, 35, 36, 43.
90. James, *Notes on Dialectics*, 55.
91. James, *Notes on Dialectics*, 51.
92. James, *Notes on Dialectics*, 100.
93. James, *Notes on Dialectics*, 101, 103.
94. James, *Notes on Dialectics*, 89.
95. Cited in James, *Notes on Dialectics*, 100.
96. James, *Notes on Dialectics*, 69.
97. James, *Notes on Dialectics*, 70.
98. James, *Notes on Dialectics*, 178.
99. Fanon, *Wretched of the Earth*, 72.
100. Hallward, "Fanon and Political Will," 125.
101. G. W. F. Hegel, *Science of Logic*, trans. A. V. Miller. London: Allen & Unwin, 1969, 126.

CHAPTER 9

A version of this chapter was previously published as "Inventions of Existence: Sylvia Wynter, Frantz Fanon, Sociogeny, and the 'Damned.'" Copyright © 2011 by Michigan State University. *CR: The New Centennial Review* 11, no. 3 (2011): 45–89.

1. Sylvia Wynter, "The Re-Enchantment of Humanism: An Interview with Sylvia Wynter," *Small Axe* 8 (2001): 197–98. Fanon's notion of the leap seems to have become an important motif for Wynter, as can be seen in the final sentences of her important paper "Unsettling the Coloniality of Being/Power/Truth/Freedom: Towards the Human. After Man. Its Overrepresentation—An Argument," *The New Centennial Review* 3, no. 3 (2003): 257–337; here 331. Unlike Fanon, however, Wynter continues to think this leap in teleological terms—a difference that I will be exploring throughout this chapter.
2. Wynter, "Re-Enchantment," 198.
3. Frantz Fanon, *Black Skin, White Masks*, trans. Charles Lam Markmann. New York: Grove Press, 1967, 10, 228.
4. Wynter, "Re-Enchantment," 199.

5. Wynter, "Re-Enchantment," 199.

6. The term "stricture" is taken from Derrida's *Glas*, where it refers to a tension of opposites that, though not dialectic, creates dialectic effects. See Jacques Derrida, *Glas*. Paris: Éditions Galilée, 1974. The term also features in the "Specular . . ." section of Jacques Derrida, *The Post Card*, trans. Alan Bass. Chicago: University of Chicago Press, 1987; and the "Restitutions" essay in Jacques Derrida, *The Truth in Painting*, trans. Geoffrey Bennington and Ian McLeod. Chicago: University of Chicago Press, 1987.

7. Fanon, *Black Skin, White Masks*, 111.

8. Wynter, "Re-Enchantment," 169. On the notion of the "mystical foundation of authority," see Jacques Derrida, "Force of Law: the Mystical Foundation of Authority," trans. Mary Quaintance. In *Acts of Religion*, ed. G. Anidjar. New York: Routledge, 2002, 230–98.

9. Wynter, "Re-Enchantment," 169. This critique of normality also falls into a vicious circle that consists of first determining as a priori codes that belong neither to history nor to the human but that determine our sense of reality, and then posing the question of freedom on the basis of those codes that tie the human to meanings that it can neither escape nor question. Accordingly, to conceive sociogeny scientifically means that one must recognize that the human, in Wynter, is nothing other than the genesis of an illusion whose sense continues to define us.

10. Wynter, "Re-Enchantment," 184.

11. Fanon, *Black Skin, White Masks*, 14.

12. Wynter, "Re-Enchantment," 207.

13. "Blackism" is Wynter's term for the use of race purity as a cultural weapon in the "struggle for hegemony between members of the educated middle classes [or the colonial bourgeoisie]." Wynter, "Re-Enchantment," 171.

14. Fanon, *Black Skin, White Masks*, 14.

15. Fanon, *Black Skin, White Masks*, 226.

16. Fanon, *Black Skin, White Masks*, 12.

17. Fanon, *Black Skin, White Masks*, 167, 179, 180, 151.

18. Fanon, *Black Skin, White Masks*, 197.

19. Wynter, "Re-Enchantment," 135. See also Wynter's "One Love—Rhetoric or Reality?—Aspects of Afro-Jamaicanism," *Caribbean Studies* 12, no. 3 (1972)" 64–97.

20. Wynter, "Re-Enchantment," 136, 169.

21. Wynter, "Re-Enchantment," 170.

22. Fanon, *Black Skin, White Masks*, 11.

23. Sylvia Wynter, "Towards the Sociogenic Principle: Fanon, Identity, the Puzzle of Conscious Experience, and What It Is Like to Be 'Black.'" In *National Identities and Sociopolitical Changes in Latin America*, eds. M. F. Durán-Cogan and Antonio Gómez-Moriana. London: Routledge, 2001, 30–66.

24. Wynter, "Towards the Sociogenic Principle," 31.

25. Wynter, "Towards the Sociogenic Principle," 31, 59.

26. Wynter, "Towards the Sociogenic Principle," 56, 52.

27. Wynter, "Towards the Sociogenic Principle," 48.

28. Wynter, "Towards the Sociogenic Principle," 58.

29. Wynter, "Towards the Sociogenic Principle," 55.

30. See Fanon, *Black Skin, White Masks*, Chapter One, and pages 111, 119, 120, 128, 168, and 188.

31. Wynter, "Re-Enchantment," 177.

32. Fanon, *Black Skin, White Masks*, 8.

33. Fanon, *Black Skin, White Masks*, 10.

34. In Aristotle's *Physics, tuché* is best rendered as "luck" or "fortune" and *automaton* as "accident" or "chance result." However, it is the meaning of the terms as proposed by Lacan, in Seminar 11 on *The Four Fundamental Concepts of Psychoanalysis*, that interests me here. Lacan renders *tuché* as "encounter with the real" and *automaton* as the "network of signifiers" or "return, the coming back, the insistence of the signs." Jacques Lacan, *The Seminar of Jacques Lacan, Book 11. The Four Fundamental Concepts of Psychoanalysis*, trans. A. Sheridan. New York: W. W. Norton, 1998, 53.

35. Lacan, *The Seminar of Jacques Lacan*, 192.

36. For an elegant summary of Freud's (and Lacan's) use of the term, see the entry for "deferred action" in J. Laplance and J. B. Pontalis, *The Language of Psychoanalysis*, trans. D. Nicholson-Smith. London: Hogarth Press, 1973.

37. Jacques Lacan, *Ecrits*, trans. B. Fink. New York: W. W. Norton, 2002, 213.

38. Fanon, *Black Skin, White Masks*, 139.

39. Jacques Derrida, *Psyche: Inventions of the Other*, Vol. 1, trans. P. Kamuf and E. Rottenberg. Stanford: Stanford University Press, 2007, 28.

40. Fanon, *Black Skin, White Masks*, 135.

41. Fanon, *Black Skin, White Masks*, 145.

42. Fanon, *Black Skin, White Masks*, 191.

43. Fanon, *Black Skin, White Masks*, 147.

44. Lacan, *The Seminar of Jacques Lacan*, 54–55.

45. Lacan, *The Seminar of Jacques Lacan*, 66; Fanon, *Black Skin, White Masks*, 122.

46. Fanon, *Black Skin, White Masks*, 120.

47. Fanon, *Black Skin, White Masks*, 193.

48. Fanon, *Black Skin, White Masks*, 65.

49. For the difference between the "organic" and "structure," which are part of a debate with Lacan's early work, see Fanon, *Black Skin, White Masks*, 80–81.

50. Fanon, *Black Skin, White Masks*, 12, 23.

51. Frantz Fanon, *Toward the African Revolution. Political Essays*, trans. Haakon Chevalier. New York: Grove Books, 1988, 17–29; Fanon, *Black Skin, White Masks*, 147.

52. Fanon, *Black Skin, White Masks*, 222.

53. Fanon, *Black Skin, White Masks*, 231.

54. Fanon, *Black Skin, White Masks*, 121.

55. Fanon, *Black Skin, White Masks*, 192.

56. Fanon, *Black Skin, White Masks*, 224–25, my emphasis.

57. "The partisans of integration, for their part, saw a new occasion to affirm 'French Algeria' by making the language of the occupation the sole practical means of communications placed at the disposal of the Kabyle, Arabs, Chaoulas, Mozabites, etc. . . . This thesis, on the level of discourse, recalled the very doctrine of colonialism: it is the intervention of the foreign nation that puts order into the original anarchy of the colonized country. Under these conditions, French, the language of the occupier, has thus attributed to it the function of *Logos*, with the [attendant] ontological implications within Algerian society." Frantz Fanon, *Studies in a Dying Colonialism*, trans. Haakon Chevalier. London: Earthscan, 1989, 92.

58. Fanon, *Black Skin, White Masks*, 20.

59. Fanon, *Black Skin, White Masks*, 24. For a more detailed commentary on language in the colony, see Part One, Chapter Four.

60. Fanon, *Black Skin, White Masks*, 20, 191.

61. Fanon, *Black Skin, White Masks*, 191.

62. Fanon, *Black Skin, White Masks*, 83–109.

63. Wynter, "Re-Enchantment," 183.

64. Wynter, "Re-Enchantment," 183.

65. Wynter, "Re-Enchantment," 184.

66. Cited in Wynter, "Towards the Sociogenic Principle," 45.

67. Wynter, "Towards the Sociogenic Principle," 60–61.

68. Wynter, "Re-Enchantment," 186; "Towards the Sociogenic Principle," 46.

69. Wynter, "Re-Enchantment," 189–90.

70. Wynter, "Re-Enchantment," 190.

71. Wynter, "Re-Enchantment," 31.

72. Wynter, "Towards the Sociogenic Principle," 32.

73. Wynter, "Towards the Sociogenic Principle," 37.

74. Fanon, *Black Skin, White Masks*, 23.

75. Wynter, "Towards the Sociogenic Principle," 59.

76. Wynter, "Towards the Sociogenic Principle," 60.

77. Wynter, "Towards the Sociogenic Principle," 60.

78. Wynter, "Towards the Sociogenic Principle," 60.

79. Wynter, "Towards the Sociogenic Principle," 59.

80. Wynter, "Towards the Sociogenic Principle," 53.

81. Wynter, "Towards the Sociogenic Principle," 60.

82. Wynter, "Towards the Sociogenic Principle," 58.

83. Wynter, "Towards the Sociogenic Principle," 58.

84. Wynter, "Towards the Sociogenic Principle," 58.

85. Frantz Fanon, *The Wretched of the Earth*, trans. Charles Lam Markmann. New York: Grove Press, 1967, 103.

86. Fanon, *Wretched of the Earth*, 31.

87. Fanon, *Black Skin, White Masks*, 12.

88. Fanon, *Black Skin, White Masks*, 19.

89. Fanon, *Black Skin, White Masks*, 19.

90. Sigmund Freud, *Studies on Hysteria*, trans. J. Strachey. London: Basic Books, 2000, 290, my emphasis.

CHAPTER 10

1. Frantz Fanon, *The Wretched of the Earth*, trans. Constance Farrington. London: Penguin Books, 1967, 171, 174.

2. Aimé Césaire, "Letter to Maurice Thorez," trans. Chike Jeffers. *Social Text* 28, no. 2 (2010): 145–52; here 152.

3. Césaire, "Letter to Maurice Thorez," 152.

4. Césaire, "La Poésie . . . ," in *La poésie*, ed. Daniel Maximin and Gilles Carpentier. Paris: Seuil, 1994, 5.

5. David Marriott, *On Black Men*. Columbia University Press: New York, 2000, 15; and David Marriott, *Haunted Life: Visual Culture and Black Modernity*. Rutgers University Press: New Brunswick, 2007.

6. The word "nigger" in an absolute sense signifies either a drive to life and pleasure that acknowledges itself as contrary to law or, in the same fixed and determined way, a form of life that is also the performance of a kind of death, as in the trope "If I were a nigger, I would kill myself." In both instances, blackness is taken to be a role that is at odds with life itself, or is aberrant with regards to right, life, and value.

7. Jared Sexton, "Unbearable Blackness," *Cultural Critique* 90 (Spring 2015): 173.

8. For an example, see A.L. Massa, "Implications of Wilderson's Afro-Pessimism," *The Historical Nerds* (December 16, 2014). And for a contrasting response see K. Arons, "No Selves to Abolish: AfroPessimism, Anti-Politics and the End of the World." *Anarchistnews.org* (March 1, 2016).

9. See Part One, Chapter Seven, "The Condemned."

10. See Frank Wilderson, *Red, White & Black: Cinema and the Structure of U.S. Antagonisms*. Durham: Duke University Press, 2010; Jared Sexton, *Amalgamation Schemes: Antiblackness and the Critique of Multiracialism*. Minneapolis: University of Minnesota Press, 2008; Sora Han, *Letters of the Law: Race and the Fantasy of Colorblindness in American Law*. Redwood City: Stanford University Press, 2015; Christina Sharpe, *Monstrous Intimacies: Making Post-Slavery Subjects*. Durham: Duke University Press, 2010; and Kara Keeling, *The Witch's Flight: The Cinematic, the Black Femme, and the Image of Common Sense*. Durham: Duke University Press, 2007.

11. Jared Sexton, "The Social Life of Social Death: On Afro-Pessimism and Black Optimism," *InTensions* 5 (Fall/Winter 2011): 1–47; here 24.

12. Frank Wilderson, "Grammar and Ghosts: The Performative Limits of African Freedom," *Theater Survey* 50, no. 1: 123.

13. Wilderson, *Red, White & Black*, 249.
14. Wilderson, *Red, White & Black*, 251.
15. Wilderson, *Red, White & Black*, 262.
16. Wilderson, *Red, White & Black*, 333.
17. Wilderson, *Red, White & Black*, 249.
18. The literature on negritude and Césaire's poem is vast, but see in particular Gregson Davis, *Aimé Césaire*. Cambridge: Cambridge University Press, 1997; Brent Edwards, "Aimé Césaire: The Syntax of Influence," *Research in African Literatures* 36, no. 2 (2005): 1–18; Nick Nesbitt, *Voicing Memory: History and Subjectivity in French Caribbean Literature*. Charlottesville: University of Virginia Press, 2003; and Robert Bernasconi, "The Assumption of Negritude: Aimé Césaire, Frantz Fanon, and the Vicious Circle of Racial Politics," *Parallax* 8, no. 2 (2002): 69–83.
19. See André Breton, *Martinique. Snake Charmer*, trans. David W. Seaman. Austin: University of Texas Press, 2008.
20. Jean-Paul Sartre, "Black Orpheus," trans. J. MacCombie, in *Race*, ed. Robert Bernasconi. Blackwells: Oxford, 2001, 115–43.
21. M. NourbeSe Philip, *Zong!* Wesleyan: Wesleyan University Press, 2011.
22. Césaire, *Notebook of a Return to My Native Land*, trans. Mirielle Rosello and Annie Pritchard. Durham: Bloodaxe Books, 1995.
23. Cited in Gregson Davis, *Aimé Césaire*. Cambridge: Cambridge University Press, 1997, 59.
24. Sartre, "Black Orpheus," 121.
25. Sartre, "Black Orpheus," 137.
26. Sartre, "Black Orpheus," 138.
27. Sartre, "Black Orpheus," 138.
28. Sartre, "Black Orpheus," 129.
29. Sartre, "Black Orpheus," 123.
30. Sartre, "Black Orpheus," 123.
31. Sartre, "Black Orpheus," 119.
32. Sartre, "Black Orpheus," 120.
33. Sartre, "Black Orpheus," 122.
34. Sartre, "Black Orpheus," 122.
35. Sartre, "Black Orpheus," 123; 125.
36. Sartre, "Black Orpheus," 126.
37. Sartre, "Black Orpheus," 124.
38. Sartre, "Black Orpheus," 125.
39. Sartre, "Black Orpheus," 125.
40. Frantz Fanon, *Black Skin, White Masks*, trans. Richard Philcox. New York: Grove Press, 2008, 10.
41. Fanon, *Black Skin, White Masks*, 11.
42. Sartre, "Black Orpheus," 137.
43. Sartre, "Black Orpheus," 139.
44. Fanon, *Black Skin, White Masks*, 133.

45. Aimé Césaire, *Discourse on Colonialism*. New York: Monthly Review Press, 2001, 78.

46. Fanon, *Black Skin, White Masks*, 134.

47. Sartre, "Black Orpheus," 130.

48. Sartre, "Black Orpheus," 139.

49. Sartre, "Black Orpheus," 139.

50. Fanon, *Black Skin, White Masks*, 135.

51. Sartre, "Black Orpheus," 128.

52. Sartre, "Black Orpheus," 130.

53. Fanon, *Black Skin, White Masks*, 109–10, translation modified.

54. Werner Hamacher, *Pleroma—Reading in Hegel*, trans. Nicholas Walker and Simon Jarvis. Stanford: Stanford University Press, 1998, 10.

55. Fanon, *Black Skin, White Masks*, 219.

56. Fanon, *Black Skin, White Masks*, 220ff.

57. G. W. F. Hegel, *Lectures on the Philosophy of World History: Introduction, Reason in History*, trans. H. B. Nisbet. Cambridge: Cambridge University Press, 1992, 177.

58. Cited in Jacques Derrida, *Glas*, trans. John P. Leavey and Richard Rand. Lincoln: University of Nebraska Press, 1990, 208.

59. Hegel, *Lectures on the Philosophy of World History*, 295.

60. Fanon, *Black Skin, White Masks*, 134.

61. Fanon, *Black Skin, White Masks*, 135.

62. Fanon, *Black Skin, White Masks*, 134, 135.

63. Hamacher, *Pleroma*, 16–17.

Index

Cultural Memory in the Present

Jacques Derrida, *Monolingualism of the Other; or, The Prosthesis of Origin*

Andrew Baruch Wachtel, *Making a Nation, Breaking a Nation: Literature and Cultural Politics in Yugoslavia*

Niklas Luhmann, *Love as Passion: The Codification of Intimacy*

Mieke Bal, ed., *The Practice of Cultural Analysis: Exposing Interdisciplinary Interpretation*

Jacques Derrida and Gianni Vattimo, eds., *Religion*